Madsen-Bibeau

W9-AYC-593

Timothy Dansdill
Quinnipiac University

The Individual in the Community

Fifth Edition

CONTENTS

17   21

No *Malls R Us*?

PREFACE

In September 2002, the Quinnipiac University curriculum committee asked the faculty to consider two questions as part of the review of general education goals and structure: what do the faculty want students to gain from their general education at Quinnipiac University and what common set of educational philosophies unites us as a learning community? In August 2004, the first ten sections of the freshman seminar, QU101: "The Individual in the Community," were piloted. The first of three interdisciplinary seminars at the heart of our innovative general education curriculum, it introduces our freshmen to the core value that most fully encompasses Quinnipiac's stated mission as a university: community. Accordingly, the course introduces students to academic perspectives that address human nature, individuality, and the goals of community, while easing their transition into a new community—Hamden, Connecticut—and a new *type* of community—Quinnipiac University. By challenging students with an academically rigorous experience within a supportive environment, I hope to produce intentional learners who confidently take control of their own educational decisions and success. Finally the general subjects of individual and community examined throughout this first seminar provide the base for the university seminar series which will further explore the concept of community but at the national and global levels.

This volume brings together selected writings intended to facilitate the exploration of important ideas regarding the dialectical tensions between the individual and the community. It is a work in progress, but has already benefited from the positive contributions of many members of Quinnipiac's faculty and staff.

I would be negligent if we failed to acknowledge the superior efforts of the ten "pioneers" who designed and offered the first ten sections of QU101: Cheryl Barnard, Crystal Brian, Eric Bronson, Debbie Clark, Ray Foery, Jill Martin, Scott McLean, Bruce Saulnier, Bob Smart, and Allison Stratton. Their contributions can never be surpassed. In addition, I would like to thank Walter Mullen, Quinnipiac's former Coordinator of Assessment and Academic Research, who was a part of the planning process for QU101 from the beginning. I also thank Linda Broker, former Director of Academic Programs, for her organizational genius in helping to start up and sustain QU101. Their contributions in building QU101 went farther than their "official" roles. Both kept me mindful of whether the objectives I intend are being met.

The course, and the readings included in this volume, continues to reflect the contributions of the faculty who have taught the course and shared their ideas with their colleagues—both formally and informally. Their numbers are too great to thank them each individually; nevertheless, this volume is a testament to their continued support and generosity.

For this 5th edition of the QU101 Reader, I would like to recognize below a true, continuing community of collaborative Full and Part Time faculty, students, and administrators who have shared their views on the teaching QU101 using such important common methods as Annotation, Discussion Circles and Writing to Learn Assignments. Part time QU101 faculty colleagues who have been consistently insightful and committed to best practices in QU101 over the course of regularly scheduled QU101 faculty meetings during the Fall semester include: **Lori Amann-Chetcuti, Bruce Fox, Bruce Franklin, David Gross, Sharon Jenkins, Jill McKeon, Siggy Nystrom, Betsy Rosenblum, Bill Schwanbeck, and Lyneene Richards.**

I am also thankful for the work and insights of my colleagues who made the second year of the QU101 Peer Catalyst Initiative a success: **Aileen Dever, David Herscovici, Mark Hoffman, and Joan Kreiger.** Our sophomore student Peer Catalysts made each of our QU101 sections a great experience for our students, and their weekly reports on our teaching and their observations of students' growth in such "essential learning proficiency" areas as "social intelligence," "oral communication," and "responsible citizenship" are rich with assessment data. Their perspective on what works best in QU101 is unique and will continue in their role this year as "Meta-Catalysts." Kudos to: **Sara McKersie, Rebecca Muller, Kasey Quinlan, and Danielle Susi.**

Any new readings that appear in the 5th edition of QU101 Reader, as well as the many deletions of both long standing and more recent additions, ultimately come down to my decision as Coordinator of QU101. I would like to thank, however, a diverse mix of QU101 teachers, QU administrators, or those who wear both hats. **Andrew Delohery; Berny Grindel; Richard Kamins; Janice Swiatek-Kelley, and Joan Kreiger.** They either made excellent suggestions for addition or deletion, or else took the time to let me bounce my thinking off them about how best to keep the Reader's original core texts in place, while making changes that either address generational and cultural shifts, or redress long standing oversights in representation.

Thanks to **John Hassett**, Quinnipiac University photographer, for the cover photo of graduating Quinnipiac students.

I continue to extend special thanks to a number of long standing colleagues and administrators who have been patient with my sometimes overly passionate and mercurial approach to ensuring that QU101 not become irrelevant as Quinnipiac University continues to undergo breath taking change, or that it not become hollowed out by contending curricular agendas. Thanks to: **QU Seminars Director, Jill Shahverdian; QU201 Coordinator, Raymond Foery; QU301 Coordinator, Ewa Callahan; Director of Academic Programming, Angela Skyers; Associate Vice President for Academic Affairs, Edward Kavanagh; and lastly, thanks to Senior Vice President for Academic Affairs, Mark Thompson** for his wise and energetic vision regarding the future of greater Intellectual Community at Quinnipiac University.

I also recognize the indefatigable and enthusiastic work of Deborah Clark, whose coordination of the Faculty Collaborative Seminars enables QU101 to share its vision and best practices for advancing the University Curriculum.

Finally, I would like to recognize the lasting legacy of Sean Duffy—the first coordinator of QU101, and the QU Seminars Series' first Director. I know of no one at Quinnipiac University who so consistently and graciously combines the intellectual, civic, and collegial virtues most valued in higher education.

INTRODUCTION TO THE 5TH EDITION OF
QU101 READER
"THE INDIVIDUAL IN THE COMMUNITY"
A PRIMER FOR INSTRUCTORS AND STUDENTS

THREE INNOVATIVE AND COLLABORATIVE FEATURES
OF THE QU101 READER

The fifth edition of the QU101 Reader retains three important features that were first introduced in the 2010, fourth edition. First, please find and detach the bookmark at the back of this reader and use it to locate your place in your reading and to refer quickly to the six common course questions all of us are seeking answers to—not only in QU101, but over the course of our lives. On the other side of this bookmark is a passage from Amin Maalouf's *In the Name of Identity*, (which also appears in a selection in this reader). This quotation distills the conceptually complex and lived nature of individuality and how its "heritages" can be mapped onto the various communities within which all individuals must affiliate. Next, please note that each page of every reading provides wide, ample margins so that we can continue to advance the basic method of annotation we practiced in our summer reading and opening discussions of Barack Obama's *Dreams from My Father*. Finally, at the end of every reading, please find a "Notes" section with blank pages for advancing and deepening the basic practice of marginal annotation. A book with blank pages—open locations—at the end of each reading enables us to expand and deepen our individual and collaborative ownership of what we are learning. Instead of using a separate "notebook," we can now account for and integrate into a single book a number of "Writing-to-Learn" activities that will advance one of the most valued and essential proficiencies for life-long learning: "Critical Thinking and Reasoning." These open "Notes" sections of your Reader can serve as the place where:

- you transfer "teachable moments" from your teacher's board work or from peers' small group findings;
- you collect, select, and reflect on earlier annotations in light of later ones;
- you reflect on or synthesize new questions or problems;
- you respond to a standard set of questions about what is most clear, what is most puzzling, and what counts as "new knowledge" from any individual text, or from two or more texts.

The triple rationale and result of these format innovations lead us to a new understanding of what a "common reader" is for. In ascending importance of its "use-value," we should recognize: **first, that the QU101 Reader is a common "textbook"; second, that it is a multi-use, yet commonplace, "notebook"; and third, that if you take full ownership of it, your QU101 Reader becomes a highly individualized *work book*.** In other words, the book you now hold in your hands has best served its purpose when its pages and spaces for critical thinking, reasoning, and reflection through writing have been so much (re)marked upon, that it has become, in the common course of its use in QU101, a uniquely individual possession, one rendered unusable by others, totally unsuitable for resale, or to be "rented" by any future first year student of QU101.

TAKING OWNERSHIP OF YOUR QU101 READER

As new college students, you should never underestimate the power of recording your identifying information in a book dedicated to the most fundamental questions of who you are and why you have joined Quinnipiac University's community of higher education. By identifying your selves as unique, individual owners of a book you all hold in common with your teacher—by "making your mark"—literally—inside its cover, you are setting in motion a series of written acts of ownership and relationship as reader-annotators that will represent some broad and deep changes to the "high school" identity and community you were part of only two months before your first QU101 class. Another very important reason for taking full, intentional ownership of your QU101 Reader is that you will have a permanent, accessible record of your mind at work during your first semester as a university student. Keeping this book close at hand as you advance in your studies will serve you well as you complete the requirements of The University Curriculum, and most especially as you will be taking on and completing:

- **QU201 ("The Individual in the National Community")**
- **QU301, ("The Individual in the Global Community")**
- ***Quinnipiac University's Electronic Portfolio of Student Learning Proficiencies (Scheduled for Rollout In Fall 2012)***

For now, though, here you are as a member of Quinnipiac University's Class of 2015, trying to understand what it means to initiate the taking of full, intentional ownership of your QU101 Common Reader. During the May orientation that I coordinate for all QU101 teachers, I make the case that no ongoing, authentic discussion about how we form and sustain individual identities within our various communities can happen until every QU101 teacher has set a basic standard of identity and ownership. Well before he or she learns your name, your QU101 teacher will ask that you write in the inside cover of this book some information that answers four common questions of: **Who; Where; When; Why?** By writing your name, your place of residence (at home and at QU), the starting date of your first QU101 class, and a brief description of why you have chosen to pursue a University education, you are claiming an ***indelible individual ownership*** of your QU101 Common Reader.

Your QU101 teacher will also be asked to print out your QU101 class roster that is on *Blackboard* with the names and photographs of you and your peers. He or she might even go so far as to ask you to keep a copy of this key community identification document in your common reader to help you more quickly identify the members of your QU101 seminar discussion. Some teachers will insist on experimenting with the power of "face-to-face" interactions with various "social ice breakers" so that you become more comfortable with the art of student-focused discussion, instead of teacher-focused lecture. They will try to actualize the rich inter-dependence of our personal and intellectual responsibilities by requiring that you own up to identifying yourself as an emerging college student who is curious to form and sustain various kinds of circles of participation and discussion according to our common goals.

QU101'S "GEOGRAPHIC" GOAL: LOCATING OURSELVES AS MEMBERS OF A UNIVERSITY COMMUNITY

Because of my ever-shifting, double identity as both a teacher and the coordinator of QU101, I find it helpful to imagine this course, this reader, and the questions and methods we hold in common, in *geographic* and *logistical* terms. I see both individual and communal opportunities for "charting," "mapping," and "locating" ourselves within and across the intellectual *landscapes* and conceptual *locales* of our reading, writing, listening and speaking. In a "geographic" sense, the custom book mark, for example, acts as both our map's "legend," (6 Course Questions), and as a "location device," (Maalouf's axial concept of "vertical and horizontal" heritages), as we set the course of our common intellectual adventure. Nor do I think it an accident of random word choice that the original meaning of "legend" comes from the ancient Greek, *legein*: "to choose, collect, speak." Are not these acts integral to annotated-driven discussion based on our common course questions? Note, too, that *legend* in turn derives from *logos,* meaning: "word, reason, speech, account."

In effect, teachers and students "coordinate" and map out together an intellectual journey whose *logical* destinations are reached through reading, writing, speaking, listening. In the words of Stephen Brookfield and Stephen Preskill, we can also undertake the "co-creation" of the many *geographic* analogies that spring into view as we better understand the singularly collaborative purpose of QU101, in which "the responsibility for teaching and learning is held in common"(13). **Our sense of a strong intellectual community thus begins in each QU101 class.** Teachers and students need to recognize and negotiate the opportunities and obligations for teaching and learning that is held in common. Yet our local, distributed responsibilities across individual QU101 sections are ultimately beholden to an even larger landscape of teaching and learning we hold in common: The Quinnipiac University Curriculum and the **"Essential Learning Proficiencies."**

QU101 AND THE PRACTICE OF SIX "ESSENTIAL LEARNING PROFICIENCIES"

Quinnpiac University has identified ten "Essential Learning Proficiencies" that all students are expected to achieve as they fulfill the course requirements of both the University Curriculum and their chosen majors. When students begin activating their "E-Portfolios" in Fall 2012, the written, spoken, and visual artifacts documenting their learning will be tied to these Learning Proficiencies. In my half decade of teaching and coordinating experience in QU101, I will stake my credibility as an educator on the "logical"—in the fullest sense of *legendary*—powers of *Annotation* for initiating, modeling, and advancing the stated outcomes of six of these university-wide proficiencies. They are:

> *Oral Communication*: an ability to think critically, clearly, and creatively as both intentional speakers and listeners.
>
> *Written Communication: an ability to think critically, clearly, and creatively as intentional readers and writers.*
>
> *Critical Thinking and Reasoning*—An ability to recognize problems, and to acquire, assess and synthesize information in order to derive creative and appropriate solutions.
>
> *Social Intelligence*—An ability to work effectively with others, to understand and manage interactions, and to act ethically, constructively, and responsibly to achieve individual and common goals.
>
> *Diversity Awareness and Sensitivity*—An understanding of, and respect for, the similarities and differences among human communities. This includes a recognition and appreciation for the unique talents and contributions of all individuals.
>
> *Responsible Citizenship*—An ability to recognize, analyze and influence decisions and actions at the local, national and global community, and to engage with these communities as responsible citizens.

Obviously, the extraordinary "dialectical" premise of QU101, wherein the concept and experience of "individuality" is placed in continuous, ever changing, and inter-dependent tension with that of "community," holds forth the **promise** that teachers and students, as themselves individuals in our local (university) community, will experience some basic level of "oral communication" through a teacher who asks questions and students who answer them. More certainly, QU101's six common questions, when replicated in a course syllabus, or broadcasted on a bookmark, should signal explicitly to teachers and students that any authentic answers to these questions will need to draw on the powers of "critical thinking and reasoning" we have developed over the course of a K-12 education. Finally, and most certainly, the texts selected for a course that focuses on how individuals and communities form and sustain themselves could not ignore such issues as "diversity awareness and sensitivity" and "responsible citizenship." In other words, in hypothetical terms, QU101 should fulfill four of six essential learning proficiencies by simply running as a teacher-driven lecture course with required readings and some form of assessment to determine what students have "learned."

QU101 has evolved, however—especially in light of the above "essential learning proficiencies"—to ensure that students and teachers become both more "intentional as readers and writers," and more "intentional as speakers and listeners." To achieve this variable, four square goal means that teachers and students will need to adopt and adapt some multi-purpose methods that will practice and integrate both our inter-personal and our intellectual dispositions. Annotation is one such method that has now been tried and tested by many QU101 teachers and students who will confirm that it is an effective, deeply intentional, method. (For some ringing student testimonials, please see the closing pages of this introduction.)

QU101'S BOOKFACE COMMUNITY: WHY ANNOTATION INTENSIFIES INTENTIONAL DISCUSSION

"Annotation"—also known as "marginalia"—has been in evidence for over two thousand years. In her marvelous history of the subject—*Marginalia: Readers Writing in Books*—H. J. Jackson reminds us that, "[i]ndeed the habit may be as old as script itself, for readers have to interpret writing, and note follows text as thunder follows lightning" (44). In his recent New York Times report, "Book Lovers Fear Dim Future for Notes in the Margins," Dirk Johnson reminds us of the lasting value and power of such "thunder." "Like many readers, Mark Twain [engaged] in marginalia, writing comments alongside passages and giving an author a piece of his mind." His annotations now enable us to more deeply understand the mind and times of one of America's greatest writers because, rather than leaving his books blank, he left behind "a literary archaeology." Johnson tells us that Studs Terkel, America's great oral historian, "was known to admonish friends who would read his books but leave them free of markings. He told them that reading a book should not be a passive exercise, but rather a raucous conversation."

For students of QU101, the essential proficiency of more "intentional" "oral communication" begins when, with this book and pens in their hands, they "speak" to the author with fundamental questions in mind. In effect, active, habitual annotation merges the acts of writing and speaking; the record of our marginalia holds, potentially, the communal "thunder" and "raucous conversation" of class discussion that follows from the many strikes of "lightning" that we bring as individual, intentional readers to class. When we write in the margins of books, we do so for many reasons: we pretend to be "talking back" to what a writer is telling us; we are keeping a record of what is most important—our "notes to self"—depending on our purposes. Annotation always begins as an individual, solitary, intimately focused exercise in which we exchange a piece of our mind with that of the writer's.

Annotation, as an educational end, however, represents the "*social network*" of learning in QU101. Reading with a pen poised in one's hand slows down what I like to call "the pulse rate of our reading's purpose." Interrupting—"intentionally"—our reading to interject our own thinking into the margins of our common reader is what I call *Bookface.* **When we are annotating responsively and responsibly, when we are sharing a focused piece of our mind with an expert writer in anticipation that we will be asked to share our marginalia with our intellectual peers "intentionally," we are on** *Bookface.* Therefore, to best form and cultivate this time-tested habit of mind as new members of our university's intellectual community, don't you *think* that it might be useful to experiment with annotation as an essential proficiency of intellectual *uni-tasking*, to **turn off** *Facebook* and other virtual social networking sites that appeal to our questionable proficiencies as multitaskers?

vs. Facebook

QU101 teachers and students should discuss the above question, particularly in the language of how we form "habits" and the essential defining and balancing of our "social" and "intellectual" habits of mind. H. J. Jackson reflects on that species of reader "for whom annotating books is an act of love, transforming monologues into dialogues" (242). While not every QU101 teacher will agree that writing in all books is an act of love, he or she has been oriented to understand that the QU101 Common Reader is designed to be written in habitually, that it is a work(ing) book in process, and that its blank spaces and pages need to be filled in with the intellectually—and socially, and emotionally—focused pieces of our minds.

QU101 teachers also understand that teaching this course is not a platform for lecturing on their annotations exclusively; it is not a place for a professor's "monologue," but is, rather, an opportunity for a dialogue that is intentionally focused on and driven by a community of close and curious readers. Jackson's description of the annotator's "dialogue" allows us to adapt and expand her idea of "a second voice"—and a "third voice," and a fourth . . . and so forth, to the purposes of annotation-driven class discussions in QU101.

> Set aside for the moment the fact that annotation is not a dialogue since the author cannot (normally) reply. Annotation introduces a second voice where writers and publishers intended only one; the reader talks to the book. For the initial annotating reader, marginalia articulate some of the thoughts stimulated by the act of reading. This second voice is the reader's own, and the resulting "dialogue" is a partial record of the reader's participation in the book, the naturally occurring transaction between text and reader (242).

Only by intentionally locating ourselves in the margins of what we are reading together in QU101 do we create the literal *response-ability* of gathering ourselves and our new voices as questioning readers. Just consider for a moment the discussion multiplier effect of 22 students and their teacher, each of whom brings a second voice as an annotator that he or she then gives a new and third voice to in group dialogue. I would go so far as to describe QU101's method of annotation as *intentionality squared.* **When charged with annotating our common readings with common questions always in mind, we become doubly intentional in a course that requires us to discover and share ourselves as one intellectual community. This is a bold claim.** Students who might associate their daily *Facebook* habits with exercising their "social intelligence," for example, are now challenged to think of this "essential learning proficiency" as the practice of more intentional reading: *individual acts of annotation that also will be shared face-to-face in QU101's communal acts of discussion.* At the risk of redundancy, this is, again, what I mean by QU101 as an opportunity to join *Bookface*. In effect, by practicing more intentional acts of reading and writing synthesized by annotation, we **join an intellectual networking site where unrehearsed, face-to-face discussion is not mediated by our screens,** nor by our virtual "relationship status" on *Facebook*, but by our *actual* **face-to-face responses.**

Students reading this will ask: "Ok, I think I understand what you mean by *Bookface*, especially when I compare really reading a book to going on *Facebook*. But how can annotating my reading to be ready to talk to kids my own age—and who are not my "friends"—make me more "responsive"? I mean, when you add all the "texting" I do on top of my *Facebook* time, I don't think I can focus just on my reading—never mind acquire the habit of *Bookface*." My answer is that when—or if—you force yourself to focus on annotating your QU101 Reader, you do so because you are equally interested in becoming a "responsible citizen" of your new University Community. You are interested in recognizing new faces, speaking and listening to the diverse interpretations of your new social and intellectual peers as you share and compare your annotations with them. The challenge of ***Bookfacing*** is that you are being asked to give up some part of your ***Facebooking*** habit so that you can experience and achieve what your university education has identified as more "essential learning proficiencies." *Bookface,* though, needs "co-creators"—not only of the intentionally annotated results of our common reading, but of our willingness to speak and listen through more intentional discussion.

QU101 AND THE CIRCULATION OF
MORE INTENTIONAL DISCUSSION

From its common motivating questions, to its "work-book" assumptions of how to locate and allocate our common pursuit of the six essential learning proficiencies, we now better understand that QU101's *Bookface Community* stands or falls on the use of annotation in a course designated to be run as *a seminar-discussion, rather than a teacher-centered lecture.* The word "note" is at the center of annotation, and according to the *Oxford English Dictionary*, it came in the 12th century to mean: "to notice, pay attention to, to perceive, to indicate, to put down in writing, to mention." So just in case you haven't yet noticed, *please note the following: the intellectual and inter-personal habits of mind intended by the six "essential learning proficiencies" are central to stimulating and achieving an engaged intellectual community of intentional learners who join with their QU101 teacher in the "co-creation of knowledge" through discussion of their annotations.*

That last phrase is from Stephen Brookfield's and Stephen Preskill's *Discussion as a Way of Teaching: Tools and Techniques for Democratic Classrooms*. "Co-creation of knowledge" epitomizes the design and purpose of QU101. Such co-operative creation becomes a reality in our QU101 classes when teachers and students **inhabit discussion circles**, and develop together the **habits of intellectual and social openness** that such democratic arrangements enable. Years of experiential research have led Brookfield and Preskill to conclude that discussion circles instill in students

> *. . . the confidence to be both teacher and student.* Instead of being passive recipients of the instructor's wisdom, students alternate between the roles of teacher and learner, sometimes explaining and conveying information and at other times actively absorbing and interpreting what others have to share. To allow the traditional dividing line between teacher and student to become blurred in this way requires teachers and students to view their enterprise as truly collaborative. *In collaborative classrooms, the responsibility for teaching and learning is held in common* (13, emphasis added).

To bolster their claim that discussion as a way of teaching is most effective for teachers and learners held to a common—and thus higher—standard of collaboration, take notice of how Brookfield and Preskill use a series of classic "binary oppositions" in the above passage. They explicitly pose passive versus active learning; teacher-centeredness versus student centeredness; teacher wisdom versus student acceptance. Less obvious are the authors' implicit, but much more compelling, precepts for blending and synthesizing such binaries. Namely, when discussion-based seminars are working best, our educationally defined *roles alternate; traditional dividing lines become blurred;* and taken together, all of us, when held to collaborating within QU101's common learning community, gain new forms of *confidence to be both teacher and student*.

Let's pause to consider what this *both<>and logic* means for both students and teachers of QU101. It means that together we need to acknowledge, and then work to move beyond, binary oppositional thinking and *either/or* per-spectives. Identifying and capturing the tension and energy of *either/or* think-ing so as to transform it into *both<>and* thinking is called *dialectical rea-soning*. Dialectical reasoning seeks to find some shared territory or unforeseen common ground for understanding complex questions and problems. It puts a premium on "thinking outside the box" of binary thinking. Throughout their book, Brookfield and Preskill consistently pose and expose key binaries in how we teach and learn. They then work toward helping us to understand a "dialectical" approach to finding a shared, mutual—even a new 3rd—way of transforming ourselves as co-creators of knowledge.

Both And = Dialectical

3rd Place

Here is summary of how they line up the most important binary opposi-tions that inform the most common room arrangement for discussion-based classrooms: the circle. In their section, "Discussion in the Round: Hearing All Voices," they first describe all of the obvious, community-minded reasons for using circles to form and sustain discussion. In the second group, the authors expose the potential perils of circles, which can favor certain indi-viduals and intimidate others.

☺ **In circles everyone has the same chance of being seen and heard.**
☺ **In circles, the teacher is not front and center; all face one another around a common center.**
☺ **The circle literally shapes expectations for equal participation.**
☺ **The circle is thus a physical manifestation of democracy (81).**

☹ **Circles favor only confident and talkative individuals.**
☹ **Circles strip individuals of the right to privacy.**
☹ **Circles deny individuals distance to assess a teacher's good will and trustworthiness.**
☹ **Circles can be experienced as zones of forced disclosure (81).**

Brookfield and Preskill believe that by acknowledging these contending assumptions about discussion circles will make for a far more engaged, high stakes investment for teachers and students. They have created a number of "tools and techniques" that enable us to move past the idea of the circle as *either* an ideal speech situation that is unattainable for all, *or* a hypothetical ordeal for some. They have experimented with a range of procedures, includ-ing: "The Circle of Voices"; "Circular Response Discussions"; "Snowballing"; "Rotating Groups"; "Relaxed and Structured Buzz Groups"; "The Encircled Circle." *Your QU101 teacher has been oriented to using discussion circles in all of their great variety. After all, with 22 students in a section, and designated as a seminar, rather than a lecture, it would be a wasted opportunity if a given QU101 teacher is not at least willing to acknowl-edge and work toward blending the virtues, and minimizing the vices, within that most fundamental, either/or educational binary of all: Lec-ture Versus Discussion as a Way of Teaching.*

✱ Handout? Ask Tim/Lori

Before we can understand that the *Form* of the QU101 discussion circle requires a particular intellectual *Content* to make it truly circulate into the co-creator's "confidence to be both teacher and student," we should understand that there are many virtues to teacher-lecture that can be adapted to circle discussions. Brookfield and Preskill are quite instructive on the need for transcending the binary opposition between lecture mode and discussion mode. They believe that lectures, if used tactically and tactfully, can also model "democratic" and communal discussion. Using dialectical reasoning, they dismiss "the false dichotomy between lecturing and discussion" this way: "Lectures are not, by definition, oppressive and authoritarian. . . . Similarly, discussions are not, in and of themselves, liberating and spontaneous. . . . Instead of reducing questions of pedagogical method to a simplistic dichotomy—discussion good, lecture bad—we see these methods as complementary" (45). They then offer several techniques that in my own QU101 experience have been proven to work particularly well *both within and without the circle of discussion in an alternating role reversal.* Three of these techniques are particularly custom-made for QU101, given that we all are asking and answering the same set of six common course questions.

> *"Begin every lecture with one or more questions. . . .* [B]y raising a series of framing questions, [students will] be more accepting when [teachers] frame discussions around a question or questions to be explored" (46).
>
> *"End every lecture with one or more questions. . . .* This prepares students for the practice we advocate—of ending discussion sessions by asking students to volunteer the questions the discussion has raised for them, rather than by giving a summary of 'what we learned today in our discussion'—" (46).
>
> *"Deliberately introduce periods of silence. . . .* We believe that periods of reflective silence are as integral to good discussion as the most animated speech. . . . [Students and teachers] need to learn that silence does not represent a vacuum in discussion. Rather, it signifies a different but equally significant and intense engagement with the subject of discussion" (46).

Former QU101 students have testified to the generative, democratic space of the discussion circle in which the teacher becomes almost unnoticeable. He or she becomes more of listening, note-taking student, an auditor and annotator of what he or she hears from fellow co-creators of knowledge. Students need to understand that your QU101 teachers are not born with "the confidence to be both teacher and student." We need to practice intentional listening over speaking, to balance monologue with dialogue. Yet I, and even my former QU101 students will also tell you that QU101 teachers have the clear responsibility to seize upon "teachable moments" from robust circle discussions, and to model for their students any number of "lecture-style" moves like those endorsed by Brookfield and Preskill. They can do so both inside and outside the space of the discussion circle. Here are several more that I recommend to teachers who come from a lecture-culture, and wish to alternate their position and place at—and as—"the head of the class" in a seminar setting.

- At the start of the class, stay in your seat in the circle and model— briefly—your response to one of your own annotations of the text in question to get the discussion started.
- Half way through the class session, take up your own "annotations" of your students' discussion, and leave your seat in the circle discussion to summarize and synthesize key issues, binaries, dilemmas, new questions, and "dialectical" opportunities. Do a brief (5–10 minute) "chalk and talk" session on the board and return to the circle.
- Toward the end of the class, leave your seat in the circle to perform a summary and synthesis session based on notes and listening to students' discussion, or on a complex passage that not only exemplifies a course questions, but raises other questions and complexities for next class.
- Begin a big circle discussion for 20 minutes, then break students into smaller groups(circles) to focus on particular course questions or repeated cited/annotated passages. Have them decide on the 1 most puzzling question they would like the teacher to "lecture on" to open the next class.
- Use the "natural" silences that occur and evolve in a discussion-based seminar such as QU101. This means that teachers should not only wait as long as need be for students to answer questions posed, but that they should also call for silence so that all students have time to locate and reflect on annotations that are appropriate for advancing or restarting a discussion.

The dynamic point of all of these techniques taken together is to recall the ancient and original meaning of "lecture." From *legere*, "to read," the good "lecturer" knew how best "to gather, collect, pick out, choose" the most important passages for sharing with an otherwise illiterate and "unread" audience. Thus, in a contemporary college course that introduces new students to such "essential learning proficiencies" as more "intentional" reading, listening, speaking, and writing, the best "lecture" is one in which students and teacher gather and choose what needs to be read and annotated—together. Now we can see that the best student-led discussion is, in fact, an intentionally shared lecture, just as the best teacher-lecture tends toward shared discussion. If we can ever begin to understand the potential for sharing ourselves—students and teachers together—as co-creators of knowledge, then teachers must alternate their roles to the point where ***the confidence to be both lecturer and listener" is circulated, transferred, and modeled by***

QU101 students themselves, who in turn gain the confidence to become lecturers in common.

Yet for all of their rich, methodological and practical experience as students of, and teachers in, circles, Brookfield and Preskill nevertheless fall short in helping us to ensure that the collaborative consistency and variety of discussion can be sustained in intellectually rigorous and socially substantial ways. At the risk of holding the power of the discussion circle captive to one side of a very familiar "binary opposition"—that of *Form/Content*—the circle as a *form* for discussion does not guarantee that the *content* of discussion will be collaborative and conducive to realizing the essential learning proficiencies. That is why QU101 requires that we pursue a set of *common* questions, readings, and methods. When *both* the discussion circle *and* a series of annotation-related methods are *held in common*, only then can individual students and their teachers begin to realize the goal of a strong, collaborative, intentional learning community.

Based on five years of teaching QU101, I am certain that annotation's "legendary" power to gather and share the intellectual "Content" of any act of reading is greatly intensified and made even more intentional through QU101's common course questions. I am equally certain that by annotating our common reading according to these common questions—and to the new questions teachers and students will intentionally create and adapt as their discussions mature and deepen—we will experience a tremendous growth in "Oral Communication," "Social Intelligence," "Diversity Awareness," and "Responsible Citizenship." In the next three sections, I will make the case that annotation is also the essential foundation for creating and realizing more intentional writing and critical reasoning in QU101.

FROM ANNOTATION TO DIALECTICAL REASONING: MORE INTENTIONAL WRITING IN QU101

Older than the act of annotation is the art of *Dialectic*, which was perfected in Greece over 2500 years ago by the philosopher, Socrates. Apparently, Socrates never learned how to read or to write, but his student, Plato, must have carefully "annotated" his teacher's lectures and discussions about the power of *dialectic*—the practice of focused *conversation*. Most simply, the art of *dialectic* can be equated with conducting a *dialogue*. According to *The Oxford English Dictionary*, the original meaning of dialectic is to "speak through" or "speak across." I think it is no stretch of this definition to assert that the annotation-based discussions at the heart of every QU101 class qualify them as intentionally "dialectical." We need to speak through and across our annotations, and across the discussion circles we form throughout the semester if we are to come close to achieving the essential learning proficiencies noted above. For both Plato and Socrates, there was no difference between "dialectical reasoning" and what we today define as the essential learning proficiency of "critical thinking and reasoning."

As set forth in Plato's *The Republic*, (selections of which appear in this QU101 Reader), Socrates elevates *Dialectic* to the most important position in the studies one would undertake to become a "Guardian" of an ideal community. *The Republic* is a wide-ranging investigation into the best—and worst—ways to form and sustain a community of informed, responsible citizens. In this "dialogue," Socrates and his "students" are, in the words of QU's definition of "critical thinking and reasoning," trying "to recognize problems" posed by too much individuality in a community—wherein everyone enjoys certain common rights, and are "wise" to their liberties, but might be loathe to accept, or are ignorant of equally critical responsibilities. They are trying "to acquire, assess and synthesize information in order to derive creative and appropriate solutions" to this problem. They are seeking an ideal balance, a way to continuously ad*just*—through proper education—the contending forces of Individuality and Community. *The Republic*—whether or not we agree with the vision of its ideal community—is an exercise in using critical reasoning to seek *Justice*. **It considers how to find the most *just* outcome for any given group of individuals who find themselves in tension with the communities they form, join, and sustain according to regulatory principles that are themselves in continuous tension and contention as to rights and responsibilities.**

Because QU101 students have just graduated from high school, let's consider how Joe Greenwald, a high school teacher who teaches dialectical reasoning to his students, defines *dialectic*. "A method of reasoning that compares and contrasts opposing points of view in order ***to find a new point of view that will incorporate whatever is true in the originals***" (Greenwald, emphasis added). In other words, to think or reason in *dialectical* terms requires that we move between and across two aspects or alternatives. This definition accords with our sense of the opposition, tension, and opportunity within the grand theme of QU101: ***The Individual In the Community.*** Using a table of "binary oppositions," we can begin to visualize opposing concepts or points of view. Look at this stack of juxtaposed boxes divided by an apparently impassable vertical line. We could add endlessly to this list.

Light	Dark
Good	Evil
Wisdom	Ignorance
Master	Slave
Self	Other
One	Many
Sovereign	Subject
Citizen	Alien
Male	Female
Authority	Freedom
Right	Responsibility
Community	Individual

For Joe Greenwald, his central learning outcome for his high school students is to have them *recognize* just how fundamental "binary thinking" is to the way humans process reality, and how prevalent and dominant it is as a method of learning and argument. His second goal is to have his students *re-think* the apparently un-passable boundary between a given binary opposition. He will conduct, in effect, a "dialectical" conversation with his students. So, for example, he will ask, much like Socrates does with his students, a set of questions about the binary opposition of "light" and "dark."

For our purposes in QU101, I have moved students in the first week of class to using dialectical reasoning in a brief, but very intentional exercise that will not only help them to appreciate the "dialectical" energy residing in QU101's grand theme, but also to set the teaching and learning stage for three of the six essential learning proficiencies: "oral communication; "critical thinking/reasoning"; and "written communication." I take 15 minutes, at most, to complete with students the following "writing-to-learn" assignment on the first blank "Notes" page following this introduction to the QU101 Reader.

1. Define light as the opposite of dark.
2. Define dark as the opposite of light.
3. Using your definitions from 1 and 2, define that which is composed of both light and dark.

Students' answers are illuminating, confused, and amusing, but what comes through from individual reports generally is the following, which I then synthesize on the board. *Light is the absence of dark. Dark is the absence of light. Sundown (or dusk) is the presence of both light and dark.* I then ask the class whether *dusk* is *more* or *less* than the sum of its light and dark parts. All tentatively agree that it is more. I then ask them: **Is it reasonable to think that 1(light) plus 2(dark) equals 3(dusk)?** And the students agree that this new "arithmetic" is reasonable. I then tell them: **When we try to critically reason using binary terms to achieve dialectical, rather than *arithmetical, reasoning, we have to be curious, willing, and creative to seek a new "thirdness"—a conception that would not otherwise "add up" or occur to us. 1+1=3 is therefore a reasonable formula for practicing the essential learning proficiency of "critical thinking and reasoning."** Once students accept that this kind of "dialectical" reasoning might be useful for investigating, for example, their summer reading of Obama's memoir and his struggle with his identity as to whether he is either "white" or "black," or whether he is part of one community or another, class discussions—and the kinds of "writing-to-learn" assignments teachers can ask for—become more focused on the stated outcome of "critical thinking and reasoning": "to synthesize information in order to derive creative and appropriate solutions."

Students very soon recognize, for example, the dialectical form and opportunity of Course Questions 1–2 and 5–6 as we dive right into our annotation-driven, dialectically charged discussions that always end up circling Obama's provisional, but key conclusion on page 100: "Don't you know who I am? I'm an *individual!*"

As a matter of fact, QU101's majority of "white" students and teachers could begin to recognize the dialectically transformative opportunities of thinking differently—beyond binaries; that **an individual can be both white and black—or neither-nor.** In using dialectical reasoning in brief, writing-to-learn exercises, and through new, more advanced annotation codes, they could recognize that Obama, America's first "black" president, was, and still is, struggling to recognize and move himself, and all of us, *beyond* America's racialized, binary calculations. But most of all, by introducing dialectical reasoning into our QU101 reading, discussion, and writing, we begin to recognize a much deeper meaning behind Obama's remark on page 105: "Strange how a single conversation can change you." In QU101, we have the opportunity to have multiple, truly *dialectical* and deeply *methodical* conversations—from within the margins of our annotated reading, to the writing-to-learn assignments that capture the otherwise ephemeral voices of our discussion circles.

We have now understood that Annotation can serve as our workaday, multi-purpose method for locating and transferring our common practices of reading and discussion in QU101. We also now recognize that a very strong case can be made for further pursuing and achieving our mastery of the six essential learning proficiencies by experimenting with the basic and intermediate phases of what Plato somewhat mystically refers to in *The Republic* as "Dialectic"—"the only method of inquiry which . . . gently draws and leads [students' souls] upward, using as assistants and helpers the arts we have described—which we often through force of habit call branches of knowledge." By moving to the third, most advanced form of dialectical reasoning, we can set the stage for a new kind of method that is, in fact, the seeking of dialectical "thirdness" through recourse to the literal visualization of such— *Triangulation.*

MOVING FROM DIALECTICAL REASONING
TO THEMATIC TRIANGULATION

In his comprehensive history, *Dialectical Thinking and Adult Development*, the psychologist Michael Basseches reminds us that dialectical reasoning is a **dynamic movement** of mature thought that transforms binary oppositional thinking through the practice of three distinct phases. At the risk of repetition of our **1+1=3** example above, Basseches is describing the same three phased movement, but instead of using numbers, he uses a descriptor that we are all familiar with from our high school five paragraph format days—**thesis.**

The first phase involves reflection upon a thought—the thesis—to a new thought—the antithesis. A thesis is any idea or element of thought. An antithesis is . . . any idea or element of thought excluded from, outside of, or contrary to the thesis.

The second phase involves movement from reflection upon both thesis and antithesis to a third thought—the synthesis—in which the thesis and the antithesis (or some aspect of each) are related to each other. The synthesis usually has a more complex form than either the thesis of the antithesis, since it includes aspects of thesis and antithesis within itself and binds those aspects together. . . .

The overall movement toward a *synthesis* may be *cyclical* in that it can become *a new thesis*, reflection upon which can then lead to a thought which is alternative to or omitted from it, (that is, *a new antithesis*). (Basseches 77–78, emphasis added).

What Basseches is describing really just boils down to noticing how or whether the key concept(s) in a particular passage we have annotated in light of a particular course question is exhibiting a strict "binary oppositional" (*either/or*) point of view, or is perhaps moving toward a more open "dialectical" (*both<>and*) point of departure that enables us to cycle and newly "synthesize." For example, if we are asked to review our annotations of a particular reading—or between two, even three readings—with an eye to answering a particular course question in a **"writing-to-learn synthesis"** assignment, we will quickly discover conceptual patterns and movements that will qualify as "first phase" or "second phase."

If, however, QU101 students and teachers are uncertain about how to get to what Basseches calls "a third thought—*the synthesis*"—I ask that you remain open and willing to **look back at, and reflect upon, your annotations as they have developed and matured across the texts of this book.** It is not enough to annotate a particular reading by dutifully populating its margins with course question codes. QU101 teachers and students also need to use the "Notes" section following each reading so as to bring forward and "synthesize" whatever movements and phases you deem important toward exercising the all important proficiency of "critical thinking and reasoning." If QU101 teachers and their students have an equally effective method for doing this, one that doesn't traffic in the logics of binaries, dialectics, and synthesis, and you can document this hard won, new knowledge in writing, then bravo! Indeed, the most compelled annotators among my many former QU101 students, those who worked hardest at dialectical reasoning, have discovered that there are certain ideas, points of view, or ways of the world, that simply will not settle down as co-operative binaries to be made into some new (un)common ground of knowing that has, heretofore, eluded the best minds humanity have beheld.

When they report on their findings, I must again proclaim: Bravo! For when students and teachers push and apply annotation consistently and rigorously, the method leads to great teachable moments that a lecture-driven course cannot deliver, because these moments are co-created by students. What the most intentional QU101 students have discovered—without their teacher imposing it upon them—is that *the persistent attempt to critically reason from a dialectical approach to reading and writing can sometimes pitch us not into some "new synthesis," but instead onto the horns of a dilemma*. That is, many QU101 students find themselves struggling with two alternatives that cannot possibly coexist with each other—at least at this stage of their lives. *Examples abound: The Mandatory versus the Voluntary; Narcissism versus Altruism; Individual Right versus Community Responsibility; and, of course, Facebook versus Bookface!*

Nevertheless, we must remember that *QU101 is the first of three courses about Community.* QU101 and the QU101 Common Reader will have done its work when students and teachers **recognize that the Theme of the QU Seminars is part of a much larger thematic "logic of triangulation."**

PRACTICING THEMATIC TRIANGULATION IN QU101

In his book, *The Research Act*, sociologist Norman Denzin adapts dialectical reasoning into "the logic of triangulation." After all the 1, 2, 3 arithmetical and philosophical propositions, perhaps the triangle is the most useful analogy for visualizing and activating my running argument to QU101 students and teachers that we need to cultivate common, rigorous and intentional methods of intellectual inquiry and inter-personal engagement in our courses.

Connects to syllabus

For Denzin, who is concerned to improve the research acts of social scientists, *"data triangulation"* is at the heart of "[a]ll sociological observations [and] relates to activities of socially situated *persons*—whether they are in groups, or organizations, or aggregately distributed over some social area or community. A focus on *time* and *space* as observational units, recognizes their relationship to the observations of *persons*" (301–302, author's emphasis). For Denzin, time, space and persons are what he calls the three most important "conceptual sensitizers" for doing research. **So how does *"data triangulation,"* as a social scientific method, involving the observation of *persons* in *time* and *space*, transfer to what we do in QU101 as a general educational principle for building intellectual community?**

Based on my teaching experience in QU101, I have evolved into an *observer* of how students will take up and share the role and responsibility of the *lecturer* through annotation-driven discussion circles. I have become an *observer* of my *time* spent listening to and synthesizing QU101 students' struggles to achieve the essential learning proficiencies. I have become an *observer* of knowing my place in the *space* of the discussion circle to guide QU101 students toward synthesizing their annotations to achieve the essential learning proficiencies. I have become far more "sensitized" to students' conceptualizations of what they have noticed in their reading and wish to discuss in a community of their peers. And I am absolutely certain that discussion circles, driven by annotation and dialectically inspired acts of "data triangulation," are crucial "conceptual sensitizers" that have helped me produce brief, but bracing "writing-to-learn" outcomes. Here are several. Many QU101 faculty have created equally challenging writing assignments derived from their willingness to reverse their roles and responsibilities as lecturers into those of "participant observers."

- **Require that students select three annotated passages from within a single reading or three from across three different readings, and ask them to work out a "triangulation" that will produce a new way of understanding a course question or theme.**
- **Require that students select three annotated passages—a total of six—between two different readings, and ask them to work out a "triangulation" that will produce some new way of understanding a course question or theme.**
- **Require that students select three annotated passages—a total of nine—across three different readings, and ask them to work out a "triangulation" that will produce a new way of understanding a course question or theme.**
- **Allow students to propose variations upon, and to experiment with, any of the graduated "writing-to-learn" assignments suggested above. Students and teachers should discuss the active, "dialectical" possibilities that exist between Annotation, as an act of "Reading to Learn," and Data Triangulation as both an intellectual and very "social" act of *"Writing-to-Learn"* that is part of a sequence of "Low Stakes," assignments that all QU instructors are encouraged to assign.**

QU101: COMING FULL CIRCLE

I will close by reminding all students and teachers of QU101 that the methods I am espousing have placed me under *observation* by my own QU101 students in my Fall 2010 class. Here is a broadly representative selection of their 21 comments, solicited by me through a group email request during the present, spring 2001 semester.

Being required to annotate the texts we read and discuss them in a circle format really helped me in class. Not only did it give me the opportunity to feel like everyone was listening when I talked, but it also taught me to be more prepared for class. In order to participate in the discussions, I knew I had to fully understand the readings and be able to quickly reference my point in the text before the discussion moved on, so annotating was important. Annotation also forced me to read with the possible topics of discussion always in mind and think critically about how the texts relate to individuals, communities, the course questions, and even other readings or situations. (Danielle Burns)

Annotation is the vehicle by which our QU101 discussions underwent critical and analytical discussions. Through these discussions, we learned various techniques which helped us understand different views and look at certain topics through different perspectives. The way these discussions were able to work so progressively— aside the usage of the powerful tool of annotation—was by facing each other congruently by being seated in a circle. The face-to-face interaction among the students in our classroom triggered the dialectical means of learning by helping us interpose from one idea to another. This combined method of learning increasingly changed my reasoning experience by empowering me with a higher level of social understanding among the people in my community. (Sheryl Rosario)

The use of discussion circles allows students to develop oral communication skills such as speaking in a clear and cogent manner, looking your audience in the eyes, and displaying confident body language. Unlike in a normal lecture with rows, the use of discussion circles allows for the formation of an interpersonal relationship between students. The use of annotation paired with the classroom discussion circles initiates a positive environment for oral communication, discussion, and interaction between the whole class. Annotation is a method of note taking done "in the margin", where the reader is able to identify key points of interest that can be used for class discussion. Students who annotate critical readings, prior to class, are able to form cogent arguments that can be used during class. This gives students time to activate their thought processes and critical thinking before entering the classroom. Skills developed, in result of these methods, can be used in the classroom, workplace, and social environment. (Gregory Foster)

After being involved in your section of QU101 I now have firsthand experience as to why annotating texts prior to class and discussing these annotations in a circle form can help improve the outcome of a class. By reading and annotating the required texts prior to class this gave me the opportunity to think about the important points that I wanted to bring up in class discussion. It also allowed the conversation to flow more freely in the class room, instead of sitting there and trying to find our points in the text during class we had already marked them off and written down what we thought. Aside from annotations sitting in a circle instead of rows also improved my class room experience. The circle allowed students to look at each other while talking, and the class discussions were more of a conversation then a lecture. By having a conversation with the class and watching each other speak we learned each others names allowing us to have a better relationship with our classmates. If the class had been in rows we would not have had such good relationships with each other, and this would have negatively impacted our class discussions. (Sam Lagani)

Circles during this course are essential to the discussion based structure. It is important to look at the person talking so that, ultimately, the discussion as a whole can continue with every individual's thoughts about the specific topic. Since this course is based upon individuals in the community, the circle acts as a community where the individuals can use their beliefs to dissect the given texts and portray their ideas to the rest of the community. (Alyssa Magri)

QU101's annotation driven discussions were the turning point in my transition from an immature high school graduate to a mature, well-spoken college student. Without circles, I wouldn't have been able to become as comfortable as I have with speaking to a large group while making eye contact and taking control of discussions. The annotations we were asked to make in our readings helped me become a more productive reader as well as a more effective writer. The readings required by QU101 were about extremely intellectual topics, forcing us as students to think more critically and more like adults. Without QU101, I feel that I would never have changed from an innocent, naïve high school student to a mature, critical thinking college student. (Michael Alfano)

In the deepest *dialectical* sense, academic freedom is inseparable from intellectual responsibility. Given the original meaning of *educate*, QU101 teachers must "bring out," and "lead forth," both in themselves and in students, a more responsible freedom "by developing," in the words of Mark Thompson, our Senior Vice-President for Academic Affairs, "a culture of intellectual vitality . . . to more readily recognize how our individual efforts contribute to the common purpose of excellence in education." Let us take ownership of this opportunity for building one intellectual community through the work of our Common Reader, and of QU101 itself, a course we hold in common as critical and creative thinkers, and as engaged citizens responsible for our local, national, and global communities of the 21st century.

WORKS CITED OR CONSULTED

Basseches, Michael. *Dialectical Thinking and Adult Development*, Ablex, NJ: 1984

Brookfield, Steven and Steven Preskill. *Discussion as a Way of Teaching: Tools and Techniques for Democratic Classrooms*. Jossey-Bass, San Francisco, 1999.

Clark, L. http://legacy.lclark.edu/~krauss/russiaweb2005/wrworkshop/imagestriangle.gif

Denzin, Norman. *The Research Act*. Butterworths: London, 1970

Greenwald, Joe. http://ablemedia.com/ctcweb/showcase/greenwaldgreece11.html

Jackson, H.J. *Marginalia: Readers Writing in Books*. R.R Donnelly & Sons: Harrisonberg, VA, 2001.

Johnson, Dirk. "Book Lovers Fear Dim Future for Notes in the Margins." *The New York Times*, February 20, 2011.

Oxford English Dictionary Online, Oxford University Press. http://www.oed.com/

Biopoem ▉
later?

THE UNKNOWN CITIZEN
W. H. Auden

(To JS/07 M 378 This Marble Monument Is Erected by the State)

He was found by the Bureau of Statistics to be   1
One against whom there was no official complaint,
And all the reports on his conduct agree
That, in the modern sense of an old-fashioned word, he was a saint,
For in everything he did he served the Greater Community.
Except for the War till the day he retired
He worked in a factory and never got fired,
But satisfied his employers, Fudge Motors Inc.
Yet he wasn't a scab or odd in his views,
For his Union reports that he paid his dues,   10
(Our report on his Union shows it was sound)
And our Social Psychology workers found
That he was popular with his mates and liked a drink.
The Press are convinced that he bought a paper every day
And that his reactions to advertisements were normal in every way.
Policies taken out in his name prove that he was fully insured,
And his Health-card shows he was once in hospital but left it cured.
Both Producers Research and High-Grade Living declare
He was fully sensible to the advantages of the Installment Plan
And had everything necessary to the Modern Man,   20
A phonograph, a radio, a car and a frigidaire.
Our researchers into Public Opinion are content
That he held the proper opinions for the time of year;
When there was peace, he was for peace: when there was war, he went.
He was married and added five children to the population,
Which our Eugenist says was the right number for a parent of his generation.
And our teachers report that he never interfered with their education.
Was he free? Was he happy? The question is absurd:
Had anything been wrong, we should certainly have heard.

[handwritten margin notes: #1 #2; #5 – none are acknowledged; – what do you think Auden's poem's point is? – what is freedom? – what is happiness?]

Reprinted from *Another Time* (1940), Random House, Inc.

THE BETRAYAL OF THE MENTORS
Mark Bauerlein

It is the nature of adolescents to believe that authentic reality begins with themselves, and that what long preceded them is irrelevant. For 15-year-olds in the United States in the twenty-first century, the yardstick of pertinence is personal contact, immediate effects. Space and time extend not much further than their circumstances, and what does Holbein's portrait of Sir Thomas More have to say to a kid who works at Wendy's, struggles with algebra, and can't find a girlfriend? The attitude marks one of the signal changes of the twentieth century in the United States. It insists that a successful adolescence and rightful education entail growing comfortable with yourself, with who you are at age 17. Many generations ago, adolescent years meant preparation for something beyond adolescence, not authentic selfhood but serious work, civic duty, and family responsibility, with parents, teachers, ministers, and employers training teens in grown-up conduct. Adolescence formed a tenuous middle ground between the needs of childhood and the duties of adulthood, and the acquisition of the virtues of manhood and womanhood was an uncertain progress. It did not terminate with an acceptance and approval of the late-teen identity. The shrewdest approach was not to prize the interval but to escape it as efficiently as possible.

Not anymore. For a long time now, adolescence has claimed an independent value, an integrity all its own. The rise of adolescence is too long a story to tell, but the stance of teachers and researchers that fostered it may be indicated by a few highlights. In one of its first authoritative expressions, Professor G. Stanley Hall, president of Clark University and head of the American Psychological Association, composed a massive volume outlining the uniqueness of the stage. In *Adolescence: Its Psychology and Its Relations to Physiology* . . . (1904), he observed in glorious cadences, "Self-feeling and ambition are increased, and every trait and faculty is liable to exaggeration and excess. It is all a marvelous new birth, and those who believe that nothing is so worthy of love, reverence, and service as the body and soul of youth, and who hold that the best test of every human institution is how much it contributes to bring youth to the ever fullest possible development, may well review themselves and the civilization in which we live to see how far it satisfies this supreme test."

A cover story in *Time* magazine exemplifies it well (24 Jan 2005). The article profiles a new youth phenomenon, an unforeseen generational sub-cohort termed the "Twixters." This curious social outcropping rests in a novel cluster of demographic traits. Twixters:

- are 22 to 30 years old;
- have a college degree, or substantial college coursework;

Reprinted from *The Dumbest Generation: How the Digital Age Stupefies Young Americans and Jeopardizes Our Future* (2008), by permission of Penguin Group.

40   • come from middle-class families; and

• reside in cities and large suburban centers.

These features embody nothing unusual, certainly, but where they lead is surprising. What makes the Twixters different from other people with the same demographics from the past is the lifestyle they pursue after college.

Despite their circumstances, Twixters aren't marginal youngsters sinking into the underclass. They drift through their twenties, stalled at work and saving no money, but they like it that way. They congregate just as they did before college, hopping bar to bar on Friday night and watching movies on Saturday. They have achieved little, but they feel good about themselves. Indeed,
50   precisely along the lines of Reich's understanding, they justify their aimless lifestyle as a journey of self-discovery. Yes, they put off the ordinary decisions of adulthood (career, marriage), but with a tough job market and so many divorced parents, their delays mark a thoughtful desire to "search their souls and choose their life paths," to find a livelihood right for their "identity." So Lev Grossman, the author of the story, phrases it. Social scientists quoted in the article, too, ennoble the lifestyles, judging Twixter habits (in Grossman's paraphrase) "important work to get themselves ready for adulthood." These young people take adulthood "so seriously, they're spending years carefully choosing the right path into it." University of Maryland psychologist Jeffrey
60   Arnett dislikes the "Twixter" label, preferring "emerging adulthood." They assume no responsibilities for or to anyone else, he concedes, but that only permits them "this wonderful freedom to really focus on their own lives and work on becoming the kind of person they want to be." Sociologist James Côté blames their delay on the economy: "What we're looking at really began with the collapse of the youth labor market," he says, which persists today and means that young people simply can't afford to settle down until their late twenties. Marshall Heskovitz, creator of the television shows *thirtysomething* and *My So-Called Life*, gives the problem a social/emotional angle: "it's a result of the world not being particularly welcoming when they come into it. Lots
70   of people have a difficult time dealing with it, and they try to stay kids as long as they can because they don't know how to make sense of all this. We're interested in this process of finding courage and one's self." And a Dartmouth neuroscientist backs the economic and social resistances with brain chemistry: "We as a society deem an individual at the age of 18 ready for adult responsibility. Yet recent evidence suggests that our neuropsychological development is many years from being complete."

Their comments apply a positive spin to what less sympathetic elders would call slacker ways. But even if we accept the characterizations—their brains aren't ready, the cost of living is high, they take marriage too seriously to plunge
80   into it—there is something missing from the expert observations in the article, an extraordinary absence in the diagnosis. In casting Twixter lifestyle as genuine exploration and struggle, neither the author nor the researchers nor

the Twixters themselves whisper a single word about intellectual labor. Not one of the Twixters or youth observers mentions an idea that stirs them, a book that influenced them, a class that inspired them, or a mentor who guides them. Nobody ties maturity to formal or informal learning, reading or studying, novels or paintings or histories or syllogisms. For all the talk about life concerns and finding a calling, none of them regard history, literature, art, civics, philosophy, or politics a helpful undertaking. Grossman speaks of Twixter years as "a chance to build castles and knock them down," but these castles haven't a grain of intellectual sand in them. As these young people forge their personalities in an uncertain world, they skirt one of the customary means of doing so—that is, acquainting themselves with the words and images, the truths and beauties of the past—and nobody tells them they have overlooked anything. Social psychologists don't tell them so, nor do youth experts and educators, but the anti-intellectual banality of their choices is stark. What is the role of books in the Twixter's world? Negligible. How has their education shaped their lives? Not at all. This is what the Twixters themselves report. One of them remarks, "Kids used to go to college to get educated. That's what I did, which I think now was a bit naïve. Being smart after college doesn't really mean anything."

In a word, the Twixter vision aligns perfectly with that of their wired younger brothers and sisters. It's all social, all peer-oriented. Twixters don't read, tour museums, travel, follow politics, or listen to any music but pop and rap, much less do something such as lay out a personal reading list or learn a foreign language. Rather, they do what we expect an average 19-year-old to do. They meet for poker, buy stuff at the mall, and jump from job to job and bed to bed. The maturity they envision has nothing to do with learning and wisdom, and the formative efforts that social scientists highlight don't include books, artworks, ideologies, or Venn diagrams. For the Twixters, mature identity is entirely a social matter developed with and through their friends. The intellectual and artistic products of the past aren't stepping-stones for growing up. They are the fading materials of meaningless schooling.

Does tradition have to retire so conspicuously in order for the adolescent self to come into its own?

Spend some hours in school zones and you see that the indulgent attitude toward youth, along with the downplaying of tradition, has reached the point of dogma among teachers, reporters, researchers, and creators in arts and humanities fields, and pro-knowledge, pro-tradition conceptions strike them as bluntly unpleasant, if not reactionary and out of touch. Indeed, the particular mode of sympathy for the kids has taken such a firm hold that offering education as a fruitful dialectic of tradition and individuality looks downright smothering. Uttered so rarely in education circles, a modest opinion in favor of tradition comes across to experts and mentors as an aggression against the students, a curmudgeon's grievance. For many of them, the power of cultural tradition sounds authoritarian and retrograde, or aligned with a Eurocentric, white male

syllogism

banality

curmudgeon

retrograde

lineage, their view recalling the Culture Wars of the 1980s when conservative activists battled liberal professors over the content of the curriculum in English classes. In truth, however, the indulgence crosses ideological boundaries, touching generational feelings that mix widely among liberals and conservatives alike. It's not a political conflict. It's a cultural condition, a normative sentiment positioning young people in relation to a past and a future, the cultural inheritance and their prospective adulthood. Instead of charting as Left or Right, it charts as traditionalist or self-centered (or youth-centered, present-fixated, individualist). And while traditionalists lean toward conservative opinion, many liberals feel a similar respect for the past and impatience with youth self-absorption, and many conservatives no longer set their moral values, religious faith, and civic pride under the long shadow of great books and thoughts and artworks.

What makes someone say to an adolescent, "Before you sally forth into the world, heed the insight of people long dead who possessed a lot more talent and wisdom than you," is more a personal ethic than a political creed. The ethic has seeped down to the level of etiquette, so that when a dissenting voice calls for more traditional knowledge, it sounds not just wrong, but wrongheaded, mean-spirited, bad form. The intellectual force of the call is obscured by its impropriety. This is the natural course of a norm. It begins as a fresh and unusual idea, then passes through the stages of argument, clarification, revision, and acceptance. It may have been radical or controversial once, but over time, adopted by more and more people, it turns into common sense and its distinctiveness dims. When an idea becomes a habit, it stops sparking thought. When everybody accepts it, it abides without evidence. At that point, the idea acts as a tacit premise, like travel directions you print out from Mapquest when taking a trip for the first time. You follow the route and arrive at Point B. You don't ponder alternatives. In a traditional classroom from way back when, a youth-centered approach might have appeared iconoclastic and provocative, triggering disputes over learning, maturity, and selfhood. Now it passes without a murmur.

iconoclastic

The sentimentality justifies mentors in downgrading their mentoring task. They can't produce much solid evidence of youth brilliance and drive, and so they resort to lofty and flushed language to make the case. "Young adults are fiercely individualistic. . . . They are still incredibly open to new ideas and they want to dabble and experiment." So enthuses a report from the Advertising Council (with funding from MTV and the Pew Research Center), though providing little evidence of the good of their "dabbling." The *Philadelphia Inquirer*'s columnist Jane Eisner acknowledges the embarrassing voting rates of 18- to 29-year-olds, but shifts the issue: "Only if we address the structural reasons that young people don't vote can we begin to count on them to infuse our democracy with the ideas and idealism for which young Americans have always been prized" (Sept 2004). "Always been prized" for their "ideas and idealism"? Since 1965, perhaps, but not before.

Young people pick up these rationalizations and run with them. For a study of news consumption entitled *Tuned Out: Why Americans Under 40 Don't Follow the News* (2005), journalist David Mindich interviewed hundreds of young adults who told him that "the political process is both morally bankrupt and completely insulated from public pressure," a sentiment whose truth is doubtful—how do *they* know?—but that saves them the trouble of civic action. In a 1999 survey by Northwestern University's Medill School of Journalism ("Y Vote 2000: Politics of a New Generation"), 69 percent of 15- to 24-year-olds concurred with the statement "Our generation has an important voice, but no one seems to hear it." The cliché is so hollow it could rank with the statement "Our generation has sexual desires, but no one satisfies them," but it has acquired a seriousness that 50 years ago would have been inconceivable. It is normal for young people, temporarily, to act disaffected and feel unheard, but for the mentors to turn this condition into an injustice is to downgrade their position, with youths only too eager to play along. No matter how benevolent the rhetoric of the mentors, though, the thing it bestows—intellectual independence—does the majority of youths no favors. And this isn't only because most youths aren't ready to exercise it wisely, to their long-term benefit. It's also because, while the indulgence emancipates the young mind, it sends an implicit and far-reaching message, too, one the kids handily discern. It sabotages something that may, perhaps, be more fragile than the transmission of knowledge from old to young, namely, the simple, sturdy conviction that knowledge itself is worth receiving, the conviction that traditions remote from their daily circumstances have any bearing.

When teachers stand before the young and assure them of the integrity and autonomy of what adolescents think and say and write, teachers expect the young to respond affirmatively, to seek out knowledge and truth on their own. And maybe that works for the upper-crust students, those contending zealously for a place at Yale or an internship on the Hill. But beyond that talented tenth or twentieth student, something different happens. All of them expect the mentors to enter the room with credentialed authority, some know-how that justifies their position, even if some of the kids begrudge and reject it. When the mentors disavow their authority, when they let their discipline slacken, when they, in the language of the educators, slide from the "sage on the stage" to the "guide on the side," the kids wonder what goes. They don't consider the equalizing instructor a caring liberator, and they aren't motivated to learn on their own. They draw another, immobilizing lesson. If mentors are so keen to recant their expertise, why should students strain to acquire it themselves?

The opposite of what the indulgers intend sets in. Knowledge and tradition are emptied of authority. Ronald Reagan once declared, "Freedom is never more than one generation away from extinction," but a more elemental rule may be, "Knowledge is never more than one generation away from oblivion." If the guardians of tradition claim that the young, though ignorant, have a special perspective on the past, or if teachers prize the impulses of tenth-graders more than the thoughts of the wise and the works of the masters, learning loses its point. The thread of intellectual inheritance snaps. The young man from Boston who announces with pride that he cares nothing about Rembrandt and Picasso typifies the outcome. His disregard follows from the mentors' disregard, their own infidelity to tradition, and the transfer affects all students more or less, the best and brightest as well as the dropouts. The indulgers assume that their approval will bring teachers and students closer together, throwing students further into academic inquiry, inspiring them to learn and study, but the evidence shows that this does not happen.

One pertinent measure of the trend appears as an item on the *National Survey of Student Engagement* (NSSE). The question tallies how many first-year and senior undergraduates "Discussed ideas from your readings or classes with faculty members outside of class." The activity goes beyond course requirements, the tests and papers, and thus charts how many students are inspired by lectures and homework to confer with the instructor on their own. The numbers are disappointing. In 2003, fully 40 percent of the first-year respondents "Never" exchanged a word with a teacher beyond the classroom. Seniors that year displayed more engagement—only 25 percent responded "Never"—although that is still too high a figure after three years of coursework. Normally, as students proceed, they pursue more specialization in a major and form shared interests and career concerns with teachers. Nevertheless, one quarter of all seniors ignore their professors outside the classroom. Worse, three years later, both ranks increased their disengagement. In 2006, first-year students raised the "Never talk to my teacher" rate to 43 percent, and seniors to 28 percent. More students tune their professors out once the hour is up, and the engagement score gap between seniors and freshmen still stands at only 15 points—a sign that the curriculum hasn't improved.

Notwithstanding the disengagement numbers, however, researchers summarizing the 2003 NSSE survey commend precisely the pedagogical methods of the indulgers. The report observes,

> One of the pleasant surprises from the first few years of NSSE findings was the substantial number of students engaged in various forms of active and collaborative learning activities. This shift from passive, instructor-dominated pedagogy to active, learner-centered activities promises to have desirable effects on learning.

A nice prediction, but wholly without support. As "instructor domination" dwindles, as "learner-centered" classrooms multiply, then students should feel empowered to hunt down their profs at other times and places. But while "active, learner-centered" pedagogies have proliferated, more student-teacher contact hasn't happened, as subsequent NSSE reports show. In a "passive" mode, with an authoritative teacher before them, students may feel more secure and encouraged to consult one-on-one. Once "activated" by power-sharing profs, though, students head elsewhere. A paradox may have set in: the more equal and accessible the teachers, the less accessed they are by the students.   260 Nonetheless, NSSE researchers buy the "learner-centered" assumption. They assert that youth-approving teaching strategies "take students to deeper levels of understanding and meaning," but if deeper understanding entails closer engagement with instructors, their own data don't correlate with the theory.

The researchers could find other noncorrelations elsewhere, too. For instance, *Your First College Year*, a survey of first-year students, sponsored by the Higher Education Research Institute at UCLA, provided the following summary in 2005:

> Although most respondents studied and discussed their courses with other students during the first year, findings suggest that many   270 remain disengaged from their coursework: over half "frequently" or "occasionally" came late to class; almost half turned in course assignments that did not reflect their best work or felt bored in class; and approximately one-third skipped class at least "occasionally" in the first year.

College delinquency of this kind says nothing about these students' intelligence. It marks an attitude, a sign of disrespect, and we may blame several influences for its spread. When colleges treat students as consumers and clients, they encourage it, as does pop culture when it elevates hooky-playing tricksters such as Ferris Bueller into heroes. College professors complain all the   280 time about it, but they have their own part in the students' negligence, for they pass it along whenever they esteem the students' knowledge and deauthorize their own.

That isn't what they think they do, of course, but the effect is the same. Many indulgers believe that teacher-centered instruction bores the kids into diffidence or proves too difficult to handle, and that student-centered instruction will inspire the lesser-caliber students to work harder and stay in school, but in fact those lesser students say otherwise. In a National Governors Association poll of 10,378 teenagers (reported in July 2005), nearly 90 percent intended to graduate, and more than one-third of them stated that high school   290 has been "easy" (less than 10 percent called it "very hard"). Surprisingly, the future dropouts scored similarly on the "hardness" index. Of the 11 percent who admitted that they didn't intend to graduate from high school, only one in nine gave as a reason, "schoolwork is too hard." At the top, at 36 percent, was the claim that they were "not learning anything," 12 points higher than sheer "hate" for the school they attend. The reactions of delinquent college students are less extreme than that, but they echo the high school dropouts' motives. When "instructor-domination" decreases, a few students step up

diffidence

their learning, but most of them cut their discipline, now and then blowing
off in-class duties and all the time ignoring their teachers out of class. A 2005
report sponsored by Achieve, Inc., on college and workplace readiness heard
less than one-quarter of high school graduates say that they were "significantly challenged and faced high expectations" (*Rising to the Challenge: Are
High School Graduates Prepared for College and Work?*). In the *First-Year* study,
only 30 percent of students studied 11 or more hours per week, and 39 percent did six hours or less. Only 24 percent "frequently" felt that their courses
inspired them "to think in new ways." Half the students (49 percent) visited an instructor's office hours a sorry two times or fewer per term. Let the
students guide themselves, and they'll do so happily.

As they glide through their courses, they seem unaware of the long-term
disadvantages. Here, too, the abnegation of the mentors plays a role, for in
releasing students from the collective past they deny students a resource to
foster a healthy and prosperous future. Dissociated from tradition, with nobody
telling them that sometimes they must mute the voices inside them and heed
instead the voices of distant greatness, young people miss one of the sanative,
humbling mechanisms of maturity. This is the benefit of tradition, the result
of a reliable weeding-out process. At any present moment, a culture spills over
with ideas and images, sayings and symbols and styles, and they mingle promis-
cuously. Many of them arise passing only a commercial standard, not a critical or moral one, and in the rush of daily life it's hard to discriminate them,
the significant from the insignificant, trendy from lasting, tasteful from vulgar. As time goes by, though, the transient, superficial, fashionable, and hack-
neyed show up more clearly and fall away, and a firmer, nobler continuity forms.
We think of jazz, for instance, as the tradition of Armstrong, Ellington, Parker,
Monk, Fitzgerald, Getz, and the rest, but at the time when they recorded their
signature pieces, jazz looked much different. The cream hadn't fully risen to
the top, and "Parker's Mood" and "Blue 7" appeared amid a thousand other,
now forgotten songs in the jazz landscape. Only with the passage of time does
the field refine and settle into its superior creations.

The tradition-making process, then, somewhat distorts the actual historical
genesis of its ingredients. But it serves a crucial moral and intellectual function.
Tradition provides a surer standard, a basis for judgment more solid than present comparisons, than political, practical, and commercial grounds. Young Americans exist amidst an avalanche of input, and the combination overwhelms their
shaky critical sense. Tradition provides grounding against and refuge from the
mercurial ebb and flow of youth culture, the nonstop marketing of youth products to youths. The great nineteenth-century critic Matthew Arnold explained
the benefits of connecting to "the ancients" in precisely these "steadying" terms:

> The present age makes great claims upon us: we owe it service, it will
> not be satisfied without our admiration. I know not how it is, but their
> commerce with the ancients appears to me to produce, in those who

constantly practice it, a steadying and composing effect upon their judgment, not of literary works only, but of men and events in general.

Contact with the past steadies and composes judgment of the present. That's the formula. People who read Thucydides and Caesar on war, and Seneca and Ovid on love, are less inclined to construe passing fads as durable outlooks, to fall into the maelstrom of celebrity culture, to presume that the circumstances of their own life are worth a Web page. They distinguish long-term meanings in the sequence of "men and events," and they gamble on the lasting stakes of life, not the meretricious ones.

maelstrom

350 *meretricious*

Nobody likes a scold, but the critical filter has never been more needed. The rush of the "present age" noted by Arnold in 1853 has cascaded into a deluge. Digital technology has compounded the incoming flow, and young adults flounder in it the most. Their grandparents watch them at the keyboard, on the cell phone, with the BlackBerry, etc., and it looks like delirium. All the more reason, then, to impart the unchanging and uncompromising examples, in Arnold's words, the "best that is known and thought in the world." Without the anchor of wise and talented men and women long gone, of thoughts and works that have stood the test of time, adolescents fall back upon the meager, anarchic resources of their sole selves. They watch a movie—say, *Pretty Woman*—and see it in the light of real and imagined high school romances instead of, in this case, fairy tales and 1980s finance wizards. Asked for a political opinion, they recall the images they catch on television, not the models of Washington, Churchill, and Pope John Paul II. Instead of understanding the young adult roller coaster of courtship and rejection with the help of novels by Jane Austen, they process their miasmic feelings by themselves or with sympathetic friends. And why should they do otherwise when the counsel of mentors, not to mention the avalanche of movies, music, and the rest, upholds the sovereignty of youth perspective? The currents of social life press upon them hourly, while the pages within *The Decline and Fall of the Roman Empire* and *Wuthering Heights* seem like another, irrelevant universe. They don't know much about history and literature, but they have feelings and needs, and casualty figures from Shiloh and lines from Donne don't help.

360

miasmic

370 *Plays "don't know much" song*

No wonder psychological assessments show rising currents of narcissism among Americans who haven't yet joined the workforce. In one study publicized in early 2007, researchers analyzed the responses of more than 16,000 college students on the Narcissistic Personality Inventory going back to the early 1980s. Undergraduates in 2006, it turned out, scored 30 percent higher than students in 1982 on the narcissism scale, with two-thirds of them reaching above-average levels. The researchers traced the rise directly to self-esteem orientations in the schoolroom, and lead author Jean Twenge groused, "We need to stop endlessly repeating, 'You're special,' and having children repeat that back. Kids are self-centered enough already."

380

The behavioral features of narcissism are bad enough, but a set of other studies demonstrates just how disabling it proves, particularly with schoolwork. One consequence of narcissism is that it prevents young people from weighing their own talents and competencies accurately. Narcissists can't take criticism, they hate to hand power over to others, and they turn disappointments into the world's fault, not their own. These are the normal hurdles of growing up, but for narcissists they represent a hostile front advancing against them. It's a distorted and destroying mirror, as Narcissus himself showed when he fixed upon his own reflection in the pool and snubbed the calls of love and caution he'd heard before, unable to leave his lovely countenance until the end. Education requires the opposite, a modicum of self-doubt, a capacity for self-criticism, precisely what the narcissist can't bear.

The attitude is even more harmful than the knowledge deficiencies we've seen earlier. An ignorant but willing mind can overcome ignorance through steady work and shrewd guidance. Read a few more books, visit a museum, take some classes, and knowledge will come. An unwilling mind can't, or won't. It already knows enough, and history, civics, philosophy, and literature have too little direct application to satisfy. For many young Americans, that translates into a demoralizing perception problem, a mismatch of expectation and ability. An October 2005 report by the U.S. Department of Education drew the distinction in gloomy forecasts. Titled *A Profile of the American High School Senior in 2004: A First Look,* it culled four traits out, of the academic lives of more than 13,000 students from across the country. They were: tested achievement, educational intentions, reasons for choosing a particular college, and life goals. Set alongside each other, the first two characteristics settled so far apart as to signal a national pathology. The study focused on student achievement ratings on math scores and derived the usual abysmal picture. Only "a third (35 percent) showed an understanding of intermediate-level mathematical concepts," and 21 percent of them could not perform "simple operations with decimals, fractions, powers, and roots." More than one-third of high school seniors (37.6 percent) could not complete "simple problem solving, requiring the understanding of low-level mathematical concepts," and a tiny 3.9 percent reached proficiency in "complex multistep word problems."

A troubling outcome, but no shocker. The surprise comes with the second trait, the students' expectations. The survey asked high school seniors how much education they expected to complete—not *wanted* to complete, but would successfully complete—and their answers bounded far beyond trait #1. Fully 69 percent of the respondents "expected to complete college with a 4-year degree," and of that group 35 percent believed that they would proceed further to earn a professional or postbaccalaureate degree. Of the others, 18 percent predicted that they would earn a two-year degree or attend college for some period of time. That left 8 percent who had no prediction, and only 5 percent who admitted that they would never attend college.

Broken down by proficiency, the expectations looked downright heartbreaking. Nearly one-third (31.7 percent) of the students who expected to graduate from college could handle, at best, simple problem solving, and one-fifth of those anticipating an advanced degree could do no better. Only 7.6 percent of the I-expect-an-advanced-degree group reached advanced proficiency in mathematics, while 9.4 percent of graduate-degree intenders compiled a transcript with the highest mathematics coursework as pre-algebra or lower.

In the National Governors Association poll cited on page 21, similar misestimations came up. When asked "How well do you think your high school prepares you in each of the following areas?" 80 percent replied "Excellent/Good" in basic reading skills and math skills—a number far exceeding the actual percentage. Three-quarters of them claimed "Ability to read at a high level," and 71 percent boasted excellent/good algebra talents. Furthermore, they demanded more courses in senior year "related to the kind of job I want," not realizing that they can't proceed to more specialized courses until they improve their basic proficiencies in standard subjects.

Indeed, when comparing the self-image of the students and the knowledge/ skill deficits that emerge whenever they undergo objective tests, one has to wonder: What are they thinking? Optimism is nice, but not when it reaches delusional limits. Soon enough, the faulty combo of aptitude and ambition will explode, and the teenagers won't understand why. Michael Petrilli of the Fordham Foundation terms it "the reality gap between students' expectations and their skills" (see McCluskey), and the illusion gets punctured all too readily not long after high school graduation. General education requirements in college include a math course, and any degree in the sciences entails more than that. One week in calculus sends them scurrying to drop/add, and many end up in remediation or disappear altogether. It doesn't make sense. The math skills they lack are requisite for the degrees they expect, but they don't make the connection. They must get their college readiness conceits from somewhere besides test scores and coursework, partly, no doubt, from teachers who, with the best intentions, tell middling students that they're doing great, that they should follow their dreams, be all they can be . . .

All too often, the mentors don't see the results of their indulgence, which emerge only after students leave their class, leaving teachers unaware of how the approach misleads their charges. A recent study of teachers' expectations touches one of the significant thresholds in a person's educational life: graduation. When a student graduates from high school, the diploma is supposed to signify a certain level of skill and knowledge, but the teachers who have graded them don't seem to realize the levels actually expected of students at the next stage. Instead, high school teachers consistently assess the skills of their graduating students much more highly than college teachers assess the skills of their entering students. That's the finding of companion surveys sponsored by the *Chronicle of Higher Education* in 2006, one of them directed at high school teachers, the other at college professors (see *Chronicle of Higher Education,* "What Professors and Teachers Think"). Researchers asked 746 high school teachers and 1,098 college professors specifically about the college readiness of the kids they instructed, and the variance was huge. On the general question "How well prepared are your students for college-level work?" 31 percent of the teachers stated "Very well," while only 13 percent of professors stated "Very well." In the "Not well" category, professors doubled the teacher score, 24 percent to 12 percent, meaning that while only one in eight high school teachers found among

480 the students "large gaps in preparation" that left them "struggling," one in four college teachers found them. In certain subject areas, the discrepancy between high school and college perceptions increased to a ratio of nine to one. In mathematics, fully 37 percent of teachers estimated that the students were "Very well prepared," while a meager 4 percent of professors agreed. For science, 38 percent of teachers gave them "Very well prepared," but only 5 percent of professors did. In writing, nearly half the professors (44 percent) rated the freshman class "Not well prepared," while only 10 percent of teachers were equally judgmental. Interestingly, for motivational traits the discrepancy shrank significantly, for example, with teach-

490 ers and professors differing by only three points in judging students "Very well prepared" to "work hard." The decrease indicates that the problem lies not in the students' diligence but in their intellectual tool kits, and that the energy students devote to schoolwork (and leisure play) often dodges activities that build college-level knowledge and skills.

One of the most precious tools they lack does not appear in predominant education philosophies, however, nor does it shape training programs for teachers and professors, nor does it arise in discussions of American competitiveness and innovation among business leaders and politicians interested in education. When foundation personnel talk of school improvement and

500 education officers announce academic outcomes, they cite test scores, retention rates, school choice plans, technology, and a dozen other topics, but not this one. And if it were posed to intellectuals, academics, educators, and journalists, a few might seize it as crucial but most would give it a limp nod of approval, or stare blankly, or reject it outright. It sounds fainthearted to them, or outmoded, moralistic, or irrelevant. The tool is precisely what has been lost in the shifting attitude in favor of youth: self-criticism in the light of tradition.

Adolescents are painfully self-conscious, to be sure, and they feel their being intensely, agonizing over a blemish on the cheek and a misstep in the lunch-

510 room. But the yardstick of their judgment comes not from the past but from the present, not from wise men and women but from cool classmates, not from art and thought through the ages but from pop culture of the moment. They pass through school and home ever aware of inadequacy, but the ideals they honor raise them only to the condition of peer respect. Their idols are peer idols, their triumphs the envy of friends, not adults. Their self-criticism isn't enlightened and forward-looking, nor is it backward-looking. It's social and shortsighted.

<u>What young Americans need isn't more relevance in the classroom, but less.</u> A June 2006 op-ed in *Education Week* on student disengagement in class, "The Small World of Classroom Boredom," concludes, "Instead of responding to our students as individuals with their own interests and knowledge, the school curriculum is, by and large, remote, providing little connection between the classroom and students' lives" (see Schultz). Yes, the coursework is remote, but instead of blaming the curriculum and offering more blather about sparking "intellectual curiosity" and "independent thinking," as the author does, let's blame "students' lives" for stretching the divide. Young people need mentors not to go with the youth flow, but to stand staunchly against it, to represent something smarter and finer than the <u>cacophony</u> of social life. They don't need more pop culture and youth perspectives in the classroom. They get enough of those on their own. Young Americans need someone somewhere in their lives to reveal to them bigger and better human stories than the sagas of summer parties and dormitory diversions and Facebook sites.

cacophony

In slighting the worth of tradition, in allowing teenagers to set their own concerns before the civilization of their forebears, mentors <u>have only opened more minutes to youth contact and youth media.</u> And not just school time, but leisure time, too, for the betrayal of the mentors ripples far beyond the campus. In the past, as long as teachers, parents, journalists, and other authorities insisted that young people respect knowledge and great works, young people devoted a portion of out-of-class hours to activities that complement in-class work. These include the habits we've already charted: books for fun, museums, "art music," dance and theater, politics.

The more mentors have engaged youth in youth terms, though, the more youth have disengaged from the mentors themselves and from the culture they are supposed to represent. To take one more example: in 1982, 18- to 24-year-olds made up 18.5 percent of the performing arts attendance. In 2002, the portion fell to 11.2 percent, a massive slide in audience makeup, and an ominous sign for the future of arts presenters (National Endowment for the Arts, *Survey of Public Participation in the Arts*).

The decline of school-supporting leisure habits—lower reading rates, fewer museum visits, etc.—created a vacuum in leisure time that the stuff of youth filled all too readily, and it doesn't want to give any of it back. Digital technology has fostered a segregated social reality, peer pressure gone wild, distributing youth content in an instant, across continents, 24/7. Television watching holds steady, while more screens mean more screen time. What passes through them locks young Americans ever more firmly into themselves and one another, and whatever doesn't pass through them appears irrelevant and profitless. Inside the classroom, they learn a little about the historical past and civic affairs, but once the lesson ends they swerve back to the youthfull, peer-bound present. Cell phones, personal pages, and the rest unleash persistent and simmering forces of adolescence, the volatile mix of cliques

and loners, rebelliousness and conformity, ambition and self-destruction, idol-
atry and irreverence, know-nothing-ness and know-it-all-ness, all of which tradition and knowledge had helped to contain. The impulses were always there,
but the stern shadow of moral and cultural canons at home and in class managed now and then to keep them in check. But the guideposts are now
unmanned, and the pushback of mentors has dwindled to the sober objections
of a faithful few who don't mind sounding unfashionable and insensitive.

abdicate

The ingredients come together into an annihilating recipe. Adolescent urg-
ings, a teen world cranked up by technology, a knowledge world cranked down
by abdicating mentors . . . they commingle and produce young Americans
whose wits are just as keen as ever, but who waste them on screen diversions;
kids whose ambitions may even exceed their forebears', but whose aims merge
on career and consumer goals, not higher learning; youths who experience a
typical stage of alienation from the adult world, but whose alienation doesn't
stem from countercultural ideas and radical mentors (Karl Marx, Herbert Mar-
cuse, Michel Foucault, etc.), but from an enveloping immersion in peer stuff.
Their lengthening independence has shortened their mental horizon. Teen
material floods their hours and mentors esteem them, believing the kids more
knowledgeable and skilled than they really are, or, perhaps, thinking that assurance will make them that way.

Peter Principle

Few things are worse for adolescent minds than overblown appraisals of
their merits. They rob them of constructive self-criticism, and obscure the lessons of tradition. They steer their competitive instincts toward peer triumphs,
not civic duty. They make them mistrust their guides, and interpret cynically
both praise and censure. They set them up for failure, a kind of Peter Principle in young people's lives whereby they proceed in school and in social circles without receiving correctives requisite to adult duties and citizenship. They
reach a level of incompetence, hit a wall in college or the workplace, and never
understand what happened. The rising cohort of Americans is not "The Next
Great Generation," as Strauss and Howe name them in their hagiographic
book *Millennials Rising*. We wish they were, but it isn't so. The twenty-first-
century teen, connected and multitasked, autonomous yet peer-mindful, marks
no great leap forward in human intelligence, global thinking, or "netizen"-
ship. Young users have learned a thousand new things, no doubt. They upload
and download, surf and chat, post and design, but they haven't learned to analyze a complex text, store facts in their heads, comprehend a foreign policy
decision, take lessons from history, or spell correctly. Never having recognized

fissure

their responsibility to the past, they have opened a fissure in our civic foundations, and it shows in their halting passage into adulthood and citizenship.
They leave school, but peer fixations continue and social habits stay the same.
They join the workforce only to realize that self-esteem lessons of home and
class, as well as the behaviors that made them popular, no longer apply, and
it takes them years to adjust. They grab snatches of news and sometimes
vote, but they regard the civic realm as another planet. And wherever they end
up, whomever they marry, however high they land in their careers, most of

them never acquire the intellectual tools they should have as teenagers and young adults. Perhaps during their twenties they adapt, acquiring smarter work and finance habits. But the knowledge and culture traits never catch up.

A few years of seasoning in the American workplace may secure their income and inculcate maturity in private life, but it won't sustain the best civic and cultural traditions in American history. If young people don't read, they shut themselves out of public affairs. Without a knowledge formation in younger years, adults function as more or less partial citizens. Reading and knowledge have to enter their leisure lives, at their own initiative. Analyzing Pew Research data from 2002 and 2004, political scientists Stephen and Linda Bennett lay out the simple fact: "People who read books for pleasure are more likely than non-readers to report voting, being registered to vote, 'always' voting, to pay greater attention to news stories about national, international, and local politics, and to be better informed."

As the rising generation reaches middle age, it won't re-create the citizenship of its precursors, nor will its ranks produce a set of committed intellectuals ready to trade in ideas, steer public policy, and espouse social values on the basis of learning, eloquence, and a historical sense of human endeavor. This is one damaging consequence of the betrayal of the mentors that is often overlooked. When people warn of America's future, they usually talk about competitiveness in science, technology, and productivity, not in ideas and values. But the current domestic and geopolitical situation demands that we generate not only more engineers, biochemists, nanophysicists, and entrepreneurs, but also men and women experienced in the ways of culture, prepared for contest in the marketplace of ideas. Knowledge-workers, wordsmiths, policy wonks . . . they don't emerge from nowhere. They need a long foreground of reading and writing, a home and school environment open to their development, a pipeline ahead and behind them. They need mentors to commend them when they're right and rebuke them when they're wrong. They need parents to remind them that social life isn't everything, and they need peers to respect their intelligence, not scrunch up their eyes at big words. It takes a home, and a schoolhouse, and a village, and a market to make a great public intellectual and policy maker. The formula is flexible, but with the Dumbest Generation its breakdown is under way, and with it the vitality of democracy in the United States.

TWO ESSENTIAL GOALS
Ernest L. Boyer

An effective college has a clear and vital mission. Administrators, faculty, and students share a vision of what the institution is seeking to accomplish. The goals at such an institution flow from the needs of society and also from the needs of the persons seeking education.

But can the modern college, with all its separations and divisions, be guided by a common vision? And can the search for goals be something more than a diversion?

America's first colleges were guided by a vision of coherence. The goal was to train not only the clergy, but a new civic leadership as well. These struggling institutions sought "to develop a sense of unity where, in a society created from many of the nations of Europe, there might otherwise be aimlessness and uncontrolled diversity" [said Frederick Rudolph in *The American College and University*].

The confidence of professors and their students in this era "owed much to their membership in an established middle class, a commitment to European learning, and a Christian conception of character and culture." Within that framework, bitter disputes sometimes did rage, but from today's perspective the colonial college seems stiflingly monolithic.

The first students at tiny Harvard College advanced in lockstep fashion, studied a common curriculum, one subject a day, from 8:00 A.M. until 5:00 P.M., Monday through Friday, and a half day on Saturday. In the first year, there was logic, Greek and Hebrew, rhetoric, divinity catechetical, history, and the nature of plants. The second year included ethics and politics, Aramaic, and further studies in rhetoric and divinity catechetical. The final year of college was capped by arithmetic, astronomy, Syriac, more Greek, rhetoric, and, of course, divinity catechetical.

This academic core was considered absolute and immutable, to be accepted, not criticized or questioned. The goal was to discipline the mind and, through such training, graduates were to move comfortably into prestigious professions—the clergy, business, medicine, law, and civic leadership.

Our present academic world would be unrecognizable to the men who founded Harvard College in 1636. The fixed curriculum of the colonial era is as much an anachronism today as the stocks in the village square. Separations and divisions, not unity, mark the undergraduate program. Narrow departmentalization divides the campus. So distinctive are the different disciplines in method and content, the argument goes, that there is no way to connect them in the minds of students. Knowledge is so vast and specialization so persistent that shared goals cannot be defined.

Reprinted from *College: The Undergraduate Experience in America* (1987), HarperCollins.

There is, we believe, a way out of our dilemma. While preparing this report we repeatedly were reminded that two powerful traditions—*individuality* and *community*—have been at the heart of the undergraduate experiences. These two priorities have defined throughout the years the boundaries of the collegiate debate about purposes and goals and within these traditions there is, perhaps, sufficient common ground on which a vital academic program can be built.

The focus on individuality, on the personal benefits and the utility of education, has a rich tradition in American higher education. Throughout the years, students have come to college to pursue their own goals, to follow their own aptitudes, to become productive, self-reliant human beings, and, with new knowledge, to continue learning after college days are over. Serving individual interests has been a top priority in higher education.

But amidst diversity, the claims of community must be vigorously affirmed. By community we mean an undergraduate experience that helps students go beyond their own private interests, learn about the world around them, develop a sense of civic and social responsibility, and discover how they, as individuals, can contribute to the larger society of which they are a part.

Robert Bellah, co-author of *Habits of the Heart,* observes that "since World War II, the traditions of atomistic individualism have grown stronger, while the traditions of the individual in society have grown weaker. The sense of cohesive community is lost." In an era when an emphasis on narrow vocationalism dominates many campuses, the challenge is to help students relate what they have learned to concerns beyond themselves.

Individuals should become empowered [or enabled] to live productive, independent lives. They also should be helped to go beyond private interests and place their own lives in larger context. When the observant Frenchman Alexis de Tocqueville visited the United States in the 1830s, he warned that "as individualism grows, people forget their ancestors and form the habit of thinking of themselves in isolation and imagine their whole destiny is in their hands." To counter this cultural disintegration, Tocqueville argued, "Citizens must turn from the private inlets and occasionally take a look at something other than themselves."

We suggest, then, that within the traditions of individuality and community, educational and social purposes for the undergraduate experience can be defined. The individual preferences of each student must be served. But beyond diversity, the college has an obligation to give students a sense of passage toward a more coherent view of knowledge and a more integrated life.

Individualism is necessary for a free and creative society, and the historic strength of our democracy lies in its commitment to personal improvement and fulfillment. We need individualism but, at the same time, we must be mindful of the consequences of selfishness. It is appropriate, therefore, for educational institutions that are preparing students to be citizens in a participatory democracy to understand the dilemmas and paradoxes of individualistic culture.

Just as we search culturally to maintain the necessary balance between private and public obligations, in education we seek the same end. The college, at its best, recognizes that, although we live alone, we also are deeply dependent on each other. Through an effective college education, students should become personally empowered and also committed to the common good.

ALL SUMMER IN A DAY
Ray Bradbury

No one in the class could remember
a time when there wasn't rain.

"Ready?"   1

"Ready."

"Now?"

"Soon."

"Do the scientists really know? Will it happen today, will it?"

"Look, look; see for yourself!"

The children pressed to each other like so many roses, so many weeds,
intermixed, peering out for a look at the hidden sun.

It rained.   10

It had been raining for seven years; thousand upon thousands of days
compounded and filled from one end to the other with rain, with the drum
and gush of water, with the sweet crystal fall of showers and the concussion
of storms so heavy they were tidal waves come over the islands. A thousand
forests had been crushed under the rain and grown up a thousand times to
be crushed again. And this was the way life was forever on the planet Venus,
and this was the schoolroom of the children of the rocket men and women
who had come to a raining world to set up civilization and live out their lives.

"It's stopping, it's stopping!"

"Yes, yes!"   20

Margot stood apart from these children who could never remember a
time when there wasn't rain and rain and rain. They were all nine years old,
and if there had been a day, seven years ago, when the sun came out for an
hour and showed its face to the stunned world, they could not recall. Sometimes, at night, she heard them stir, in remembrance, and she knew they were
dreaming and remembering and old or a yellow crayon or a coin large
enough to buy the world with. She knew they thought they remembered a
warmness, like a blushing in the face, in the body, in the arms and legs and
trembling hands. But then they always awoke to the tatting drum, the endless shaking down of clear bead necklaces upon the roof, the walk, the gar-   30
dens, the forests, and their dreams were gone.

All day yesterday they had read in class about the sun. About how like a
lemon it was, and how hot. And they had written small stories or essays or
poems about it:

I think the sun is a flower,
That blooms for just one hour.

Reprinted from *The Stories of Ray Bradbury* (1980), by permission of Don Congdon Associates.

That was Margot's poem, read in a quiet voice in the still classroom while the rain was falling outside.

"Aw, you didn't write that!" protested one of the boys.

"I did," said Margot. "I *did*."

40 "William!" said the teacher.

But that was yesterday. Now the rain was slackening, and the children were crushed in the great thick windows.

"Where's teacher?"

"She'll be back."

"She'd better hurry, we'll miss it!"

They turned on themselves, like a feverish wheel, all tumbling spokes.

Margot stood alone. She was a very frail girl who looked as if she had been lost in the rain for years and the rain had washed out the blue from her eyes and the red from her mouth and the yellow from her hair. She was an old

50 photograph dusted from an album, whitened away, and if she spoke at all her voice would be a ghost. Now she stood, separate, staring at the rain and the loud wet world beyond the huge glass.

"What're *you* looking at?" said William.

Margot said nothing.

"Speak when you're spoken to." He gave her a shove. But she did not move; rather she let herself be moved only by him and nothing else.

They edged away from her, they would not look at her. She felt them go away. And this was because she would play no games with them in the echoing tunnels of the underground city. If they tagged her and ran, she stood

60 blinking after them and did not follow. When the class sang songs about happiness and life and games her lips barely moved. Only when they sang about the sun and the summer did her lips move as she watched the drenched windows.

And then, of course, the biggest crime of all was that she had come here only five years ago from Earth, and she remembered the sun and the way the sun was and the sky was when she was four in Ohio. And they, they had been on Venus all their lives, and they had been only two years old when last the sun came out and had long since forgotten the color and heat of it and the way it really was. But Margot remembered.

70 "It's like a penny," she said once, eyes closed.

"No it's not!" the children cried.

"It's like a fire," she said, "in the stove."

"You're lying, you don't remember!" cried the children.

But she remembered and stood quietly apart from all of them and watched the patterning windows. And once, a month ago, she had refused to shower in the school shower rooms, had clutched her hands to her ears and over her head, screaming the water mustn't touch her head. So after that, dimly, dimly, she sensed it, she was different and they knew her difference and kept away.

There was talk that her father and mother were taking her back to Earth   80
next year; it seemed vital to her that they do so, though it would mean the
loss of thousands of dollars to her family. And so, the children hated her for
all these reasons of big and little consequence. They hated her pale snow face,
her waiting silence, her thinness, and her possible future.

"Get away!" The boy gave her another push. "What're you waiting for?"

Then, for the first time, she turned and looked at him. And what she was
waiting for was in her eyes.

"Well, don't wait around here!" cried the boy savagely. "You won't see
nothing!"

Her lips moved.   90

"Nothing!" he cried. "It was all a joke, wasn't it?" He turned to the other
children. "Nothing's happening today. *Is* it?"

They all blinked at him and then, understanding, laughed and shook
their heads. "Nothing, nothing!"

"Oh, but," Margot whispered, her eyes helpless. "But this is the day, the
scientists predict, they say, they *know*, the sun. . . ."

"All a joke!" said the boy, and seized her roughly. "Hey, everyone, let's put
her in a closet before teacher comes!"

"No," said Margot, falling back.

They surged about her, caught her up and bore her, protesting, and then   100
pleading, and then crying, back into a tunnel, a room, a closet, where they
slammed and locked the door. They stood looking at the door and saw it
tremble from her beating and throwing herself against it. They heard her
muffled cries. Then, smiling, they turned and went out and back down the
tunnel, just as the teacher arrived.

"Ready, children?" she glanced at her watch.

"Yes!" said everyone.

"Are we all here?"

"Yes!"

The rain slackened still more.   110

They crowded to the huge door.

The rain stopped.

It was as if, in the midst of a film, concerning an avalanche, a tornado, a
hurricane, a volcanic eruption, something had, first, gone wrong with the
sound apparatus, thus muffling and finally cutting off all noise, all of the
blasts and repercussions and thunders, and then, second, ripped the film
from the projector and inserted in its place a peaceful tropical slide which did
not move or tremor. The world ground to a standstill. The silence was so
immense and unbelievable that you felt your ears had been stuffed or you had
lost your hearing altogether. The children put their hands to their ears. They   120
stood apart. The door slid back and the smell of the silent, waiting world
came in to them.

The sun came out.

It was the color of flaming bronze and it was very large. And the sky around it was a blazing blue tile color. And the jungle burned with sunlight as the children, released from their spell, rushed out, yelling, into the spring-time.

"Now don't go too far," called the teacher after them. "You've only two hours, you know. You wouldn't want to get caught out!"

130 But they were running and turning their faces up to the sky and feeling the sun on their cheeks like a warm iron; they were taking off their jackets and letting the sun burn their arms.

"Oh, it's better than the sun lamps, isn't it?"

"Much, much better!"

They stopped running and stood in the great jungle that covered Venus, that grew and never stopped growing, tumultuously, even as you watched it. It was a nest of octopi, clustering up great arms of flesh-like weed, wavering, flowering this brief spring. It was the color of rubber and ash, this jungle, from the many years without sun. It was the color of stones and white cheeses

140 and ink, and it was the color of the moon.

The children lay out, laughing, on the jungle mattress, and heard it sigh and squeak under them, resilient and alive. They ran among the trees, they slipped and fell, they pushed each other, they played hide-and-seek and tag, but most of all they squinted at the sun until the tears ran down their faces, they put their hands up to that yellowness and that amazing blueness and they breathed of the fresh, fresh air and listened and listened to the silence which suspended them in a blessed sea of no sound and no motion. They looked at everything and savored everything. Then, wildly, like animals escaped from their caves, they ran and ran in shouting circles. They ran for

150 an hour and did not stop running.

And then—

In the midst of their running one of the girls wailed.

Everyone stopped.

The girl, standing in the open, held out her hand.

"Oh, look, look," she said, trembling.

They came slowly to look at her opened palm.

In the center of it, cupped and huge, was a single raindrop.

She began to cry, looking at it.

They glanced quietly at the sky.

160 "Oh. Oh."

A few cold drops fell on their noses and their cheeks and their mouths. The sun faded behind a stir of mist. A wind blew cool around them. They turned and started to walk back toward the underground house, their hands at their sides, their smiles vanishing away.

A boom of thunder startled them and like leaves before a new hurricane, they tumbled upon each other and ran. Lightening struck ten miles away, five miles away, a mile, a half mile. The sky darkened into midnight in a flash.

They stood in the doorway of the underground for a moment until it was raining hard. Then they closed the door and heard the gigantic sound of the rain falling in tons and avalanches, everywhere and forever.   170

"Will it be seven more years?"

"Yes. Seven."

Then one of them gave a little cry.

"Margot!"

"What?"

"She's still in the closet where we locked her."

"Margot."

They stood as if someone had driven them, like so many stakes, into the floor. They looked at each other and then looked away. They glanced out at the world that was raining now and raining and raining steadily. They could   180 not meet each other's glances. Their faces were solemn and pale. They looked at their hands and feet, their faces down.

"Margot."

One of the girls said, "Well . . . ?"

No one moved.

"Go on," whispered the girl.

They walked slowly down the hall in the sound of the cold rain. They turned through the doorway to the room in the sound of the storm and thunder, lightening on their faces, blue and terrible. They walked over to the closest door slowly and stood by it.   190

Behind the closed door was only silence.

They unlocked the door, even more slowly, and let Margot out.

Circle of Conversation

Then write 3 best insights from the conversation independently,
or unresolved questions

ACADEMIC ADMINISTRATORS AND THE CHALLENGE OF SOCIAL-NETWORKING WEBSITES
Karen M. Bradshaw and Souvik Saha

There exists a divide between users and nonusers of social-networking websites. For users, such websites are generally an integral part of social interaction used daily for information sharing, event planning, and reputation building. In contrast, nonusers typically fail to grasp the extent to which social-networking websites influence in-person interactions. Consequently, university professors and administrators who do not participate in online communities may underestimate the extent to which interactions occurring in the virtual realm affect their academic institutions. This divide can produce serious, negative consequences, particularly when students engage in behavior online that would be unacceptable in a traditional, live setting.

Millions of college students are members of social-networking websites and belong to online groups. The majority of groups on social-networking websites are devoted to shared interests, such as a sport or geographical connection. Other groups, however, are focused on individuals, including faculty members and fellow students. Such groups share candid photos and threads of commentary about their targets. Some are complimentary and are of a fan club nature. Others are not. Bitter comments and untruthful rants about students and faculty at a number of educational institutions are easily found using a quick search of social-networking websites. The existence of these groups raises many questions: When does a thread of commentary transform from acceptably critical to abusive? When do unflattering photos taken and posted without permission become a violation of privacy? Why do students feel free to post lewd comments that they would not say in person?

Abusive behavior taking place online, known as "cyber bullying," is easy to dismiss as harmless pestering that is unlikely to affect a serious graduate student or tenured professor. Yet, online communities often engage in targeted hate speech and defamation that academic communities would not accept in a live setting. These abuses have serious consequences, including professional and reputational damage, sexual harassment, and perhaps even increased suicide rates.

What nonusers fail to recognize is the potency of social-networking websites as compared with other virtual communication tools, such as chat rooms or instant messaging systems. Rather than just a means of communication, Facebook and similar websites—like MySpace and Bebo—are functional communities that happen to exist on the Internet. Technological or generational barriers often render these online communities void of administrators and faculty, allowing students to feel removed from the supervision that exists in classrooms or campuses. We argue that, as a result, online communities lack many of the positive social norms found in traditional academic communities. Without these norms, individuals are emboldened to engage in strikingly abusive harassment of students and faculty. Administrators who are not a part of online

Reprinted from *The Offensive Internet* (2011), edited by Nussbaum and Levmore, by permission of Harvard University Press.

social networks tend to underestimate the impact online communities have on classrooms and campuses.

In this essay, we survey administrators' attempts to engage with online communities, and argue that many current approaches fail to appreciate that Facebook is a fundamental component of social dynamics among students. Some schools focus on classroom dynamics by limiting or restricting in-class Internet use. Other academic institutions focus more broadly on monitoring and disciplining inappropriate behavior. These approaches are controversial: privacy concerns, free speech issues, and the appropriate reach of institutional authority are all fodder for heated debates. More importantly, continued, widespread cyber bullying demonstrates that these regulations are ineffective as currently applied. In looking to alternative approaches, we argue that methods designed to inject social norms into the online environment and introduce the metaphorical adult into the room are important, achievable steps toward addressing the most blatant online abuses.

INTERACTIONS BETWEEN ONLINE AND ACADEMIC COMMUNITIES

We posit that two communities exist simultaneously in the modern academic setting. First, there is the obvious traditional community in which students, faculty, and administrators interact with one another in the physical space of the institution. A second community has arisen among the millions of students who participate daily in social-networking websites. Administrators have yet to fully grasp the extent to which the traditional academic community is affected by what occurs in these virtual communities. Though a multitude of positive outcomes are generated through student participation in online communities, so too are abuses. This essay focuses on two forms of abuse: obvious in-class use of the Internet, and cyber bullying that may impact the academic community even though it occurs outside the physical classroom.

Social-networking websites provide hundreds of millions of users with a forum for online interaction. According to the website of one popular online community, "Facebook helps you connect and share with the people in your life." These websites are stunningly popular and widely used. University students rely on social-networking websites to keep in touch with friends, organize activities, and pursue information and groups that interest them. Social-networking websites are distinct from previous forms of online communications because they do more than facilitate interaction. Unlike chat rooms or instant messaging, social-networking websites continue to convey and send information about participants even when they are not logged on.

Facebook groups are of particular interest because they are an example of online communities that coexist or even supplant traditional communities. Students can create and join groups focused on varied interests. Group "administrators" provide a title and description of the groups and monitor who can join. Members of the group may post pictures, events, and comments viewable by every group member.

Although social-networking websites provide a new forum for interaction, abusive behavior by college students against a particular target is not new. Facebook groups are somewhat like fraternities that engage in targeted rumor spreading and information sharing. Just as fraternity behavior can become abusive toward individual targets—by spreading lies around campus about a fellow student or creating hateful reviews of professors—online groups may also provide a forum that encourages group members to act increasingly abusively toward targeted persons. Such analogies are helpful in contextualizing the problem for administrators, but can minimize the unique features of cyber bullying that can make it especially difficult but important to discourage.

Some features of social-networking websites, particularly the vast audience and constancy of interaction, make them particularly prone to abuse. Social-networking groups constitute a broadcasting mechanism that permits hundreds of students to see the same information simultaneously. The reach of the broadcasting capability is exponentially magnified when coupled with Facebook's ability to synthesize information from multiple sources, such as other groups or applications on Facebook. Unlike traditional academic communities, Facebook groups can span geographical distances, and members may simultaneously view and share information. The number of potential group members is far greater than in physical communities; on Facebook, elementary school friends and potential employers may have access to the same information that would previously have been available only to students in the academic setting. While strangers may care little about a target, people with minimal external context about a person—especially potential employers—may rely upon the information. This becomes especially damaging when the archiving of Internet pages is taken into account; it can take years for negative messages to disappear from search engine results. Combined, these characteristics create a new and powerful communication tool that is different from previous forms of social information sharing.

Educators mistakenly believe that they understand the depth of concerns presented by social-networking websites because the *symptoms* of in-class Facebook use are obvious. Faculty can easily detect inattention, reduced participation, and distraction. It is perhaps too easy to attribute this inattention to Internet use. For example, Norman Garrett, a professor of Computer Information Systems at Eastern Illinois University, wonders: "Are [students] not even in the same universe as I'm in because they're looking at the Internet?" Studies reporting high in-class use of social-networking websites lead administrators to wrongly conclude that the extent of problems caused by the Internet is limited to inappropriate use within the classroom.

Administrators fail to recognize that the *causes* behind the symptoms outlined above are not obvious. It is certainly possible that a student may not participate in class because she is instead looking at a friend's photos or writing a message. But more troubling and less obvious causes of distraction or unwillingness to participate also exist. These problems seem largely unknown to faculty and administrators, even though they have substantial impact on classroom and social dynamics at academic institutions. For example, a student who is *not* online during class may not be willing to participate in class because

130   she fears her comments will be critiqued online.

Studies of cyber bullying among girls indicate that one form of cyber bullying involves being teased by peers for sharing opinions. Unlike the teasing that occurs in traditional academic communities, targeted communications in online communities have the potential to be more widely broadcast, to take place in groups rather than individual capacities, and to occur without monitoring by educators and administrators. Their spread and impact can be even broader, extending well beyond the confines of the traditional academic community. Fear of this particular form of cyber bullying—rather than actual in-class Internet use—may be the true cause of a student's silence. Other,

140   similar causes abound.

It is easy for administrators, particularly those who are unfamiliar with social-networking websites, to be dismissive of how the effects of online harassment may impact the academic setting. Suicide, significant damage to professional and personal reputation, and the inability of instructors to function in their professional capacities are among the many outcomes of extreme cyber bullying.

Facebook groups most threaten academic environments when they are used to bully, defame, or engage in hate speech against students, administrators, and faculty. Recent reports of campus-related cyber bullying highlight the

150   gravity of this problem. At Syracuse University, sixteen students joined a Facebook group solely devoted to criticizing an English doctoral student teaching a writing class. They engaged in crass and sexualized criticism of the instructor. One entry was described by a different instructor as "level[ing] a crude and personal accusation of possessing an infectious disease, which, though meant hyperbolically, crosses a . . . line. At a Canadian University, a post written to a 200-student Facebook group ridiculed a business student and even acknowledged that "[w]e are pretty much ruining someone's life here." Three hundred sixty students in the United Kingdom joined a Facebook group targeting a library worker at Kent University that included physical threats and

160   speculation about his sexual orientation. Students at a high school posted a false profile of a school principal with lewd language implying he was a pedophile who propositioned students. They also leveled attacks on his wife and child.

Significant anecdotal evidence demonstrates that what occurs in online communities affects traditional academic communities. At an extreme, several student suicides have been attributed to cyber bullying. A study conducted by researchers at the Yale School of Medicine found no direct links but indicated that there is a likely association between bullying and suicide. Less dramatic cases illustrate that cyber bullying negatively impacts traditional academic communities. While no studies were found illustrating this point, anecdotal evidence abounds. For example, one post-graduate student who was a victim of cyber bullying reported that online harassment affected his ability to study. Educators targeted by students online have filed suits pursuing claims for intentional infliction of emotional distress.

Cyber bullying is a small but pervasive negative aspect of a social network that produces many positive effects. It is likely, however, that less obvious but more widespread impacts of cyber bullying may harm classroom and academic dynamics. For example, the potential for online harassment may chill class participation. Some Facebook groups are specifically designed to target students who are active classroom participants. Fear of becoming the target of such groups may cause many students to reduce their in-class participation. Studies exploring the link between online cyber bullying and in-class participation are both lacking and necessary. Classrooms and schools no longer exist as a closed, protected sphere with limited outside influence. The extent, detection, and addressing of concerns stemming from social-networking sites present unique problems. Each of these is exacerbated because those responsible for monitoring and enforcing social norms in traditional communities are functionally excluded from online communities.

ACADEMIC RESPONSE TO ONLINE COMMUNITIES

Given the potential for social-networking tools to disrupt the academic environment, school administrators face a challenge. The first is recognizing the seriousness of cyber bullying. While some administrators have begun to mobilize in response, there exists a legal debate concerning the extent to which administrators may restrict or punish certain forms of online behavior—whether in class or off campus—that disrupt the integrity of the learning environment. Despite a lack of clear legal precedent, school administrators have adopted strategies to combat the negative effects of online communities on students and academic culture. Surveying administrative approaches designed to lessen inappropriate online behavior illustrates both the strengths and shortcomings of current strategies.

Many current strategies demonstrate the failure of administrators to understand the complex and widespread nature of online communities. Some academic institutions believe they have addressed the problems presented by Facebook by taking technological measures to regulate Internet use within the classroom. For example, some institutions allow only selective use of the Internet in the classroom. Modern technology enables administrators to implement Internet "kill switches" that allow selective access to various websites and course management systems, while temporarily banning all other access. While a testament to increased sophistication in science and technology, students can circumvent these "kill switches" through open wireless (WiFi) networks that are not subject to such regulation. Further, as information technology officials at the University of North Carolina-Chapel Hill found, these technological measures can be extremely time-consuming and costly. And as the director of Computing Services at the University of Michigan Business School states, "There's nothing you can do to keep a student from getting on the Internet." Limiting Internet use through selective website blocking presents cost and efficacy concerns.

Another, more radical approach is to ban Internet use altogether. The University of Chicago Law School has adopted this approach. Disconnecting in-class Internet availability reduces the symptoms of inattention and poor par-

220   ticipation. Additionally, for the period of time that students are in the classroom, it limits them to a single community, in which the professor plays the central role. However, while this solves the immediate problem of distracting sub-communities within the classroom, it fails to recognize that Facebook dynamics outside of the classroom can still affect in-class dynamics. Banning Internet use entirely in classrooms may provide a partial answer. However, it would be an error to think that by doing so administrators have protected their students. Taking away in-class Internet use to prevent cyber bullying is like unplugging a television set to prevent violence on television: it fails to address the core concern.

230   Other institutions refrain from banning Internet use in the classroom on principle. They suggest that the benefits of Internet access in the classroom outweigh the potential for distraction and reputational concerns. The argument underpinning this hands-off approach—that students online will be driven by the same social norms as those in traditional settings—fails to capture the unmonitored nature of the Internet. Administrators have firmly established that they will step in if students begin to abuse one another in the classroom or even at the fraternity house. In contrast, most administrators have yet to establish that their school norms extend to the Internet.

While each in-class Internet policy has certain advantages, none fully
240   addresses the extent to which Facebook use—in and out of the classroom— may affect the academic environment. More important, these approaches undercut the value of the Internet as a powerful learning tool. As one official at the University of Louisiana at Baton Rouge states, these solutions are tantamount to "throwing the baby out with the bathwater." It is therefore necessary to evaluate new and more comprehensive approaches to controlling the impact of Facebook in academic settings.

One reason for abuses in online communities is that they do not have a metaphorical adult in the room. Some school officials address this problem by taking an active role in online communities. "Administrators within higher
250   ed[ucation] are finding ways of embracing the technology, using it as a new medium for interacting with students while tackling these very problems rather than ignore them." Administrators join websites like Facebook to monitor or engage with their students online.

Some administrators join online communities to monitor their students. For example, some school officials pose as students online by creating "dummy Facebook profiles." Administrators use these Facebook profiles to "friend" students, so they can view their profile pages. Once they have access to a student's profile, administrators may view their photos, comments, and group memberships. This information may be used to warn or discipline students. For example, "four Northern Kentucky students received University Code of Conduct violations based on pictures posted on Facebook that showed them drinking." Monitoring students' online activities gives administrators information that would be less available if they relied only upon traditional sources.

Should administrators actively monitor students' online behavior? Opponents of monitoring cite privacy concerns, boundaries between school and other areas of life, and chilling of free speech. They suggest it is deceptive for administrators to pose as students, and costly to pay people to do so. Proponents of monitoring assert that schools have an obligation to protect academic communities from online abuses. At Brandeis University, administrators screen student Facebook profiles for campus-related employment. Both academic and outside employers are increasingly using Facebook searches as part of the hiring process.

Other administrators are actively, publically participating in online communities rather than simply monitoring activity. School administrators urge faculty to become members of the Facebook community in order to temper student behavior online by injecting an authority figure into a previously unregulated community. At Brown University, several high-ranking school administrators have Facebook accounts. Participants include the associate dean for judicial affairs, associate vice president of campus life and dean for student life, a psychotherapist, and three members of the Department of Public Safety. This approach addresses one of the fundamental challenges of Facebook by placing an authority figure into the setting. Embedding an authority figure to enforce rules of conduct and assert social norms makes online communities more analogous to traditional communities. One analogy is to the "mother," whose presence checks the behavior of members of the fraternity. However, there are roadblocks to such interactions. A faculty member or school administrator who fails to identify himself on Facebook might later be held to have violated a student's right to privacy. It is possible that student monitoring could fill this void, inasmuch as students surely expect fellow students to be present in the networking site.

Finally, school administrators have adopted punitive measures to mitigate the growing challenge that off-campus Facebook use presents for the academic environment. Increasing awareness of the potential ugliness of online social-networking communities has produced punitive responses to cyber bullying and other forms of inappropriate online student conduct. Students face suspension and expulsion for their actions, as well as potential criminal charges. At Syracuse University, four students were expelled from their writing class and placed under "disciplinary reprimand" for creating a Facebook group with vulgar comments about an instructor. In reacting to the disciplinary measure, the students' primary concern was that the university failed to provide adequate notice that Facebook posts could lead to punishment. As one of the students implicated in the Syracuse scandal said, "The student body needs to be aware of the [the administration's] expectations and if Facebook is fair grounds for policing, they need to make us aware of it." Without clear guidelines, harsh punishment will be controversial. As an associate dean at the Newhouse School of Public Communications at Syracuse University argues, "If [the judicial office] wants to operate on a case-by-case basis, that doesn't seem like a standard process. . . . What can and cannot be said on the internet should be spelled out clearly."

310   This need for *ex-ante* rule making is illustrated through one student's battle against the administration at Ryerson University; he was expelled for contributing to a Facebook group dedicated to peer discussion of physics homework. The student, who faces 147 violations of the code of conduct, argues, "If this kind of help is cheating, then so is tutoring and all the mentoring programs the university runs and the discussions we do in tutorials." If a school chooses to punish students for their online communication, it must clearly delineate the boundaries of acceptable and prohibited interaction. In response to such criticisms, some administrators have clarified rules to reflect the claim that online behavior is subject to school regulations. By extension, online

320   abuses fall under the purview of acceptable disciplinary action if the behavior disrupts the learning environment.

Administrators and courts face difficult line-drawing questions. May schools discipline students who cyber bully from home? Is it the student's behavior or the school's reaction that disrupts a student body? As academic responses to cyber bullying become more robust, it will be necessary to address these concerns. The challenge Facebook presents to school administrators to monitor online communities highlights the shortcomings of current policies to combat the potential negative effects of online social-networking tools. Disallowing Internet use in the classroom may reduce the symptoms of Facebook

330   use in the real-time classroom. However, this fails to address the extent to which online community dynamics impact traditional communities. Administrators seem unaware of the extent to which Facebook and other online-networking tools permeate the academic culture, and indeed form unmonitored social communities within the classroom. The primary approach to infusing online communities with the norms present in other areas of an institution is to introduce an authority figure into such communities. Regulating and normalizing online behavior is necessary to maintaining cohesive traditional academic environments. Doing so requires accountability for action and involvement by administration when abuses do occur.

340   Freedom of expression and privacy rights must be balanced against protecting students. One approach is for school administrators to use social-networking tools while continuing to respect student privacy as they would in traditional settings. For instance, the possibility of educating and encouraging students to self-monitor and report instances of cyber bullying can be an important first step in combating the most serious symptoms of Facebook. This would also address the second shortcoming of administrators' current

approaches: the failure to understand how off-campus Facebook use affects in-class dynamics.

At present, many administrators fail to appreciate the pervasive nature and potentially harmful impact of Facebook on campus. A crucial first step in tackling this problem is for school officials to clearly amend academic codes of conduct regarding permissible behavior to include online networking both on and off campus. One legal expert argues, "Policies should inform students [and their parents] that disciplinary action may be taken against them when their off-campus speech causes a substantial disruption to the education environment or interferes with another student's rights." This would be an important first step in notifying students that their actions, statements, use, and involvement with social-networking tools such as Facebook are subject to university policing and punitive standards. Clear policies alone may substantially chill online abuses and allow schools to sidestep the costs of dedicated monitoring of online communities. Extending the academic administrative reach to Facebook can inject the social norms of traditional academic communities into the online realm, which in turn will deter students from cyber bullying.

Administrators underestimate the detrimental impacts of social-networking groups on traditional academic communities. First, the negative impacts of inappropriate use of online-networking websites are real and serious. They include reputational damage, inability to function in academic settings, and links to suicide risks. Although similar to fraternity activity that has long been associated with campus life, the danger of cyber bullying lies in its ability to pervade many aspects of a target's life, while flying under the radar of campus administrators who may be reticent to block it. Second, what happens in online communities tangibly affects traditional communities, even if students are not online during class. The technology presented by these networking sites provides a forum for online communities. At present, many such communities are unmonitored by academic administrators, thus providing a haven for those who engage in hate speech or bullying behavior that would be blatantly unacceptable in traditional academic environments.

The responses by academic administrators to the challenges presented by online-networking sites reflect some progress in addressing the most serious concerns. However, much remains to be decided and enacted. First, courts, legislators, and administrators will need to define the role that academic institutions may play in regulating acts of bullying that do not physically occur on school grounds. Next, administrators must find a balance that simultaneously protects the norms of their institutions and protects the privacy and free speech of its students. Doing so without incurring tremendous monitoring costs is a challenge. Among current approaches, attempts to merely ban Internet use at school seem incomplete in addressing the widespread sense of community provided by online-networking sites. Attempts to actively monitor websites present privacy and cost concerns. Clearly defining standards formally through codes of conduct and informally through

350

What does all have now?

360

Won't students just invent new social places?

370

380

390

administrators' public engagement with the issue is a good foundation. Encouraging student monitoring of peers for truly egregious violations provides a backstop against extreme abuse.

Deputization

Social-networking websites present new and largely unrecognized challenges to academic administrators who are unaware of the pervasiveness and potential for abuse within online communities. Understanding the severity of the problems that may arise, and surveying the available approaches, provides administrators with the information necessary to begin considering and addressing these concerns effectively.

EASY CHAIR
Servile Disobedience
Thomas Frank

Class has long been a topic of sociological scrutiny. Psychological experiments on the subject, however, are a relatively novel thing. So I was surprised to discover that, over the past few years, psychologists have published a series of papers on the behavioral aspects of social status—and that their findings have so far been almost uniformly unflattering toward society's winners.

One 2009 study in *Psychological Science* found that, in conversations with strangers, higher-status people tend to do more doodling and fidgeting and also to use fewer "engagement cues"—looking at the other person, laughing, and nodding their heads. A 2010 paper published in the *Journal of Personality and Social Psychology* found that "lower-class individuals" turned out to be better performers on measures of such "prosocial" virtues as generosity, charity, and helpfulness. A third study found that those of higher status were noticeably worse at assessing the emotions of others or figuring out what facial expressions meant.

All of which is to say, The rich are different from you and me. They are ruder and less generous. They don't get what others are thinking. And apparently they don't really care.

If you stop and think about it for a second, you understand that all of this makes sense. People don't craft poisoned collateralized debt obligations by calling on what they learned in Sunday school. Still, the research aroused media interest. *The Christian Science Monitor*'s account of one study ends with this quotation from Michael Kraus of the University of California, San Francisco, one of the researchers:

> *Being empathic is one of the first steps to helping other people. . . . One of the first things we're really interested in is what can make wealthy people—affluent people, the people with the largest capacity to give—what can make them empathic?*

I think I see the urgency of Dr. Kraus's question. After all, we have spent the past thirty years doing everything we could to transfer the wealth of the nation into the bank accounts of the affluent, to send them victorious, happy and glorious, long to reign over us.

Oh, we've cut their taxes, gladly transferring much of the cost of keeping their holdings safe onto our own shoulders. We've furnished them with special megaphones so that their voices might be heard over the hubbub of the crowd. We have conferred upon them separate and better schools, their very own transportation system, and a full complement of private security guards.

Reprinted from *Harper's Magazine*, February 2011, by permission of Harper's Magazine.

We've built an entire culture of courtiers and sycophants to make their every waking hour an otherworldly delight.

40   We let them build a system of bonuses and "executive compensation" on the theory that it would be good for everyone if the people on top got to take home much, much more. And when it turned out that the theory was wrong—that in the most famous cases the rich chased bonuses not to the shareholders' benefit but at their expense—why, we promptly bailed them out. We allowed them to step up to the Fed's discount window and fill their pockets, we generously transferred their dumb investments to our balance sheet, and we sent them off with little more than a request that they please not do it again. We've done everything we can to lift them up and exalt them as a new leviathan; the least they can do in return, one feels, is show a little empathy.

50   Besides, look what we've done with the old leviathan, the government. For decades we have attacked it, redirected it, outsourced it, and filled it with incompetents and cronies. Yes, it still works well enough when we need it to replenish the accounts of investment banks or bang some small country against a wall, but those branches of it designed to help out Americans of "lower socioeconomic status," as the scientists would put it, are now bare. The government fails the people of New Orleans when they are hit by a hurricane, fails to notice the cadmium paint in the marketplace, does a lousy job educating our kids, can't keep the libraries open or the park lawns mowed, overlooks the catastrophic shortcuts taken by its pals in the oil-drilling industry—

60   and all we can do to express our frustration is elect candidates who promise to hack it down even more.

We need the rich to be nice. We need them to stop doodling, pay attention, and get generous. Now that the government has divested from the empathy business, we need the rich to discover brotherly love, and fast.

Come to think of it, wasn't that supposed to be the deal in the first place, the arrangement Andrew Carnegie brokered over a century ago, when he made his big career move from steel king to public-library baron? The laissez-faire social contract would offer a free hand for private business, but in exchange those who piled up massive wealth were supposed to extend a magnanimous

70   hand to the rest of us. As Carnegie wrote in his famous 1889 essay, "The Gospel of Wealth," we didn't need socialism to solve our problems; philanthropy is "the true antidote for the temporary unequal distribution of wealth, the reconciliation of the rich and the poor. . . ." Going further, Carnegie argued that the "duty of the man of wealth" was

> to consider all surplus revenues which come to him simply as trust funds, which he is called upon to administer in the manner which, in his judgment, is best calculated to produce the most beneficial results for the community—the man of wealth thus becoming the mere trustee and agent for his poorer brethren. . . .

The same way of thinking led Carnegie to support the estate tax—"of all   80
forms of taxation this seems the wisest," he wrote. It was wise because it would
"induce the rich man to attend to the administration of wealth during his
life," and if he didn't it would return most of his hoardings to the "community from which it chiefly came."

Vestiges of the Carnegie attitude survive to this day. A recent study of high-
net-worth individuals by Barclays Wealth ("a leading global wealth manager")
confirmed that American philanthropists tend to understand their giving in
a context in which the state is either absent or irrelevant.

And, of course, there are plenty of nice plutocrats who don't fidget or doo-
dle when talking to strangers, and no doubt their robust "empathic" instincts   90
will someday bring many of them to endow a ward or a wing in return for a
commemorative plaque. The business headlines have been filled of late with
stories of billionaires coming together under the leadership of Warren Buffett and Bill Gates to donate their fortunes to worthy causes. Or to promise
to donate them, anyway.

But the billionaires with the strongest sense of class solidarity have another
plan for their disposable income: activating their lobbyists in Washington,
building grassroots movements to march on their behalf, and using their media
properties to run experiments on human credulity. Even their giving is a form
of taking. For example, Charles Koch, of Wichita oil fame, recently circulated   100
to his "network of business and philanthropic leaders" an invitation to a meeting at which—if their last meeting's agenda is any indication—they will discuss strategies for beating back environmentalism and the "threat" of financial regulation. This is a kind of philanthropy that pays dividends.

If the affluent no longer possess the capacity to interpret facial expressions, let alone maintain a social conscience, can we find a way, with the
help of behavioral economics, to make them act as if they do? One idea out
there is to turn the rich, via a little marketing jiujitsu that exploits their
well-known taste for prestigious consumer goods, into slaves of "prosocial" trends. The means by which this might be done have actually been   110
the subject of a recent study on "green" consumerism by a psychologist and
two marketing professors. Summarizing their results in the *Journal of Personality and Social Psychology*, the academics announced that "activating status motives" can push people to choose environmentally friendly products over luxury goods and thereby ensnare consumers in a race to niceness
that the scholars call "competitive altruism." The conditions have to be just
right, of course: People will pay more for a green product, the researchers
found, if they are buying it in public, where everybody can see them doing
it. They will also be drawn to "prosocial" products if the prices are artifi-
cially high; that way their sacrifice will be especially acute and their   120
status-bump that much more noticeable. The preeminent example is the
Toyota Prius, a hybrid car that "essentially functions as a mobile, self-
promoting billboard for proenvironmentalism."

All that remains is to give the rich some form of psychic gratification that can outweigh the profits that would come from their usual routine. At one of Warren Buffett's gatherings of the superwealthy, according to *Fortune* magazine, a number of such inducements were discussed: "national recognition of great philanthropists (presidential medals, for example), or a film, or a philanthropy guidebook." The idea Buffett's group finally settled upon was to
130   persuade their peers to take a pledge. Not exactly the most innovative or inspiring answer to the question, although it's worth noting that a number of billionaires signed up anyway.

Another approach would be to leverage the human accessories that are so much in vogue these days—in Hollywood, nothing says *I care* like a Sri Lankan war orphan. And so perhaps we can, with some deft cultural manipulation, make it equally rewarding for a billionaire to adopt, say, the entire blue-collar population of Rockford, Illinois. The city can rename itself in the billionaire's honor, and in return all the kids might get college educations and a start in some industry other than fastener manufacturing.

140   But then there's the bummer backlash that inevitably overtakes all such plans. What happens to green consumerism, for example, when all those canny shoppers figure out that marketers are making high-minded things seem expensive just to trigger the buyer's status anxiety? What will those consumers do when it becomes plain how absurd it is to show off by wearing $120 fair-trade hemp tennis shoes, or when their vain pretensions to thrift expose them to the derision of consumers even more environmentally savvy than themselves? How will they react when they discover that those hair shirts aren't really trendy at all, just uncomfortable? What happens when they figure out that altruism isn't really in their self-interest?

150   Among those who make it their business to manipulate the attitudes of the rich, one of the hottest trends is the zero option. Attend a few Tea Party rallies around the country and you'll be passed a platter of Ayn Rand's spiciest hors d'oeuvres. She is hot stuff these days. True, her philosophy of market rationality and bankerly heroism influenced the disastrous policymaking of the conservatives who brought us to economic ruin, and it was even a former member of her inner circle, Alan Greenspan, who personally prescribed much of the snake oil, but by the curious homeopathy of American politics that merely means we need a larger dose of the same poison; it means Ms. Rand is the rightest dame who ever lived.

160   Back in her heyday, Rand would occasionally address audiences of businessmen, exhorting them to understand that they had few moral obligations to others. Altruism, she told one such gathering in 1981, was "a contemptibly evil idea" promulgated by guilt-slinging "humanitarians" in order to shake down the productive. Insofar as they accepted this "altruism," the business class committed "treason against themselves." And so the novelist inveighed against philanthropic donations to universities, where altruists twisted the

minds of the young. "It is a moral crime to give money to support your own destroyers," she scolded.

In *Atlas Shrugged*, Rand also proposed a famous antidote to all this mawk- 170 ish nonsense: a union of class-conscious plutocrats that would go on strike and bring the world to its knees. *Atlas Shrugged* is in some ways a prophetic book: Ms. Rand's imagined future has in effect come to pass. After all, what is the phrase "too big to fail" but a standing threat to shut down the system unless the firm in question gets its way? In 2008, Wall Street essentially held the nation's 401(k)s hostage until it was bailed out. American business is sitting today on an immense reservoir of cash that it refuses to invest until the economic situation is more to its liking. And as I write this, business's pet political party is holding the legislative process itself hostage until its favorite tax cuts are extended.

As both rejoinder and homage to Ayn Rand, let us consider a different sort 180 of strike, one that might help the emotionally arrested rich in their time of need. I propose a twenty-four-hour refusal to fawn. A servility strike. A day without deference.

For one day, let the nation's doormen do their jobs without smiling. Let waiters at suburban restaurants leave their flair at home; let waiters at downtown restaurants neglect to compliment the good taste of their customers. Let the janitors at Princeton mop no vomit from the dormitory stairwells. Let retail greeters of every description call in sick. Let the first-class passengers board at someone else's leisure. Let the nation's limo drivers require their passengers to open their own damn doors. Let the production interns at CNBC 190 send the on-air "talent" to fetch the coffee. And, for just one day, let the talent ask their interviewees hard questions.

It wouldn't change much, of course. It would do nothing to alter the economic system that produced all those affluent louts in the first place, or the way that system divvies up what we produce, suborns the state, sends your job to China, and smashes your retirement fund for good measure. A day without deference will do nothing to fix the faithless machinery that assembles winners in its own churlish image. But as a form of therapy for those winners it might just work. It might help them to actualize their true selves, overcome their inner barriers to sharing. And maybe that's what vast indus- 200 trial actions ought to be about in the first place.

After all, Americans are born to serve and assist the wealthy; it is our inalienable duty. We like to think of ourselves as a people of untamed independence, but any observer not steeped in our culture would quickly conclude that we are in fact a nation of footmen. We cater to the wealthy in our work lives and we glorify them in our leisure. Our dueling political parties are dedicated to the principle of serving them (although they approach the directive in slightly different ways), and even our seething antielitist movements are carefully designed to build even further the affluence of the affluent. We take

210 up collections for our public schools because we feel the fortunes of the rich ought to go unencumbered by that burden. Our leaders in Washington are considering cutting Social Security because retaining it might require the rich to chip in more than their current percentage. If it's a choice between us spending our dotage in helplessness and filth and our high-net-worth friends having to forgo next year's Learjet, Americans will choose the personal sacrifice every time.

By withholding niceness for a day we might, surprisingly, inculcate niceness in our charges. So let's teach the rich to listen. Not because we have anything interesting to say, of course. Not for our own sake. But for theirs.

INDIVIDUAL AND SOCIAL NARCISSISM
Erich Fromm

One of the most fruitful and far-reaching of Freud's discoveries is his con- 1
cept of narcissism. Freud himself considered it to be one of his most
important findings, and employed it for the understanding of such distinct
phenomena as psychosis ("narcissistic neurosis"), love, castration fear, jealousy, sadism, and also for the understanding of mass phenomena, such as the
readiness of the suppressed classes to be loyal to their rulers. In this chapter
I want to continue along Freud's line of thought and examine the role of narcissism for the understanding of nationalism, national hatred, and the psychological motivations for destructiveness and war . . .

. . . What is the development of narcissism in the "normal" person? Freud 10
sketched the main lines of this development, and the following paragraph is
a short summary of his findings.

The fetus in the womb still lives in a state of absolute narcissism. "By
being born", says Freud, "we have made the step from an absolutely self-
sufficient narcissism to the perception of a changing external world and the
beginning of the discovery of objects,"[1] It takes months before the infant can
even perceive objects outside as such, as being part of the "not me." By many
blows to the child's narcissism, his ever increasing acquaintance with the outside world and its laws, thus of "necessity," man develops his original narcissism into "object love." But, says Freud, "a human being remains to some 20
extent narcissistic even after he has found external objects for his libido."[2]
Indeed, the development of the individual can be defined in Freud's term as
the evolution from absolute narcissism to a capacity for objective reasoning
and object love, a capacity, however, which does not transcend definite limitations. The "normal," "mature" person is one whose narcissism has been
reduced to the socially accepted minimum without ever disappearing completely. Freud's observation is confirmed by everyday experience. It seems
that in most people one can find a narcissistic core which is not accessible
and which defies any attempt at complete dissolution.

Those not sufficiently acquainted with Freud's technical language will 30
probably not obtain a distinct idea of the reality and power of narcissism,
unless some more concrete description of the phenomenon is forthcoming.
This I shall try to give in the following pages. Before I do so, however, I wish
to clarify something about the terminology. Freud's views on narcissism are
based on his concept of sexual libido. As I have already indicated, this mech-
anistic libido concept proved more to block than to further the development
of the concept of narcissism. I believe that the possibilities of bringing it to
its full fruition are much greater if one uses a concept of psychic energy
which is not identical with the energy of the *sexual* drive. This was done by
Jung; it even found some initial recognition in Freud's idea of desexualized 40

49

libido. But although nonsexual psychic energy differs from Freud's libido it is, like libido an *energy* concept; it deals with psychic forces, visible only through their manifestations, which have a certain intensity and a certain direction. This energy binds, unifies, and holds together the individual within himself as well as the individual in his relationship to the world outside. Even if one does not agree with Freud in his earlier view that aside from the drive for survival, the energy of the sexual instinct (libido) is the only important motive power for human conduct, and if one uses instead a general concept of psychic energy, the difference is not as great as many who think in dogmatic terms are prone to believe. The essential point on which any theory or therapy which could be called psychoanalysis depends, is the *dynamic* concept of human behavior; that is, the assumption that highly charged forces motivate behavior, and that behavior can be understood and predicted only by understanding these forces. This dynamic concept of human behavior is the center of Freud's system. How these forces are theoretically conceived, whether in terms of a mechanistic-materialistic philosophy or in terms of humanistic realism, is an important question, but one which is secondary to the central issue of the dynamic interpretation of human behavior.

Let us begin our description of narcissism with two extreme examples: the "primary narcissism" of the newborn infant, and the narcissism of the insane person. The infant is not yet related to the outside world (in Freudian terminology his libido has not yet cathexed outside objects). Another way of putting it is to say that the outside world does not exist for the infant, and this to such a degree that it is not able to distinguish between the "I" and the "not I". We might also say that the infant is not "interested" (inter-esse) = "to be in") in the world outside. The only reality that exists for the infant is itself: its body, its physical sensations of cold and warmth, thirst, need for sleep and bodily contact.

The insane person is in a situation not essentially different from that of the infant. But while for the infant the world outside has *not yet emerged* as real, for the insane person it *has ceased* to be real. In the case of hallucinations, for instance, the senses have lost their function of registering outside events—they register subjective experience in categories of sensory response to objects outside. In the paranoid delusion the same mechanism operates. Fear or suspicion, for instance, which are subjective emotions, become objectified in such a way that the paranoid person is convinced that others are conspiring against him; this is precisely the difference to the neurotic person: the latter may be constantly afraid of being hated, persecuted, etc., but he still knows that this is what he *fears*. For the paranoid person the fear has been transformed into a fact.

A particular instance of narcissism which lies on the borderline between sanity and insanity can be found in some men who have reached an extraordinary degree of power. The Egyptian pharaohs, the Roman Caesars, the Borgias, Hitler, Stalin, Trujillo—they all show certain similar features. They have attained absolute power; their word is the ultimate judgment of every-

thing, including life and death; there seems to be no limit to their capacity
to do what they want. They are gods, limited only by illness, age and death.
They try to find a solution to the problem of human existence by the desperate attempt to transcend the limitation of human existence. They try to
pretend that there is no limit to their lust and to their power, so they sleep
with countless women, they kill numberless men, they build castles everywhere, they "want the moon," they "want the impossible."[3] This is madness,
even though it is an attempt to solve the problem of existence by pretending
that one is not human. It is a madness which tends to grow in the lifetime of
the afflicted person. The more he tries to be god, the more he isolates himself from the human race; this isolation makes him more frightened, everybody becomes his enemy, and in order to stand the resulting fright he has to
increase his power, his ruthlessness, and his narcissism. This Caesarian madness would be nothing but plain insanity were it not for one factor: by his
power Caesar has bent reality to his narcissistic fantasies. He has forced everybody to agree that he is god, the most powerful and the wisest of men—
hence his own megalomania seems to be a reasonable feeling. On the other
hand, many will hate him, try to overthrow and kill him—hence his pathological suspicions are also backed by a nucleus of reality. As a result he does
not feel disconnected from reality—hence he can keep a modicum of sanity,
even though in a precarious state.

Psychosis is a state of absolute narcissism, one in which the person has broken all connection with reality outside, and has made his own person the sub-
stitute for reality. He is entirely filled with himself, he has become "god and
the world" to himself. It is precisely this insight by which Freud for the first
time opened the way to the dynamic understanding of the nature of psychosis.

However, for those who are not familiar with psychosis it is necessary to
give a picture of narcissism as it is found in neurotic or "normal" persons. One
of the most elementary examples of narcissism can be found in the average
person's attitude toward his own body. Most people like their own body, their
face, their figure, and when asked whether they would want to change with
another perhaps more handsome person, very definitely say no. Even more
telling is the fact that most people do not mind at all the sight or smell of their
own feces (in fact, some like them), while they have a definite aversion for
those of other people. Quite obviously there is no aesthetic or other judgment
involved here; the same thing which when connected with one's own body is
pleasant, is unpleasant when connected with somebody else's . . .

. . . Let us look at two phenomena which are apparently extremely different, and yet both of which are narcissistic. A woman spends many hours every
day before the mirror to fix her hair and face. It is not simply that she is vain.
She is obsessed with her body and her beauty, and her body is the only important reality she knows. She comes perhaps nearest to the Greek legend which
speaks of Narcissus, a beautiful lad who rejected the love of the nymph Echo,
who died of a broken heart. Nemesis punished him by making him fall in love
with the reflection of his own image in the water of the lake; in self-admiration

he fell into the lake and died. The Greek legend indicates clearly that this kind of "self-love" is a curse, and that in its extreme form it ends in self-destruction.[4] Another woman (and it could well be the same one some years later) suffers from hypochondriasis. She is also constantly preoccupied with her body although not in the sense of making it beautiful, but in fearing illness. Why the positive, or the negative, image is chosen has, of course, its reasons; however, we need not deal with these here. What matters is that behind both phenomena lies the same narcissistic preoccupation with oneself, with little interest left for the outside world . . .

140   . . . How does one recognize the narcissistic person? There is one type which is easily recognized. That is the kind of person who shows all the signs of self-satisfaction; one can see that when he says some trivial words he feels as if he has said something of great importance. He usually does not listen to what others say, nor is he really interested. (If he is clever, he will try to hide this fact by asking questions and making it a point to seem interested.) One can also recognize the narcissistic person by his sensitivity to any kind of criticism. This sensitivity can be expressed by denying the validity of any criticism, or by reacting with anger or depression. In many instances the narcissistic orientation may be hidden behind an attitude of modesty and humility;
150   in fact, it is not rare for a person's narcissistic orientation to take his humility as the object of his self-admiration. Whatever the different manifestations of narcissism are, a lack of genuine interest in the outside world is common to all forms of narcissism.[5]

Sometimes the narcissistic person can also be recognized by his facial expression. Often we find a kind of glow or smile, which gives the impression of smugness to some, of beatific, trusting, childlikeness to others. Often the narcissism, especially in its most extreme forms, manifests itself in a peculiar glitter in the eyes, taken by some as a symptom of half-saintliness, by others of half-craziness. Many very narcissistic persons talk incessantly—often at
160   a meal, where they forget to eat and thus make everyone else wait. Company or food are less important than their "ego."

The narcissistic person has not even necessarily taken his whole person as the object of his narcissism. Often he has cathexed a partial aspect of his personality with his narcissism; for instance, his honor, his intelligence, his physical prowess, his wit, his good looks (sometimes even narrowed down to such details as his hair or his nose). Sometimes his narcissism refers to qualities about which normally a person would not be proud, such as his capacity to be afraid and thus to foretell danger. "He" becomes identified with a partial aspect of himself. If we ask who "he" is, the proper answer would be that "he"
170   is his brain, his fame, his wealth, his penis, his conscience, and so on. All the idols of the various religions represent so many partial aspects of man. In the narcissistic person the object of his narcissism is any one of these partial qualities which constitute for him his self. The one whose self is represented by his property can take very well a threat to his dignity, but a threat to his property is like a threat to his life. On the other hand, for the one whose self is

represented by his intelligence, the fact of having said something stupid is so painful that it may result in a mood of serious depression. However, the more intense the narcissism is, the less will the narcissistic person accept the fact of failure on his side, or any legitimate criticism from others. He will just feel outraged by the insulting behavior of the other person, or believe that the other person is too insensitive, uneducated, etc., to have proper judgment. (I think, in this connection, of a brilliant, yet highly narcissistic man who, when confronted with the results of a Rorschach test he had taken and which fell short of the ideal picture he had of himself, said, "I am sorry for the psychologist who did this test: he must be very paranoid.")

We must now mention one other factor which complicates the phenomenon of narcissism. Just as the narcissistic person has made his "self-image" the object of his narcissistic attachment, he does the same with everything connected with him. *His* ideas, *his* knowledge, *his* house, but also people in *his* "sphere of interest" become objects of his narcissistic attachment. As Freud pointed out, the most frequent example is probably the narcissistic attachment to one's children. Many parents believe that their own children are the most beautiful, intelligent, etc., in comparison with other children. It seems that the younger the children are, the more intense is this narcissistic bias. The parents' love, and especially the mother's love for the infant, is to a considerable extent love for the infant as an extension of oneself. Adult love between man and woman also has often a narcissistic quality. The man who is in love with a woman may transfer his narcissism to her once she has become "his." He admires and worships her for qualities which he has conferred upon her; precisely because of her being part of him, she becomes the bearer of extraordinary qualities. Such a man will often also think that all things he possesses are extraordinarily wonderful, and he will be "in love" with them.

Narcissism is a passion the intensity of which in many individuals can only be compared with sexual desire and the desire to stay alive. In fact, many times it proves to be stronger than either. Even in the average individual in whom it does not reach such intensity, there remains a narcissistic core which appears to be almost indestructible. This being so we might suspect that like sex and survival, the narcissistic passion also has an important *biological function.* Once we raise this question the answer comes readily. How could the individual survive unless his bodily needs, his interests, his desires, were charged with much energy? Biologically, from the standpoint of survival, man must attribute to himself an importance far above what he gives to anybody else. If he did not do so, from where would he take the energy and interest to defend himself against other, to work for his subsistence, to fight for his survival, to press his claims against those of others? Without narcissism he might be a saint—but do saints have a high survival rate? What from a spiritual standpoint would be most desirable—absence of narcissism—would be most dangerous from the mundane standpoint of survival. Speaking teleologically, we can say that nature had to endow man with a great amount of narcissism to enable him to do what is necessary for survival. This is true especially because nature has not endowed man with well-developed instincts such as the animal has. The animal has no "problems" of survival in the sense that its built-in instinctive nature takes care of survival in such a way that the animal does not have to consider or decide whether or not it wants to make an effort. In man the instinctive apparatus has lost most of its efficacy—hence narcissism assumes a very necessary biological function.

However, once we recognize that narcissism fulfills an important biological function, we are confronted with another question. Does not extreme narcissism have the function of making man indifferent to others, incapable of giving second place to his own needs when this is necessary for co-operation with others? Does not narcissism make man asocial and, in fact, when it reaches an extreme degree, insane? There can be no doubt that extreme individual narcissism would be a severe obstacle to all social life. But if this is so, narcissism must be said to be in *conflict* with the principle of survival, for the individual can survive only if he organizes himself in groups; hardly anyone would be able to protect himself all alone against the dangers of nature, nor would he be able to do many kinds of work which can only be done in groups.

We arrive then at the paradoxical result that narcissism is necessary for survival, and at the same time that it is a threat to survival. The solution of this paradox lies in two directions. One is that *optimal* rather than *maximal* narcissism serves survival; that is to say, the biologically necessary degree of narcissism is reduced to the degree of narcissism that is compatible with social co-operation. The other lies in the fact that individual narcissism is transformed into group narcissism, that the clan, nation, religion, race, etc., become the objects of narcissistic passion instead of the individual. Thus, narcissistic energy is maintained but used in the interests of the survival of the group rather than for the survival of the individual . . .

. . . There is, however, still another solution to the threat to narcissism which is more satisfactory to the individual, although more dangerous to others. This solution consists in the attempt to transform reality in such a way as to make it conform, to some extent, with his narcissistic self-image. An example of this is the narcissistic inventor who believes he has invented a *perpetuum mobile*, and who in the process has made a minor discovery of some significance. A more important solution consists in getting the consensus of one other person, and, if possible, in obtaining the consensus of millions. The former case is that of a *folie à deux* (some marriages and friendships rest on this basis), while the latter is that of public figures who prevent the open outbreak of their potential psychosis by gaining the acclaim and consensus of millions of people. The best-known example for this latter case is Hitler. Here was an extremely narcissistic person who probably could have suffered a manifest psychosis had he not succeeded in making millions believe in his won self-image, take his grandiose fantasies regarding the millennium of the "Third Reich" seriously, and even transforming reality in such a way that it seemed proved to his followers that he was right. (After he had failed he had to kill himself, since otherwise the collapse of his narcissistic image would have been truly unbearable.)

There are other examples in history of megalomaniac leaders who "cured" their narcissism by transforming the world to fit it; such people must also try to destroy all critics, since they cannot tolerate the threat which the voice of sanity constitutes for them. From Caligula and Nero to Stalin and Hitler we see that their need to find believers, to transform reality so that it fits their narcissism, and to destroy all critics, is so intense and so desperate precisely because it is an attempt to prevent the outbreak of insanity. Paradoxically, the element of insanity in such leaders makes them also successful. It gives them that certainty and freedom from doubt which is so impressive to the average person. Needless to say, this need to change the world and to win others to share in one's ideas and delusions requires also talents and gifts which the average person, psychotic or nonpsychotic, lacks.

In discussing the pathology of narcissism it is important to distinguish between two forms of narcissism—one *benign*, the other *malignant*. In the benign form, the object of narcissism is the result of a person's effort. Thus, for instance, a person may have a narcissistic pride in his work as a carpenter, as a scientist, or as a farmer. Inasmuch as the object of his narcissism is something he has to work for, his exclusive interest in what is *his* work and *his* achievement is constantly balanced by his interest in the process of work itself, and the material he is working with. The dynamics of this benign narcissism thus are self-checking. The energy which propels the work is, to a large extent, of a narcissistic nature, but the very fact that the work itself makes it necessary to be related to reality, constantly curbs the narcissism and keeps it within bounds. This mechanism may explain why we find so many narcissistic people who are at the same time highly creative.

In the case of malignant narcissism, the object of narcissism is not anything the person does or produces, but something he *has;* for instance, his body, his looks, his health, his wealth, etc. The malignant nature of this type of narcissism lies in the fact that it lacks the corrective element which we find in the benign form. If I am "great" because of some quality I *have*, and not because of something I *achieve*, I do not need to be related to anybody or anything; I need not make any effort. In maintaining the picture of my greatness I remove myself more and more from reality and I have to increase the narcissistic charge in order to be better protected from the danger that my narcissistically inflated ego might be revealed as the product of my empty imagination. Malignant narcissism, thus, is not self-limiting, and in consequence it is crudely solipsistic as well as xenophobic. One who has learned to achieve cannot help acknowledging that others have achieved similar things in similar ways—even if his narcissism may persuade him that his own achievement is greater than that of others. One who has achieved nothing will find it difficult to appreciate the achievements of others, and thus he will be forced to isolate himself increasingly in narcissistic splendor.

We have so far described the dynamics of individual narcissism: the phenomenon, its biological function, and its pathology. This description ought to enable us now to understand the phenomenon of *social narcissism* and the role it plays as a source of violence and war.

The central point of the following discussion is the phenomenon of the transformation of personal into group narcissism. We can start with an observation about the sociological function of group narcissism which parallels the biological function of individual narcissism. From the standpoint of any organized group which wants to survive, it is important that the group be invested by its members with narcissistic energy. The survival of a group depends to some extent on the fact that its members consider its importance as great as or greater than that of their own lives, and furthermore that they believe in the righteousness, or even superiority, of their group as compared with others. Without such narcissistic cathexis of the group, the energy necessary for serving the group, or even making severe sacrifices for it, would be greatly diminished.

In the dynamics of group narcissism we find phenomena similar to those we discussed already in connection with individual narcissism. Here too we can distinguish between benign and malignant forms of narcissism. If the object of group narcissism is an achievement, the same dialectical process takes place which we discussed above. The very need to achieve something creative makes it necessary to leave the closed circle of group solipsism and to be interested in the object it wants to achieve. (If the achievement which a group seeks is conquest, the beneficial effect of truly productive effort will of course be largely absent.) If, on the other hand, group narcissism has as its object the group as it is, its splendor, its past achievements, the physique of its members, then the countertendencies mentioned above will not develop, and the narcissistic orientation and subsequent dangers will steadily increase. In reality, of course, both elements are often blended.

There is another sociological function of group narcissism which has not been discussed so far. A society which lacks the means to provide adequately for the majority of its members, or a large proportion of them, must provide these members with a narcissistic satisfaction of the malignant type if it wants to prevent dissatisfaction among them. For those who are economically and culturally poor, narcissistic pride in belonging to the group is the only—and often a very effective—source of satisfaction. Precisely because life is not "interesting" to them, and does not offer them possibilities for developing interests, they may develop an extreme form of narcissism. Good examples of this phenomenon in recent years are the racial narcissism which existed in Hitler's Germany, and which is found in the American South today. In both instances the core of the racial superiority feeling was, and still is, the lower middle class; this backward class, which in Germany as well as in the American South has been economically and culturally deprived, without any realistic hope of changing its situation (because they are the remnants of an older and dying form of society) has only one satisfaction: the inflated image of itself as the most admirable group in the world, and of being superior to another racial group that is singled out as inferior. The member of such a backward group feels: "Even though I am poor and uncultured I am somebody important because I belong to the most admirable group in the world—I am white"; or, "I am an Aryan."　　360

Group narcissism is less easy to recognize than individual narcissism. Assuming a person tells others, "I (and my family) are the most admirable people in the world; we alone are clean, intelligent, good, decent; all others are dirty, stupid, dishonest and irresponsible," most people would think him crude, unbalanced, or even insane. If, however, a fanatical speaker addresses a mass audience, substituting the nation (or race, religion, political party, etc.) for the "I" and "my family," he will be praised and admired by many for his love of country, love of God, etc. Other nations and religions, however, will resent such a speech for the obvious reason that they are held in contempt. *Within* the favored group, however, everybody's personal narcissism is flat-　　370 tered and the fact that millions of people agree with the statements makes them appear as reasonable. (What the majority of people consider to be "reasonable" is that about which there is agreement, if not among all, at least among a substantial number of people; "reasonable," for most people, has nothing to do with reason, but with consensus.) Inasmuch as the group as a whole requires group narcissism for its survival, it will further narcissistic attitudes and confer upon them the qualification of being particularly virtuous.

The group to which the narcissistic attitude is extended has varied in structure and size throughout history. In the primitive tribe or clan it may comprise only a few hundred members; here the individual is not yet an　　380 "individual" but is still united to the blood group by "primary bonds"[6] which have not yet been broken. The narcissistic involvement with the clan is thus strengthened by the fact that its members emotionally have still no existence of their own outside of the clan.

In the development of the human race we find an ever increasing range of socialization; the original small group based on blood affinity gives way to ever larger groups based on a common language, a common social order, a common faith. The larger size of the group does not necessarily mean that the pathological qualities of narcissism are reduced. As was remarked earlier, the group narcissism of the "whites" or the "Aryans" is as malignant as the　　390 extreme narcissism of a single person can be. Yet in general we find that in the process of socialization which leads to the formation of larger groups, the need for co-operation with many other and different people not connected among themselves by ties of blood, tends to counteract the narcissistic charge within the group. The same holds true in another respect, which we have discussed in connection with benign individual narcissism: Inasmuch as the large group (nation, state, or religion) makes it an object of its narcissistic pride to achieve something valuable in the fields of material, intellectual, or artistic production, the very process of work in such fields tends to lessen the narcissistic charge. The history of the Roman Catholic Church is one of　　400 many examples of the peculiar mixture of narcissism and the counteracting forces within a large group. The elements counteracting narcissism within the Catholic Church are, first of all, the concept of the universality of man and of a "catholic" religion which is no longer the religion of one particular tribe or nation. Second, the idea of personal humility which follows from the idea of God and the denial of idols. The existence of God implies that no man can be God, that no individual can be omniscient or omnipotent. It thus sets a definite limit to man's narcissistic self-idolatry. But at the same time the Church has nourished an intense narcissism; believing that the Church is the only chance of salvation and that the Pope is the Vicar of Christ, its members were able to develop an intense narcissism inasmuch as they were members of such an extraordinary institution. The same occurred in relation to God; while the omniscience and omnipotence of God should have led to man's humility, often the individual identified himself with God and thus developed an extraordinary degree of narcissism in this process of identification.

This same ambiguity between a narcissistic or an antinarcissistic function has occurred in all the other great religions, for example, in Buddhism, Judaism, Islam, and Protestantism. I have mentioned the Catholic religion not only because it is a well-known example, but mainly because the Roman Catholic religion was the basis both for humanism and for violent and fanatical religious narcissism at one and the same historical period: the fifteenth and sixteenth centuries. The humanists within the Church and those outside spoke in the name of a humanism which was the fountainhead of Christianity . . .

. . . Looking back to the religious hatred of the sixteenth and seventeenth centuries, its irrationalities are clear. Both sides spoke in the name of God, of Christ, of love, and they differed only in points which, if compared with the general principles, were of secondary importance. Yet they hated each other, and each was passionately convinced that humanity ended at the frontiers of his own religious faith. The essence of this over-estimation of ones' own position and the hate for all who differ from it is narcissism. "We" are admirable; "they" are despicable. "We" are good; "they" are evil. Any criticism of one's own doctrine is a vicious and unbearable attack; criticism of the others' position is a well-meant attempt to help them to return to the truth.

From the Renaissance onward, the two great contradictory forces, group narcissism and humanism, have each developed in its own way. Unfortunately the development of group narcissism has vastly outstripped that of humanism. While it seemed possible in the late Middle Ages and at the time of the Renaissance that Europe was prepared for the emergence of a political and religious humanism, this promise failed to materialize. New forms of group narcissism emerged, and dominated the following centuries. This group narcissism assumed manifold forms: religious, national, racial, political. Protestants against Catholics, French against Germans, whites against blacks, Aryans against non-Aryans, Communists against capitalists; different as the contents are, psychologically we deal with the same narcissistic phenomenon and its resulting fanaticism and destructiveness.[7]

While group narcissism grew, its counterpart—humanism—also developed. In the eighteenth and nineteenth centuries—from Spinoza, Leibniz, Rousseau, Herder, Kant, to Goethe and Marx—the thought developed that mankind is one, that each individual carries within himself all of humanity, that there must be no privileged groups claiming that their privileges are based on their intrinsic superiority . . .

larger community   450

. . . As a reaction to this threat to humanity, a renaissance of humanism can be observed today in all countries and among the representatives of diverse ideologies; there are radical humanists among Catholic and Protestant theologians, among socialist and nonsocialist philosophers. Whether the danger of total destruction, the ideas of the neohumanists and the bonds created between all men by the new means of communication will be sufficient to stop the effects of group narcissism is a question which may determine the fate of mankind . . .

Ask what was happening in Cold war than   460

ENDNOTES

1. Freud, *Group Psychology* (Standard Edition), Vol. XVIII, p. 130.
2. Freud, *Totem and Taboo* (Standard Edition), Vol. XIII, p. 89.
3. Camus, in his drama *Caligula*, has portrayed this madness of power most accurately.
4. Cf. my discussion of self-love in *Man for Himself.* I try to show there that true love for self is not different from love for others; that "self-love" in the sense of egoistic, narcissistic love is to be found in those who can love neither others nor themselves.
5. Sometimes it is not easy to distinguish between the vain, narcissistic person and one with a low self-evaluation; the latter often is in need of praise and admiration, not because he is not interested in anyone else, but because of his self-doubts and low self-evaluation. There is another important distinction which is also not always easy to make: that between narcissism and egotism. Intense narcissism implies an inability to experience reality in its fullness; intense egotism implies to have little concern, love or sympathy for others but it does not necessarily imply the overevaluation of one's subjective processes. In other words the extreme egotist is not necessarily extremely narcissistic; selfishness is not necessarily blindness to objective reality.
6. Cf. the discussion of primary bonds in E. Fromm, *Escape From Freedom* (New York: Holt, Rinehart & Winston, 1941).
7. There are other more harmless forms of group narcissism directed toward small groups like lodges, small religious sects, "the old school tie," etc. While the degree of narcissism in these cases may not be less than in those of the larger groups, the narcissism is less dangerous simply because the groups involved have little power, and hence little capacity to cause harm.

Hardin

1) Start with game of tick-tack-toe

2) Technical problems — what is?

                which is Hardin concerned with?

3) Population issue
- Show NPR piece
- Show Friedman Clip on one lightbulb
- Story of Stuff?

4) Show Trag of Commons Game website

Relate back to Leopold
  + Rousseau

What if ½ not allowed to have children?

THE TRAGEDY OF THE COMMONS
Garrett Hardin

At the end of a thoughtful article on the future of nuclear war, Wiesner and York[1] concluded that: "Both sides in the arms race are . . . confronted by the dilemma of steadily increasing military power and steadily decreasing national security. *It is our considered professional judgment that this dilemma has no technical solution.* If the great powers continue to look for solutions in the area of science and technology only, the result will be to worsen the situation."

I would like to focus your attention not on the subject of the article (national security in a nuclear world) but on the kind of conclusion they reached, namely that there is no technical solution to the problem. An implicit and almost universal assumption of discussions published in professional and semipopular scientific journals is that the problem under discussion has a technical solution. A technical solution may be defined as one that requires a change only in the techniques of the natural sciences, demanding little or nothing in the way of change in human values or ideas of morality.

[margin note: Definition of Technical Solution]

In our day (though not in earlier times) technical solutions are always welcome. Because of previous failures in prophecy, it takes courage to assert that a desired technical solution is not possible. Wiesner and York exhibited this courage; publishing in a science journal, they insisted that the solution to the problem was not to be found in the natural sciences. They cautiously qualified their statement with the phrase, "It is our considered professional judgment. . . ." Whether they were right or not is not the concern of the present article. Rather, the concern here is with the important concept of a class of human problems which can be called "no technical solution problems," and, more specifically, with the identification and discussion of one of these.

It is easy to show that the class is not a null class. Recall the game of tick-tack-toe. Consider the problem, "How can I win the game of tick-tack-toe?" It is well known that I cannot, if I assume (in keeping with the conventions of game theory) that my opponent understands the game perfectly. Put another way, there is no "technical solution" to the problem. I can win only by giving a radical meaning to the word "win." I can hit my opponent over the head; or I can drug him; or I can falsify the records. Every way in which I "win" involves, in some sense, an abandonment of the game, as we intuitively understand it. (I can also, of course, openly abandon the game—refuse to play it. This is what most adults do.)

[margin note: math term]

The class of "No technical solution problems" has members. My thesis is that the "population problem," as conventionally conceived, is a member of this class. How it is conventionally conceived needs some comment. It is fair

[margin note: 7 BILLION MONDAY]

Reprinted from *Science Magazine*, December 1968, by permission of The American Association for the Advancement of Science.

to say that most people who anguish over the population problem are trying
to find a way to avoid the evils of overpopulation without relinquishing any
of the privileges they now enjoy. They think that farming the seas or developing new strains of wheat will solve the problem—technologically. I try to
show here that the solution they seek cannot be found. The population problem cannot be solved in a technical way, any more than can the problem of
winning the game of tick-tack-toe.

WHAT SHALL WE MAXIMIZE?

Population, as Malthus said, naturally tends to grow "geometrically," or, as
we would now say, exponentially. In a finite world this means that the per
capita share of the world's goods must steadily decrease. Is ours a finite world?

A fair defense can be put forward for the view that the world is infinite;
or that we do not know that it is not. But, in terms of the practical problems
that we must face in the next few generations with the foreseeable technology, it is clear that we will greatly increase human misery if we do not, during the immediate future, assume that the world available to the terrestrial
human population is finite. "Space" is no escape.[2]

A finite world can support only a finite population; therefore, population
growth must eventually equal zero. (The case of perpetual wide fluctuations
above and below zero is a trivial variant that need not be discussed.) When
this condition is met, what will be the situation of mankind? Specifically, can
Bentham's goal of "the greatest good for the greatest number" be realized?

No—for two reasons, each sufficient by itself. The first is a theoretical
one. It is not mathematically possible to maximize for two (or more) variables
at the same time. This was clearly stated by von Neumann and Morgenstern,[3]
but the principle is implicit in the theory of partial differential equations,
dating back at least to D'Alembert (1717–1783).

The second reason springs directly from biological facts. To live, any
organism must have a source of energy (for example, food). This energy is
utilized for two purposes: mere maintenance and work. For man, maintenance of life requires about 1600 kilocalories a day ("maintenance calories").
Anything that he does over and above merely staying alive will be defined as
work, and is supported by "work calories" which he takes in. Work calories
are used not only for what we call work in common speech; they are also
required for all forms of enjoyment, from swimming and automobile racing
to playing music and writing poetry. If our goal is to maximize population it
is obvious what we must do: We must make the work calories per person
approach as close to zero as possible. No gourmet meals, no vacations, no
sports, no music, no literature, no art. . . . I think that everyone will grant,
without argument or proof, that maximizing population does not maximize
goods. Bentham's goal is impossible.

In reaching this conclusion I have made the usual assumption that it is
the acquisition of energy that is the problem. The appearance of atomic

energy has led some to question this assumption. However, given an infinite source of energy, population growth still produces an inescapable problem. The problem of the acquisition of energy is replaced by the problem of its dissipation, as J. H. Fremlin has so wittily shown.[4] The arithmetic signs in the analysis are, as it were, reversed; but Bentham's goal is still unobtainable.

The optimum population is, then, less than the maximum. The difficulty of defining the optimum is enormous; so far as I know, no one has seriously tackled this problem. Reaching an acceptable and stable solution will surely require more than one generation of hard analytical work—and much persuasion.

We want the maximum good per person; but what is good? To one person it is wilderness, to another it is ski lodges for thousands. To one it is estuaries to nourish ducks for hunters to shoot; to another it is factory land. Comparing one good with another is, we usually say, impossible because goods are incommensurable. Incommensurables cannot be compared.

Theoretically this may be true; but in real life incommensurables are commensurable. Only a criterion of judgment and a system of weighting are needed. In nature the criterion is survival. Is it better for a species to be small and hideable, or large and powerful? Natural selection commensurates the incommensurables. The compromise achieved depends on a natural weighting of the values of the variables.

Man must imitate this process. There is no doubt that in fact he already does, but unconsciously. It is when the hidden decisions are made explicit that the arguments begin. The problem for the years ahead is to work out an acceptable theory of weighting. Synergistic effects, nonlinear variation, and difficulties in discounting the future make the intellectual problem difficult, but not (in principle) insoluble.

Has any cultural group solved this practical problem at the present time, even on an intuitive level? One simple fact proves that none has: there is no prosperous population in the world today that has, and has had for some time, a growth rate of zero. Any people that has intuitively identified its optimum point will soon reach it, after which its growth rate becomes and remains zero.

Of course, a positive growth rate might be taken as evidence that a population is below its optimum. However, by any reasonable standards, the most rapidly growing populations on earth today are (in general) the most miserable. This association (which need not be invariable) casts doubt on the optimistic assumption that the positive growth rate of a population is evidence that it has yet to reach its optimum.

We can make little progress in working toward optimum population size until we explicitly exorcize the spirit of Adam Smith in the field of practical demography. In economic affairs, *The Wealth of Nations* (1776) popularized the "invisible hand," the idea that an individual who "intends only his own gain," is, as it were, "led by an invisible hand to promote . . . the public interest."[5] Adam Smith did not assert that this was invariably true, and perhaps

Adam Smith's legacy

neither did any of his followers. But he contributed to a dominant tendency of thought that has ever since interfered with positive action based on rational analysis, namely, the tendency to assume that decisions reached individually will, in fact, be the best decisions for an entire society. If this assump-
130   tion is correct it justifies the continuance of our present policy of laissez-faire in reproduction. If it is correct we can assume that men will control their individual fecundity so as to produce the optimum population. If the assumption is not correct, we need to reexamine our individual freedoms to see which ones are defensible.

TRAGEDY OF FREEDOM IN A COMMONS

The rebuttal to the invisible hand in population control is to be found in a scenario first sketched in a little-known pamphlet[6] in 1833 by a mathematical amateur named William Forster Lloyd (1794–1852). We may well call it "the tragedy of the commons," using the word "tragedy" as the philosopher Whitehead used it:[7] "The essence of dramatic tragedy is not unhappiness. It
140   resides in the solemnity of the remorseless working of things." He then goes on to say, "This inevitableness of destiny can only be illustrated in terms of human life by incidents which in fact involve unhappiness. For it is only by them that the futility of escape can be made evident in the drama."

the scenario

The tragedy of the commons develops in this way. Picture a pasture open to all. It is to be expected that each herdsman will try to keep as many cattle as possible on the commons. Such an arrangement may work reasonably satisfactorily for centuries because tribal wars, poaching, and disease keep the numbers of both man and beast well below the carrying capacity of the land. Finally, however, comes the day of reckoning, that is, the day when the long-
150   desired goal of social stability becomes a reality. At this point, the inherent logic of the commons remorselessly generates tragedy.

As a rational being, each herdsman seeks to maximize his gain. Explicitly or implicitly, more or less consciously, he asks, "What is the utility *to me* of adding one more animal to my herd?" This utility has one negative and one positive component.

1) The positive component is a function of the increment of one animal. Since the herdsman receives all the proceeds from the sale of the additional animal, the positive utility is nearly +1.

2) The negative component is a function of the additional overgrazing
160   created by one more animal. Since, however, the effects of overgrazing are shared by all the herdsmen, the negative utility for any particular decision-making herdsman is only a fraction of −1.

p 245 Rousseau

Adding together the component partial utilities, the rational herdsman concludes that the only sensible course for him to pursue is to add another animal to his herd. And another; and another. . . . But this is the conclusion reached by each and every rational herdsman sharing a commons. Therein is the tragedy. Each man is locked into a system that compels him to increase his herd without limit—in a world that is limited. Ruin is the destination toward which all men rush, each pursuing his own best interest in a society that believes in the freedom of the commons. Freedom in a commons brings ruin to all.

170 *Freedom = Ruin*

Some would say that this is a platitude. Would that it were! In a sense, it was learned thousands of years ago, but natural selection favors the forces of psychological denial.[8] The individual benefits as an individual from his ability to deny the truth even though society as a whole, of which he is a part, suffers.

Education can counteract the natural tendency to do the wrong thing, but the inexorable succession of generations requires that the basis for this knowledge be constantly refreshed.

A simple incident that occurred a few years ago in Leominster, Massachusetts, shows how perishable the knowledge is. During the Christmas shopping season the parking meters downtown were covered with plastic bags that bore tags reading: "Do not open until after Christmas. Free parking courtesy of the mayor and city council." In other words, facing the prospect of an increased demand for already scarce space, the city fathers reinstituted the system of the commons. (Cynically, we suspect that they gained more votes than they lost by this retrogressive act.)

180

In an approximate way, the logic of the commons has been understood for a long time, perhaps since the discovery of agriculture or the invention of private property in real estate. But it is understood mostly only in special cases which are not sufficiently generalized. Even at this late date, cattlemen leasing national land on the western ranges demonstrate no more than an ambivalent understanding, in constantly pressuring federal authorities to increase the head count to the point where overgrazing produces erosion and weed-dominance. Likewise, the oceans of the world continue to suffer from the survival of the philosophy of the commons. Maritime nations still respond automatically to the shibboleth of the "freedom of the seas." Professing to believe in the "inexhaustible resources of the oceans," they bring species after species of fish and whales closer to extinction.[9]

190

Show post peak images?

The National Parks present another instance of the working out of the tragedy of the commons. At present, they are open to all, without limit. The parks themselves are limited in extent—there is only one Yosemite Valley—whereas population seems to grow without limit. The values that visitors seek in the parks are steadily eroded. Plainly, we must soon cease to treat the parks as commons or they will be of no value to anyone.

200

What shall we do? We have several options. We might sell them off as private property. We might keep them as public property, but allocate the right to enter them. The allocation might be on the basis of wealth, by the use of an auction system. It might be on the basis of merit, as defined by some agreed-upon standards. It might be by lottery. Or it might be on a first-come, first-served basis, administered to long queues. These, I think, are all the reasonable possibilities. They are all objectionable. But we must choose—or acquiesce in the destruction of the commons that we call our National Parks.

options for limiting use

vote on which they like

210

POLLUTION

In a reverse way, the tragedy of the commons reappears in problems of pollution. Here it is not a question of taking something out of the commons, but of putting something in—sewage, or chemical, radioactive, and heat wastes into water; noxious and dangerous fumes into the air, and distracting and unpleasant advertising signs into the line of sight. The calculations of utility are much the same as before. The rational man finds that his share of the cost of the wastes he discharges into the commons is less than the cost of purifying his
220   wastes before releasing them. Since this is true for everyone, we are locked into a system of "fouling our own nest," so long as we behave only as independent, rational, free-enterprisers.

The tragedy of the commons as a food basket is averted by private property, or something formally like it. But the air and waters surrounding us cannot readily be fenced, and so the tragedy of the commons as a cesspool must be prevented by different means, by coercive laws or taxing devices that make it cheaper for the polluter to treat his pollutants than to discharge them untreated. We have not progressed as far with the solution of this problem as we have with the first. Indeed, our particular concept of private property,
230   which deters us from exhausting the positive resources of the earth, favors pollution. The owner of a factory on the bank of a stream—whose property extends to the middle of the stream, often has difficulty seeing why it is not his natural right to muddy the waters flowing past his door. The law, always behind the times, requires elaborate stitching and fitting to adapt it to this newly perceived aspect of the commons.

The pollution problem is a consequence of population. It did not much matter how a lonely American frontiersman disposed of his waste. "Flowing water purifies itself every 10 miles," my grandfather used to say, and the myth was near enough to the truth when he was a boy, for there were not too many
240   people. But as population became denser, the natural chemical and biological recycling processes became overloaded, calling for a redefinition of property rights.

HOW TO LEGISLATE TEMPERANCE?

Analysis of the pollution problem as a function of population density uncovers a not generally recognized principle of morality, namely: *the morality of an act is a function of the state of the system at the time it is performed.*[10] Using the commons as a cesspool does not harm the general public under frontier conditions, because there is no public, the same behavior in a metropolis is unbearable. A hundred and fifty years ago a plainsman could kill an American bison, cut only the tongue for his dinner, and discard the rest of the ani-
250   mal. He was not in any important sense being wasteful. Today, with only a few thousand bison left, we would be appalled at such behavior.

In passing, it is worth noting that the morality of an act cannot be determined from a photograph. One does not know whether a man killing an elephant or setting fire to the grassland is harming others until one knows the total system in which his act appears. "One picture is worth a thousand words," said an ancient Chinese; but it may take 10,000 words to validate it. It is as tempting to ecologists as it is to reformers in general to try to persuade others by way of the photographic shortcut. But the essence of an argument cannot be photographed: it must be presented rationally—in words.   260

That morality is system-sensitive escaped the attention of most codifiers of ethics in the past. "Thou shalt not . . ." is the form of traditional ethical directives which make no allowance for particular circumstances. The laws of our society follow the pattern of ancient ethics, and therefore are poorly suited to governing a complex, crowded, changeable world. Our epicyclic solution is to augment statutory law with administrative law. Since it is practically impossible to spell out all the conditions under which it is safe to burn trash in the back yard or to run an automobile without smog-control, by law we delegate the details to bureaus. The result is administrative law, which is rightly feared for an ancient reason—*Quis custodiet ipsos custodes?*—"Who   270 shall watch the watchers themselves?" John Adams said that we must have "a government of laws and not men." Bureau administrators, trying to evaluate the morality of acts in the total system, are singularly liable to corruption, producing a government by men, not laws.

Prohibition is easy to legislate (though not necessarily to enforce); but how do we legislate temperance? Experience indicates that it can be accomplished best through the mediation of administrative law. We limit possibilities unnecessarily if we suppose that the sentiment of *Quis custodiet* denies us the use of administrative law. We should rather retain the phrase as a perpetual reminder of fearful dangers we cannot avoid. The great challenge fac-   280 ing us now is to invent the corrective feedbacks that are needed to keep custodians honest. We must find ways to legitimate the needed authority of both the custodians and the corrective feedbacks.

FREEDOM TO BREED IS INTOLERABLE

The tragedy of the commons is involved in population problems in another way. In a world governed solely by the principle of "dog eat dog"—if indeed there ever was such a world—how many children a family had would not be a matter of public concern. Parents who bred too exuberantly would leave fewer descendants, not more, because they would be unable to care adequately for their children. David Lack and others have found that such a negative feedback demonstrably controls the fecundity of birds.[11] But men are   290 not birds, and have not acted like them for millenniums, at least.

If each human family were dependent only on its own resources; if the children of improvident parents starved to death; *if,* thus, overbreeding brought its own "punishment" to the germ line—*then* there would be no public interest in controlling the breeding of families. But our society is deeply committed to the welfare state,[12] and hence is confronted with another aspect of the tragedy of the commons.

In a welfare state, how shall we deal with the family, the religion, the race, or the class (or indeed any distinguishable and cohesive group) that adopts overbreeding as a policy to secure its own aggrandizement?[13] To couple the concept of freedom to breed with the belief that everyone born has an equal right to the commons is to lock the world into a tragic course of action.

Unfortunately this is just the course of action that is being pursued by the United Nations. In late 1967, some 30 nations agreed to the following:[14]

> The Universal Declaration of Human Rights describes the family as the natural and fundamental unit of society. It follows that any choice and decision with regard to the size of the family must irrevocably rest with the family itself, and cannot be made by anyone else.

It is painful to have to deny categorically the validity of this right; denying it, one feels as uncomfortable as a resident of Salem, Massachusetts, who denied the reality of witches in the 17th century. At the present time, in liberal quarter, something like a taboo acts to inhibit criticism of the United States. There is a feeling that the United States is "our last and best hope," that we shouldn't find fault with it; we shouldn't play into the hands of arch-conservatives. However, let us not forget what Robert Louis Stevenson said: "The truth that is suppressed by friends is the readiest weapon of the enemy." If we love the truth, we must openly deny the validity of the Universal Declaration of Human Rights, even though it is promoted by the United Nations. We should also join with Kingsley Davis[15] in attempting to get Planned Parenthood-World Population to see the error of its ways in embracing the same tragic ideal.

CONSCIENCE IS SELF-ELIMINATING

It is a mistake to think that we can control the breeding of mankind in the long run by an appeal to conscience. Charles Galton Darwin made this point when he spoke on the centennial of the publication of his grandfather's great book. The argument is straightforward and Darwinian.

People vary. Confronted with appeals to limit breeding, some people will undoubtedly respond to the plea more than others. Those who have more children will produce a larger fraction of the next generation than those with more susceptible consciences. The difference will be accentuated, generation by generation.

In C. G. Darwin's words: "It may well be that it would take hundreds of generations for the progenitive instinct to develop in this way, but if it should do so, nature would have taken her revenge, and the variety *Homo contracipiens* would become extinct and would be replaced by the variety *Homo progenitivus*."[16]

The argument assumes that conscience or the desire for children (no matter which) is hereditary—but hereditary only in the most general formal sense. The result will be the same whether the attitude is transmitted through germ cells, or exosomatically, to use A. J. Lotka's term. (If one denies the latter possibility as well as the former, then what's the point of education?) The argument has here been stated in the context of the population problem, but it applies equally well to any instance in which society appeals to an individual exploiting a commons to restrain himself for the general good—by means of his conscience. To make such an appeal is to set up a selective system that works toward the elimination of conscience from the race.

PATHOGENIC EFFECTS OF CONSCIENCE

The long-term disadvantage of an appeal to conscience should be enough to condemn it; but has serious short-term disadvantages as well. If we ask a man who is exploiting a commons to desist "in the name of conscience," what are we saying to him? What does he hear?—not only at the moment but also in the wee small hours of the night when, half asleep, he remembers not merely the words we used but also the nonverbal communication cues we gave him unawares? Sooner or later, consciously or subconsciously, he senses that he has received two communications, and that they are contradictory: (i) (intended communication) "If you don't do as we ask, we will openly condemn you for not acting like a responsible citizen"; (ii) (the unintended communication) "If you do behave as we ask, we will secretly condemn you for a simpleton who can be shamed into standing aside while the rest of us exploit the commons."

Everyman then is caught in what Bateson has called a "double bind." Bateson and his co-workers have made a plausible case for viewing the double bind as an important causative factor in the genesis of schizophrenia.[17] The double bind may not always be so damaging, but it always endangers the mental health of anyone to whom it is applied. "A bad conscience," said Nietzsche, "is a kind of illness."

To conjure up a conscience in others is tempting to anyone who wishes to extend his control beyond the legal limits. Leaders at the highest level succumb to this temptation. Has any President during the past generation failed to call on labor unions to moderate voluntarily their demands for higher wages, or to steel companies to honor voluntary guidelines on prices? I can recall none. The rhetoric used on such occasions is designed to produce feelings of guilt in noncooperators.

For centuries it was assumed without proof that guilt was a valuable, perhaps even an indispensable, ingredient of the civilized life. Now, in this post-Freudian world, we doubt it.

Paul Goodman speaks from the modern point of view when he says: "No good has ever come from feeling guilty, neither intelligence, policy, nor compassion. The guilty do not pay attention to the object but only to themselves, and not even to their own interests, which might make sense, but to their anxieties."[18]

380   One does not have to be a professional psychiatrist to see the consequences of anxiety. We in the Western world are just emerging from a dreadful two-centuries-long Dark Ages of Eros that was sustained partly by prohibition laws, but perhaps more effectively by the anxiety-generating mechanism of education. Alex Comfort has told the story well in *The Anxiety Makers;*[19] it is not a pretty one.

Since proof is difficult, we may even concede that the results of anxiety may sometimes, from certain points of view, be desirable. The larger question we should ask is whether, as a matter of policy, we should ever encourage the use of a technique the tendency (if not the intention) of which is psychologically pathogenic. We hear much talk these days of responsible parenthood; the coupled words are incorporated into the titles of some organizations devoted to birth control. Some people have proposed massive propaganda campaigns to instill responsibility into the nation's (or the world's) breeders. But what is the meaning of the word responsibility in this context? Is it not merely a synonym for the word conscience? When we use the word responsibility in the absence of substantial sanctions are we not trying to browbeat a free man in a commons into acting against his own interest? Responsibility is a verbal counterfeit for a substantial *quid pro quo.* It is an attempt to get something for nothing.

400   If the word responsibility is to be used at all, I suggest that it be in the sense Charles Frankel uses it.[20] "Responsibility," says this philosopher, "is the product of definite social arrangements." Notice that Frankel calls for social arrangements—not propaganda.

MUTUAL COERCION MUTUALLY AGREED UPON

The social arrangements that produce responsibility are arrangements that create coercion, of some sort. Consider bank-robbing. The man who takes money from a bank acts as if the bank were a commons. How do we prevent such action? Certainly not by trying to control his behavior solely by a verbal appeal to his sense of responsibility. Rather than rely on propaganda we follow Frankel's lead and insist that a bank is not a commons; we seek the definite social arrangements that will keep it from becoming a commons. That we thereby infringe on the freedom of would-be robbers we neither deny nor regret.

The morality of bank-robbing is particularly easy to understand because we accept complete prohibition of this activity. We are willing to say "Thou shalt not rob banks," without providing for exceptions. But temperance also can be created by coercion. Taxing is a good coercive device. To keep downtown shoppers temperate in their use of parking space we introduce parking meters for short periods, and traffic fines for longer ones. We need not actually forbid a citizen to park as long as he wants to; we need merely make it increasingly expensive for him to do so. Not prohibition, but carefully biased options are what we offer him. A Madison Avenue man might call this persuasion; I prefer the greater candor of the word coercion.

Coercion is a dirty word to most liberals now, but it need not forever be so. As with the four-letter words, its dirtiness can be cleansed away by exposure to the light, by saying it over and over without apology or embarrassment. To many, the word coercion implies arbitrary decisions of distant and irresponsible bureaucrats; but this is not a necessary part of its meaning. The only kind of coercion I recommend is mutual coercion, mutually agreed upon by the majority of the people affected.

To say that we mutually agree to coercion is not to say that we are required to enjoy it, or even to pretend we enjoy it. Who enjoys taxes? We all grumble about them. But we accept compulsory taxes because we recognize that voluntary taxes would favor the conscienceless. We institute and (grumblingly) support taxes and other coercive devices to escape the horror of the commons.

An alternative to the commons need not be perfectly just to be preferable. With real estate and other material goods, the alternative we have chosen is the institution of private property coupled with legal inheritance. Is this system perfectly just? As a genetically trained biologist I deny that it is. It seems to me that, if there are to be differences in individual inheritance, legal possession should be perfectly correlated with biological inheritance—that those who are biologically more fit to be the custodians of property and power should legally inherit more. But genetic recombination continually makes a mockery of the doctrine of "like father, like son" implicit in our laws of legal inheritance. An idiot can inherit millions, and a trust fund can keep his estate intact. We must admit that our legal system of private property plus inheritance is unjust—but we put up with it because we are not convinced, at the moment, that anyone has invented a better system. The alternative of the commons is too horrifying to contemplate. Injustice is preferable to total ruin.

It is one of the peculiarities of the warfare between reform and the status quo that it is thoughtlessly governed by a double standard. Whenever a reform measure is proposed it is often defeated when its opponents triumphantly discover a flaw in it. As Kingsley Davis has pointed out,[21] worshippers of the status quo sometimes imply that no reform is possible without unanimous agreement, an implication contrary to historical fact. As nearly as I can make out, automatic rejection of proposed reforms is based

[handwritten margin note: Voting for imperfect change because we know the status quo is also imperfect]

on one of two unconscious assumptions: (i) that the status quo is perfect; or
(ii) that the choice we face is between reform and no action; if the proposed
reform is imperfect, we presumably should take no action at all, while we
460   wait for a perfect proposal.

But we can never do nothing. That which we have done for thousands of
years is also action. It also produces evils. Once we are aware that the status
quo is action, we can then compare its discoverable advantages and disadvantages with the predicted advantages and disadvantages of the proposed
reform, discounting as best we can for our lack of experience. On the basis
of such a comparison, we can make a rational decision which will not involve
the unworkable assumption that only perfect systems are tolerable.

RECOGNITION OF NECESSITY

Perhaps the simplest summary of this analysis of man's population problems
is this: the commons, if justifiable at all, is justifiable only under conditions
470   of low-population density. As the human population has increased, the commons has had to be abandoned in one aspect after another.

First we abandoned the commons in food gathering, enclosing farm land
and restricting pastures and hunting and fishing areas. These restrictions are
still not complete throughout the world.

Somewhat later we saw that the commons as a place for waste disposal
would also have to be abandoned. Restrictions on the disposal of domestic
sewage are widely accepted in the Western world; we are still struggling to
close the commons to pollution by automobiles, factories, insecticide
sprayers, fertilizing operations, and atomic energy installations.

480   In a still more embryonic state is our recognition of the evils of the commons in matters of pleasure. There is almost no restriction on the propaga-
tion of sound waves in the public medium. The shopping public is assaulted
with mindless music, without its consent. Our government is paying out billions of dollars to create supersonic transport which will disturb 50,000 people for every one person who is whisked from coast to coast 3 hours faster.
Advertisers muddy the airwaves of radio and television and pollute the view
of travelers. We are a long way from outlawing the commons in matters of
pleasure. Is this because our Puritan inheritance makes us view pleasure as
something of a sin, and pain (that is, the pollution of advertising) as the sign
490   of virtue?

Every new enclosure of the commons involves the infringement of somebody's personal liberty. Infringements made in the distant past are accepted
because no contemporary complains of a loss. It is the newly proposed infringements that we vigorously oppose; cries of "rights" and "freedom" fill the air. But
what does "freedom" mean? When men mutually agreed to pass laws against
robbing, mankind became more free, not less so. Individuals locked into the
logic of the commons are free only to bring on universal ruin once they see the

[handwritten margin note: Rousseau]

necessity of mutual coercion, they become free to pursue other goals. I believe it was Hegel who said, "Freedom is the recognition of necessity."

The most important aspect of necessity that we must now recognize, is   500 the necessity of abandoning the commons in breeding. No technical solution can rescue us from the misery of overpopulation. Freedom to breed will bring ruin to all. At the moment, to avoid hard decisions many of us are tempted to propagandize for conscience and responsible parenthood. The temptation must be resisted, because an appeal to independently acting consciences selects for the disappearance of all conscience in the long run, and an increase in anxiety in the short.

The only way we can preserve and nurture other and more precious freedoms is by relinquishing the freedom to breed, and that very soon. "Freedom is the recognition of necessity"—and it is the role of education to reveal to all   510 the necessity of abandoning the freedom to breed. Only so, can we put an end to this aspect of the tragedy of the commons.

ENDNOTES

1. J. B. Wiesner and H. F. York, *Sci. Amer.* **211** (No. 4), 27 (1964).
2. G. Hardin, *J. Hered.* **50,** 68 (1959); S. von Hoernor, *Science* **137,** 18 (1962).
3. J. von Neumann and O. Morgenstern, *Theory of Games and Economic Behavior* (Princeton Univ. Press, Princeton, N.J., 1947), p. 11.
4. J. H. Fremlin, *New Sci.,* No. 415 (1964), p. 285.
5. A. Smith, *The Wealth of Nations* (Modern Library, New York, 1937), p. 423.
6. W. F. Lloyd, *Two Lectures on the Checks to Population* (Oxford Univ. Press, Oxford, England, 1833), reprinted (in part) in *Population, Evolution, and Birth Control,* G. Hardin, Ed. (Freeman, San Francisco, 1964), p. 37.
7. A. N. Whitehead, *Science and the Modern World* (Mentor, New York, 1948), p. 17.
8. G. Hardin, Ed. *Population, Evolution, and Birth Control* (Freeman, San Francisco, 1964), p. 56.
9. S. McVay, *Sci. Amer.* **216** (No. 8), 13 (1966).
10. J. Fletcher, *Situation Ethics* (Westminster, Philadelphia, 1966).
11. D. Lack, *The Natural Regulation of Animal Numbers* (Clarendon Press, Oxford, 1954).
12. H. Girvetz, *From Wealth to Welfare* (Stanford Univ. Press, Stanford, Calif., 1950).
13. G. Hardin, *Perspec. Biol. Med.* **6,** 366 (1963).
14. U. Thant, *Int. Planned Parenthood News,* No. 168 (February 1968), p. 3.
15. K. Davis, *Science* **158,** 730 (1967).

16. S. Tax, Ed., *Evolution after Darwin* (Univ. of Chicago Press, Chicago, 1960), vol. 2, p. 469.
17. G. Bateson, D. D. Jackson, J. Haley, J. Weakland, *Behav. Sci.* **1,** 251 (1956).
18. P. Goodman, *New York Rev. Books* 10(8), 22 (23 May 1968).
19. A. Comfort, *The Anxiety Makers* (Nelson, London, 1967).
20. C. Frankel, *The Case for Modern Man* (Harper, New York, 1955), p. 203.
21. J. D. Roslansky, *Genetics and the Future of Man* (Appleton-Century-Crofts, New York, 1966), p. 177.

CARING AS A FEMINIST PRACTICE OF MORAL REASON
Alison M. Jaggar

In less than two decades, the ethics of care has achieved a spectacular rise to   1
fame and fortune, at least in North America.[1] Almost unheard of in 1980,
today caring is widely regarded as a moral perspective that is both distinctively feminine and peculiarly appropriate for feminists; it has even been
institutionalized in establishments such as the Center for Human Caring,
run by the School of Nursing at my own University of Colorado.[2] Although
the ethics of care has been variously described, it is typically portrayed as a
moral orientation that not only produces assessments of action different from
those provided by traditional Western moralities, especially the ethics associated with the European Enlightenment, but that also arrives at those assess-   10
ments through an alternative process of moral thinking.[3] My present interest
is not in care as a moral ideal or value or virtue but rather in the potential
of care thinking as a feminist mode or "style" of practical moral reasoning
(Hacking 1985).

Practical moral reasoning is intended to identify morally desirable, or at
least morally permissible, actions and practices, although it cannot, of course,
be expected to do so infallibly. Since feminism, by definition, revolves around
moral opposition to women's subordination, a mode of moral reasoning adequate for feminism should be capable of critiquing conventionally accepted
practices of male dominance and identifying actions and practices that pro-   20
mote feminist ideals and values. Since male dominance is manifested in both
institutional arrangements and personal relationships and in both the so-
called public and private domains, feminist moral reasoning must be able to
address all these aspects of social life. In addition, since feminist thought and
action occur by definition in a world that is morally imperfect, a feminist
mode of moral reasoning must be applicable to circumstances that are less
than morally ideal.

This chapter discusses what I find to be two limitations of care thinking
as a practice of moral reasoning suitable for feminism. My arguments suggest
that although care thinking may have considerable utility for feminists, fem-   30
inist practical ethics cannot rely exclusively on care but must supplement it
with other modes of moral reasoning.

DISTINCTIVE FEATURES OF CARE REASONING

As a practice of moral thinking, care involves a distinctive moral orientation
toward another person or persons. This orientation has both affective and
cognitive dimensions: the caring individual is simultaneously concerned
about the other's welfare and perceives acutely and insightfully how it is with

Reprinted from *Justice and Care: Essential Readings in Feminist Ethics*, edited by Virginia Held
(1995), by permission of the author.

the other. The carer recognizes and takes pleasure in the other's happiness and identifies and is concerned about her needs (Blum 1992). Descriptions of care thinking often take as paradigmatic situations in which the other is in
40 need, but Sara Ruddick notes that participants in caring relations also strive to delight and empower each other (Ruddick, personal correspondence).

Care thinking is generally explained by contrasting it with so-called justice thinking. One contrast lies in the structure of moral reasoning attributed to each mode of thinking. Justice thinking is portrayed as appealing to rational and universalizable moral principles, applied impartially, whereas accounts of care thinking emphasize its responsiveness to particular situations whose morally salient features are perceived with an acuteness thought to be made possible by the carer's emotional posture of empathy, openness, and receptiveness (Blum 1992). Care theorists' emphasis on moral perception is
50 sometimes taken to imply that care is immediate rather than deliberate, but several authors assert that it may be thoughtful and reflective (Blum 1991:706). However, rather than validating its responses by reference to general principles, care reasoning is likely to take the form of a narrative in which the concrete details of specific situations become intelligible in the context of people's ongoing lives and relationships (Walker 1992:167).

Perhaps the most distinctive and controversial feature attributed to care thinking is its particularity, which means not only that it addresses the needs of others in their concrete specificity but that it is unmediated by general principles. Addressing the needs of others in their concrete specificity is
60 understood as responding to them as unique, irreplaceable individuals rather than as "generalized" others regarded simply as representatives of a common humanity (Benhabib 1986). Such responsiveness requires paying as much moral attention to the ways in which people differ from each other as to the ways in which they are the same (Dillon 1992). Care's intense focus on particular others is taken to entail the denial that it is impartial in the sense of universalizable; thus, asserting the moral propriety of a particular caring response is claimed to carry no implication that someone else in a similar situation should do something similar (Walker 1987).

Care and justice thinking have sometimes been portrayed by contrasting
70 allegedly dispassionate justice with supposedly nonrational care, but in fact such portrayals caricature both justice and care. Although traditional accounts of moral reason often neglected or disparaged the moral significance of emotion, recent accounts increasingly acknowledge that even justice involves characteristic emotions such as respect and indignation. Similarly, theorists of care resist reducing it to a simple feeling, insisting that its cognitive elements be recognized. They consider care not simply as a motivation to right action, itself conceived as established through a process of rational calculation, but also as a distinct moral capacity with cognitive dimensions, necessary to determining what actions are morally appropriate (Blum
80 1992:125). The significant contrast seems to be not that care is emotional whereas justice is rational but rather that, as Virginia Held points out, the emotions play a different epistemic role in each perspective: the justice per-

abortion

spective limits the role of emotion to that of motivating actions whose moral permissibility must be determined by reason; the care perspective regards emotions as having "an important function in developing moral understanding itself, in helping us decide what the recommendations of morality themselves ought to be." Specifically, caring "involves feelings and requires high degrees of empathy to enable us to discern what morality recommends in our caring activities" (Held 1993:30).

Care is not rational in the senses of being purely intellectual, deductive, or even egoistic, but Nel Noddings asserts that "rationality and reasoning involve more than the identification of principles and their deductive application" (Noddings 1990a:27). Proponents of care thinking regard it as rational in a broader, honorific sense of being a distinctively human way of engaging with others that produces morally appropriate action.

WOMEN AND THE ETHICS OF CARE

There is nothing new in the assertion that women are uninterested in—often, indeed, neglectful of—justice. This claim has been made not only by antifeminists, such as Sigmund Freud, who thought that lack of concern for justice was inherent in women's nature (Freud 1933), but also by feminists, such as John Stuart Mill, who thought that women would develop a greater concern for justice if they were allowed to extend their sphere of activity beyond the home (Mill 1980). Until the 1970s, antifeminists and feminists alike assumed that to establish women's lack of concern about justice would be tantamount to demonstrating that women were morally inferior to men. The contemporary feminist counterclaim, that an exclusive preoccupation with *justice* reflects a moral sensibility that is also defective, is quite uncharacteristic of modern Western moral philosophy—although we shall see that it is not entirely unprecedented in it.

Even though the ethics of care is widely associated with women, some critics contend that the alleged connection between women and caring cannot be validated empirically. Some studies have found no sex differences emerging on tests of moral development when subjects are matched for education and occupation: with the exception of women who work in the home, males and females are said to achieve almost identical scores on Kohlbergian tests (Walker 1984:677–691). Moreover, many men as well as women have been asserted to employ care thinking, including members of traditional African societies (Harding 1987), African Americans migrating back from the northern to the southern United States (Stack 1986:321–324), and the members of some Native American cultures—not to mention so-called new age men.

Even within male-dominated Western philosophy, the themes that define the ethics of care are not entirely novel. Apart from Christ's injunction to love our neighbors, we may think of Aristotle's remark in Book VIII of his *Nicomachean Ethics* that "when we have justice, we also need friendship but when we have friends, we no longer need justice" echoed by Aquinas's assertion in his ethics commentaries that "a moralist should be more profoundly concerned with friendship than justice." Annette Baier regards David Hume's moral thought as congenial with Gilligan's account of the ethics of care (Baier 1987b), and Joan Tronto finds caring themes in the work of two other Scottish Enlightenment thinkers, Francis Hutcheson and Adam Smith (Tronto 1993).[4] Such examples are more than sufficient to discredit any simple claims that the ethics of justice and care reflect invariable differences between the moral thinking of men and women.

None of the major theorists of care makes any such simple claim, though many have been misread as doing so. Even in her early work, Carol Gilligan[5] asserted that as men and women age, their moral thinking converges, and in a later study of "educationally advantaged Americans" she found that a third of the women focused on justice, a third on care, and a third raised considerations of both justice and care (Gilligan 1987:25–26). Even though men thought about situations almost exclusively in terms of justice and failed to raise concerns of care spontaneously, both sexes were able to recognize both moral orientations when these were suggested to them. Virginia Held and Sara Ruddick both associate care thinking with mothering, but Ruddick asserts that men as well as women are able to mother and Held speaks of "mothering persons" with pointed gender neutrality. Noddings attributes care thinking to those who saved Jews during the Holocaust, people who certainly included men as well as women (Noddings 1990a:27–28).

Although feminist proponents of the ethics of care recognize that some women think in terms of justice and some men think in terms of care, they still associate caring with women because they believe that the care perspective emerges from forms of socialization and experience that, in contemporary Western society, are predominantly feminine. Gilligan suggests that women's affinity for the ethics of care and men's preference for the ethics of justice may be explained at least partly in terms of Nancy Chodorow's version of neo-Freudian object relations theory, which claims that because children are reared primarily by women, girls' gender identity is defined through connection with others whereas boys' gender identity must be established through separation from others (Gilligan 1987:28). Although Held and Ruddick both assert that mothering may be performed by men, they are clear that male mothering is the exception rather than the rule. Noddings connects care with the feminine work of raising children, tending to the elderly, maintaining a supportive home environment, nursing, and teaching (Noddings 1990a:26).

Joan Tronto argues that in contemporary Western society, care is linked not only with gender but also with race and class. Defining care as those practices aimed at "maintaining, continuing and repairing the world," she associates the moral perspective of care with the work of cleaning up after bodily functions, tasks that in Western history have been relegated primarily to women, but not to women exclusively and not to all women (Tronto 1993:104). Tronto asserts that in "modern industrial societies, these tasks of caring continue to be disproportionately carried out by the lowest ranks of society: by women, the working class, and in most of the West, by people of color" (Tronto 1993:113). She argues, therefore, that it is misleading to associate care with femininity *simpliciter:* the ethics of care reflects primarily the experience of women of certain races and classes—as well as of some racial/ethnic men of those classes (Tronto 1993:112). Tronto's analysis of the social genesis of care thinking fits well with Lawrence Blum's characterization of two prominent versions of the ethics of justice, the moral rationalisms of Kant and Hegel, as expressing a juridical-administrative perspective that, in modern Western societies, is typically masculine (Blum 1982). Blum's view suggests that the justice orientation does not reflect the moral perspective of men universally, but only the perspective of men from the professional, administrative, and managerial classes—leaving open the possibility that the ethics of justice may well be adopted by the increasing numbers of women currently entering professional and administrative occupations. Tronto's and Blum's work suggests several reasons that caring themes are recessive rather than dominant in modern Western moral philosophy; such themes appear to characterize the thinking not only of women but also of people in premodern societies and of lower-class people, including people of color—none of whom are well represented among modern Western philosophers.

In addition to reflecting a social experience that is usually but not invariably or inevitably feminine, care may also be feminine in a symbolic or normative sense. Marilyn Friedman asserts that the genders are "moralized" in that

> specific moral ideals, values, virtues, and practices are culturally conceived as the special projects or domains of specific genders. These conceptions determine which commitments and behaviors are to be considered normal, appropriate, and expected of each gender, which commitments and behaviors are to be considered remarkable or heroic, and which commitments and behaviors are to be considered deviant, improper, outrageous, and intolerable. (Friedman 1993:123)

Friedman reports that the moralization of gender is commonplace at the level of popular perception in contemporary Western societies. Both men and women expect women to be more empathic and altruistic, to display concern for the welfare of others, to be caring and nurturant and, to a lesser extent, to be interpersonally sensitive, emotionally expressive, and gentle in personal style. By contrast, men are expected to be assertive, dominant, independent, self-confident, personally efficacious, and direct and adventurous in personal style (Friedman 1993:124). Friedman concludes that the ethics of care is feminine not simply in springing from types of labor assigned generally to women but also in reflecting moral ideals that are culturally feminine.

That the ethics of care is in some plausible senses feminine does not of course establish it as a mode of moral reasoning that is especially appropriate for feminism. Although Western feminists in both the nineteenth and twentieth centuries have occasionally attempted to reclaim the culturally feminine, including the domestic and the emotional,[6] most feminists, and certainly most Western philosophers who have promoted women's equality, such as Plato, Marx, and Mill, have been concerned to challenge and even reject the feminine (Coole 1988). Developing the ethics of care is clearly one means of reappropriating the feminine in the area of moral philosophy, but to evaluate the possibilities for the success of this project requires a critical examination of the strengths and weaknesses of care reasoning for feminist purposes.

ARE CARE AND JUSTICE THINKING COMPATIBLE?

In her early accounts of the ethics of care, Gilligan spoke of the need to marry care with justice, but she did not explain how this might be possible (Gilligan 1982:174). Several philosophers have explored how such a marriage might be consummated, suggesting ways in which care and justice might not only coexist but even presuppose each other. Susan Okin, for instance, argues both that justice is needed to frame caring relationships and that care for others is the value implicit in impartiality (Okin 1989). Friedman argues both that being just is one form of caring and that caring should be done justly so that, for instance, one partner does not bear most of the burden of sustaining the personal relationship or accomplishing the family or parenting labor (Friedman 1993:127–130).

If care and justice are construed as values or ideals, there seems no reason to doubt that both may be part of the same value system and compatibility in this sense is not threatened by occasional uncertainty over which ideal should take precedence, just as liberty and equality may both be part of a single value system even though there may be occasional tension between them. But when care and justice are construed as alternative modes of moral thinking or reasoning, it is harder to see how they may be compatible. As Friedman expresses the opposition between them, care thinking emphasizes moral commitments to particular individuals and justice thinking, to general principles (Friedman 1993:136). Although Friedman asserts that the two modes of thinking may be integrated, her own argument, which recognizes the difficulty of choosing between them, suggests that they are compatible only in the sense that a moral agent may elect at one time to use one mode of thinking, at another time, the other (Friedman 1993:138–139). Friedman does not show that care and justice thinking are compatible in that both may be used on the same occasion, let alone that each implies the other.

Some philosophers have attempted to make precisely such an argument, suggesting that care and justice reasoning be interpreted not as independent practices of moral thinking but rather as aspects of a single practice. With such an interpretation, the ethics of care would not identify a different voice, new at least to philosophy, but would rather present a somewhat different way of listening to a familiar voice, emphasizing elements previously ignored by moral philosophers.

Various suggestions have been offered for construing care as one aspect of a complex practice of moral reasoning. Some Kantian feminists have suggested that care might be interpreted as a moral motive operating within a frame- 260 work of morally permissible action determined by the Categorical Imperative (Herman 1983; Baron 1984; O'Neill 1984). Other philosophers have suggested that care be equated with the faculty that Kant calls judgment, which is a direct and non-rule-governed but nonetheless moral assessment of the nature of the situation (Kant 1965:177). Still other moral theorists redescribe care reasoning as universalizable, whether or not agents appeal consciously to the Categorical Imperative, arguing that it involves a suppressed major premise (Kohlberg 1982:513–528; Sher 1987:187–188). If accounts of care thinking do not designate a hitherto unrecognized mode or practice of moral reasoning but instead highlight unremarked aspects of a familiar practice, it is 270 plausible to suppose that both aspects must be included in a complete account of moral reasoning and thus that justice and care are not only logically compatible with but even logically indispensable to each other.

Suggesting that justice and care ethics each represent different aspects of moral reasoning is not the only way of arguing for their compatibility. Another approach is to recognize them as distinct practices of moral thinking but, assuming that they originate in the experience of public and private life respectively, to suggest that they complement each other in the sense of being appropriate for different domains. Not only Kohlberg and his colleagues (Kohlberg, Levine, and Hewer 1983) but also Blum (1992:126) have 280 suggested that care is especially appropriate for intimate relations or one-to-one encounters.

A third strategy for viewing care and justice as compatible and even complementary is to construe each as addressing a different set of issues. Jürgen Habermas suggests that care thinking is concerned with "evaluative questions of the good life" and "the evaluation of personality types and modes of action." He regards these as "personal" issues of self-realization, not truly moral, unlike the questions of universal obligation, which he takes to be the subject of justice thinking. For Habermas, care is distinguished from justice in reflecting *Sittlichkeit* rather than *Moralitaet* and addressing questions of 290 the good rather than the right, the content of morality rather than its form (Habermas 1990:178–180).

Although compatibility claims are accepted by some advocates of the ethics of care, they are made more frequently by those committed to the primacy of justice. Often compatibility claims are presented in a way that is deflationary, minimizing the moral and theoretical significance of care by reducing it to one aspect of a morality whose essential constituents are the impartiality and universalizability thought to be defining characteristics of the ethics of justice. George Sher, for instance, denies firmly that the articulation of the ethics of care provides any reason to suppose that moral theory 300 needs radical revision; he states that "far from being novel, this approach [making moral decisions on the basis of care and sympathy] . . . is central to the existing tradition" (Sher 1987:184).

Advocates of care thinking are especially resistant to compatibility proposals that trivialize the concerns raised by the ethics of care, proposals that Barbara Houston has diagnosed as expressing a "politics of dismissal" (Houston 1988). Blum, for instance, has objected to several attempts to assimilate caring to one aspect of justice thinking. He insists that care cannot be reconstructed in terms of rules that are in principle universalizable (Blum 310   1987:326–327), and he distinguishes moral perception from the Kantian notion of moral judgment on the grounds that its task is not to apply moral principles but rather to individuate the situations in which moral judgment operates (Blum 1991:708–714). Margaret Walker argues that some moral reasoning is irreducibly particular and nonuniversalizable because those practicing it assign a discretionary weight, rank, or value to moral particulars, in the process defining their own moral personae, the kind of persons they are (Walker 1987).

Many care advocates reject also the suggestion that care and justice are each appropriate for a different domain. Apart from Noddings's attempt to extend 320   care thinking to handle all moral concerns in all domains (Noddings 1991:97), some argue that justice as well as care is needed in the household (Ruddick) and many assert that care as well as justice is needed in the public domain (Walker 1991; Tronto 1993; Held 1993; Ruddick). Dividing the moral labor so that justice and care regulate the public and private domains, respectively, makes justice primary over care because justice regulates the domain that not only has the higher status but also controls how the domains are demarcated. Care ethics, symbolically gendered feminine, then becomes analogous to housework: despite its indispensability, its contribution to the larger economy is disregarded or marginalized.

330   Although Seyla Benhabib retains a strong commitment to a universal ethics of justice, she seeks to rescue care thinking from what she calls Habermas's relegation of it "to the margins of ethical theory." Benhabib complains that, on Habermas's construal, the issues with which he takes care to be concerned become "'anomalies' or residual problems of an otherwise adequate scientific paradigm" (Benhabib 1992:183). She challenges Habermas's sharp distinction between the right and the good, noting, "The line between matters of justice and those of the good life is not given by some moral dictionary, but evolves as a result of historical and cultural struggles" (Benhabib 1992:75). In her view, questions of the good life are also susceptible to inter-340   subjective debate and reflection, although she concedes that consensus here may not be possible, and she insists, in opposition to Habermas, that "questions of care are moral issues" (Benhabib 1992:186).

Most proponents of the ethics of care now dispute the possibility of any easy synthesis of care with justice. They note that in her later work, Gilligan presents care and justice as "two moral perspectives that organize thinking in different ways" (Gilligan 1987:20), dropping her early metaphor of a marriage in favor of explaining care and justice by reference to ambiguous figures that may be given alternative and incompatible interpretations. Rather than seeking to include care and justice in a unified account of moral reasoning, most contemporary advocates of an ethics of care are committed to exploring care's strengths as an independent style or practice of moral thinking. They present the ethics of care as a complete moral orientation or perspective or outlook, "a unified perspective on morality" (Walker 1989:123). In this view, care and justice both involve distinctive ontological, epistemological, and practical commitments, though this is not to deny that the concepts, themes, and priorities associated with both orientations are often loosely defined, permitting considerable disagreement between them. Sara Ruddick speaks for many in asserting that "justice" and "care" are "two non-assimilable moral orientations . . . which foster distinctive cognitive capacities, appeal to distinctive ideals of rationality, elicit distinctive moral emotions, presume distinctive conceptions of identity and relationships, recognize distinctive virtues and make distinctive requirements on institutions." On Ruddick's view, "justice" and "care" each offer

> "a point of view from which alone a certain sort of understanding of human life is possible." That is to say, each orientation is genuinely moral; neither can be replaced by or subsumed under the other; each covers the whole of the moral domain and therefore can check and inform the other; there is no third, "mature," single integrative moral perspective within which each orientation has its place. (Ruddick)

CARE THINKING'S SIGNIFICANCE FOR MORAL PHILOSOPHY

Even if the new interest in caring did no more than focus philosophical attention on previously disregarded aspects of moral thinking, it would have considerable significance for moral philosophy. Cheshire Calhoun has argued that the historical neglect of these aspects has produced a distorted and misleading representation of moral life (Calhoun 1988). For instance, focusing exclusively on people's shared humanity and equal membership in the moral community diverts attention from the ways in which people's basic interests and empirical desires may differ depending on their social location. Focusing exclusively on the adult capacity for consistent and universalizable moral reflection diverts attention from the indispensability of moral motivation and education and from the social availability of morally relevant information. Focusing exclusively on the dangers of egoism and partiality to one's own diverts attention from the dangers of self-sacrifice and devalues the moral significance of special relations. Calhoun argues that the traditional focus of Western moral philosophy has created a lopsided ideology of moral life and thought that reflects the moral preoccupations of propertied males and obscures the moral concerns of (among others) many women. The ethics of care, construed as a focus on hitherto neglected aspects of moral life and thought, can help to redress this gendered bias in moral theory.

390   If care thinking is construed in a stronger sense, as an independent style or practice of moral reasoning, then its advocates contend that it may generate actions morally superior to those that result from a concern for justice. Many examples purport to illustrate how people motivated primarily by justice frequently ignore the pressing needs of real people, often those closest to them, or subordinate individuals to abstract principle, with a "blind willingness to sacrifice people to truth" (Gilligan 1982:104; compare Baier 1987a and Noddings 1984). Care's ability to generate actions morally preferable to those produced by justice reasoning is credited in part to its reliance on the direct perception of particular situations. This direct perception is said to

400   facilitate action that is more context-sensitive than actions guided by moral rules that, because of their generality, are necessarily indeterminate.

Care is also asserted to be more reliable than justice thinking in motivating right action because justice often presents right action as requiring the sacrifice of one's own self-interest, whereas care thinking regards the interests of the self as inseparable from those of others. Unlike acting from a concern for justice, therefore, acting caringly does not require a prior act of moral will strong enough to overcome one's inclinations, and so caring action, unlike justice-motivated action, can hardly be inhibited by "weakness of the will." For instance, Noddings reports that of the non-Jews who risked their own

410   safety to save Jews during the Holocaust, only 11 percent acted on principle; the rest "responded either directly out of compassion or from a sense of themselves as decent, caring people" (Noddings 1990a:27).

Finally, the process of responding in a caring manner itself is said to have moral value, unlike the intellectual appeal to principle characteristic of the ethics of justice. As Blum observes, "Accurate moral perception is a good in its own right," expressing a praiseworthy moral sensitivity (Blum 1991:714).

Many of these claims seem to me persuasive, but rather than developing them here, I intend to discuss two features of care reasoning that I find especially problematic. Gilligan chose the analogy of the ambiguous figure to sug-

420   gest that the ethics of care draws attention to some things only at the expense of obscuring others. I am concerned about two of care thinking's apparent blind spots, which hamper and may even disable care from addressing certain questions crucial for feminist ethics.

JUSTIFYING "TRUE CARE"

In this section, I criticize the care tradition for failing to explain how care thinking may be properly critical of the moral validity of felt, perceived, or expressed needs, so that it can avoid permitting or even legitimating morally inadequate responses to them. I attribute this failure to the relative lack of attention to moral justification given so far by theorists of care ethics.

It would not be true to say that the tradition of care ethics fails to acknowledge any distinction between real necessities and objects of empirical desire, between felt or expressed needs, on the one hand, and genuine needs, on the other. On the contrary, such a distinction runs through the work of Gilligan, it is implicit in Ruddick's definition of caring in terms of what may usefully be given and received (Ruddick), and it is explicit in Tronto's observation that "a patient in the hospital who refuses to get up may be forced to do so. A child who wishes only to eat junk food may be disappointed by parents' reluctance to meet this wish" (Tronto 1989:177). But although most accounts of care reasoning assume such a distinction, they have provided only scanty explanations of how it should be drawn.

Accounts of care thinking that emphasize the directness of caring perception sometimes discourage even raising this epistemological question by treating care as a "success" concept. On this construal, caring perception of another's need is by definition veridical; if someone fails to assess another's situation accurately, she is not practicing care thinking. Tronto's assertion that hospital patients may be forced to get up and children prevented from eating junk food is followed immediately by the remark, "Genuine attentiveness would presumably allow the caretaker to see through these pseudo-needs and come to appreciate what the other really needs" (Tronto 1989:177). Such comments tend to obscure the question of how we distinguish "pseudo-needs" from "real needs" by suggesting that "genuine attentiveness," which Tronto takes as central to caring, is self-authenticating. From here, it is easy to slide into paternalism, authoritarianism, and dogmatism.

Many care theorists, including Tronto, are aware of these dangers and discuss such concerns as vicarious identification, projection, and carers' desires to control those for whom they care or to maintain them in a state of dependence. Frequently, care theorists maintain that these dangers may be avoided through improved practices of attentiveness, portraying attentiveness as a kind of discipline whose prerequisites include attitudes and capacities such as openness, receptivity, empathy, sensitivity, and imagination. Margaret Walker writes, "Acuity of moral perception, especially as regards the interests and perspectives of people, must result from the exercise of many complex, learned, and indefinitely improvable skills of attention, communication, and interpretation" (Walker 1991:771).

Among contemporary care theorists, Walker is probably the most insistent on the need that caring intentions be validated through communication with those cared-for. But Ruddick also mentions mothers attempting to figure out how to care for their children by talking with each other (Ruddick 1989), and Held emphasizes the need "to listen to each other in actual conversations in actual communities" (Held 1993:41). Noddings's argument that there must be fairly tight limits on the circle of those for whom we care depends partly on her insistence that the caring relation be completed by the recognition of those who are cared-for, and this insistence is in turn at least partially motivated by an epistemological concern. She says that if we do not "check on the effects of our efforts" and attend to a "living other speaking to us directly—informing us, persuading us, getting us to change our minds," we can be led into "a dangerous inauthenticity" (Noddings 1991:98). In a similar vein, Walker writes, "A great deal of our best evidence about how it is with others requires talking with and listening to them . . . . Asking, telling, repeating, mutually clarifying, mulling over, and checking back are the most 480 dependable, accessible, and efficient devices for finding out how it is with others" (Walker 1991:769).

Theorists influenced by Simone Weil and Iris Murdoch sometimes speak as though care thinking requires forgetting the self; Noddings, for instance, asserts that "our attention, our mental engrossment is on the cared-for, not on ourselves" (Noddings 1984:24). But other theorists emphasize that care thinking also requires self-awareness and self-knowledge; Tronto says that attentiveness requires "a tremendous self-knowledge so that the caretaker does not simply transform the needs of the other into a projection of the self's own needs" (Tronto 1989:178).

490   The care perspective's attention to the subjects of moral consciousness contrasts with the justice perspective's efforts to disregard or bracket individual subjectivity through ingenious theoretical devices designed to approximate an impersonal "view from nowhere." Not only that strand of the justice tradition concerned primarily with rights but also the strand that concerns itself with welfare or utility typically focuses on relations "out there" in the world external to the self. This is not to say that the justice tradition dismisses all questions about the interests and obligations of the moral subject or about personal relationships but that, in both teleological and neo-Kantian deontological ethics, relationships between particular selves and particular others 500 are regarded as likely to be epistemologically subversive or morally corrupting. Theoretical postulates such as the ideal observer, the disinterested judge, the archangel, the original position, and the view from nowhere are designed to correct for the assumed bias of particular points of view.

Care reasoning is unlike justice reasoning in that it does not attempt to bracket or disregard the self, whose appropriate motivations, attitudes, sensibilities, and qualities of character are thought indispensable to morally acute perception. Furthermore, these qualities are regarded not simply as instrumental to producing a morally desirable outcome but as intrinsic to the quality of the caring relationship. Care thinking thus not only pays more atten- 510 tion than justice thinking to the subject or moral consciousness but also conceptualizes differently the relation between that subject and the objects of her moral concern. Justice thinking is impersonal and general because it regards both moral subjects and the objects of their moral concern in terms of their moral status as representatives of humanity or as beings capable of pleasure and pain rather than in terms of their concrete specificity; care thinking is personal and particularized in that both carers and those cared-for regard each other as unique, irreplaceable individuals.

The justice perspective's concern to depersonalize moral thinking reflects its interest in epistemological issues and its eagerness to identify a method for discovering which moral principles are most objectively just. Justice thinking   520 often prides itself on being objective precisely insofar as it distances itself from the self and particular relationships and dismisses care thinking as subjective and therefore unreliable precisely because successful caring by definition involves particular relations between carers and those cared-for. However, it is mistaken to assume that bracketing subjectivity is the best way of achieving moral objectivity, in the sense of trustworthy moral responses.

Care's focus on the relation between the carer and the cared-for is valuable in raising questions often ignored by justice reasoning, questions that are important both morally and epistemologically. Turning our attention inward as well as outward encourages reflexive consideration of what the agent brings   530 to the situation, her interests, her location, the context, her warrant for intervention. Conceiving moral reasoning as interactive encourages reflection not only on the moral implications for others of action or inaction but also on the implications for the self, how it expresses or develops her moral character. As Walker puts it, it encourages us to ask, What kind of person do I want to become? (Walker 1987). Acknowledging the moral dimension of perception and the epistemic dimension of emotion also encourages consideration of how people may develop the moral abilities for morally sensitive perception and loving attention. Finally, insisting on the importance of checking with the one cared-for, rather than assuming that we know her needs in   540 advance, avoids the arrogance and presumptiveness of postulating hypothetical consent in what Walker calls "round robins of role-taking" in what she regards as the "alarming" "philosophical predilection for the game of imagination" (Walker 1991:769).

Although it is not true that moral objectivity is best achieved by bracketing subjectivity, it is equally mistaken to suppose that morally appropriate responses can be determined by focusing exclusively either on the attitude of the moral subject or even on the caring relationship. Yet care theorists often seem to assume that even if adequate caring cannot be guaranteed by the carer's intentions alone, the carer/cared-for dyad between them can be   550 counted on to identify truly caring behavior.

On reflection, it is immediately evident that such an assumption is unwarranted. Overindulgence or "spoiling" are only the least of the moral mistakes that may be carried out in the name of care. Other, more clearly gendered, abuses include incest and even footbinding. Incestuous fathers often portray themselves as caring for their daughters, even as nurturing or initiating them, and the Chinese women who bound the feet of their daughters and granddaughters also equated the pain they caused with care (Blake 1994:682).[7] These examples show not only that appropriate caring is not guaranteed by the intentions of the one who claims to care but that such a guarantee is not   560 supplied even by agreement on the part of the one who is cared-for. Children characteristically retain a tenacious trust in the goodness of their "caretakers" intentions, finding it less psychologically devastating to interpret neglect or abuse as care than to believe that they are not cared for. Abused women also often regard violence as an expression of caring or love, and they may even identify empathically with their abusers. "Co-dependents" appeal to care to justify their facilitation of destructive or self-destructive behavior on the part of others. These examples demonstrate clearly that so long as care thinking focuses exclusively on the carer/cared-for dyad, it cannot reliably assess the adequacy and appropriateness of responses that claim to be caring.

The care perspective is not necessarily without resources for addressing this issue, but so far few care theorists have given it more than perfunctory attention, perhaps because they have not yet clearly acknowledged it as a problem. The care literature contains relatively few direct discussions of how to identify care that is morally appropriate and has shown limited interest in moral justification. Noddings, here as often elsewhere the most radical of the care theorists, even explicitly rejects traditional concerns about justification. She writes,

> An ethic of caring does not emphasise justification. As one-caring, I am not seeking justification for my action; I am not standing alone before some tribunal. What I seek is completion in the other—the sense of being cared-for and, I hope, the renewed commitment of the cared-for to turn about and act as one-caring in the circles and chains within which he is defined. Thus, I am not justified but somehow fulfilled and completed in my own life and in the lives of those I have thus influenced. (Noddings 1984:95)

This passage may be read as expressing lack of concern for any perspectives external to the caring relation.

The recent work of Joan Tronto is one exception to care theorists' lack of interest in justification. Because she recognizes that identifying and ranking needs is inherently contestable, Tronto asserts that care is a desirable political ideal only in the context of a just, pluralistic, democratic society in which open and equal discussion about needs and justice occurs (Tronto 1993:154–172). But in asserting the necessity of societywide dialogue about needs, which presumably involves assessing and ranking the needs of classes of people rather than specific individuals, Tronto seems to be concerned primarily with care as a political ideal and to depart from classic accounts of care thinking that describe it as distinguished by its focus on particular others.

These considerations suggest that care thinking, at least as it has been described so far in the literature, is incomplete as a feminist account of moral rationality. The suggestion that dyadic relations of care are somehow self-justifying, a suggestion more often implied than explicit, is not only mystifying but evidently false. I suggest that claims to care, like other perceptual and moral claims, can be justified only by widening the circle of intersubjective validation.

CARE'S FOCUS ON THE PARTICULAR

Care reasoning is often described as responding directly to particular persons and situations, whereas justice reasoning is supposedly concerned with universal principles. Like several other alleged contrasts between care and justice, this contrast is often overstated, since justice and care reasoning each necessarily recognize both particular and universal aspects of situations. Justice reasoning, as we have seen already, requires perceiving and assessing the morally salient features of particular situations in order to know which general principles should be brought to bear. Similarly, care's recognition of particular situations necessarily utilizes general concepts; for instance, recognizing a particular individual's need for companionship presupposes an ability to deploy the concepts of person and loneliness in a range of relevantly similar situations. Since both care and justice reasoning logically involve reference to both particular and universal aspects of situations, this distinction between them may be regarded as one of degree rather than kind, a difference of emphasis or attention or focus.

Justice reasoning regards particular situations as tokens of more general types and so attends to what they have in common with other situations. Care reasoning, by contrast, focuses on the specificities of each situation, emphasizing the ways in which it is unique and responding to those involved as particular in the sense of nonsubstitutable or irreplaceable (Friedman 1993:136–137). Accounts of care reasoning emphasize its attentiveness to detail, its deep and rather narrow focus, whereas justice reasoning, which requires explicit comparisons, tends to have a wider but shallower focus. Although the state of the nation, the world, and the universe are all, in a logical sense, particular states of affairs, care reasoning, with its emphasis on detail, depth, and specificity, is typically practiced in small-scale or micro situations involving a very few people whom the carer knows or comes to know personally. Justice reasoning, by contrast, has often been thought inappropriate for small-scale situations involving personal relations (Sandel 1982) and is paradigmatically used to address large-scale or macro situations involving people not known by the agent in their concrete specificity. On those somewhat exceptional occasions when agents apply justice reasoning to situations in which they are personally acquainted with those involved, they are expected to bracket or discount their personal knowledge and feelings. Care thinking celebrates minute perception of detail, but justice is supposed to be blind to all aspects of situations other than the limited number of generalizable features taken to be morally salient.

Some critics of the ethics of care complain that care thinking is unable to address large-scale social or global problems, but that is not precisely my concern here. Instead, I want to discuss one limitation of care reasoning not in terms of its applicability or otherwise to large-scale situations or the so-called public realm but rather in terms of what care makes visible in any situation regardless of scale or publicity. Accepting that one strength of care reasoning lies in its ability to draw moral attention to aspects of situations often disregarded by justice reasoning, I shall argue that its weakness lies in its inability

650 to bring into focus other morally salient features of situations. When some things are foregrounded, others recede into the background; in making some things visible, care obscures others.

The distinctive feature of care reasoning that I address here is its focus on the specificities of particular situations, especially the needs of particular individuals. This focus is valuable in encouraging awareness of the moral complexities of situations, which are always open to a variety of interpretations, and of individuals' responsibilities within situations. Its weakness is that its attention to situations' specificity and particularity diverts attention away from their general features such as the social institutions and groupings that
660 give them their structure and much of their meaning (Card 1990:205; Hoagland 1991:253, 260). For instance, care's emphasis on responding to immediate needs simultaneously takes those needs as givens, failing to question their source or why they are presently unfulfilled.

My point is not that the care perspective excludes awareness of social identities and structures; on the contrary, care presupposes such awareness, since the identity of particular individuals is constituted partly by their group membership and since particular actions or situations are made possible by and gain their meaning from social structures. Thus, recognizing a situation of racial privilege or sexual abuse inevitably presupposes an awareness of the
670 race or sex of the individuals involved and of the way that these aspects of their identity influence particular situations. In an example of Lawrence Blum's, for instance, when a taxi driver chooses a white male customer over an African American woman, it would be impossible to perceive the affront to the dignity of the African American woman unless one were aware of the social meanings assigned to the skin colors of those involved; without this awareness, one's perception would be aesthetic rather than moral. Conversely, social structures, such as race and sex, exist only in their specific manifestations, and understanding them requires recognizing their operation in particular situations and experiences. The universal and particular aspects of sit-
680 uations, what might be called their form and content, thus presuppose each other in a way that the images of the duck and the rabbit in the ambiguous duck-rabbit figure do not presuppose each other. It is no more than a contingent fact that the outline of the duck can also be seen as the shape of a rabbit and vice versa, whereas it is not contingent that particular situations gain their meaning from social structures and that social structures exist only through their instantiation in particular situations. Despite this disanalogy, reference to the ambiguous duck-rabbit figure helps illustrate one important feature of the relationship between justice and care. This is that even when one is aware of the presence of both images, one cannot focus on both at
690 once; when one is visible, the other becomes invisible. Similarly, when an agent is focusing on the concrete specificities of a situation, she is not attending directly to the social institutions that structure it and vice versa. When one is at the center of her consciousness, the other is at the margins. In care

You can't focus on both approaches/aspects at once

thinking, social structure occupies a place comparable to the frame of a picture one is viewing; one must be aware of it in some sense but one pays it little direct attention.

From a feminist perspective, care's exclusive focus on particularity is sometimes a significant liability, since an important concern of feminist ethics must be the ways in which male-dominant social structures limit the life chances of women and men. Close attention to the specificities of small-scale situations may well obscure perception of the larger social context in which they are embedded. For instance, focusing on particular examples of oppression may facilitate perception of insensitive and bullying behavior on the part of individuals, but it can also divert moral attention away from the social structures of privilege that legitimate such behavior. Moral thinking that focuses on the specificities of particular situations is likely to see the source of problems as lying in the personal attitudes of individual men, whites or heterosexuals who benefit, sometimes unwittingly or unwillingly, from sexism, racism, and heterosexism, rather than in those larger institutions that give some individuals power and privilege over others. Similarly, attending to an individual's immediate needs for food, shelter, comfort, or companionship is likely to distract from moral scrutiny of the social structures that create those needs or leave them unfulfilled.

I do not wish to argue that individual attitudes and immediate needs are morally insignificant. On the contrary, social structures and institutions are human inventions that survive only because people conform their behavior to them; racism and sexism outlive legal prohibition because of individuals' insensitivity or callousness. Care reasoning encourages personal accountability and individual resistance to oppressive structures. But care's emphasis on individual responses to immediate needs also encourages what are sometimes called band-aid or social work approaches to moral problems rather than efforts to solve them institutionally or prevent their occurrence through social changes.

The characteristic strengths and limitations of the care perspective are revealed in Noddings's response to the criticism most commonly made of caring, namely, that it is partial or parochial because attention to intimates and proximate strangers can lead to neglecting those who are further away. Noddings readily acknowledges the legitimacy of moral concern for distant strangers or humanity at large but insists it is not properly addressed in ways such as giving money to famine-relief organizations, which she calls "caring about." "Caring about" is "a poor second-cousin to caring," in Noddings's view, (1984:112) because caring, as she defines it, is an interactive relation in which people recognize each other as particular individuals. When others are too distant or too numerous for personal caring relations to be established with them, Noddings suggests that we either press their neighbors to care for them or seek to empower them to help themselves (Noddings 1991:97–98). "Instead of presenting ourselves to the

world as heroes, gangbusters, or saviors, we would act as friends and partners, carefully building and maintaining stable relations on which we as
740   well as others could depend in times of need" (Noddings 1991:97).

> From the perspective of caring, when we empower a group, we do not
> just give them things. Rather we help them to gain control over their
> own lives and, especially, to develop the resources and commitment to
> help others. The process of empowering is thus a part of caring. It nec-
> essarily requires a sort of "staying with" or "holding" as Sara Ruddick
> describes it, and this is a longterm program that involves the contin-
> uous construction and maintenance of caring relations. *It is still lim-
> ited in the individualist sense.* I have to trust others to do the direct
> work of caring when I cannot be present." (1991:98, emphasis added)

750   Care's insistence on personal engagement and individual responsibility is
a useful corrective to the impersonality, insensitivity, and frequent ineffec-
tiveness of social engineering. It reminds us not only that a new society needs
new people to make it work but that social change requires individual action
and challenges each of us to act now rather than wait for the authorities or
the revolution. Noddings's rejection of the masculine models of hero, gang-
buster, and savior is a characteristically feminist response to the "grandiose
universality" of the justice orientation (Friedman 1993:109) and the postur-
ing of leaders, paradigmatically male (Fisher 1980:12–13), who infantilize
and disempower their followers, positioning them as victims awaiting rescue
760   or salvation.

Despite the virtues of care thinking, its emphasis on the quality of individual relations seems to preclude its addressing the structural oppositions
between the interests of social groups that make caring difficult or unlikely
between members of those groups. Similarly, care's reliance on individual
efforts to meet individual needs disregards the social structures that make this
virtually impossible in many cases. Care thinking seems unable to focus on the
social causes of many individual problems, such as widespread homelessness
and hunger, both of which have disproportionately severe effects on women.

I am not aware that care theorists have addressed the question of home-
770   lessness in North America, but it seems compatible with the spirit of care
ethics to encourage moral responses such as personally helping homeless individuals or families rehabilitate or build houses or even taking them into one's
own home, as opposed to challenging zoning and credit restrictions, pressing
for governmental provision of housing, or even questioning why so many
people, especially women, lack the money for housing. With respect to the
question of Third World hunger, we have seen that care thinking encourages
local people to give food to individuals with whom they are acquainted and
even to help them grow their own food. But care thinking does not question
why some "neighbors" have food while others do not, let alone identify the

larger social forces causing peasant dislocation and dispossession, the assign-   780
ment of land to cash crops for export rather than food for local people, Third
World deforestation and desertification, and the draining of Third World
resources to service its debt to international financial institutions. Even if caring is capable eventually of producing a social transformation that is evolutionary rather than revolutionary, the slowness and uncertainty of this
approach make it morally inadequate for tackling existing problems of home-
lessless or hunger, given the level and extent of dislocation, malnutrition, and
starvation as well as the interlinked and accelerating social and environmental crises.

Some care theorists have talked about making care applicable to large-   790
scale social or global issues by enlarging our moral imagination, learning to
care for distant others, including large populations with whom we have no
personal contact. But this is to treat care merely as a moral motive, not as a
distinctive mode of moral response, and it is incompatible with the characteristically interactive and personal relation that defines care thinking. At
best, it is what Noddings calls "caring about." At worst, it appropriates the
language of caring to refer to "caring that is *directed toward* inert and
unknown recipients" and is thus a form of colonization, "oblivious to the
possibility that [its] 'targets' might experience the proffered caring as insulting and invasive" (Code 1992:1–2).   800

Significantly improving the lives of the world's women certainly requires
the empathy, imagination, and responsiveness that distinguish care thinking;
but it also requires a kind of moral thinking that focuses not only on meeting immediate needs but on problematizing the structures that create those
needs or keep them unfulfilled. This is as true on the familial and local levels as it is on the national and international levels, and it presents a major
challenge for care theorists.

To note care thinking's difficulty in addressing some crucial questions of
feminist practical ethics is not necessarily to assume that justice thinking is
capable of dealing adequately with those questions. For instance, care rea-   810
soning addresses instances of rape and domestic violence by "strongly disap-
proving" of them (Noddings 1990b:125) and tries to protect victims and sur-
vivors by establishing moral authority over their assailants; justice reasoning,
as commonly construed, is likely to condemn these assaults as violations by
individuals of other individuals' rights. In order to fully comprehend sexual
violence, however, its meanings and functions as a systematic social practice
must be addressed, together with the ways in which many social institutions
implicitly condone and legitimate it. Neither care nor justice reasoning, as
ordinarily construed, constitutes the kind of hermeneutical moral thinking
capable of questioning conventional definitions of assault as well as of explor-   820
ing the complex assumptions about sexuality, aggression, and gender that
make rape not only thinkable but predictable and even normal. The feminists
of the late 1960s called this kind of thinking consciousness-raising.

CONCLUSION

At least as so far described by its theorists, care thinking has severe limitations. Its inability to focus on social structures restricts the scope of its moral critiques, and its lack of theoretical interest in justification renders its critical perspective unreliable even on those issues that it does address. Despite these shortcomings, the recent recognition of care thinking has made valuable contributions to philosophical understandings of moral rationality. Through
830 studying empirical examples of moral thinking, care theorists have raised questions hitherto largely neglected by moral philosophers and revealed that the conception of practical reason associated with the European Enlightenment has its own limitations. Among these are an inadequate portrayal of moral thinking that exaggerates the significance of principles and fails to recognize that affectively laden aspects of moral thinking have epistemic as well as motivational functions. In addition, and because care is generally associated with the personal realm, the ethics of care has contributed to rehabilitating personal life as an arena for moral scrutiny; it has thus expanded the domain of practical morality, exposing further limitations in traditional theory. Finally,
840 the ethics of care has revealed damaging biases, including gender biases, in Enlightenment moral theory, which has not only devalued the caring work assigned primarily to women, especially women of the lower classes, but also functioned as an ideology to rationalize selfishness as natural and normal.

ENDNOTES

1. Virginia Held and Sara Ruddick both read several earlier drafts of this essay and discussed them with me at length. I am deeply grateful for their help, although I must make the usual disclaimer that the views expressed here are still, in the end, not theirs but mine.

2. The Center for Human Caring was established in 1986 and its history and mission statement describes it as "the nation's first interdisciplinary center with an overall commitment to develop and use knowledge of human caring and healing as the foundation for transforming the health care system."

3. The contemporary ethics of care was pioneered by Milton Mayeroff's 1971 book, *On Caring,* (New York: Harper & Row) but this did not explore care's gendered dimensions and so was largely ignored by feminists. The name most widely associated with the contemporary feminist ethics of care is that of Nel Noddings (1984, 1989) but other philosophers who have endorsed some version of this approach to ethics include, but are not limited to Annette Baier (1987a, 1987b, 1994), Lawrence Blum (1988, 1991), Marilyn Friedman (1993), Virginia Held (1993), Rita Manning (1992), Sara Ruddick (1987, 1989, 1995), Joan Tronto (1993), and Margaret Urban Walker (1987, 1989, 1991, 1992).

4. There also appear to be convergences between the ethics of care and some non-Western moral thought. For instance, a recent article likens the ethics of care to the Confucian ethics of *Jen* (Chenyang Li 1994).

5. Contemporary feminist claims that women's morality is different from men's were foreshadowed in theories developing the neo-Marxist notion of a feminist standpoint (Smith 1974; Hartsock 1983), but the claims became best known in their psychological versions, through the work of Jean Baker Miller (1976), Nancy Chodorow (1978) and especially Carol Gilligan. In two influential articles published in the late 1970s in the *Harvard Educational Review*, followed by her landmark book, *In a Different Voice*, Gilligan argued that most accepted accounts of moral development were male biased not simply in focusing primarily on males but, more seriously, in measuring the development of both males and females by a standard derived exclusively from the study of men and boys (Gilligan 1982). Reflecting on the responses of girls and women interviewed initially about their abortion decisions, Gilligan claimed to hear "a different voice" expressing an understanding of morality that she called the ethics of care. She argued that this understanding contrasted in significant ways with what she called the ethics of justice assumed by her teacher and mentor Lawrence Kohlberg, whose own studies of moral development had drawn on the Kantian conception of morality embodied in the work of Jean Piaget and John Rawls.

6. Some suffragists argued for the vote on grounds that women's moral superiority would encourage cleaning up politics, and the "moral mothers" in Britain and the United States drew on cultural myths of women's innate peacefulness to oppose World War I. Contemporary feminist peace and environmental activists have sometimes portrayed their political work as a kind of global housekeeping.

7. The Chinese word *teng* may mean "pain," "care," or a conflation of both, as in the proverb that translates as "Beating is caring, scolding is loving" (Blake 1994).

REFERENCES

Baier, Annette C. 1987a. "The Need for More than Justice." *Science, Morality and Feminist Theory*, edited by Marsha Hanen and Kai Nielsen. Calgary, Canada: University of Calgary Press (*Canadian Journal of Philosophy*, Supplementary Volume 13).

——. 1987b. "Hume, the Women's Moral Theorist?" In *Women and Moral Theory*, edited by Eva Feder Kittay and Diana T. Meyers. Totowa, NJ: Rowman and Littlefield.

——. 1994. *Moral Prejudices: Essays on Ethics.* Cambridge, MA: Harvard University Press.

Baron, Marcia. 1984. "The Alleged Moral Repugnance of Acting from Duty." *Journal of Philosophy* 81:4 (April), 197–220.

Benhabib, Seyla. 1986. "The Generalized and the Concrete Other: The Kohlberg-Gilligan Controversy and Feminist Theory." *Praxis International* 5:4 (January), 402–424.

———. 1992. *Situating the Self: Gender, Community and Postmodernism in Contemporary Ethics.* New York: Routledge.

Blake, C. Fred. 1994. "Footbinding in Neo-Confucian China and the Appropriation of Female Labor." *Signs: Journal of Women in Culture and Society* 19:3 (Spring).

Blum, Lawrence. 1982. "Kant's and Hegel's Moral Rationalism: A Feminist Perspective." *Canadian Journal of Philosophy* 12:2 (June), 287–302.

———. 1987. "Particularity and Responsiveness." *The Emergence of Morality in Young Children*, edited by Jerome Kagan and Sharon Lamb. Chicago: University of Chicago Press.

———. 1988. "Gilligan and Kohlberg: Implications for Moral Theory." *Ethics* 98 (April), 472–491.

———. 1991. "Moral Perception and Particularity." *Ethics* 101:4 (July), 701–725.

———. 1992. "Care." In *Encyclopedia of Ethics*, edited by Lawrence C. Becker. New York: Garland.

Calhoun, Cheshire. 1988. "Justice, Care, Gender Bias." *Journal of Philosophy* 85:9 (September).

Card, Claudia. 1990. "Gender and Moral Luck." In *Identity, Character and Morality*, edited by Owen Flanagan and Amelie Oksenberg Rorty. Cambridge, MA: MIT Press.

Chodorow, Nancy. 1978. *The Reproduction of Mothering: Psychoanalysis and the Sociology of Gender.* Berkeley: University of California Press.

Code, Lorraine. 1992."Who Cares? The Poverty of Objectivism for a Moral Epistemology." *The Annals of Scholarship* 9:1–2, 1–17.

Coole, Diana. 1988. *Women in Political Theory: From Ancient Misogyny to Contemporary Feminism.* Brighton, UK, and Boulder, CO: Wheatsheaf and Lynne Rienner.

Dillon, Robin S. 1992. "Care and Respect." In *Explorations in Feminist Ethics: Theory and Practice*, edited by Eve Browning Cole and Susan Coultrap McQuin. Bloomington and Indianapolis: Indiana University Press.

Fisher, Berenice. 1980. "Who Needs Woman Heroes?" *Heresies* 3:1 (issue 9).

Flanagan, Owen, and Kathryn Jackson. 1987. "Justice, Care and Gender: The Kohlberg-Gilligan Debate Revisited." *Ethics* 97, 622–637.

Freud, Sigmund. 1933. "Femininity." In *New Introductory Lectures on Psychoanalysis*, translated from the German and edited by James Strachey. New York: W. W. Norton.

Friedman, Marilyn. 1993. *What Are Friends For? Feminist Perspectives on Personal Relationships and Moral Theory.* Ithaca: Cornell University Press.

Gilligan, Carol. 1982. *In a Different Voice: Psychological Theory and Women's Development.* Cambridge, MA: Harvard University Press.

———. 1987. "Moral Orientation and Moral Development." In *Women and Moral Theory*, edited by Eva Feder Kittay and Diana T. Meyers. Totowa, NJ: Rowman and Littlefield.

Habermas, Jürgen. 1990. "Moral Consciousness and Communicative Action." In *Moral Consciousness and Communicative Action*, translated by Christian Lenhardt and Shierry Weber Nicholsen. Boston: MIT Press, pp. 178–180.

Hacking, Ian. 1985. "Styles of Scientific Reasoning." In *Post-Analytic Philosophy*, edited by John Rajchman and Cornel West. New York: Columbia University Press.

Harding, Sandra. 1987. "The Curious Coincidence of Feminine and African Moralities: Challenges in Feminist Theory." In *Women and Moral Theory*, edited by Eva Feder Kittay and Diana T. Meyers. Totowa, NJ: Rowman and Littlefield.

Hartsock, Nancy. 1983. *Money, Sex and Power: Toward a Feminist Historical Materialism.* New York: Longman.

Held, Virginia. 1993. *Feminist Morality: Transforming Culture, Society and Politics.* Chicago: University of Chicago Press.

Herman, Barbara. 1983. "Integrity and Impartiality." *Monist* 66, 233–250.

Hoagland, Sarah Lucia. 1991. "Some Thoughts About 'Caring.'" In *Feminist Ethics*, edited by Claudia Card. Lawrence: University of Kansas Press.

Houston, Barbara. 1988. "Gilligan and the Politics of a Distinctive Women's Morality." In *Feminist Perspectives: Philosophical Essays on Method and Morals*, edited by Lorraine Code, Sheila Mullett, and Christine Overall. Toronto: University of Toronto Press.

Kant, Immanuel. 1965. *Critique of Pure Reason*, translated by L. W. Beck. New York: St. Martin's Press, p. 177:A133–A134.

Kohlberg, Lawrence. 1982. "A Reply to Owen Flanagan." *Ethics* 92, 513–528.

Kohlberg, Lawrence, Charles Levine, and Alexandra Hewer. 1983. *Moral Stages: A Current Reformulation and Response to Critics.* Basel: S. Karger.

Li, Chenyang. 1994. "The Confucian Concept of *Jen* and the Feminist Ethics of Care: A Comparative Study." *Hypatia* 9:1 (Winter), 70–89.

Mill, John Stuart. 1980. *The Subjection of Women.* Arlington Heights, IL: Harlan Davidson. Originally published in 1869.

Miller, Jean Baker. 1976. *Toward a New Psychology of Women.* Boston: Beacon Press.

Noddings, Nel. 1984. *Caring: A Feminine Approach to Ethics and Moral Education.* Berkeley: University of California Press.

———. 1989. *Women and Evil.* Berkeley: University of California Press.

———. 1990a. "Feminist Fears in Ethics." *Journal of Social Philosophy* 21:2–3 (Fall-Winter), 25–33.

———. 1990b. "A Response." *Hypatia* 5:1 (Spring).

———. 1991. "The Alleged Parochialism of Caring." *American Philosophical Association Newsletter on Feminism and Philosophy* 90:2 (Winter).

Okin, Susan. 1989. "Reason and Feeling in Thinking About Justice." *Ethics* 99:2 (January), 229–249.

O'Neill, Onora. 1984. "Kant After Virtue." *Inquiry* 26, 387–405.

Ruddick, Sara. 1987. "Remarks on the Sexual Politics of Reason." In *Women and Moral Theory*, edited by Eva Feder Kittay and Diana T. Meyers. Totowa, NJ: Rowman and Littlefield.

———. 1989. *Maternal Thinking: Towards a Politics of Peace.* Boston: Beacon Press.

Sandel, Michael. 1982. *Liberalism and the Limits of Justice.* Cambridge: Cambridge University Press.

Sher, George. 1987. "Other Voices, Other Rooms? Women's Psychology and Moral Theory." In *Women and Moral Theory*, edited by Eva Feder Kittay and Diana T. Meyers. Totowa, NJ: Rowman and Littlefield.

Smith, Dorothy. 1974. "Women's Perspective as a Radical Critique of Sociology." *Sociological Inquiry* 44.

Stack, Carol. 1986. "The Culture of Gender: Women and Men of Color." *Signs: Journal of Women in Culture and Society* 11:2 (Winter), 321–324.

Tronto, Joan. 1989. "Women and Caring: What Can Feminists Learn About Morality from Caring?" In *Gender/Body/Knowledge: Feminist Reconstructions of Being and Knowing*, edited by Alison M. Jaggar and Susan R. Bordo. New Brunswick, NJ: Rutgers University Press.

———. 1993. *Moral Boundaries: A Political Argument for the Ethics of Care.* New York: Routledge.

Walker, Lawrence J. 1984. "Sex Differences in the Development of Moral Reasoning." *Child Development* 55:3, 677–691.

Walker, Margaret Urban. 1987. "Moral Particularity." *Metaphilosophy* 18:3–4 (July-October).

———. 1989. "What Does the Different Voice Say? Gilligan's Women and Moral Philosophy." *Journal of Value Inquiry* 23, 123–134.

———. 1991. "Partial Consideration." *Ethics* 101:4 (July), 758–774.

———. 1992. "Moral Understandings: Alternative 'Epistemology' for a Feminist Ethics." In *Explorations in Feminist Ethics: Theory and Practice*, edited by Eve Browning Cole and Susan Coultrap McQuin. Bloomington and Indianapolis: Indiana University Press.

"CONQUERING SELF-CENTEREDNESS"
The Reverend Martin Luther King, Jr.

Sermon Delivered at Dexter Avenue Baptist Church
[11 August 1957]
Montgomery, Ala.

I want to continue the series of sermons this morning that I started several weeks ago. The series dealing with problems of personality integration. This morning our subject is: "Conquering Self-Centeredness." . . . . An individual has not begun to live until he can rise above the narrow horizons of his particular individualistic concerns to the broader concerns of all humanity. And this is one of the big problems of life; that so many people never quite get to the point of rising above self. And so they end up the tragic victims of self-centeredness. They end up the victims of distorted and disrupted personality.

Life has its beginning and its maturity comes into being when an individual rises above self to something greater. Few individuals learn this. And so they go through life merely existing and never living. Now you see signs all along in your everyday life with individuals who are the victims of self-centeredness. They are the people who live an eternal "I." They do not have the capacity to project the "I" into the "Thou." They do not have the mental equipment for an eternal, dangerous and sometimes costly altruism. They live a life of perpetual egotism. And they are the victims all around of the egocentric predicament. They start out, the minute you talk with them, talking about what they can do, what they have done. They're the people who will tell you, before you talk with them five minutes, where they have been and who they know. They're the people who can tell you in a few seconds, how many degrees they have and where they went to school and how much money they have. We meet these people every day. And so this is not a foreign subject. It is not something far off. It is a problem that meets us in everyday life. We meet it in ourselves, we meet in other selves: the problem of self-centeredness.

Now, we can say to a certain extent that persons in this situation are persons who have really never grown up. They are still children, at a point. For you see, a child is inevitably, necessarily egocentric. He is a bundle of his own sensations, clamoring to be cared for. And, to be sure, he has his own social context. He belongs to his mother but he cares for her only because he wants to be fed and protected. He does not care for his mother for her sake but he cares for his mother for his own sake. And so a child is inevitably egocentric, inevitably self-centered. And that is why Dr. Burnham says that during the first six or seven years of development, the ego is dominant within the child. And both in behavior and in attitudes, a child is a victim of self-centeredness. This is a part of the early development of a little child. When

Reprinted from *Sermon delivered at Dexter Avenue Baptist Church* (1957), Writers House.

people become mature, they are to rise above this. I look at my little daughter every day and she wants certain things and when she wants them, she wants them. And she almost cries out, "I want what I want when I want it." She is
40 not concerned about what I think about it or what Mrs. King thinks about it. She wants it. She's a child and that's very natural and normal for a child. She is inevitably self-centered because she's a child.

But when one matures, when one rises above the early years of childhood, he begins to love people for their own sake. He turns himself to higher loyalties. He gives himself to something outside of himself. He gives himself to causes that he lives for and sometimes will even die for. He comes to the point that now he can rise above his individualistic concerns. . . And so you see people who are apparently selfish; it isn't merely an ethical issue but it is a psychological issue. They are the victims of arrested development and they are still
50 children. They haven't grown up. And like a modern novelist says about one of his characters, "Edith is a little country, bounded on the east and the west, on the north and the south, by Edith." And so many people are little countries, bounded all around by themselves and they never quite get out of themselves. And these are the persons who are victimized with arrested development.

Now the consequences, the disruptive effects of such self-centeredness, such egocentric desires are tragic. And we see these every day. At first, it leads to frustration and disillusionment and unhappiness at many points. For usually when people are self-centered, they are self-centered because they are seeking attention, they want to be admired and this is the way they set out to do
60 it. But in the process, because of their self-centeredness, they are not admired; they are mawkish and people don't want to be bothered with them. And so the very thing they seek, they never get. And they end up frustrated and unhappy and disillusioned.

I'm sure you have seen people in life who are so desirous of gaining attention that if they cannot have and gain attention through normal channels, through normal social channels, they will gain it through anti-social means. There are those people who are so desirous of gaining attention that if everybody says, "Yes," they automatically say, "No," in order to be seen and to be heard. They are so self-centered that they must gain attention and they must
70 be seen in order to survive. They want to be admired and in their quest for admiration, they don't gain it and in their failure to gain it, they become frustrated and bewildered and disillusioned.

Also, it leads to extreme sensitiveness. The individual who is self-centered, the individual who is egocentric ends up being very sensitive, a very touchy person. And that is one of the tragic effects of a self-centered attitude, that it leads to a very sensitive and touchy response toward the universe. These are the people you have to handle with kid gloves because they are touchy, they are sensitive. And they are sensitive because they are self-centered. They are too absorbed in self and anything gets them off, anything makes them angry.
80 Anything makes them feel that people are looking over them because of a tragic self-centeredness. That even leads to the point that the individual is

not capable of facing trouble and the hard moments of life. One can become so self-centered, so egocentric that when the hard and difficult moments of life come, he cannot face them because he's too centered in himself. These are the people who cannot face disappointment. These are the people who cannot face being defeated. These are the people who cannot face being criticized. These are the people who cannot face these many experiences of life which inevitably come because they are too centered in themselves. In time, somebody criticizes them, time somebody says something about them that they don't like too well, time they are disappointed, time they are defeated, even in a little game, they end up broken-hearted. They can't stand up under it because they are centered in self.

Then, finally, it can become so morbid that it rises to ominous proportions and leads to a tragic sense of persecution. There are persons who come to the point that they are so self-centered that they end up with a persecution complex and the end result is insanity. They end up thinking that the universe stands against them, that everybody is against them. They are turning around within themselves. They are little solar systems within themselves and they can't see beyond that. As a result of their failure to get out of self, they end up with a persecution complex and sometimes madness and insanity. These are some of the effects of self-centeredness.

Now one will inevitably raise the question: How then do we conquer self-centeredness? How do we get away from this thing that we call self-centeredness? How can we live in this universe with a balance and with a type of perspective that keeps us going smoothly and we are not too absorbed in self? How do we do it? Let me make two or three suggestions and I can assure you that these suggestions will not at all solve the problem. For you will have to solve it, in many points, for yourself. But at least these things, I hope, will give you some guidance.

I think one of the best ways to face this problem of self-centeredness is to discover some cause and some purpose, some loyalty outside of yourself and give yourself to that something. The best way to handle it is not to suppress the ego but to extend the ego into objectively meaningful channels. And so many people are unhappy because they aren't doing anything. They're self-centered because they aren't doing anything. They haven't given themselves to anything and they just move around in their little circles. One of the ways to rise above this self-centeredness is to move away from self and objectify yourself in something outside of yourself. Find some great cause and some great purpose, some loyalty to which you can give yourself and become so absorbed in that something that you give your life to it. Men and women have done this throughout all of the generations. And they have found that necessary ego satisfaction that life presents and that one desires through projecting self in something outside of self. As I said, you don't solve the problem by trying to trample over the ego altogether. That doesn't solve the problem. For you will always have the ego and the ego has certain desires, certain desires for significance. The three great psychoanalysts of this age, of this century pointed

out that there are certain basic desires that human beings have and that they long for and that they seek at any cost. And so for Freud the basic desire was to be loved. Jung would say that the basic desire is to be secure. But then Adler
130 comes along and says the basic desire of human nature is to feel important and a sense of significance. And I think of all of those certainly all are significant, but the one that Adler mentions is probably even more significant than any: that all human beings have a desire to belong and to feel significant and important.

And the way to solve this problem is not to drown out the ego but to find your sense of importance in something outside of the self. And you are then able to live because you have given your life to something outside and something that is meaningful, objectified. You rise above this self-absorption to something outside. We look through history. We see that biography's a running com-
140 mentary of this. . . . We see an Albert Schweitzer who looks at men in dark Africa who have been the victims of colonialism and imperialism and there he gives his life to that. He objectifies himself in this great cause. . . .

This is the way to go through life with a balance, with the proper perspective because you've given yourself to something greater than self. Sometimes it's friends, sometimes it's family, sometimes it's a great cause, it's a great loyalty but give yourself to that something and life becomes meaningful. I've seen people who discovered a great meaning in their jobs and they became so absorbed in that that they didn't have time to become self-centered. They loved their job. . . . And the great prayer that anyone could pray at that
150 point is: "O God, help me to love my job as this individual loves his or hers. O God, help me to give my self to my work and to my job and to my allegiance as this individual does." And this is the way out. And I think this is what [*Ralph Waldo*] Emerson meant when he said: "O, see how the masses of men worry themselves into nameless graves, while here and there, some great unselfish soul forgets himself into immortality." And this becomes a point of balance when you can forget yourself into immortality. You're not so absorbed in self, but you are absorbed in something beyond self.

And there is another way to rise above self-centeredness and that is by having the proper inner attitude toward your position or toward your status in
160 life or whatever it is. You conquer self-centeredness by coming to the point of seeing that you are where you are today because somebody helped you to get there. And so many people, you see, live a self-centered, egocentric life because they have the attitude that they are responsible for everything and for their position in life. For everything they do in life, they feel, somehow, that they are responsible and solely responsible for it.

An individual gets away from this type of self-centeredness when he pauses enough to see that no matter what he does in life, he does that because somebody helped him to do it. And he then gains the type of perspective and the type of balance which keeps him from becoming self-centered. He
170 comes to see that somebody stands in the background, often doing a little job in a big way, making it possible for him to do what he's doing. Can

you believe that? That no matter where you stand, no matter how much popularity you have, no matter how much education you have, no matter how much money you have, you have it because somebody in this universe helped you to get it. And when you see that, you can't be arrogant, you can't be supercilious. You discover that you have your position because of the events of history and because of individuals in the background making it possible for you to stand there.

Would you allow me to share a personal experience with you this morning? And I say it only because I think it has bearing on this message. One of   180
the problems that I have to face and even fight every day is this problem of self-centeredness. This tendency that can so easily come to my life now that I'm something special, that I'm something important. Living over the past year, I can hardly go into any city or any town in this nation where I'm not lavished with hospitality by peoples of all races and of all creeds. I can hardly go anywhere to speak in this nation where hundreds and thousands of people are not turned away because of lack of space. And then after speaking, I often have to be rushed out to get away from the crowd rushing for autographs. I can hardly walk the street in any city of this nation where I'm not confronted with people running up the street, "Isn't this Reverend King of Alabama?"   190
Living under this it's easy, it's a dangerous tendency that I will come to feel that I'm something special, that I stand somewhere in this universe because of my ingenuity and that I'm important, that I can walk around life with a type of arrogance because of an importance that I have. . . . And one of the prayers that I pray to God everyday is: . . . "O God, help me to see that where I stand today, I stand because others helped me to stand there and because the forces of history projected me there. And this moment would have come in history even if M. L. King had never been born." And when we come to see that, we stand with a humility. This is the prayer I pray to God every day, "Lord help me to see M. L. King as M. L. King in his true perspective." Because if I don't   200
see that, I will become the biggest fool in America. . . .

. . . We never get anywhere in this world without the forces of history and individual persons in the background helping us to get there. . . .

. . . And only by seeing this can we rise out. If you have the privilege of a fine education, well, you have it because somebody made it possible. If you have the privilege to gain wealth and a bit of the world's goods, well, you have it because somebody made it possible. So don't boast, don't be arrogant. You, at that moment, rise out of your self-centeredness to the type of living that makes you an integrated personality. . . .

You know, Greek mythology used to talk about the goddess of Nemesis   210   *Nemesis*
and this was one of the functions of the goddess of Nemesis. The goddess of Nemesis kept everything on a common level. If you got too low, beat down and you didn't feel that you were quite up to par, you felt a sense of inadequacy and a sense of inferiority, this goddess would pull you up. And then, if you got too high for yourself, you felt too highly of yourself, you felt too exalted, this goddess would do what the older people used to say, "Pull you

a buttonhole lower." And everything was kept on a common level. And there needs to be something in your life of a goddess of Nemesis which pulls you down when you get too high and pulls you up when you feel the sense of inad-
220   equacy and that is what religion at its best does. It keeps you to the point that you don't feel like you are too low and you don't feel like you are too high but you'll maintain that type of balance. . . .

science

And I'm so glad that the new science did something to dampen our arrogant spirits. For a long time, man felt that he was the center of the universe and all of his science had given him that. All of the days in the past he came up under what was known as the geocentric theory: the earth was the center of the universe and everything revolved around the earth. Then came Copernicus and Galileo and others said that the sun is the center, the heliocentric theory came into being. And that reminded us somehow that we are depen-
230   dent on something. We are not just at the center of this universe. . . .

And I'm so glad that the new science came into being to dampen our arrogance. It says to us that our earthly planet is a dependent planet. It is a small planet in the orbits of this universe. The sun is the center of this universe, that man must look beyond himself to discover his significance. . . .

. . . . And when you take this attitude, you go into the room of your life and take down the mirrors because you cannot any longer see yourself. But the mirrors somehow are transformed into windows and you look out into the objective world and see that you are what you are because of somebody else. . . . He who seeks to find his ego will lose it. But he who loses his ego
240   in some great cause, some great purpose, some great ideal, some great loyalty, he who discovers, somehow, that he stands where he stands because of the forces of history and because of other individuals. . . . And this is the way, it seems to me, to the integrated personality.

Narcissus + Nemesis Greek Myth

SELECTIONS FROM *A SAND COUNTY ALMANAC*
Aldo Leopold

THE LAND ETHIC

When god-like Odysseus returned from the wars in Troy, he hanged all on   1
one rope a dozen slave-girls of his household whom he suspected of misbe-
havior during his absence.

This hanging involved no question of propriety. The girls were property.
The disposal of property was then, as now, a matter of expediency, not of right
and wrong.

Concepts of right and wrong were not lacking from Odysseus' Greece: witness the fidelity of his wife through the long years before at last his black-
prowed galleys clove the wine-dark seas for home. The ethical structure of that
day covered wives, but had not yet been extended to human chattels. During   10
the three thousand years which have since elapsed, ethical criteria have been
extended to many fields of conduct, with corresponding shrinkages in those
judged by expediency only.

The Ethical Sequence

This extension of ethics, so far studied only by philosophers, is actually a
process in ecological evolution. Its sequences may be described in ecological
as well as in philosophical terms. An ethic, ecologically, is a limitation on freedom of action in the struggle for existence. An ethic, philosophically, is a
differentiation of social from anti-social conduct. These are two definitions of
one thing. The thing has its origin in the tendency of interdependent individuals or groups to evolve modes of co-operation. The ecologist calls these   20
symbioses. Politics and economics are advanced symbioses in which the original free-for-all competition has been replaced, in part, by co-operative mechanisms with an ethical content.

The complexity of co-operative mechanisms has increased with population density, and with the efficiency of tools. It was simpler, for example, to
define the anti-social uses of sticks and stones in the days of the mastodons
than of bullets and billboards in the age of motors.

The first ethics dealt with the relation between individuals; the Mosaic
Decalogue is an example. Later accretions dealt with the relation between
the individual and society. The Golden Rule tries to integrate the individual   30
to society; democracy to integrate social organization to the individual.

There is as yet no ethic dealing with man's relation to land and to the
animals and plants which grow upon it. Land, like Odysseus' slave-girls, is still
property. The land-relation is still strictly economic, entailing privileges but
not obligations.

privileges but not obligations

Reprinted from *A Sand Country Almanac* (1947), by permission of Oxford University Press.

111

The extension of ethics to this third element in human environment is, if I read the evidence correctly, an evolutionary possibility and an ecological necessity. It is the third step in a sequence. The first two have already been taken. Individual thinkers since the days of Ezekiel and Isaiah have asserted that the despoliation of land is not only inexpedient but wrong. Society, however, has not yet affirmed their belief. I regard the present conservation movement as the embryo of such an affirmation.

An ethic may be regarded as a mode of guidance for meeting ecological situations so new or intricate, or involving such deferred reactions, that the path of social expediency is not discernible to the average individual. Animal instincts are modes of guidance for the individual in meeting such situations. Ethics are possibly a kind of community instinct in-the-making.

The Community Concept

All ethics so far evolved rest upon a single premise: that the individual is a member of a community of interdependent parts. His instincts prompt him to compete for his place in that community, but his ethics prompt him also to co-operate (perhaps in order that there may be a place to compete for).

The land ethic simply enlarges the boundaries of the community to include soils, waters, plants, and animals, or collectively: the land.

This sounds simple: do we not already sing our love for and obligation to the land of the free and the home of the brave? Yes, but just what and whom do we love? Certainly not the soil, which we are sending helter-skelter downriver. Certainly not the waters, which we assume have no function except to turn turbines, float barges, and carry off sewage. Certainly not the plants, of which we exterminate whole communities without batting an eye. Certainly not the animals, of which we have already extirpated many of the largest and most beautiful species. A land ethic of course cannot prevent the alteration, management, and use of these "resources," but it does affirm their right to continued existence, and, at least in spots, their continued existence in a natural state.

In short, a land ethic changes the role of *Homo sapiens* from conqueror of the land-community to plain member and citizen of it. It implies respect for his fellow-members, and also respect for the community as such.

In human history, we have learned (I hope) that the conqueror role is eventually self-defeating. Why? Because it is implicit in such a role that the conqueror knows, *ex cathedra*, just what makes the community clock tick, and just what and who is valuable, and what and who is worthless, in community life. It always turns out that he knows neither, and this is why his conquests eventually defeat themselves.

In the biotic community, a parallel situation exists. Abraham knew exactly what the land was for: it was to drip milk and honey into Abraham's mouth. At the present moment, the assurance with which we regard this assumption is inverse to the degree of our education.

The ordinary citizen today assumes that science knows what makes the community clock tick; the scientist is equally sure that he does not. He knows that the biotic mechanism is so complex that its workings may never be fully understood.

That man is, in fact, only a member of a biotic team is shown by an ecological interpretation of history. Many historical events, hitherto explained solely in terms of human enterprise, were actually biotic interactions between people and land. The characteristics of the land determined the facts quite as potently as the characteristics of the men who lived on it.

Consider, for example, the settlement of the Mississippi valley. In the years following the Revolution, three groups were contending for its control: the native Indian, the French and English traders, and the American settlers. Historians wonder what would have happened if the English at Detroit had thrown a little more weight into the Indian side of those tipsy scales which decided the outcome of the colonial migration into the cane-lands of Kentucky. It is time now to ponder the fact that the cane-lands, when subjected to the particular mixture of forces represented by the cow, plow, fire, and axe of the pioneer, became bluegrass. What if the plant succession inherent in this dark and bloody ground had, under the impact of these forces, given us some worthless sedge, shrub, or weed? Would Boone and Kenton have held out? Would there have been any overflow into Ohio, Indiana, Illinois, and Missouri? Any Louisiana Purchase? Any transcontinental union of new states? Any Civil War?

Kentucky was one sentence in the drama of history. We are commonly told what the human actors in this drama tried to do, but we are seldom told that their success, or the lack of it, hung in large degree on the reaction of particular soils to the impact of the particular forces exerted by their occupancy. In the case of Kentucky, we do not even know where the bluegrass came from—whether it is a native species, or a stowaway from Europe.

Contrast the cane-lands with what hindsight tells us about the Southwest, where the pioneers were equally brave, resourceful, and persevering. The impact of occupancy here brought no bluegrass, or other plant fitted to withstand the bumps and buffetings of hard use. This region, when grazed by livestock, reverted through a series of more and more worthless grasses, shrubs, and weeds to a condition of unstable equilibrium. Each recession of plant types bred erosion; each increment to erosion bred a further recession of plants. The result today is a progressive and mutual deterioration, not only of plants and soils, but of the animal community subsisting thereon. The early settlers did not expect this: on the ciénegas of New Mexico some even cut ditches to hasten it. So subtle has been its progress that few residents of the region are aware of it. It is quite invisible to the tourist who finds this wrecked landscape colorful and charming (as indeed it is, but it bears scant resemblance to what it was in 1848).

This same landscape was "developed" once before, but with quite different results. The Pueblo Indians settled the Southwest in pre-Columbian times, but they happened *not* to be equipped with range livestock. Their civilization expired, but not because their land expired.

In India, regions devoid of any sod-forming grass have been settled, apparently without wrecking the land, by the simple expedient of carrying the grass to the cow, rather than vice versa. (Was this the result of some deep wisdom, or was it just good luck? I do not know.)

In short, the plant succession steered the course of history; the pioneer simply demonstrated, for good or ill, what successions inhered in the land. Is history taught in this spirit? It will be, once the concept of land as a community really penetrates our intellectual life.

The Ecological Conscience

Conservation is a state of harmony between men and land. Despite nearly a century of propaganda, conservation still proceeds at a snail's pace; progress still consists largely of letterhead pieties and convention oratory. On the back forty we still slip two steps backward for each forward stride.

The usual answer to this dilemma is "more conservation education." No one will debate this, but is it certain that only the *volume* of education needs stepping up? Is something lacking in the *content* as well?

It is difficult to give a fair summary of its content in brief form, but, as I understand it, the content is substantially this: obey the law, vote right, join some organizations, and practice what conservation is profitable on your own land; the government will do the rest.

Is not this formula too easy to accomplish anything worth-while? It defines no right or wrong, assigns no obligation, calls for no sacrifice, implies no change in the current philosophy of values. In respect of land-use, it urges only enlightened self-interest. Just how far will such education take us? An example will perhaps yield a partial answer.

By 1930 it had become clear to all except the ecologically blind that southwestern Wisconsin's topsoil was slipping seaward. In 1933 the farmers were told that if they would adopt certain remedial practices for five years, the public would donate CCC labor to install them, plus the necessary machinery and materials. The offer was widely accepted, but the practices were widely forgotten when the five-year contract period was up. The farmers continued only those practices that yielded an immediate and visible economic gain for themselves.

This led to the idea that maybe farmers would learn more quickly if they themselves wrote the rules. Accordingly the Wisconsin Legislature in 1937 passed the Soil Conservation District Law. This said to farmers, in effect: *We, the public, will furnish you free technical service and loan you specialized machinery, if you will write your own rules for land-use. Each county may write its own rules, and these will have the force of law.* Nearly all the counties promptly organized to accept the proffered help, but after a decade of operation, *no county has yet written a single rule.* There has been visible progress in such practices as strip-cropping, pasture renovation, and soil liming, but none in fencing woodlots against grazing, and none in excluding plow and cow from steep slopes. The farmers, in short, have selected those remedial practices which were profitable anyhow, and ignored those which were profitable to the community, but not clearly profitable to themselves.

When one asks why no rules have been written, one is told that the community is not yet ready to support them; education must precede rules. But the education actually in progress makes no mention of obligations to land over and above those dictated by self-interest. The net result is that we have more education but less soil, fewer healthy woods, and as many floods as in 1937.

The puzzling aspect of such situations is that the existence of obligations over and above self-interest is taken for granted in such rural community enterprises as the betterment of roads, schools, churches, and baseball teams. Their existence is not taken for granted, nor as yet seriously discussed, in bettering the behavior of the water that falls on the land, or in the preserving of the beauty or diversity of the farm landscape. Land-use ethics are still governed wholly by economic self-interest, just as social ethics were a century ago.

To sum up: we asked the farmer to do what he conveniently could to save his soil, and he has done just that, and only that. The farmer who clears the woods off a 75 per cent slope, turns his cows into the clearing, and dumps its rainfall, rocks, and soil into the community creek, is still (if otherwise decent) a respected member of society. If he puts lime on his fields and plants his crops on contour, he is still entitled to all the privileges and emoluments of his Soil Conservation District. The District is a beautiful piece of social machinery, but it is coughing along on two cylinders because we have been too timid, and too anxious for quick success, to tell the farmer the true magnitude of his obligations. Obligations have no meaning without conscience, and the problem we face is the extension of the social conscience from people to land.

No important change in ethics was ever accomplished without an internal change in our intellectual emphasis, loyalties, affections, and convictions. The proof that conservation has not yet touched these foundations of conduct lies in the fact that philosophy and religion have not yet heard of it. In our attempt to make conservation easy, we have made it trivial.

AGE, RACE, CLASS AND SEX:
WOMEN REDEFINING DIFFERENCE
Audre Lorde

*Paper delivered at the Copeland Colloquium, Amerst College,
April 1980*

Reproduced in: Sister Outsider *Crossing Press, California 1984*

Much of Western European history conditions us to see human differences in simplistic opposition to each other: dominant/subordinate,
good/bad, up/down, superior/inferior. In a society where the good is defined
in terms of profit rather than in terms of human need, there must always be
some group of people who, through systematized oppression, can be made
to feel surplus, to occupy the place of the dehumanized inferior. Within this
society, that group is made up of Black and Third World people, working-
class people, older people, and women.

As a forty-nine-year-old Black lesbian feminist socialist mother of two,
including one boy, and a member of an interracial couple, I usually find myself
a part of some group defined as other, deviant, inferior, or just plain wrong.
Traditionally, in american society, it is the members of oppressed, objectified
groups who are expected to stretch out and bridge the gap between the actu-
alities of our lives and the consciousness of our oppressor. For in order to
survive, those of us for whom oppression is as american as apple pie have
always had to be watchers, to become familiar with the language and man-
ners of the oppressor, even sometimes adopting them for some illusion of protection. Whenever the need for some pretense of communication arises, those
who profit from our oppression call upon us to share our knowledge with
them. In other words, it is the responsibility of the oppressed to teach the
oppressors their mistakes. I am responsible for educating teachers who dismiss my children's culture in school. Black and Third World people are
expected to educate white people as to our humanity. Women are expected
to educate men. Lesbians and gay men are expected to educate the heterosexual world. The oppressors maintain their position and evade responsibility for their own actions. There is a constant drain of energy which might be
better used in redefining ourselves and devising realistic scenarios for altering the present and constructing the future.

Institutionalized rejection of difference is an absolute necessity in a profit
economy which needs outsiders as surplus people. As members of such an economy, we have *all* been programmed to respond to the human differences
between us with fear and loathing and to handle that difference in one of
three ways: ignore it, and if that is not possible, copy it if we think it is dominant, or destroy it if we think it is subordinate. But we have no patterns for

Reprinted from *Paper delivered at the Copeland Colloquium, Amherst College* (April 1980), by
permission of Regula Noetzli Literary Agent.

relating across our human differences as equals. As a result, those differences have been misnamed and misused in the service of separation and confusion.

Certainly there are very real differences between us of race, age, and sex. But it is not those differences between us that are separating us. It is rather our refusal to recognize those differences, and to examine the distortions which result from our misnaming them and their effects upon human behavior and expectation.

Racism, the belief in the inherent superiority of one race over all others and thereby the right to dominance. Sexism, the belief in the inherent superiority of one sex over the other and thereby the right to dominance. Ageism. Heterosexism. Elitism. Classism.

It is a lifetime pursuit for each one of us to extract these distortions from our living at the same time as we recognize, reclaim, and define those differences upon which they are imposed. For we have all been raised in a society where those distortions were endemic within our living. Too often, we pour the energy needed for recognizing and exploring difference into pretending those differences are insurmountable barriers, or that they do not exist at all. This results in a voluntary isolation, or false and treacherous connections. Either way, we do not develop tools for using human difference as a springboard for creative change within our lives. We speak not of human difference, but of human deviance.

Somewhere, on the edge of consciousness, there is what I call a *mythical norm*, which each one of us within our hearts knows "that is not me." In america, this norm is usually defined as white, thin, male, young, heterosexual, Christian, and financially secure. It is with this mythical norm that the trappings of power reside within this society. Those of us who stand outside that power often identify one way in which we are different, and we assume that to be the primary cause of all oppression, forgetting other distortions around difference, some of which we ourselves may be practising. By and large within the women's movement today, white women focus upon their oppression as women and ignore differences of race, sexual preference, class, and age. There is a pretense to a homogeneity of experience covered by the word *sisterhood* that does not in fact exist.

Unacknowledged class differences rob women of each others' energy and creative insight. Recently a women's magazine collective made the decision for one issue to print only prose, saying poetry was a less "rigorous" or "serious" art form. Yet even the form our creativity takes is often a class issue. Of all the art forms, poetry is the most economical. It is the one which is the most secret, which requires the least physical labor, the least material, and the one which can be done between shifts, in the hospital pantry, on the subway, and on scraps of surplus paper. Over the last few years, writing a novel on tight finances, I came to appreciate the enormous differences in the material demands between poetry and prose. As we reclaim our literature, poetry has been the major voice of poor, working class, and Colored women. A room of one's own may be a necessity for writing prose, but so are reams of paper, a

[margin handwritten note:] Our own set of categories that we inflict on others is invisible because of our focus on our oppression.

[margin line numbers:] 40 50 60 70

typewriter, and plenty of time. The actual requirements to produce the visual   80
arts also help determine, along class lines, whose art is whose. In this day of
inflated prices for material, who are our sculptors, our painters, our photographers? When we speak of a broadly based women's culture, we need to be aware of the effect of class and economic differences on the supplies available for producing art.

As we move toward creating a society within which we can each flourish, ageism is another distortion of relationship which interferes without vision. *with our* By ignoring the past, we are encouraged to repeat its mistakes. The "generation gap" is an important social tool for any repressive society. If the younger members of a community view the older members as contemptible or suspect or excess, they will never be able to join hands and examine the living   90 memories of the community, nor ask the all important question, "Why?" This gives rise to a historical amnesia that keeps us working to invent the wheel every time we have to go to the store for bread.

We find ourselves having to repeat and relearn the same old lessons over and over that our mothers did because we do not pass on what we have learned, or because we are unable to listen. For instance, how many times has this all been said before? For another, who would have believed that once again our daughters are allowing their bodies to be hampered and purgatoried by girdles and high heels and hobble skirts?   100

Ignoring the differences of race between women and the implications of those differences presents the most serious threat to the mobilization of women's joint power.

As white women ignore their built-in privilege of whiteness and define woman in terms of their own experience alone, then women of Color become "other," the outsider whose experience and tradition is too "alien" to comprehend. An example of this is the signal absence of the experience of women of Color as a resource for women's studies courses. *Not true so much any more* The literature of women of Color is seldom included in women's literature courses and almost never in other literature courses, nor in women's studies as a whole. All too often,   110 the excuse given is that the literatures of women of Color can only be taught by Colored women, or that they are too difficult to understand, or that classes cannot "get into" them because they come out of experiences that are "too different." I have heard this argument presented by white women of otherwise quite clear intelligence, women who seem to have no trouble at all teaching and reviewing work that comes out of the vastly different experiences of Shakespeare, Moliere, Dostoyefsky, and Aristophanes. Surely there must be some other explanation.

This is a very complex question, but I believe one of the reasons white women have such difficulty reading Black women's work is because of their   120 reluctance to see Black women as women and different from themselves. To examine Black women's literature effectively requires that we be seen as whole people in our actual complexities—as individuals, as women, as human—rather than as one of those problematic but familiar stereotypes provided in this society in place of genuine images of Black women. And I believe this holds true for the literatures of other women of Color who are not Black.

The literatures of all women of Color recreate the textures of our lives, and many white women are heavily invested in ignoring the real differences. For as long as any difference between us means one of us must be inferior, then the recognition of any difference must be fraught with guilt. To allow women of Color to step out of stereotypes is too guilt provoking, for it threatens the complacency of those women who view oppression only in terms of sex.

Refusing to recognize difference makes it impossible to see the different problems and pitfalls facing us as women.

Thus, in a patriarchal power system where whiteskin privilege is a major prop, the entrapments used to neutralize Black women and white women are not the same. For example, it is easy for Black women to be used by the power structure against Black men, not because they are men, but because they are Black. Therefore, for Black women, it is necessary at all times to separate the needs of the oppressor from our own legitimate conflicts within our communities. This same problem does not exist for white women. Black women and men have shared racist oppression and still share it, although in different ways. Out of that shared oppression we have developed joint defenses and joint vulnerabilities to each other that are not duplicated in the white community, with the exception of the relationship between Jewish women and Jewish men.

On the other hand, white women face the pitfall of being seduced into joining the oppressor under the pretense of sharing power. This possibility does not exist in the same way for women of Color. The tokenism that is sometimes extended to us is not an invitation to join power; our racial "otherness" is a visible reality that makes that quite clear. For white women there is a wider range of pretended choices and rewards for identifying with patriarchal power and its tools.

Today, with the defeat of ERA, the tightening economy, and increased conservatism, it is easier once again for white women to believe the dangerous fantasy that if you are good enough, pretty enough, sweet enough, quiet enough, teach the children to behave, hate the right people, and marry the right men, then you will be allowed to co-exist with patriarchy in relative peace, at least until a man needs your job or the neighborhood rapist happens along. And true, unless one lives and loves in the trenches it is difficult to remember that the war against dehumanization is ceaseless.

But Black women and our children know the fabric of our lives is stitched with violence and with hatred, that there is no rest. We do not deal with it only on the picket lines, or in dark midnight alleys, or in the places where we dare to verbalize our resistance. For us, increasingly, violence weaves through the daily tissues of our living—in the supermarket, in the classroom, in the elevator, in the clinic and the schoolyard, from the plumber, the baker, the saleswoman, the bus driver, the bank teller, the waitress who does not serve us.

Now this does happen— Condi Rice

Some problems we share as women, some we do not. You fear your chil- 170
dren will grow up to join the patriarchy and testify against you, we fear our
children will be dragged from a car and shot down in the street, and you will
turn your backs upon the reasons they are dying.

The threat of difference has been no less blinding to people of Color. Those
of us who are Black must see that the reality of our lives and our struggle
does not make us immune to the errors of ignoring and misnaming difference. Within Black communities where racism is a living reality, differences
among us often seem dangerous and suspect. The need for unity is often
misnamed as a need for homogeneity, and a Black feminist vision mistaken
for betrayal of our common interests as a people. Because of the continuous 180
battle against racial erasure that Black women and Black men share, some
Black women still refuse to recognize that we are also oppressed as women,
and that sexual hostility against Black women is practiced not only by the
white racist society, but implemented within our Black communities as well.
It is a disease striking the heart of Black nationhood, and silence will not make
it disappear. Exacerbated by racism and the pressures of powerlessness, violence against Black women and children often becomes a standard within
our communities, one by which manliness can be measured. But these womanhating acts are rarely discussed as crimes against Black women.

As a group, women of Color are the lowest paid wage earners in america. 190
We are the primary targets of abortion and sterilization abuse, here and abroad.
In certain parts of Africa, small girls are still being sewed shut between their
legs to keep them docile and for men's pleasure. This is known as female cir-
cumcision, and it is not a cultural affair as the late Jomo Kenyatta insisted, it
is a crime against Black women.

Black women's literature is full of the pain of frequent assault, not only
by a racist patriarchy, but also by Black men. Yet the necessity for and history of shared battle have made us, Black women, particularly vulnerable to
the false accusation that anti-sexist is anti-Black. Meanwhile, womanhating
as a recourse of the powerless is sapping strength from Black communities, 200
and our very lives. Rape is on the increase, reported and unreported, and
rape is not aggressive sexuality, it is sexualized aggression. As Kalamu ya Salaam,
a Black male writer points out, "As long as male domination exists, rape will
exist. Only women revolting and men made conscious of their responsibility
to fight sexism can collectively stop rape."

Differences between ourselves as Black women are also being misnamed
and used to separate us from one another. As a Black lesbian feminist comfortable with the many different ingredients of my identity, and a woman committed to racial and sexual freedom from oppression, I find I am constantly
being encouraged to pluck out some one aspect of myself and present this as 210
the meaningful whole, eclipsing or denying the other parts of self. But this is
a destructive and fragmenting way to live. My fullest concentration of energy
is available to me only when I integrate all the parts of who I am, openly, allowing power from particular sources of my living to flow back and forth freely

through all my different selves, without the restrictions of externally imposed definition. Only then can I bring myself and my energies as a whole to the service of those struggles which I embrace as part of my living.

A fear of lesbians, or of being accused of being a lesbian, has led many Black women into testifying against themselves. It has led some of us into destructive alliances, and others into despair and isolation. In the white women's communities, heterosexism is sometimes a result of identifying with the white patriarchy, a rejection of that interdependence between women-identified women which allows the self to be, rather than to be used in the service of men. Sometimes it reflects a die-hard belief in the protective coloration of heterosexual relationships, sometimes a self-hate which all women have to fight against, taught us from birth.

Although elements of these attitudes exist for all women, there are particular resonances of heterosexism and homophobia among Black women. Despite the fact that woman-bonding has a long and honorable history in the African and Africanamerican communities, and despite the knowledge and accomplishments of many strong and creative women-identified Black women in the political, social and cultural fields, heterosexual Black women often tend to ignore or discount the existence and work of Black lesbians. Part of this attitude has come from an understandable terror of Black male attack within the close confines of Black society, where the punishment for any female self-assertion is still to be accused of being a lesbian and therefore unworthy of the attention or support of the scarce Black male. But part of this need to misname and ignore Black lesbians comes from a very real fear that openly women-identified Black women who are no longer dependent upon men for their self-definition may well reorder our whole concept of social relationships.

Black women who once insisted that lesbianism was a white woman's problem now insist that Black lesbians are a threat to Black nationhood, are consorting with the enemy, are basically un-Black. These accusations, coming from the very women to whom we look for deep and real understanding, have served to keep many Black lesbians in hiding, caught between the racism of white women and the homophobia of their sisters. Often, their work has been ignored, trivialized, or misnamed, as with the work of Angelina Grimke, Alice Dunbar-Nelson, Lorraine Hansberry. Yet women-bonded women have always been some part of the power of Black communities, from our unmarried aunts to the amazons of Dahomey.

And it is certainly not Black lesbians who are assaulting women and raping children and grandmothers on the streets of our communities.

Across this country, as in Boston during the spring of 1979 following the unsolved murders of twelve Black women, Black lesbians are spearheading movements against violence against Black women.

What are the particular details within each of our lives that can be scrutinized and altered to help bring about change? How do we redefine difference for all women? It is not our differences which separate women, but our reluctance to recognize those differences and to deal effectively with the distortions which have resulted from the ignoring and misnaming of those differences.

As a tool of social control, women have been encouraged to recognize only one area of human difference as legitimate, those differences which exist between women and men. And we have learned to deal across those differences with the urgency of all oppressed subordinates. All of us have had to learn to live or work or coexist with men, from our fathers on. We have recognized and negotiated these differences, even when this recognition only continued the old dominant/subordinate mode of human relationship; where the oppressed must recognize the masters' difference in order to survive.   270

But our future survival is predicated upon our ability to relate within equality. As women, we must root out internalized patterns of oppression within ourselves if we are to move beyond the most superficial aspects of social change. Now we must recognize differences among women who are our equals, neither inferior nor superior, and devise ways to use each others' difference to enrich our visions and our joint struggles. The future of our earth may depend upon the ability of all women to identify and develop new definitions of power and new patterns of relating across difference. The old definitions have not served us, nor the earth that supports us. The old patterns, no matter how cleverly rearranged to imitate progress, still condemn us to cosmetically altered   280 repetitions of the same old exchanges, the same old guilt, hatred, recrimination, lamentation, and suspicion.

For we have, built into all of us, old blueprints of expectation and response, old structures of oppression, and these must be altered at the same time as we alter the living conditions which are a result of those structures. For the master's tools will never dismantle the master's house.

As Paulo Freire shows so well in *The Pedagogy of the Oppressed,* the true focus of revolutionary change is never merely the oppressive situations which we seek to escape, but that piece of the oppressor which is planted deep within each of us, and which knows only the oppressors' tactics, the oppressors' relationships.   290

Change means growth, and growth can be painful. But we sharpen self-definition by exposing the self in work and struggle together with those whom we define as different from ourselves, although sharing the same goals. For Black and white, old and young, lesbian and heterosexual women alike, this can mean new paths to our survival.

We have chosen each other
and the edge of each others *battles*
the war *is the same*
if we lose
someday women's blood *will congeal*   300
upon *a dead planet*
if we win
there is no telling
we seek beyond history
for *a new and* more *possible meeting.*

SELECTIONS FROM *IN THE NAME OF IDENTITY*
Amin Maalouf

Identity isn't given once and for all: it is built up and changes throughout a person's lifetime. This has been pointed out in numerous books and amply explained, but it is still worth emphasising again: not many of the elements that go to make up our identity are already in us at birth. A few physical characteristics of course—sex, colour and so on. And even at this point not everything is innate. Although, obviously, social environment doesn't determine sex, it does determine its significance. To be born a girl is not the same in Kabul as it is in Oslo: the condition of being a woman, like every other factor in a person's identity, is experienced differently in the two places.

The same could be said of colour. To be born black is a different matter according to whether you come into the world in New York, Lagos, Pretoria or Luanda. One might almost say that, from the point of view of identity, we're not even talking about the same colour in the different places. For an infant who first sees the light of day in Nigeria, the operative factor as regards his identity is not whether he is black rather than white, but whether he is Yoruba, say, rather than Hausa. In South Africa, whether a person is black or white is still a significant element in his identity, but at least equally meaningful is his ethnic affiliation, whether Zulu, Xhosa or something else. In the United States it's of no consequence whether you have a Yoruba rather than a Hausa ancestor: it's chiefly among the whites—the Italians, the English, the Irish and the rest—that ethnic origin has a determining effect on identity. Moreover, someone with both whites and blacks among his ancestors would be regarded as "black" in the United States, whereas in South Africa or Angola he would be considered as "of mixed race."

Why is the idea of mixed race taken into account in some countries and not in others? Why is ethnic affiliation a determining factor in some societies but not in the rest? One could put forward various more or less convincing answers to both questions. But that is not what concerns me at this stage. I mention these examples only to underline the fact that even colour and sex are not "absolute" ingredients of identity. That being so, all the other ingredients are even more relative.

To gauge what is really innate among the ingredients that go to make up identity, we may make use of a mental exercise which is extremely revealing. Imagine an infant removed immediately from its place of birth and set down in a different environment. Then compare the various "identities" the child might acquire in its new context, the battles it would now have to fight and those it would be spared. Needless to say, the child would have no recollection of his original religion, or of his country or language. And might he not one day find himself fighting to the death against those who ought to have been his nearest and dearest?

Reprinted from *In the Name of Identity: Violence and the Need to Belong* (2000), by permission of Arcade Publishing.

125

What determines a person's affiliation to a given group is essentially the influence of others: the influence of those about him—relatives, fellow-countrymen, co-religionists—who try to make him one of them; together with the influence of those on the other side, who do their best to exclude him. Each one of us has to make his way while choosing between the paths that are urged upon him and those that are forbidden or strewn with obstacles. He is not himself from the outset; nor does he just "grow aware" of what he is; he *becomes* what he is. He doesn't merely grow aware of his identity; he acquires it step by step.

50   The apprenticeship starts very soon, in early childhood. Deliberately or otherwise, those around him mould him, shape him, instil into him family beliefs, rituals, attitudes and conventions, together of course with his native language and also certain fears, aspirations, prejudices and grudges, not forgetting various feelings of affiliation and non-affiliation, belonging and not belonging.

And soon, at home, at school and in the next street, he will suffer his first knocks. By their words and by their looks, other people will make him feel he is poor, or lame, short or lanky, swarthy or too fair, circumcised or uncircumcised, or an orphan; those innumerable differences, major and minor, 60   that define every personality and shape each individual's behaviour, opinions, fears and ambitions. Such factors may act as formative influences, but they can also cause permanent injuries.

It is these wounds that at every stage in life determine not only men's attitudes towards their affiliations but also the hierarchy that decides the relative importance of these ties. When someone has been bullied because of his religion, humiliated or mocked because of the colour of his skin, his accent or his shabby clothes, he will never forget it. Up till now I have stressed the fact that identity is made up of a number of allegiances. But it is just as necessary to emphasise that identity is also singular, something that we experience as a 70   complete whole. A person's identity is not an assemblage of separate affiliations, nor a kind of loose patchwork; it is like a pattern drawn on a tightly stretched parchment. Touch just one part of it, just one allegiance, and the whole person will react, the whole drum will sound.

People often see themselves in terms of whichever one of their allegiances is most under attack. And sometimes, when a person doesn't have the strength to defend that allegiance, he hides it. Then it remains buried deep down in the dark, awaiting its revenge. But whether he accepts or conceals it, proclaims it discreetly or flaunts it, it is with that allegiance that the person concerned identifies. And then, whether it relates to colour, religion, lan-80   guage or class, it invades the person's whole identity. Other people who share the same allegiance sympathise; they all gather together, join forces, encourage one another, challenge "the other side." For them, "asserting their identity" inevitably becomes an act of courage, of liberation.

In the midst of any community that has been wounded, agitators naturally arise. Whether they are hot-heads or cool schemers, their intransigent speeches act as balm to their audience's wounds. They say one shouldn't beg others for respect: respect is a due and must be forced from those who would withhold it. They promise victory or vengeance, they inflame men's minds, sometimes they use extreme methods that some of their brothers may merely have dreamed of in secret. The scene is now set and the war can begin. Whatever happens "the others" will have deserved it. "We" can remember quite clearly "all they have made us suffer" since time immemorial: all the crimes, all the extortion, all the humiliations and fears, complete with names and dates and statistics.

I have lived in a country at war, in a neighbourhood being shelled from a nearby part of the same city. I have spent a night or two in a basement being used as an air-raid shelter, together with my young wife, who was pregnant, and my little son. From outside came the noise of explosions; inside, people exchanged rumours of imminent attack and stories about whole families being put to the sword. So I know very well that fear might make anyone take to crime. If, instead of mere rumours, there had been a real massacre in the neighbourhood where I lived, would I have remained calm and collected? If, instead of spending just a couple of days in that shelter, I had had to stay there for a month, would I have refused to take a gun if it had been put in my hand?

I prefer not to ask myself such questions too often. I had the good luck not to be put to the test; to emerge from the ordeal with my family unharmed, with my hands clean and with a clear conscience. But I speak of "good luck" because things could have turned out very differently if I'd been 16 instead of 26 when the war began in Lebanon. Or if I'd lost someone I loved. Or if I'd belonged to a different social class, or a different community.

After each new ethnic massacre we ask ourselves, quite rightly, how human beings can perpetrate such atrocities. Certain excesses seem incomprehensible; the logic behind them indecipherable. So we talk of murderous folly, of bloodthirsty ancestral or hereditary madness. In a way, we are right to talk of madness. When an otherwise normal man is transformed overnight into a killer, that is indeed insanity. But when there are thousands, millions of killers; when this phenomenon occurs in one country after another, in different cultures, among the faithful of all religions and among unbelievers alike, it's no longer enough to talk of madness. What we conveniently call "murderous folly" is the propensity of our fellow-creatures to turn into butchers when they suspect that their "tribe" is being threatened. The emotions of fear or insecurity don't always obey rational considerations. They may be exaggerated or even paranoid; but once a whole population is afraid, we are dealing with the reality of the fear rather than the reality of the threat.

I don't think any particular affiliation, be it ethnic, religious, national or anything else, predisposes anyone to murder. We have only to review the events of the last few years to see that any human community that feels humiliated or fears for its existence will tend to produce killers. And these killers will commit the most dreadful atrocities in the belief that they are right to do so and deserve the admiration of their fellows in this world and bliss in the next. There is a Mr. Hyde inside each one of us. What we have to do is prevent the conditions occurring that will bring the monster forth.

I shall not venture to propose a universal explanation of all the massacres, still less to suggest a miracle cure. I no more believe in simplistic solutions than I do in simplistic identities. The world is a complex machine that can't be dismantled with a screwdriver. But that shouldn't prevent us from observing, from trying to understand, from discussing, and sometimes suggesting a subject for reflection.

The theme that runs like a thread through the tapestry of this book might be formulated as follows: if the men of all countries, of all conditions and faiths can so easily be transformed into butchers, if fanatics of all kinds manage so easily to pass themselves off as defenders of identity, it's because the "tribal" concept of identity still prevalent all over the world facilitates such a distortion. It's a concept inherited from the conflicts of the past, and many of us would reject it if we examined it more closely. But we cling to it through habit, from lack of imagination or resignation, thus inadvertently contributing to the tragedies by which, tomorrow, we shall be genuinely shocked.

4

From the very beginning of this book I have been speaking of murderous or mortal identities. Identities that kill. The expression doesn't strike me as inappropriate insofar as the idea I'm challenging—the notion that reduces identity to one single affiliation—encourages people to adopt an attitude that is partial, sectarian, intolerant, domineering, sometimes suicidal, and frequently even changes them into killers or supporters of killers. Their view of the world is biased and distorted. Those who belong to the same community as we do are "ours," we like to think ourselves concerned about what happens to them, but we also allow ourselves to tyrannise over them: if they are thought to be "lukewarm" we denounce them, intimidate them, punish them as "traitors" and "renegades." As for the others, those on the opposite side, we never try to put ourselves in their place, we take good care not to ask ourselves whether on some point or other they might not be entirely in the wrong, and we won't let our hearts be softened by their complaints, their sufferings or the injustices that have been inflicted on them. The only thing that counts is the point of view of "our" side; a point of view that is often that of the most militant, the most demagogic and the most fanatical members of the community.

On the other hand, when one sees one's own identity as made up of a number of allegiances, some linked to an ethnic past and others not, some linked to a religious tradition and others not; when one observes in oneself, in

one's origins and in the course one's life has taken, a number of different con- 170
fluences and contributions, of different mixtures and influences, some of
them quite subtle or even incompatible with one another; then one enters into
a different relationship both with other people and with one's own "tribe." It's
no longer just a question of "them" and "us": two armies in battle order
preparing for the next confrontation, the next revenge match. From then on
there are people on "our" side with whom I ultimately have little in common,
while on "their" side there are some to whom I might feel very close.

But to return to the earlier state of mind, it's easy to imagine how it can
drive people to the worst kind of extremities: if they feel that "others" represent a threat to their own ethnic group or religion or nation, anything they
might do to ward off that danger seems to them entirely legitimate. Even 180
when they commit massacres they are convinced they are merely doing what
is necessary to save the lives of their nearest and dearest. And as this attitude
is shared by those around them, the butchers often have a clear conscience
and are amazed to hear themselves described as criminals. How can they be
criminals when all they are doing is protecting their aged mothers, their
brothers and sisters and children?

The feeling that they are fighting for the survival of their own loved ones
and are supported by their prayers; the belief that if not in the present
instance at least over the long term they can claim to be acting in legitimate
self-defence: these characteristics are common to all those who in recent 190
years, throughout the world, from Rwanda to former Yugoslavia, have committed the most abominable crimes.

We are not talking about isolated examples. The world is full of whole
communities that are wounded—either enduring present persecution or still
overshadowed by the memory of former sufferings—and who dream of
exacting revenge. We cannot remain unmoved by their martyrdom; we can
only sympathise with their desire to speak their own language freely, to practise their own religion without fear, and to preserve their own traditions. But
compassion sometimes tends towards complaisance: those who have suffered
from colonialist arrogance, racism and xenophobia are forgiven for excesses 200
they themselves have committed because of their own nationalistic arrogance, their own racism and xenophobia. This attitude means we turn a blind
eye to the fate of their victims, at least until rivers of blood have been shed.

The fact is, it's difficult to say where legitimate affirmation of identity 5
ends and encroachment on the rights of others begins. Did I not say that the
word identity was a "false friend"? It starts by reflecting a perfectly permissible aspiration, then before we know where we are it has become an instrument of war. The transition from one meaning to the other is imperceptible,
almost natural, and sometimes we all just go along with it. We are denouncing an injustice, we are defending the rights of a suffering people—then the 210
next day we find ourselves accomplices in a massacre.

All the massacres that have taken place in recent years, like most of
the bloody wars, have been linked to complex and long-standing "cases" of

identity. Sometimes the victims are forever desperately the same; sometimes the situation is reversed and the victimisers of yesterday become victims of today; or vice versa. Such words themselves, it must be said, are meaningful only to outside observers; for people directly involved in conflicts arising out of identity, for those who have suffered and been afraid, nothing else exists except "them" and "us," the insult and the atonement. "We" are necessarily
220   and by definition innocent victims; "they" are necessarily guilty and have long been so, regardless of what they may be enduring at present.

And when we, the outside observers, go in for this game and cast one community in the role of the sheep and another in that of the wolf, what we are unwittingly doing is granting the former community impunity in advance for its crimes. In recent conflicts some factions have even committed atrocities against their own people, knowing that international opinion would automatically lay the blame on their opponents.

This first type of complacency carries with it another, equally unfortunate form, whereby, at each new massacre arising out of identity, the eternal scep-
230   tics immediately declare that things have been the same since the dawn of history, and that it would be naive and self-deluding to hope they might change. Ethnic massacres are sometimes treated, consciously or otherwise, like collective crimes of passion, regrettable but comprehensible, and anyway inevitable because they are "inherent in human nature."

The *laisser-tuer* attitude has already done great harm, and the realism invoked to justify it is in my opinion a misnomer. Unfortunately the "tribal" notion of identity is still the one most commonly accepted everywhere, not only amongst fanatics. But many ideas that have been commonly accepted for centuries are no longer admissible today, among them the "natural"
240   ascendancy of men over women, the hierarchy between races, and even, closer to home, apartheid and the various other kinds of segregation. Torture, too, was for a long time regarded as a "normal" element in the execution of justice. For centuries, slavery seemed like a fact of life, and great minds of the past took care not to call it into question.

Then new ideas gradually managed to establish themselves: that every man had rights that must be defined and respected; that women should have the same rights as men; that nature too deserved to be protected; that the whole human race has interests in common in more and more areas—the environment, peace, international exchanges, the battle against the great
250   scourges of disease and natural disaster; that others might and even should interfere in the internal affairs of countries where fundamental human rights are abused. And so on.

In other words, ideas that have hitherto prevailed throughout history are not necessarily those that ought to prevail in times to come. When new facts emerge we need to reconsider our attitudes and habits. Sometimes, when such facts emerge too rapidly, our mental attitudes can't keep up with them and we find ourselves trying to fight fires by pouring oil on them.

But in the age of globalisation and of the ever-accelerating intermingling of elements in which we are all caught up, a new concept of identity is needed, and needed urgently. We cannot be satisfied with forcing billions of bewildered human beings to choose between excessive assertion of their identity and the loss of their identity altogether, between fundamentalism and disintegration. But that is the logical consequence of the prevailing attitude on the subject. If our contemporaries are not encouraged to accept their multiple affiliations and allegiances; if they cannot reconcile their need for identity with an open and unprejudiced tolerance of other cultures; if they feel they have to choose between denial of the self and denial of the other—then we shall be bringing into being legions of the lost and hordes of bloodthirsty madmen.

But let us return for a moment to some examples I quoted at the beginning of this book. A man with a Serbian mother and a Croatian father, and who manages to accept his dual affiliation, will never take part in any form of ethnic "cleansing." A man with a Hutu mother and a Tutsi father, if he can accept the two "tributaries" that brought him into the world, will never be a party to butchery or genocide. And neither the Franco-Algerian lad, nor the young man of mixed German and Turkish origin whom I mentioned earlier, will ever be on the side of the fanatics if they succeed in living peacefully in the context of their own complex identity.

Here again it would be a mistake to see such examples as extreme or unusual. Wherever there are groups of human beings living side by side who differ from one another in religion, colour, language, ethnic origin or nationality; wherever there are tensions, more or less longstanding, more or less violent, between immigrants and local populations, Blacks and Whites, Catholics and Protestants, Jews and Arabs, Hindus and Sikhs, Lithuanians and Russians, Serbs and Albanians, Greeks and Turks, English-speaking and French-speaking Canadians, Flemings and Walloons, Chinese and Malays—yes, wherever there is a divided society, there are men and women bearing within them contradictory allegiances, people who live on the frontier between opposed communities, and whose very being might be said to be traversed by ethnic or religious or other fault lines.

We are not dealing with a handful of marginal people. There are thousands, millions of such men and women, and there will be more and more of them. They are frontier-dwellers by birth, or through the changes and chances of life, or by deliberate choice, and they can influence events and affect their course one way or the other. Those who can accept their diversity fully will hand on the torch between communities and cultures, will be a kind of mortar joining together and strengthening the societies in which they live. On the other hand, those who cannot accept their own diversity may be among the most virulent of those prepared to kill for the sake of identity, attacking those who embody that part of themselves which they would like to see forgotten. History contains many examples of such self-hatred. . . .

And this not only as regards appearance, clothes, behaviour, way of life, work, habitat and the objects that surround us, but also as regards moral concepts and habits of thought.

The same applies to belief. We may call ourselves Christians—or Muslims, Jews, Buddhists or Hindus—but our vision of both this world and the next no longer bears much resemblance to that of our "co-religionists" who lived 500 years ago. For the great majority of them, Hell was as real a place as Asia Minor or Abyssinia, complete with cloven-hoofed devils thrusting sinners into eternal fire, as in apocalyptic paintings. Practically no one thinks like that now. The example I chose was extreme, but the observation itself applies equally well to all our ideas in every field. Many types of behaviour that are perfectly acceptable to a believer today would have struck his "co-religionists" in the past as inconceivable. I put the word in quotes because the religion practised by our ancestors was not the same as ours. If we had lived among them and behaved as we do nowadays we would have been stoned in the street, thrown into prison or burned at the stake for impiety, debauchery, heresy or witchcraft.

In short, each one of us has two heritages, a "vertical" one that comes to us from our ancestors, our religious community and our popular traditions, and a "horizontal" one transmitted to us by our contemporaries and by the age we live in. It seems to me that the latter is the more influential of the two, and that it becomes more so every day. Yet this fact is not reflected in our perception of ourselves, and the inheritance we invoke most frequently is the vertical one.

This is an essential point with regard to current concepts of identity. On the one hand there is what we are in reality and what we are becoming as a result of cultural globalisation: that is to say, beings woven out of many-coloured threads, who share most of their points of reference, their ways of behaving and their beliefs with the vast community of their contemporaries. And on the other hand there is what we think we are and what we claim to be: that is to say, members of one community rather than another, adherents of one faith rather than another. I do not deny the importance of our religious, national or other affiliations. I do not question the often decisive influence of our vertical heritage. But it is necessary at this point in time to draw attention to the gulf that exists between what we are and what we think we are.

To tell the truth, if we assert our differences so fiercely it is precisely because we are less and less different from one another. Because, in spite of our conflicts and our age-old enmities, each day that goes by reduces our differences and increases our likenesses a little bit more.

I seem to be glad of this. But should one rejoice to see people growing more and more like one another? Are we heading for an insipid world where we may soon speak only one language, where everyone shares the same bunch of minimal beliefs, and where everyone watches the same American TV soaps, munching the same sandwiches?

Caricature aside, the question needs to be seriously addressed. We are living in a very bewildering age, in which many of our fellow-creatures see globalisation not as a great and enriching amalgam with advantages for all, but as a standardisation and an impoverishment, a threat that the individual needs to fight against in order to preserve his own culture, identity and values.

5

350

These may be merely rear-guard actions, but in present circumstances we must have the humility to admit we don't really know. We may not always find what we expect in the dustbins of history. In any case, if so many people see globalisation as a threat it is only natural that we should examine it more closely.

Those who feel themselves to be in danger may of course be influenced in part by the fear of change that is as old as mankind itself. But there are other, more current anxieties which I'd hesitate to dismiss as irrelevant. For globalisation draws us simultaneously towards two contrasting results, one welcome and the other not: i.e., universality and uniformity. The two tracks seem so alike and are so closely intermingled it's as if there were only one. You might almost wonder if one isn't just the presentable face of the other.

360

But for my part I'm sure there are two separate tracks, however much and however closely they intertwine. It would be over-optimistic to try to unravel the whole skein at once, but we might well attempt to tease out a thread or two.

I wonder if the realization of what is being lost will ever manifest itself in a pc'ish norm of cultural maintenance. "And of course we attend to both Bill's polka classes and my Irish knitting club - the children say they don't know why we bother, but we make them go anyway just like we promised at the altar."

WTL 10/26/11
Def. equality men + women

My definition of equality is that the value of each individual
to the community as a whole is recognized. There is room for
difference, even gendered difference, but the biological
imperative of diversity of traits is recognized as a binding
moral contract against abuse/neglect of the talents of any/all.

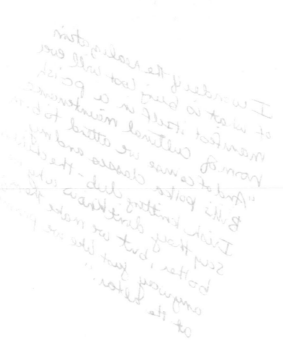

INDIVIDUALISM: A NEW VIEW OF FEMINISM
Wendy McElroy

From a talk presented for the Institute for Humane Studies, at Marymount University, Arlington, Virginia, on June 22, 2001.

Women are the equals of men and should be treated as such.   1

For most people, the foregoing statement is the core of what feminism means. But what is equal? How is equality defined?

For example, does it mean equality under existing laws and equal representation in existing institutions? Or does it involve a socio-economic equality—a redistribution of wealth and power—that, in turn, requires new laws and an overturning of existing institutions. It could involve cultural equality by which women are accorded the same level of respect as men with sexual harassment laws, for example, enforcing that respect.

The manner in which the word "equality" is defined is a litmus test by   10
which different schools of feminism can be distinguished from each other.

Throughout the 19th century, the mainstream of American feminism defined "equality" as equal treatment with men under existing laws and equal representation within existing institutions. More revolutionary feminists protested that the existing laws and institutions were the source of injustice and, as such, could not be reformed. The system had to be swept away before women's rights could be secured.

In simplistic terms, the two more revolutionary traditions were socialist feminism, from which contemporary radical feminism draws heavily, and individualist feminism, which is sometimes called libertarian feminism. These   20
two traditions differed dramatically in their approaches to equality.

To socialist feminism, equality was a socioeconomic term. Women could be equal only after private property and the economic relationships it encouraged—that is, capitalism—were eliminated. Equality was also a cultural goal. The 19th century parallel to the 20th century rebellion against 'white male culture'—against pornography, for example—is to be found in the 19th century social purity crusades over such issues as temperance. The social purity campaigns attempted to impose 'virtue'—that is, to impose a morally proper behavior upon society through the force of law—in much the same way that modern feminism attempts to impose political correctness.   30

To individualist feminism, equality was achieved when the individual rights of women were fully acknowledged under laws that identically protected the person and property of men and women. It made no reference to being economically or socially equal, only to equal treatment under the laws that governed society in such a manner as to protect person and property.

In an ideal society, the legal system would make no distinction based upon secondary characteristics, such as sex, but would protect the rights each individual equally. Women would neither be oppressed by nor receive any privileges under the law. This society does not exist. As long as the law distinguishes between the sexes, women need to stand up and demand their full and equal rights. No more, no less. This demand forms the political crux of individualist feminism.

This article focuses on the two revolutionary forms of feminism, which are diametrically opposite to each other ideologically and define the two extremes of feminism: radical feminism and individualist feminism.

Speaking in 20th century terms, how do they define equality? For radical feminism, equality is socio-economic and cultural. That is, the class distinctions between the genders must be eliminated so that men and women can enjoy social, economic, political and sexual parity. To achieve this, it is necessary to sweep away patriarchy, which is a combination of white male culture and capitalism.

For individualist feminism, equality still means equal treatment of men and women under laws that protect person and property. Individualist feminism says nothing about whether the resulting wealth should be spread equally between the sexes. That kind of division could only be achieved through the imposition of law, through State intervention over people's lives and property. This is precisely what individualist feminism opposes—the use of force in society.

Let me provide an example of why this last statement is as revolutionary. Consider the issue of marriage. Mainstream feminism says, "Reform divorce laws to make them just." Individualist feminism says, "the very existence of marriage/divorce laws is an injustice because the State has no proper authority over what should be a private contract between individuals."

The word "just" has appeared. Briefly, I want to consider how the two forms of feminism approach the concept of justice.

Radical feminism approaches justice as an end state; by which I mean, it provides a specific picture of what constitutes a just society. A just society would be one without patriarchy or capitalism in which the socio-economic and cultural equality of women was fully expressed. In other words, justice is a specific end state in which society embodies specific economic, political and cultural arrangements. It says employers shall pay men and women equally, no one should publish pornography, sexual comments in the workplace must be outlawed.

By contrast, the individualist feminist approach to justice is means-oriented: that is it refers primarily to methodology. The methodology is "anything that is peaceful." The only end-state individualist feminism envisions is the protection of person and property—that is, the removal of force and fraud from society.

Otherwise stated, justice is not embodied in a specifically defined end-state: whatever society results from the free and peaceful choices of individuals are, *politically-speaking*, a just society. Aspects of the society may not be moral and individualist feminists may use education, protest, boycott, and

Peace defined as the absence, not only of compulsion, not of the presence of justice

The artificial destruction between persuasion and force; ignoring power imbalances that make suasion a tilted playing field.

moral suasion—the whole slate of persuasive strategies—to affect change. What they will not do is use force in the form of government law to restrict peaceful choices.

The conflicting concepts of justice between radical and individualist feminism highlight one of the key differences in their approach to social problems: namely, the willingness of socialist or radical feminists to use the State. This difference is not surprising when you realize that the radical feminist ideal of justice *can* by established by the use of force, by the State. You can, for example, impose a specific economic arrangement on society. You can arrest people for overcharging or for bad hiring practices. But you cannot use force to impose a purely voluntary society: it is a contradiction in terms.

Leaving theory, I want to provide a sense of the unique history of individualist feminism within America.

As an organized force, feminism can be dated from the abolitionist movement that arose in the early 1830s. And the two dominant ideological influences on the feminism that arose were Quakerism and individualism. Many courageous women advanced the status of women prior to that date. For example, in the 17th century, Anne Hutchinson led the first organized attack on the Puritan orthodoxy of the Massachusetts Bay Colony. But these women spoke out as individuals rather than as part of a self-conscious movement dedicated to women's rights.

Abolitionism was the radical anti-slavery movement that demanded the immediate cessation of slavery on the grounds that every human being was a self-owner: every human being had a moral jurisdiction over his or her own body.

Gradually, abolitionist women began to apply the principle of self-ownership to themselves. The abolitionist feminist Abbie Kelley observed: "We have good cause to be grateful to the slave, for the benefit we have received to ourselves, in working for him. In striving to strike his irons off, we found most surely that we were manacled ourselves."

Within abolitionism, women's rights stirred hot debate. Perhaps the strongest advocate of women's rights was the libertarian William Lloyd Garrison, editor of the Liberator, who insisted that anti-slavery was a battle for human rights, not male rights.

Then, a watershed event occurred: the 1840 World Anti-Slavery Conference in London, England. The abolitionist feminism Elizabeth Cady Stanton, who attended the 1840 World Anti-Slavery Conference in London, was embittered by the dismissive treatment women received from the less-enlightened Englishmen. Garrison, who also attended, had been so outraged that he withdrew from the floor to the curtained off section to which the women were relegated.

Later, with the Quaker Lucretia Mott, Stanton planned the 1848 Seneca Falls Convention to discuss women's rights. There, women's suffrage resolution was introduced: "Resolved, that it is the duty of the women of this country to secure to themselves their sacred right to the elective franchise." The

resolution met strong resistance from Mott and other members of the old
guard of abolitionist feminists who were deeply opposed to using govern-
130 ment to solve social problems. But it passed.

Unfortunately for the American individualist tradition—in all its
manifestations—the Civil War erupted. If 'War is the health of state', as Ran-
dolph Bourne claimed, then it is the death of individualism. There are many
reasons for this; one of them being that individualism is, at its roots, an anti-
Statist ideology, and war involves an increase in State power that never seems
to roll back to its prewar level when peace is declared.

After the war, the key issue for feminism became the Constitution;
women wished to be included in the wording of the Fourteenth and Fifteenth Amendments that aimed at securing freedom for blacks. The Four-
140 teenth Amendment introduced the word "male" into the United States Constitution. The Fifteenth Amendment assured that the right to vote could not
be abridged because of "race, color, or previous condition of servitude." It
made no reference to sex. The abolitionist women felt betrayed. Susan B.
Anthony wrote, "We repudiated man's counsels forever." This became a pivotal point at which mainstream feminism became alienated from men.

At this juncture, the feminist movement diversified, with the mainstream
focusing its efforts into a drive for woman's suffrage. Other feminists were
suspicious of political solutions to social problems.

Individualist feminism found expression within a variety of social move-
150 ments, especially free love, free thought, and individualist anarchism. There,
these feminists functioned as a radical segment, where they represented and
pursued the interests of women.

The most important vehicle was the free love movement that sought to
separate the State from sexual matters such as marriage, adultery, divorce, and
birth control. Free love demanded that such matters be left to the conscience
and contracts of those involved. Consider free love, very briefly. . .

In 1889, a woman who had just risked her life in a self-induced abortion
wrote to the libertarian periodical, *Lucifer the Light Bearer*, pleading:

"I know I am dreadful wicked, but I am sure to be in the condition from
160 which I risked my life to be free, and I cannot stand it. . . Would you know
of any appliance that will prevent conception? If there is anything reliable,
you will save my life by telling me of it."

The woman wrote to Lucifer—published and edited by Moses Harman—
because, in the late 1800s, it was one of the few forums openly promoting birth
control. Moses Harman insisted that woman's self-ownership fully acknowledged in all sexual arrangements.

Unfortunately, Harman ran counter to the Comstock Act (1873), which
prohibited the mailing of obscene matter but did not define what constituted
obscenity. Whatever it was, it specifically included contraceptives and birth
170 control information. A witchhunt ensued.

Against this backdrop, Harman began his "free word" policy by which
he refused to edit correspondence to Lucifer that contained explicit lan-

guage. Harman maintained, "Words are not deeds, and it is not the province of civil law to take preventative measures against remote or possible consequences of words, no matter how violent or incendiary." He openly discussed birth control.

In 1887, the staff of Lucifer was arrested for the publication of three letters and indicted on 270 counts of obscenity. One letter had described the plight of a woman whose husband forced sex upon her even though it tore the stitches from a recent operation. It is a very early analysis of forced sex within marriage constituting rape.

Harman's legal battles against the Comstock laws continued from 1887 through to 1906, his last imprisonment during which he spent a year at hard labor, often breaking rocks for eight hours a day in the Illinois snow. Harman was 75 at the time."

Interestingly, when the authorities came to arrest Harman in 1887, his 16-year old daughter Lillian was not present. She was in jail herself, having been arrested for engaging in a private marriage—that is, a marriage that consisted of a private contract, without Church or State involvement. At that ceremony, Moses had refused to give his daughter away, stating that she was the owner of her person.

The Harman episode is not a tale of individualist feminism because he championed birth control. A number of traditions did that. Harman was an individualist feminist because of the ideology and methodology he used. He based his arguments on women's self-ownership and extended this principle to all arrangements, sexual and economic. He refused to use the State in personal relationships because he considered it to be the institutionalization of force in society. He actively opposed laws that restricted peaceful behavior.

Moses Harman—along with Voltairine de Cleyre—are the most prominent figures from the 19th century. In their own time, such figures as Harman were well recognized by contemporary radicals. Emma Goldman in her autobiography "Living My Life" credited him with being a pioneer who made her birth control work possible. In 1907, when George Bernard Shaw was asked why he did not tour America, he replied if the "brigands" could imprison Moses Harman for expressing basically the same views set forth, in his play *Man and Superman* he did not care to come to America and test his luck. It is a travesty that he is forgotten today.

So with a small taste of history, let's move back to theory.

Arguably, the most important concept in feminism today is "class." There are men, there are women, they are separate classes. . . or so the theory goes.

The foregoing statement is different than the tradition "war between the sexes." That war refers to the fact that, in the same circumstances, men and women often want different things and, so, come into conflict. For example, on a date men are typically said to want sex whereas women are said to seek a relationship. This is not the conflict to which I am referring. I am talking about a war of the gender.

A class is nothing more than an arbitrary grouping of entities that share common characteristics as determined from a certain epistemological point of view. In short, what constitutes a class is defined by the purposes of the definer. For example, a researcher studying drug addiction may break society into classes of drug using and non-drug using people. Classes can be defined by almost any factor salient to the definer.

For radical feminists, gender is the salient factor. Many fields of endeavor use biology as a dividing line. For example, medicine often separates the sexes in order to apply different medical treatment and techniques. Women are examined for breast cancer and men for prostate problems. But medicine does not claim that the basic interests of men and women as human beings conflict or even diverge. The sexes share a basic biology that requires the same approach of nutrition, exercise and common sense lifestyle choices. In short, although the biology of the sexes differs, they share the same goal of good health, which can be defined and pursued in roughly the same manner.

By contrast, radical feminism advocates a theory of fundamental class conflict based on gender. It claims that males not only share a biological identity but also a political and social one. The political interests of men are in necessary conflict with those of women.

The concept of class conflict is widely associated with Karl Marx, who popularized it as a tool to predict the political interests and social behavior of individuals. Once the class affiliation of an individual was known, his or her behavior became predictable. To Marx, the salient feature defining a person's class was his relationship to the means of production: was he a capitalist or a worker? This is a form of relational class analysis that describes a class in terms of its relationship to an institution.

Radical feminism has adapted this theory. Catherine MacKinnon refers to the analysis as "post-Marxist." By this, she means that radical feminism embraces many aspects of Marxism but rejects its insistence that economic status, not gender, is the salient political factor that determines a class. Thus, radical feminism incorporates such Marxist/socialist ideas as "surplus labor" through which one class is said to use the free market in order to commit economic theft upon another class. (An example of surplus labor in radical feminism is unsalaried housework.) The classification 'male' becomes so significant that it predicts and determines how the individuals within that class will behave. Thus, radical feminists can level accusations of "rapist" at non-violent men because they are beneficiaries of 'the rape culture' established by patriarchy.

To prevent the oppression of women, it is necessary to deconstruct the institutions through which men control women—institutions such as the free market.

This class analysis makes no sense within the framework of individualist feminism that declares all human beings to have the same political interests.

Individualism has a long and differing tradition of class analysis. The salient factor by which people are categorized is whether he or she uses force in society. Do they acquire wealth or power through merit and productivity or do they use aggression, often in the form of law, to appropriate wealth and power from others? Expressed in the most basic form, individualist feminism asks, "are you a member of the political or productive class?" This, too, is a form of relational class analysis because it asks, "What is your relationship to the State?"

Individualist feminism class analysis does not predict the behavior of individuals. Both men and women can use the political means. An individual can change his or her class affiliation at will, abandoning the use of force and adopting the economic means instead. In short, classes within individualist feminist analysis are fluid. This is not true of radical feminist analysis that is based on biology. Within radical feminism, classes are static.   270

This difference has many implications. One is that individualist feminist class analysis offers no predictive value. Just because an individual has been a member of the political class in the past says nothing about whether he or she will continue to be so in the future.

This fluidity has a further implication. Namely, there is no necessary conflict between the genders. The fact that men have oppressed women in the past says nothing about whether they will oppress women in the future. Whether an individual man is an oppressor or a friend depends on whether he uses the political means and this is a matter of his conscious choice. Men are not the enemy.   280

CONCLUSION

Radical and individualist feminism constitute the two extremes of the feminist movement. One advocates state-control; the other, self-control. One considers men to be the enemy; the other embraces men as valued partners. But the most important feature of the ideological divide is individualist feminism's insistence on applying the radically personal principle "A woman's body, a woman's right" across the board to all issues.   290

⟶ typo?

WHAT'S SO GOOD ABOUT A COLLEGE EDUCATION?
Andrew P. Mills[1]

W hy is it good to go to college? What is so valuable about a college edu- 1
cation? College is expensive, and you wouldn't spend all that money
on something that wasn't valuable. Moreover, college requires a great deal of
work, and it requires that you spend time reading and writing and studying
and going to class and taking tests—time that you could spend doing other
things—and you wouldn't spend your time on all those college-related tasks
unless you thought you were getting something valuable for all your effort.
You are in college, and so you think that getting a college education is a good
thing—that it is valuable in some way or other—but what sort of value does
it have? It's worthwhile to spend some time thinking about the answer to this 10
question, for it will affect the way you spend your time at college, and it will
affect the sort of education that you get there. If you don't know why college
is valuable, you're very likely wasting your time and money and effort during
your college years.

Most people give what I will call the simple "Can Opener Answer" to this
question. I think there are two serious problems with that answer, and that is
what I want to convince you of. Once we see what is wrong with the simple
Can Opener Answer, we can talk about some of the differences between high
school and college, and the right way to approach your college education.

THE CAN OPENER ANSWER

Why is it good to have a can opener? People pay money for can openers, and 20
people spend time with can openers, so they must think that can openers are
valuable in some way or other, but how are they valuable? The answer here is
easy: can openers are valuable because they allow you to open cans. There's
tasty stuff inside of cans, and you can't get at the tasty stuff unless the can is
open, and you can't open the can unless you've got a can opener. If you could
open cans by snapping your fingers, then you wouldn't need a can opener.
Can openers are *tools:* they are valuable, but only as tools or instruments are
valuable. That is, they are valuable because of what you can get with them.
Once we acquire the ability to open cans by snapping our fingers, or once
they stop hiding the tasty stuff inside of cans, then can openers will be use- 30
less. They will cease to have the sort of value they now have.[2]

So what's the Can Opener Answer to the question about the value of college? It's this: a college education is valuable because of what you can do with
it. In particular, it's valuable because you can trade it for a job. Crudely put,
you can take your diploma, show it to an employer, and then you'll get a job.
Of course the job interview process is not that easy, but in rough outline
that's how many people (maybe even you!) think about the value of a college

education. I hope you can see the analogy with the can opener case. The job is the analogue of the tasty stuff in the can. If you could get a job without a
40 college education, then, it would seem, it's silly and wasteful and foolish to spend all that time and money and effort at college. Just as it would be silly to spend money on a can opener if you could open the can by snapping your fingers.

People who ask the question, "So, what are you going to do with an English major?", or "How much money do Sociology majors make?" are thinking in can opener terms. They think that the only thing valuable about a college education is what sort of job (and how high-paying a job) you can get with that college education. And they also think that people who major in Classics or Philosophy or Women's Studies won't get very good jobs. So, they think, since
50 you're spending all that time and money and effort on college, you should get yourself the sort of education that is *useful* for getting a good job. So, they might say, you should major in Nursing or Education or Business or Journalism or Computer Science because those are the sort of majors that you can trade for good jobs.

Now I think there is something right about the Can Opener Answer, but there are two serious problems with it. Let me now turn to those.

THE FIRST PROBLEM WITH THE CAN OPENER ANSWER

What the Can Opener Answer has right is that a college education is useful for getting a job. After all, college graduates, in general, have better, higher paying, more interesting, potentially more fulfilling jobs than those without
60 college degrees. But that is not the only thing a college education is useful for. A college education—in particular, a broad-based, multi-disciplinary, liberal arts education—is useful for so much more. The problem with the simple Can Opener Answer is that it misses this "so much more" when it focuses merely on the job-getting features of a college degree. Here are just some of the other things that college educated people are able to do.

- College can equip us for our leisure time just as much, if not more so, than it can equip us for our working lives. College educated people are able to appreciate and enjoy literature, art, music, essays, movies, and other products of the culture. Or, to put it better, the sort of apprecia-
70   tion and enjoyment that they have is deeper because of their education: those with a liberal arts education see things in movies and music and literature that those without the education don't. And, as a consequence, their experience is richer.
- We live in a democracy, the success of which requires that each of us participates actively and intelligently in the democratic institutions. Such participation includes not simply voting, but critically examining the candidates' positions, speaking out as an advocate for policy change, perhaps even serving in a leadership role on a governmental

body. Moreover, it requires being critical of the institutions themselves, and seeing what needs changing and why. The appreciation of history, the ability to formulate a persuasive argument, an analytic skill with budgets and statistics and polling data—these are all skills you get as a college educated person and they are skills necessary for successful participation as a citizen in a democracy.

- The developments in technology and the advances in science (especially medical science) are an ever-present, and ever-more-important part of our lives. The growing presence of medications in the treatment of psychological maladies, the possibilities opened up by study and manipulation of DNA, and the prospects for artificial intelligence (just to name a few) are developments that require an intelligent response. Which of the many possibilities opened up to us by science should be pursued? How reliable is DNA testing? Should we treat depression with a drug or with traditional therapy? College graduates are well-positioned to answer these questions because they know some science, and can distinguish quackery from good scientific practice. Moreover, they are accustomed to asking questions about *value*[3] and these are the sorts of questions which very much need to be asked about technological developments.

- This last point applies not simply to the advances in science and technology, but to the information that comes to us via the media. We need to be able to distinguish the foolish fad from the important trend; we need to be able to determine which news outlets are reliable and which are overly biased; we need to be able to figure out where to turn for information and how to navigate between the twin vices of gullibility (believing everything you read in the newspaper, or see on the internet, or hear from a TV anchor) and skepticism (believing nothing that anybody else tells you). Because during your college education you will spend a significant amount of time doing research and evaluating sources, you will be, once you finish college, perfectly situated to be intelligent consumers of information.

- Finally, a college education equips people with the tools for self-examination that renders them able to make informed and intelligent choices about the direction of their own lives. College may equip you for a career, but you have to decide which career to pursue, and how to balance the competing demands of work and family. At what point do you leave the safety of an old but boring job for the insecurity of a new but exciting job? How important a role should your religious or political beliefs play in the life you lead? Should you work for (or buy the products of) a company that exploits child laborers? Should you buy your groceries from a large national chain or from the local, but perhaps more expensive, market? At what point should you put a moral principle ahead of economic interest? These are decisions that we all must make; if we don't, someone else will make them for us.

And by providing the experience and guidance at thinking through these sorts of questions (and other, much more difficult ones) a college education will turn you into a reflective, morally mature person.

The point I'm making can be put this way. A college education isn't valuable like a can opener is valuable. It's valuable like a Swiss army knife is valuable. Or like a computer is valuable. People who focus simply on the job-getting
140 feature of a college education are like people who think that the belt-punch is the only useful feature of a Swiss army knife.

I would argue that the benefits of a college education that I just listed are actually *more valuable* than the fact that you can get a good job with a college diploma. First, it is becoming increasingly unlikely you will spend the 40 years following college in one career, let alone in one job. To devote your college years to preparing for life as a lab assistant will turn out to be a waste when you leave the biomedical industry for a job in book publishing. But the features I listed above will be of use no matter what job you have. Secondly, and I think more importantly, the job you have is but one element in
150 what I would hope is a complex and multi-layered life. Living your life involves so much more than working at a job. It involves being a citizen, a spouse, a friend, a parent, a decision-maker, and someone who has leisure time to fill, and a college education contributes toward improving these aspects of your life.

THE SECOND PROBLEM WITH THE CAN OPENER ANSWER

That's the first problem with the simple Can Opener Answer: it mistakes something that has many uses for something that performs merely one task. But even when we do focus on the way in which a college education translates into a job, I think many people fail fully to grasp precisely why employers value employees who are college educated. And this failure is the second
160 problem with the simple Can Opener Answer.

The reason that college degrees translate into high-end salaries and good jobs has, I would argue, more to do with the *skills* one acquires in college than with the discipline-specific *knowledge* of the individual courses. No one is going to give you a better job because of your knowledge of Shakespeare or Plato or the Napoleonic Wars. But students who are successful in their English, philosophy, and history classes are independent and creative thinkers who can write and speak clearly, who can juggle many responsibilities, who can research a project, and who can take steps to educate themselves. And employers will be falling all over themselves to hire people with
170 these skills. Consequently, it doesn't matter so much what your major is as much as it does that you acquire these more general skills. So select a major that you find interesting, which will challenge you, which will make you smarter, and don't worry exclusively about "what you can do" with a degree in, say, religious studies.

Is it a relief to students obsessing about whether they have made a good major choice to hear this?

Even when it comes to the more vocationally-related majors like nursing or business or education or biology, it is sure to be the case that the knowledge you will need in your job will far outstrip what you will learn in your college classes. This is not a failing of the college classes, it is just a fact that specific industries and jobs require highly specific knowledge. It is also a fact that what you need to know to be an accountant or a teacher or a nurse or a biologist will change in response to advances in those fields. (Think, for example, about how much more today's middle school teachers need to know about computers compared to their predecessors 30 years ago.) One of the goals of a college education is to give you the general knowledge into which you can fit the more specific knowledge required by your particular job. And, more importantly, a college education will give you the ability to teach yourself, so that when you need a new job skill, you'll be prepared.

Do people hope learning will end?

When you get a job, the employer very likely will train you to do whatever it is that needs to be done. Large corporations have entire human resources departments and internal "universities" the sole purpose of which is to train the new employees to perform the necessary tasks. The Widget Corporation will understand if you can't come in on the first day of the job and start making the widgets; their trainers will show you how to do that. But what they won't show you is how to write clearly, how to organize your time, how to give a presentation to the Board of Directors, how to ask questions, and how to make decisions. What an employer wants above all is an employee who can *think,* and that is what they expect from people with a college education. Once you understand that it is these more generally intellectual skills which employers desire, you'll realize that they can be acquired in just about any major.

The second problem, then, with the simple Can Opener Answer is that it fails to recognize that it is the general skills and not simply the domain-specific content knowledge which turns college graduates into desirable employees. I think I can put the point this way. A college education does not, as most people believe, prepare you to do *something.* Rather, it prepares you to do *anything.*[4]

HOW TO GET THE MOST OUT OF COLLEGE

Now that we understand the value of a college education, we can think about what you should do in college, and how you can make the most of your college years. Given that college is valuable not simply because it gets you a job, but because it prepares you to be a complete person, *and* given that what you want from college in the way of job-related skills are general intellectual abilities more than particular, task-specific knowledge, what should you do? I don't have all the answers, but here are some about which I'm fairly confident.

1. Write as much as you can. Then write some more. The written word is the medium of academic communication. Academics talk to one

another through books and published articles. Students talk to their professors through exams and termpapers. If you cannot write well, you will not succeed in college, it's as simple as that. I once spoke to a group of college juniors, and I asked them what they wish they knew about college when they were entering freshmen. One of them[5] said that he wished he had known how much writing he would have to do, and to how high a standard his writing would be held. So now you know: writing is crucially important.

And since writing is a skill like juggling or playing the guitar, the only way to get better at it is to practice. Write at every opportunity. Keep a class journal. Take notes when you read (and don't simply underline or highlight your books. This is next to worthless.). Write drafts of your assigned papers. Demand feedback on your writing from your professors. The more you write, the better a writer you will become. And, you will find, the better a *thinker* you will become, because more than anything else, writing is a form of thinking out loud. Write for yourself, to clarify your own thinking, not simply because you have a paper due at the end of the term. Because writing is the medium of academic communication, you need to treat it that way—as a form of communication. Don't think of your papers as something that you turn in for a grade, but as an opportunity to talk to your professors—to tell them what you have been thinking about. I hardly need say that if you are a talented writer, you will succeed in the workplace. You won't have to write essays on Jane Austen or the Protestant Reformation once you leave college, but you will have to write memos and reports and presentations and speeches, and honing this skill in college will serve you well once you leave.

2. Talk. And not just about your weekend plans or about the details of your friends' love lives. Talk about ideas that fascinate you. Talk about politics and religion and racism and abortion and all the other issues that are important but which are not usually talked about in "polite society". It is through talking about these issues that you may very well come to turn confusion into clarity. Many of these questions can only be solved when a number of minds come together at once, and gathering in a group and talking is the best way to bring minds together. How will you know if there is a flaw in your position if you don't show it to someone else? Moreover, you can use your talking about these issues as practice for the talking that you will have to do with your spouse, your children, your coworkers, your boss, and the members of your town council. Speaking to others in private and to groups in public is one of those life and job skills that I was talking about above, and if you can treat college as an opportunity for honing that skill, you will be ready to talk in these other sorts of situations. Finally, as you will soon learn, talking about ideas is valuable for its own sake. The late-night conversations at coffee houses or

in dorm rooms about the meaning of life and the way to fix the world are just plain fun. Do it as often as you can.

3. Take responsibility for your education. Here's the part where college distinguishes itself from high school. High school students are there because they have to be. College students are in college because they want to be. (And make sure you really *want* to be in college before you go. It is a sizeable investment of time and money, and if there's something else you'd rather be doing, you should take some time and re-assess your situation. Taking a year off to figure out what you want, and entering college with a clear plan in mind can make all the difference in the world.) You are paying dearly for your college education, so you should go out and *get* it. Don't wait for someone else to hand it to you; it won't come. Taking responsibility for your own education manifests itself in small ways, and in larger ways. On the small side it means going to the dictionary when you run across a word you don't know. It also means asking your professor to read a draft of your essay, or raising your hand in class to ask for a difficult point to be repeated. But taking responsibility for your education means more than this. It means seeking out challenging courses and inspiring professors, for only if you push yourself by taking hard courses will you improve your academic and intellectual skills. It means having the courage to change your major if you find your current one uninteresting. It means engaging your friends in the dormitories and coffee shops about what you are learning in the classroom. It means speaking up and agitating for change if things aren't going the way you want. If you sit passively through your classes, skipping the readings, and taking only the easy courses, you will fail to gain the very education to which you are committing so much time and money.

It might help to think of college as a sort of health club—a health club for the mind.[6] There are all sorts of machines in the health club: these are your professors, your classes, and the many extra-curricular activity opportunities. The machines at this intellectual health club can improve your mind in the way that the weights and stair-climbers at your gym can improve your body. But, just as at the gym, the machines are useless if you don't use them. Merely buying a health club membership won't turn flab into muscle; you have to lift weights and do sit-ups. And merely enrolling in college won't turn an uneducated person into an educated one. Doing the reading, talking in class, visiting your professors in office hours, pursuing research topics outside of class—this is the sort of "machine using" behavior that will turn the gray matter inside your head into a well-toned mental muscle.

4. Do something completely different. I see so many students who take the same menu of courses they took in high school: history, English,

270

280

290

300

math, science, and a foreign language. All of those are important classes, but a quick glance at any college's course catalog will show that there are dozens if not hundreds of comparatively exotic courses. Religious studies, communication, anthropology, economics, psychology, film theory—the list goes on. Take a course that is completely different from anything you have taken before. Explore the unknown. Not only might the strange and exotic be something you like (and have a talent for!), but the challenge of these new courses will push you to develop the intellectual skills I have been talking about. This injunction to do something completely different shouldn't stop at the course catalog, however. Find the person on campus most different from you and take them out to coffee. Try out for a play, join the debate team, write for the newspaper, join a campus service organization. Try your hand at some of those activities that you would never have done in high school. Of course you will meet new people, but the primary reason for engaging in these pursuits is to discover something about yourself. Maybe you would enjoy the theatre or find that you have a talent for organizing fund-drives (and can translate that into a career!). It is foolish to commit yourself to a life-plan before you have discovered what you like and what talents you have. And after you get a "real job" and "settle down" you will find precious little time for these extra-curricular pursuits.

5. Become curious. The late Canadian novelist Robertson Davies has hit upon the essence of college. "Energy and curiosity are the lifeblood of universities," Davies had one of his characters say. "The desire to find out, to uncover, to dig deeper, to puzzle out obscurities, is the spirit of the university and it is a channeling of that unresting curiosity that holds mankind together."[7] Since this 'unresting curiosity' is the essence of any college, succeeding during the next four years requires that you tap into this energy, and that you become an unrestingly curious person yourself. Feed your curiosity by taking courses that interest you, rather than the courses which might look good on a law school application. Find those issues and problems that interest you and pursue them doggedly. Become curious about everything—about medieval history, about the structure of the cell, about what your roommates are learning in their classes, about the research interests of your professors—and you will find not only that you are getting better grades, but that you are becoming a smarter, more intellectually independent person. And that is, at the end, the goal of a college education.[8]

ENDNOTES

1. Andrew P. Mills is an assistant professor of philosophy at Otterbein College, where he teaches a wide array of philosophy courses. He received his B.A. from the University of Michigan, and his M.A. and Ph.D. in philosophy from The University of North Carolina at Chapel Hill. He is the author of scholarly articles in the philosophy of language and in philosophical logic.

2. Of course in such a situation can openers may have value as antiques, or as objects of art. And that is a real sort of value, but it is not (at least not standardly) why we think can openers are valuable now.

3. Like this very essay: it's an examination of the value of a college education.

4. I learned of this way of putting the point from Ami Berger, though I don't think she was the originator of this thought.

5. His name is Caleb Bell.

6. For this health club analogy I am indebted to Craig Froehle.

7. This is from Davies' novel, *The Rebel Angels.*

8. An earlier, abbreviated, version of this essay was published under the title "College is more than job training" in *The Blade* (Toledo, Ohio) on September 30, 2000. For helpful conversation on this essay, I would like to thank Lori Aronson, Ami Berger, Brad Cohen, Craig Froehle, Glenna Jackson, Brian Lindeman, Kristine LaLonde, Mary MacLeod, Lisa Pollak, Charles Salter, and the audiences at Otterbein College to whom I have presented the main ideas contained above. I would like to dedicate this essay to Jack Meiland, who ignited my thinking on the question of why a college education is valuable. His little book, *College Thinking* is as valuable a guide to college as I can think of.

ON LIBERTY
J. S. Mill

CHAPTER I
INTRODUCTORY

The subject of this Essay is not the so-called Liberty of the Will, so unfortunately opposed to the misnamed doctrine of Philosophical Necessity; but Civil, or Social Liberty: the nature and limits of the power which can be legitimately exercised by society over the individual. 1

The object of this Essay is to assert one very simple principle, as entitled to govern absolutely the dealings of society with the individual in the way of compulsion and control, whether the means used be physical force in the form of legal penalties, or the moral coercion of public opinion. That principle is, that the sole end for which mankind are warranted, individually or collectively, in interfering with the liberty of action of any of their number, is self-protection. That the only purpose for which power can be rightfully exercised over any member of a civilized community, against his will, is to prevent harm to others. The only part of the conduct of any one, for which he is amenable to society, is that which concerns others. In the part which merely concerns himself, his independence is, of right, absolute. Over himself, over his own body and mind, the individual is sovereign. 10

It is, perhaps, hardly necessary to say that this doctrine is meant to apply only to human beings in the maturity of their faculties. We are not speaking of children, or of young persons below the age which the law may fix as that of manhood or womanhood. Those who are still in a state to require being taken care of by others, must be protected against their own actions as well as against external injury. 20

This, then, is the appropriate region of human liberty. It comprises, first, the inward domain of consciousness; demanding liberty of conscience, in the most comprehensive sense; liberty of thought and feeling; absolute freedom of opinion and sentiment on all subjects, practical or speculative, scientific, moral, or theological. The liberty of expressing and publishing opinions may seem to fall under a different principle, since it belongs to that part of the conduct of an individual which concerns other people; but, being almost of as much importance as the liberty of thought itself, and resting in great part on the same reasons, is practically inseparable from it. Secondly, the principle requires liberty of tastes and pursuits; of framing the plan of our life to suit our own character; of doing as we like, subject to such consequences as may follow; without impediment from our fellow-creatures, so long as what we do does not harm them, even though they should think our conduct foolish, perverse, or wrong. Thirdly, from this liberty of each individual, follows the liberty, within the same limits, of combination among individuals; freedom 30

[handwritten margin note: Unions, "harm" do they harm others? Religions? Political parties? who judges the harm? what is harm but consensus of some type?]

to unite, for any purpose not involving harm to others: the persons combining being supposed to be of full age, and not forced or deceived.

Though this doctrine is anything but new, and, to some persons, may have the air of a truism, there is no doctrine which stands more directly opposed to the general tendency of existing opinion and practice. Society has expended fully as much effort in the attempt (according to its lights) to compel people to conform to its notions of personal, as of social excellence. The ancient commonwealths thought themselves entitled to practise, and the ancient philosophers countenanced, the regulation of every part of private conduct by public authority, on the ground that the State had a deep interest in the whole bodily and mental discipline of every one of its citizens.

Apart from the peculiar tenets of individual thinkers, there is also in the world at large an increasing inclination to stretch unduly the powers of society over the individual, both by the force of opinion and even by that of legislation: and as the tendency of all the changes taking place in the world is to strengthen society, and diminish the power of the individual, this encroachment is not one of the evils which tend spontaneously to disappear, but, on the contrary, to grow more and more formidable. The disposition of mankind, whether as rulers or as fellow-citizens, to impose their own opinions and inclinations as a rule of conduct on others, is so energetically supported by some of the best and by some of the worst feelings incident to human nature, that it is hardly ever kept under restraint by anything but want of power; and as the power is not declining, but growing, unless a strong barrier of moral conviction can be raised against the mischief, we must expect, in the present circumstances of the world, to see it increase.

[handwritten margin note: Chapter 2?]

CHAPTER III
OF INDIVIDUALITY, AS ONE OF THE ELEMENTS OF WELL-BEING

The liberty of the individual must be thus far limited; he must not make himself a nuisance to other people. But if he refrains from molesting others in what concerns them, and merely acts according to his own inclination and judgment in things which concern himself, the same reasons which show that opinion should be free, prove also that he should be allowed, without molestation, to carry his opinions into practice at his own cost.

It is desirable, in short, that in things which do not primarily concern others; individuality should assert itself. Where, not the person's own character, but the traditions or customs of other people are the rule of conduct, there is wanting one of the principal ingredients of human happiness, and quite the chief ingredient of individual and social progress.

In maintaining this principle, the greatest difficulty to be encountered does not lie in the appreciation of means towards an acknowledged end, but in the indifference of persons in general to the end itself. If it were felt that the free development of individuality is one of the leading essentials of well-being;

that it is not only a coördinate element with all that is designated by the terms civilization, instruction, education, culture, but is itself a necessary part and condition of all those things; there would be no danger that liberty should be undervalued, and the adjustment of the boundaries between it and social control would present no extraordinary difficulty. But the evil is, that individual spontaneity is hardly recognized by the common modes of thinking, as having any intrinsic worth, or deserving any regard on its own account. The majority, being satisfied with the ways of mankind as they now are (for it is they who make them what they are), cannot comprehend why those ways should not be good enough for everybody; and what is more, spontaneity forms no part of the ideal of the majority of moral and social reformers, but is rather looked on with jealousy, as a troublesome and perhaps rebellious obstruction to the general acceptance of what these reformers, in their own judgment, think would be best for mankind.

[margin note: I do think it ego centric.]

No one's idea of excellence in conduct is that people should do absolutely nothing but copy one another. No one would assert that people ought not to put into their mode of life, and into the conduct of their concerns, any impress whatever of their own judgment, or of their own individual character. On the other hand, it would be absurd to pretend that people ought to live as if nothing whatever had been known in the world before they came into it; as if experience had as yet done nothing towards showing that one mode of existence, or of conduct, is preferable to another. Nobody denies that people should be so taught and trained in youth, as to know and benefit by the ascertained results of human experience. But it is the privilege and proper condition of a human being, arrived at the maturity of his faculties, to use and interpret experience in his own way. It is for him to find out what part of recorded experience is properly applicable to his own circumstances and character. The traditions and customs of other people are, to a certain extent, evidence of what their experience has taught *them;* presumptive evidence, and as such, have a claim to his deference: but, in the first place, their experience may be too narrow; or they may not have interpreted it rightly. Secondly, their interpretation of experience may be correct, but unsuitable to him. Customs are made for customary circumstances, and customary characters: and his circumstances or his character may be uncustomary. Thirdly, though the customs be both good as customs, and suitable to him, yet to conform to custom, merely *as* custom, does not educate or develop in him any of the qualities which are the distinctive endowment of a human being. The human faculties of perception, judgment, discriminative feeling, mental activity, and even moral preference, are exercised only in making a choice. He who does anything because it is the custom, makes no choice. He gains no practice either in discerning or in desiring what is best. The mental and moral, like the muscular powers, are improved only by being used. The faculties are called into no exercise by doing a thing merely because others do it, no more than by believing a thing only because others believe it.

[margin note: Maybe not in his day]

It is not by wearing down into uniformity all that is individual in themselves, but by cultivating it and calling it forth, within the limits imposed by the rights and interests of others, that human beings become a noble and beautiful object of contemplation; and as the works partake the character of those who do them, by the same process human life also becomes rich, diversified, and animating, furnishing more abundant aliment to high thoughts and elevating feelings, and strengthening the tie which binds every individual to the race, by making the race infinitely better worth belonging to. In proportion to the development of his individuality, each person becomes more valuable to himself, and is therefore capable of being more valuable to others.

I insist thus emphatically on the importance of genius, and the necessity of allowing it to unfold itself freely both in thought and in practice, being well aware that no one will deny the position in theory, but knowing also that almost every one, in reality, is totally indifferent to it. People think genius a fine thing if it enables a man to write an exciting poem, or paint a picture. But in its true sense, that of originality in thought and action, though no one says that it is not a thing to be admired, nearly all, at heart, think that they can do very well without it. Unhappily this is too natural to be wondered at. Originality is the one thing which unoriginal minds cannot feel the use of. They cannot see what it is to do for them: how should they? If they could see what it would do for them, it would not be originality. The first service which originality has to render them, is that of opening their eyes: which being once fully done, they would have a chance of being themselves original. Meanwhile, recollecting that nothing was ever yet done which some one was not the first to do, and that all good things which exist are the fruits of originality, let them be modest enough to believe that there is something still left for it to accomplish, and assure themselves that they are more in need of originality, the less they are conscious of the want.

In sober truth, whatever homage may be professed, or even paid, to real or supposed mental superiority, the general tendency of things throughout the world is to render mediocrity the ascendant power among mankind. In ancient history, in the Middle Ages, and in a diminishing degree through the long transition from feudality to the present time, the individual was a power in himself; and if he had either great talents or a high social position, he was a considerable power. At present individuals are lost in the crowd. In politics it is almost a triviality to say that public opinion now rules the world. The only power deserving the name is that of masses, and of governments while they make themselves the organ of the tendencies and instincts of masses. This is as true in the moral and social relations of private life as in public transactions. Those whose opinions go by the name of public opinion, are not always the same sort of public: in America, they are the whole white population; in England, chiefly the middle class. But they are always a mass, that is to say, collective mediocrity. And what is a still greater novelty, the mass do not now take their opinions from dignitaries in Church or State, from ostensible leaders, or from books. Their thinking is done for them by men much like themselves, addressing them or speaking in their name, on the spur of the moment, through the newspapers. I am not complaining of all this. I do not assert that anything better is compatible, as a general rule, with the present low state of the human mind. But that does not hinder the government of mediocrity from being mediocre government. No government by a democracy or a numerous aristocracy, either in its political acts or in the opinions, qualities, and tone of mind which it fosters, ever did or could rise above mediocrity, except in so far as the sovereign Many have let themselves be guided (which in their best times they always have done) by the counsels and influence of a more highly gifted and instructed One or Few. The initiation of all wise or noble things, comes and must come from individuals; generally at first from some one individual. The honor and glory of the average man is that he is capable of following that initiative; that he can respond internally to wise and noble things, and be led to them with his eyes open. I am not countenancing the sort of "hero-worship" which applauds the strong man of genius for forcibly seizing on the government of the world and making it do his bidding in spite of itself. All he can claim is, freedom to point out the way. The power of compelling others into it, is not only inconsistent with the freedom and development of all the rest, but corrupting to the strong man himself. It does seem, however, that when the opinions of masses of merely average men are everywhere become or becoming the dominant power, the counterpoise and corrective to that tendency would be, the more and more pronounced individuality of those who stand on the higher eminences of thought. It is in these circumstances most especially, that exceptional individuals, instead of being deterred, should be encouraged in acting differently from the mass. In other times there was no advantage in their doing so, unless they acted not only differently, but better. In this age the mere example of non-conformity, the mere refusal to bend the knee to custom, is itself a service. Precisely because the tyranny of opinion is such as to make eccentricity a reproach, it is desirable, in order to break through that tyranny, that people should be eccentric. Eccentricity has always abounded when and where strength of character has abounded; and the amount of eccentricity in a society has generally been proportional to the amount of genius, mental vigor, and moral courage which it contained. That so few now dare to be eccentric, marks the chief danger of the time.

I have said that it is important to give the freest scope possible to uncustomary things, in order that it may in time appear which of these are fit to be converted into customs. But independence of action, and disregard of custom are not solely deserving of encouragement for the chance they afford that better modes of action, and customs more worthy of general adoption, may be struck out; nor is it only persons of decided mental superiority who have a just claim to carry on their lives in their own way. There is no reason that all human existences should be constructed on some one, or some small number of patterns. If a person possesses any tolerable amount of common sense and experience, his own mode of laying out his existence is the best, not because it is the best in itself, but because it is his own mode. Human beings are not like sheep; and even sheep are not undistinguishably alike. A man cannot get a coat or a pair of boots to fit him, unless they are either made to his measure, or he has a whole warehouseful to choose from: and is it easier to fit him with a life than with a coat, or are human beings more like one another in their whole physical and spiritual conformation than in the shape of their feet? If it were only that people have diversities of taste, that is reason enough for not attempting to shape them all after one model. But different persons also require different conditions for their spiritual development; and can no more exist healthily in the same moral, than all the variety of plants can in the same physical, atmosphere and climate. The same things which are helps to one person towards the cultivation of his higher nature, are hindrances to another. The same mode of life is a healthy excitement to one, keeping all his faculties of action and enjoyment in their best order, while to another it is a distracting burden, which suspends or crushes all internal life. Such are the differences among human beings in their sources of pleasure, their susceptibilities of pain, and the operation on them of different physical and moral agencies, that unless there is a corresponding diversity in their modes of life, they neither obtain their fair share of happiness, nor grow up to the mental, moral, and aesthetic stature of which their nature is capable.

There is one characteristic of the present direction of public opinion, peculiarly calculated to make it intolerant of any marked demonstration of individuality. The general average of mankind are not only moderate in intellect, but also moderate in inclinations: they have no tastes or wishes strong enough to incline them to do anything unusual, and they consequently do not understand those who have, and class all such with the wild and intemperate whom they are accustomed to look down upon.

The despotism of custom is everywhere the standing hindrance to human advancement, being in unceasing antagonism to that disposition to aim at something better than customary, which is called, according to circumstances, the spirit of liberty, or that of progress or improvement. The spirit of improvement is not always a spirit of liberty, for it may aim at forcing improvements on an unwilling people; and the spirit of liberty, in so far as it resists such attempts, may ally itself locally and temporarily with the opponents of improvement; but the only unfailing and permanent source of improvement is liberty, since by it there are as many possible independent centres of improvement as there are individuals. The progressive principle, however, in either shape, whether as the love of liberty or of improvement, is antagonistic to the sway of Custom, involving at least emancipation from that yoke; and the contest between the two constitutes the chief interest of the history of mankind. A people, it appears, may be progressive for a certain length of time and then stop: when does it stop? When it ceases to possess individuality. But we are progressive as well as changeable: we continually make new inventions in mechanical things, and keep them until they are again superseded by better; we are eager for improvement in politics, in education, even in morals, though in this last our idea of improvement chiefly consists in persuading or forcing other people to be as good as ourselves. It is not progress that we object to; on the contrary, we flatter ourselves that we are the most progressive people who ever lived. It is individuality that we war against: we should think we had done wonders if we had made ourselves all alike; forgetting that the unlikeness of one person to another is generally the first thing which draws the attention of either to the imperfection of his own type, and the superiority of another, or the possibility, by combining the advantages of both, of producing something better than either.

Comparatively speaking, we now read the same things, listen to the same things, see the same things, go to the same places, have our hopes and fears directed to the same objects, have the same rights and liberties, and the same means of asserting them. Great as are the differences of position which remain, they are nothing to those which have ceased. And the assimilation is still proceeding. All the political changes of the age promote it, since they all tend to raise the low and to lower the high. Every extension of education promotes it, because education brings people under common influences, and gives them access to the general stock of facts and sentiments. Improvements in the means of communication promote it, by bringing the inhabitants of distant places into personal contact, and keeping up a rapid flow of changes of residence between one place and another. The increase of commerce and manufactures promotes it, by diffusing more widely the advantages of easy circumstances, and opening all objects of ambition, even the highest, to general competition, whereby the desire of rising becomes no longer the character of a particular class, but of all classes. A more powerful agency than even all these, in bringing about a general similarity among mankind, is the complete establishment, in this and other free countries, of the ascendency of public opinion in the State. As the various social eminences which enabled persons entrenched on them to disregard the opinion of the multitude, gradually become levelled; as the very idea of resisting the will of the public, when it is positively known that they have a will, disappears more and more from the minds of practical politicians; there ceases to be any social support for non-conformity.

The combination of all these causes forms so great a mass of influences hostile to Individuality, that it is not easy to see how it can stand its ground. It will do so with increasing difficulty, unless the intelligent part of the public can be made to feel its value—to see that it is good there should be differences, even though not for the better, even though, as it may appear to them, some should be for the worse. If the claims of Individuality are ever to be asserted, the time is now, while much is still wanting to complete the enforced assimilation. It is only in the earlier stages that any stand can be successfully made against the encroachment. The demand that all other people shall resemble ourselves, grows by what it feeds on. If resistance waits till life is reduced *nearly* to one uniform type, all deviations from that type will come to be considered impious, immoral, even monstrous and contrary to nature. Mankind speedily become unable to conceive diversity, when they have been for some time unaccustomed to see it.

democracy

CHAPTER IV
OF THE LIMITS TO THE AUTHORITY OF
SOCIETY OVER THE INDIVIDUAL

What, then, is the rightful limit to the sovereignty of the individual over himself? Where does the authority of society begin? How much of human life should be assigned to individuality, and how much to society?

Each will receive its proper share, if each has that which more particularly concerns it. To individuality should belong the part of life in which it is chiefly the individual that is interested; to society, the part which chiefly interests society.

310   Though society is not founded on a contract, and though no good purpose is answered by inventing a contract in order to deduce social obligations from it, every one who receives the protection of society owes a return for the benefit, and the fact of living in society renders it indispensable that each should be bound to observe a certain line of conduct towards the rest. This conduct consists, first, in not injuring the interests of one another; or rather certain interests, which, either by express legal provision or by tacit understanding, ought to be considered as rights; and secondly, in each person's bearing his share (to be fixed on some equitable principle) of the labors and sacrifices incurred for defending the society or its members from injury

320   and molestation. These conditions society is justified in enforcing, at all costs to those who endeavor to withhold fulfilment. Nor is this all that society may do. The acts of an individual may be hurtful to others, or wanting in due consideration for their welfare, without going the length of violating any of their constituted rights. The offender may then be justly punished by opinion, though not by law. As soon as any part of a person's conduct affects prejudicially the interests of others, society has jurisdiction over it, and the question whether the general welfare will or will not be promoted by interfering with it, becomes open to discussion. But there is no room for entertaining any such question when a person's conduct affects the interests of no

330   persons besides himself, or needs not affect them unless they like (all the persons concerned being of full age, and the ordinary amount of understanding). In all such cases there should be perfect freedom, legal and social, to do the action and stand the consequences.

It would be a great misunderstanding of this doctrine, to suppose that it is one of selfish indifference, which pretends that human beings have no business with each other's conduct in life, and that they should not concern themselves about the well-doing or well-being of one another, unless their own interest is involved. Instead of any diminution, there is need of a great increase of disinterested exertion to promote the good of others. But disinterested

340   benevolence can find other instruments to persuade people to their good, than whips and scourges, either of the literal or the metaphorical sort. I am the last person to undervalue the self-regarding virtues; they are only second in importance, if even second, to the social. It is equally the business of education to cultivate both. But even education works by conviction and per-

suasion as well as by compulsion, and it is by the former only that, when the period of education is past, the self-regarding virtues should be inculcated. Human beings owe to each other help to distinguish the better from the worse, and encouragement to choose the former and avoid the latter. They should be forever stimulating each other to increased exercise of their higher faculties, and increased direction of their feelings and aims towards wise instead of foolish, elevating instead of degrading, objects and contemplations. But neither one person, nor any number of persons, is warranted in saying to another human creature of ripe years, that he shall not do with his life for his own benefit what he chooses to do with it. He is the person most interested in his own well-being: the interest which any other person, except in cases of strong personal attachment, can have in it, is trifling, compared with that which he himself has; the interest which society has in him individually (except as to his conduct to others) is fractional, and altogether indirect: while, with respect to his own feelings and circumstances, the most ordinary man or woman has means of knowledge immeasurably surpassing those that can be possessed by any one else. The interference of society to overrule his judgment and purposes in what only regards himself, must be grounded on general presumptions; which may be altogether wrong, and even if right, are as likely as not to be misapplied to individual cases, by persons no better acquainted with the circumstances of such cases than those are who look at them merely from without. In this department, therefore, of human affairs, Individuality has its proper field of action. In the conduct of human beings towards one another, it is necessary that general rules should for the most part be observed, in order that people may know what they have to expect; but in each person's own concerns, his individual spontaneity is entitled to free exercise. Considerations to aid his judgment, exhortations to strengthen his will, may be offered to him, even obtruded on him, by others; but he, himself, is the final judge. All errors which he is likely to commit against advice and warning, are far outweighed by the evil of allowing others to constrain him to what they deem his good.

The distinction here pointed out between the part of a person's life which concerns only himself, and that which concerns others, many persons will refuse to admit. How (it may be asked) can any part of the conduct of a member of society be a matter of indifference to the other members? No person is an entirely isolated being; it is impossible for a person to do anything seriously or permanently hurtful to himself, without mischief reaching at least to his near connections, and often far beyond them. If he injures "his" property, he does harm to those who directly or indirectly derived support from it, and usually diminishes, by a greater or less amount, the general resources of the community. If he deteriorates his bodily or mental faculties, he not only brings evil upon all who depended on him for any portion of their happiness, but disqualifies himself for rendering the services which he owes to his fellow-creatures generally; perhaps becomes a burden on their affection or benevolence; and if such conduct were very frequent, hardly any offence that

390 is committed would detract more from the general sum of good. Finally, if by his vices or follies a person does no direct harm to others, he is nevertheless (it may be said) injurious by his example; and ought to be compelled to control himself, for the sake of those whom the sight or knowledge of his conduct might corrupt or mislead.

less compelling →

And even (it will be added) if the consequences of misconduct could be confined to the vicious or thoughtless individual, ought society to abandon to their own guidance those who are manifestly unfit for it? If protection against themselves is confessedly due to children and persons under age, is not society equally bound to afford it to persons of mature years who are equally

400 incapable of self-government? If gambling, or drunkenness, or incontinence, or idleness, or uncleanliness, are as injurious to happiness, and as great a hindrance to improvement, as many or most of the acts prohibited by law, why (it may be asked) should not law, so far as is consistent with practicability and social convenience, endeavor to repress these also? And as a supplement to the unavoidable imperfections of law, ought not opinion at least to organize a powerful police against these vices, and visit rigidly with social penalties those who are known to practise them? There is no question here (it may be said) about restricting individuality, or impeding the trial of new and original experiments in living. The only things it is sought to prevent are things

410 which have been tried and condemned from the beginning of the world until now; things which experience has shown not to be useful or suitable to any person's individuality. There must be some length of time and amount of experience, after which a moral or prudential truth may be regarded as established: and it is merely desired to prevent generation after generation from falling over the same precipice which has been fatal to their predecessors.

what could these be?

I fully admit that the mischief which a person does to himself, may seriously affect, both through their sympathies and their interests, those nearly connected with him, and in a minor degree, society at large. When, by conduct of this sort, a person is led to violate a distinct and assignable obligation

420 to any other person or persons, the case is taken out of the self-regarding class, and becomes amenable to moral disapprobation in the proper sense of the term. Whenever, in short, there is a definite damage, or a definite risk of damage, either to an individual or to the public, the case is taken out of the province of liberty, and placed in that of morality or law.

But I cannot consent to argue the point as if society had no means of bringing its weaker members up to its ordinary standard of rational conduct, except waiting till they do something irrational, and then punishing them, legally or morally, for it. Society has had absolute power over them during all the early portion of their existence: it has had the whole period of childhood and nonage in which to try whether it could make them capable of rational con-

430 duct in life. The existing generation is master both of the training and the entire circumstances of the generation to come; it cannot indeed make them perfectly wise and good, because it is itself so lamentably deficient in goodness and wisdom; and its best efforts are not always, in individual cases, its

So inconsistent w/ the practice of conservatism → who talk of "moral failure" of welfare moms, control sexuality, etc. could I contemplate a theoretical libertarianism with a defin of environmental harm? Would lib's contemplate voluntary support of govt institutions of social aid as a fairer mechanism of charity than the chance of donations?

most successful ones; but it is perfectly well able to make the rising generation, as a whole, as good as, and a little better than, itself. If society lets any
considerable number of its members grow up mere children, incapable of being
acted on by rational consideration of distant motives, society has itself to blame
for the consequences. Armed not only with all the powers of education, but
with the ascendency which the authority of a received opinion always exercises over the minds who are least fitted to judge for themselves; and aided
by the *natural* penalties which cannot be prevented from falling on those who
incur the distaste or the contempt of those who know them; let not society
pretend that it needs, besides all this, the power to issue commands and enforce
obedience in the personal concerns of individuals, in which, on all principles
of justice and policy, the decision ought to rest with those who are to abide
the consequences.

CHAPTER V
APPLICATIONS

I have already observed that, owing to the absence of any recognized general
principles, liberty is often granted where it should be withheld, as well as withheld where it should be granted; and one of the cases in which, in the modern European world, the sentiment of liberty is the strongest, is a case where,
in my view, it is altogether misplaced. A person should be free to do as he likes
in his own concerns; but he ought not to be free to do as he likes in acting
for another under the pretext that the affairs of another are his own affairs.
The State, while it respects the liberty of each in what specially regards himself, is bound to maintain a vigilant control over his exercise of any power
which it allows him to possess over others. This obligation is almost entirely
disregarded in the case of the family relations, a case, in its direct influence
on human happiness, more important than all others taken together. The
almost despotic power of husbands over wives needs not be enlarged upon
here, because nothing more is needed for the complete removal of the evil,
than that wives should have the same rights, and should receive the protection of law in the same manner, as all other persons; and because, on this
subject, the defenders of established injustice do not avail themselves of the
plea of liberty, but stand forth openly as the champions of power. It is in the
case of children, that misapplied notions of liberty are a real obstacle to the
fulfilment by the State of its duties. One would almost think that a man's children were supposed to be literally, and not metaphorically, a part of himself,
so jealous is opinion of the smallest interference of law with his absolute and
exclusive control over them; more jealous than of almost any interference with
his own freedom of action: so much less do the generality of mankind value
liberty than power. Consider, for example, the case of education. Is it not
almost a self-evident axiom, that the State should require and compel the education, up to a certain standard, of every human being who is born its citizen? Yet who is there that is not afraid to recognize and assert this truth? Hardly

any one indeed will deny that it is one of the most sacred duties of the parents (or, as law and usage now stand, the father), after summoning a human being into the world, to give to that being an education fitting him to perform his part well in life towards others and towards himself. It still remains unrecognized, that to bring a child into existence without a fair prospect of being able, not only to provide food for its body, but instruction and training for its mind, is a moral crime, both against the unfortunate offspring and against society; and that if the parent does not fulfil this obligation, the State ought to see it fulfilled at the charge, as far as possible, of the parent.

Were the duty of enforcing universal education once admitted, there would be an end to the difficulties about what the State should teach, and how it should teach, which now convert the subject into a mere battle-field for sects and parties, causing the time and labor which should have been spent in educating, to be wasted in quarrelling about education. If the government would make up its mind to *require* for every child a good education, it might save itself the trouble of *providing* one. It might leave to parents to obtain the education where and how they pleased, and content itself with helping to pay the school fees of the poorer classes of children, and defraying the entire school expenses of those who have no one else to pay for them. The objections which are urged with reason against State education, do not apply to the enforcement of education by the State, but to the State's taking upon itself to direct that education: which is a totally different thing. That the whole or any large part of the education of the people should be in State hands, I go as far as any one in deprecating. All that has been said of the importance of individuality of character, and diversity in opinions and modes of conduct, involves, as of the same unspeakable importance, diversity of education. A general State education is a mere contrivance for moulding people to be exactly like one another: and as the mould in which it casts them is that which pleases the predominant power in the government, whether this be a monarch, a priesthood, an aristocracy, or the majority of the existing generation, in proportion as it is efficient and successful, it establishes a despotism over the mind, leading by natural tendency to one over the body. An education established and controlled by the State, should only exist, if it exist at all, as one among many competing experiments, carried on for the purpose of example and stimulus, to keep the others up to a certain standard of excellence. Unless, indeed, when society in general is in so backward a state that it could not or would not provide for itself any proper institutions of education, unless the government undertook the task; then, indeed; the government may, as the less of two great evils, take upon itself the business of schools and universities, as it may that of joint-stock companies, when private enterprise, in a shape fitted for undertaking great works of industry, does not exist in the country. But in general, if the country contains a sufficient number of persons qualified to provide education under government auspices, the same persons would be able and willing to give an equally good education on the voluntary principle, under the assurance of remu-

[handwritten margin notes:]
Ah—so there are things that need done... that we'd done... Wise people who ought to do them to pay for... but they won't always and so the State becomes the patron using $ from its corporate members.

we wish!
Don't you have to necessarily judge the content/quality of the education to know it to be adequate education?

neration afforded by a law rendering education compulsory, combined with State aid to those unable to defray the expense.

The instrument for enforcing the law could be no other than public examinations, extending to all children, and beginning at an early age. An age might be fixed at which every child must be examined, to ascertain if he (or she) is able to read. If a child proves unable, the father, unless he has some sufficient ground of excuse, might be subjected to a moderate fine, to be worked out, if necessary, by his labor, and the child might be put to school at his expense. Once in every year the examination should be renewed, with a gradually extending range of subjects, so as to make the universal acquisition, and what is more, retention, of a certain minimum of general knowledge, virtually compulsory. Beyond that minimum, there should be voluntary examinations on all subjects, at which all who come up to a certain standard of proficiency might claim a certificate. A government cannot have too much of the kind of activity which does not impede, but aids and stimulates, individual exertion and development. The mischief begins when, instead of calling forth the activity and powers of individuals and bodies, it substitutes its own activity for theirs; when, instead of informing, advising and, upon occasion, denouncing, it makes them work in fetters, or bids them stand aside and does their work instead of them. The worth of a State, in the long run, is the worth of the individuals composing it; and a State which postpones the interests of *their* mental expansion and elevation, to a little more of administrative skill, or that semblance of it which practice gives, in the details of business; a State which dwarfs its men, in order that they may be more docile instruments in its hands even for beneficial purposes, will find that with small men no great thing can really be accomplished; and that the perfection of machinery to which it has sacrificed everything, will in the end avail it nothing, for want of the vital power which, in order that the machine might work more smoothly, it has preferred to banish.

530

540

With $ from taxes presumably

Unintended consequence: The NCLB Law has done more to fetter and take over the work of educators than any other force!

THE ARTIFICIAL NIGGER
Flannery O'Connor

Mr. Head awakened to discover that the room was full of moonlight. He sat up and stared at the floor boards—the color of silver—and then at the ticking on his pillow, which might have been brocade, and after a second, he saw half of the moon five feet away in his shaving mirror, paused as if it were waiting for his permission to enter. It rolled forward and cast a dignifying light on everything. The straight chair against the wall looked stiff and attentive as if it were awaiting an order and Mr. Head's trousers, hanging to the back of it, had an almost noble air, like the garment some great man had just flung to his servant; but the face on the moon was a grave one. It gazed across the room and out the window where it floated over the horse stall and appeared to contemplate itself with the look of a young man who sees his old age before him.

Mr. Head could have said to it that age was a choice blessing and that only with years does a man enter into that calm understanding of life that makes him a suitable guide for the young. This, at least, had been his own experience.

He sat up and grasped the iron posts at the foot of his bed and raised himself until he could see the face on the alarm clock which sat on an overturned bucket beside the chair. The hour was two in the morning. The alarm on the clock did not work but he was not dependent on any mechanical means to awaken him. Sixty years had not dulled his responses; his physical reactions, like his moral ones, were guided by his will and strong character, and these could be seen plainly in his features. He had a long tube-like face with a long rounded open jaw and a long depressed nose. His eyes were alert but quiet, and in the miraculous moonlight they had a look of composure and of ancient wisdom as if they belonged to one of the great guides of men. He might have been Vergil summoned in the middle of the night to go to Dante, or better, Raphael, awakened by a blast of God's light to fly to the side of Tobias. The only dark spot in the room was Nelson's pallet, underneath the shadow of the window.

Nelson was hunched over on his side, his knees under his chin and his heels under his bottom. His new suit and hat were in the boxes that they had been sent in and these were on the floor at the foot of the pallet where he could get his hands on them as soon as he woke up. The slop jar, out of the shadow and made snow-white in the moonlight, appeared to stand guard over him like a small personal angel. Mr. Head lay back down, feeling entirely confident that he could carry out the moral mission of the coming day. He meant to be up before Nelson and to have the breakfast cooking by the time he awakened. The boy was always irked when Mr. Head was the first

Reprinted from *A Good Man Is Hard to Find* (1977), by permission of Harold Matson Company.

40   up. They would have to leave the house at four to get to the railroad junction by five-thirty. The train was to stop for them at five forty-five and they had to be there on time for this train was stopping merely to accommodate them.

This would be the boy's first trip to the city though he claimed it would be his second because he had been born there. Mr. Head had tried to point out to him that when he was born he didn't have the intelligence to determine his whereabouts but this had made no impression on the child at all and he continued to insist that this was to be his second trip. It would be Mr. Head's third trip. Nelson had said, "I will've already been there twict and
50   I ain't but ten."

Mr. Head had contradicted him.

"If you ain't been there in fifteen years, how you know you'll be able to find your way about?" Nelson had asked. "How you know it hasn't changed some?"

"Have you ever," Mr. Head had asked, "seen me lost?"

Nelson certainly had not but he was a child who was never satisfied until he had given an impudent answer and he replied, "It's nowhere around here to get lost at."

"The day is going to come," Mr. Head prophesied, "when you'll find you
60   ain't as smart as you think you are." He had been thinking about this trip for several months but it was for the most part in moral terms that he conceived it. It was to be a lesson that the boy would never forget. He was to find out from it that he had no cause for pride merely because he had been born in a city. He was to find out that the city is not a great place. Mr. Head meant him to see everything there is to see in a city so that he would be content to stay at home for the rest of his life. He fell asleep thinking how the boy would at last find out that he was not as smart as he thought he was.

He was awakened at three-thirty by the smell of fatback frying and he leaped off his cot. The pallet was empty and the clothes boxes had been
70   thrown open. He put on his trousers and ran into the other room. The boy had a corn pone on cooking and had fried the meat. He was sitting in the half-dark at the table, drinking cold coffee out of a can. He had on his new suit and his new gray hat pulled low over his eyes. It was too big for him but they had ordered it a size large because they expected his head to grow. He didn't say anything but his entire figure suggested satisfaction at having arisen before Mr. Head.

Mr. Head went to the stove and brought the meat to the table in the skillet. "It's no hurry," he said. "You'll get there soon enough and it's no guarantee you'll like it when you do neither," and he sat down across from the boy whose
80   hat teetered back slowly to reveal a fiercely expressionless face, very much the same shape as the old man's. They were grandfather and grandson but they looked enough alike to be brothers and brothers not too far apart in age, for Mr. Head had a youthful expression by daylight, while the boy's look was ancient, as if he knew everything already and would be pleased to forget it.

Mr. Head had once had a wife and daughter and when the wife died, the daughter ran away and returned after an interval with Nelson. Then one morning, without getting out of bed, she died and left Mr. Head with sole care of the year-old child. He had made the mistake of telling Nelson that he had been born in Atlanta. If he hadn't told him that, Nelson couldn't have insisted that this was going to be his second trip.

"You may not like it a bit," Mr. Head continued. "It'll be full of niggers."

The boy made a face as if he could handle a nigger.

"All right," Mr. Head said. "You ain't ever seen a nigger."

"You wasn't up very early," Nelson said.

"You ain't ever seen a nigger," Mr. Head repeated. "There hasn't been a nigger in this county since we run that one out twelve years ago and that was before you were born." He looked at the boy as if he were daring him to say he had ever seen a Negro.

"How you know I never saw a nigger when I lived there before?" Nelson asked. "I probably saw a lot of niggers."

"If you seen one you didn't know what he was," Mr. Head said, completely exasperated. "A six-month-old child don't know a nigger from anybody else."

"I reckon I'll know a nigger if I see one," the boy said and got up and straightened his slick sharply creased gray hat and went outside to the privy.

They reached the junction some time before the train was due to arrive and stood about two feet from the first set of tracks. Mr. Head carried a paper sack with some biscuits and a can of sardines in it for their lunch. A coarse-looking orange-colored sun coming up behind the east range of mountains was making the sky a dull red behind them, but in front of them it was still gray and they faced a gray transparent moon, hardly stronger than a thumbprint and completely without light. A small tin switch box and a black fuel tank were all there was to mark the place as a junction; the tracks were double and did not converge again until they were hidden behind the bends at either end of the clearing. Trains passing appeared to emerge from a tunnel of trees and, hit for a second by the cold sky, vanish terrified into the woods again. Mr. Head had had to make special arrangements with the ticket agent to have this train stop and he was secretly afraid it would not, in which case, he knew Nelson would say, "I never thought no train was going to stop for you." Under the useless morning moon the tracks looked white and fragile. Both the old man and the child stared ahead as if they were awaiting an apparition.

Then suddenly, before Mr. Head could make up his mind to turn back, there was a deep warning bleat and the train appeared, gliding very slowly, almost silently around the bend of trees about two hundred yards down the track, with one yellow front light shining. Mr. Head was still not certain it would stop and he felt it would make an even bigger idiot of him if it went by slowly. Both he and Nelson, however, were prepared to ignore the train if it passed them.

130   The engine charged by, filling their noses with the smell of hot metal and then the second coach came to a stop exactly where they were standing. A conductor with the face of an ancient bloated bulldog was on the step as if he expected them, though he did not look as if it mattered one way or the other to him if they got on or not. "To the right," he said.

Their entry took only a fraction of a second and the train was already speeding on as they entered the quiet car. Most of the travelers were still sleeping, some with their heads hanging off the chair arms, some stretched across two seats, and some sprawled out with their feet in the aisle. Mr. Head saw two unoccupied seats and pushed Nelson toward them. "Get in there by

140   the winder," he said in his normal voice which was very loud at this hour of the morning. "Nobody cares if you sit there because it's nobody in it. Sit right there."

"I heard you," the boy muttered. "It's no use in you yelling," and he sat down and turned his head to the glass. There he saw a pale ghost-like face scowling at him beneath the brim of a pale ghost-like hat. His grandfather, looking quickly too, saw a different ghost, pale but grinning, under a black hat.

Mr. Head sat down and settled himself and took out his ticket and started reading aloud everything that was printed on it. People began to stir. Several woke up and stared at him. "Take off your hat," he said to Nelson and took

150   off his own and put it on his knee. He had a small amount of white hair that had turned tobacco-colored over the years and this lay flat across the back of his head. The front of his head was bald and creased. Nelson took off his hat and put it on his knee and they waited for the conductor to come ask for their tickets.

The man across the aisle from them was spread out over two seats, his feet propped on the window and his head jutting into the aisle. He had on a light blue suit and a yellow shirt unbuttoned at the neck. His eyes had just opened and Mr. Head was ready to introduce himself when the conductor came up from behind and growled, "Tickets."

160   When the conductor had gone, Mr. Head gave Nelson the return half of his ticket and said, "Now put that in your pocket and don't lose it or you'll have to stay in the city."

"Maybe I will," Nelson said as if this were a reasonable suggestion.

Mr. Head ignored him. "First time this boy has ever been on a train," he explained to the man across the aisle, who was sitting up now on the edge of his seat with both feet on the floor.

Nelson jerked his hat on again and turned angrily to the window.

"He's never seen anything before," Mr. Head continued. "Ignorant as the day he was born, but I mean for him to get his fill once and for all."

170   The boy leaned forward, across his grandfather and toward the stranger. "I was born in the city," he said. "I was born there. This is my second trip." He said it in a high positive voice but the man across the aisle didn't look as if he understood. There were heavy purple circles under his eyes.

Mr. Head reached across the aisle and tapped him on the arm. "The thing to do with a boy," he said sagely, "is to show him all it is to show. Don't hold nothing back."

"Yeah," the man said. He gazed down at his swollen feet and lifted the left one about ten inches from the floor. After a minute he put it down and lifted the other. All through the car people began to get up and move about and yawn and stretch. Separate voices could be heard here and there and then a general hum. Suddenly Mr. Head's serene expression changed. His mouth almost closed and a light, fierce and cautious both, came into his eyes. He was looking down the length of the car. Without turning, he caught Nelson by the arm and pulled him forward. "Look," he said.

A huge coffee-colored man was coming slowly forward. He had on a light suit and a yellow satin tie with a ruby pin in it. One of his hands rested on his stomach which rode majestically under his buttoned coat, and in the other he held the head of a black walking stick that he picked up and set down with a deliberate outward motion each time he took a step. He was proceeding very slowly, his large brown eyes gazing over the heads of the passengers. He had a small white mustache and white crinkly hair. Behind him there were two young women, both coffee-colored, one in a yellow dress and one in a green. Their progress was kept at the rate of his and they chatted in low throaty voices as they followed him.

Mr. Head's grip was tightening insistently on Nelson's arm. As the procession passed them, the light from a sapphire ring on the brown hand that picked up the cane reflected in Mr. Head's eye, but he did not look up nor did the tremendous man look at him. The group proceeded up the rest of the aisle and out of the car. Mr. Head's grip on Nelson's arm loosened. "What was that?" he asked.

"A man," the boy said and gave him an indignant look as if he were tired of having his intelligence insulted.

"What kind of a man?" Mr. Head persisted, his voice expressionless.

"A fat man," Nelson said. He was beginning to feel that he had better be cautious.

"You don't know what kind?" Mr. Head said in a final tone.

"An old man," the boy said and had a sudden foreboding that he was not going to enjoy the day.

"That was a nigger," Mr. Head said and sat back.

Nelson jumped up on the seat and stood looking backward to the end of the car but the Negro had gone.

"I'd of thought you'd know a nigger since you seen so many when you was in the city on your first visit," Mr. Head continued. "That's his first nigger," he said to the man across the aisle.

The boy slid down into the seat. "You said they were black," he said in an angry voice. "You never said they were tan. How do you expect me to know anything when you don't tell me right?"

"You're just ignorant is all," Mr. Head said and he got up and moved over in the vacant seat by the man across the aisle.

220   Nelson turned backward again and looked where the Negro had disappeared. He felt that the Negro had deliberately walked down the aisle in order to make a fool of him and he hated him with a fierce raw fresh hate; and also, he understood now why his grandfather disliked them. He looked toward the window and the face there seemed to suggest that he might be inadequate to the day's exactions. He wondered if he would even recognize the city when they came to it.

After he had told several stories, Mr. Head realized that the man he was talking to was asleep and he got up and suggested to Nelson that they walk over the train and see the parts of it. He particularly wanted the boy to see
230   the toilet so they went first to the men's room and examined the plumbing. Mr. Head demonstrated the ice-water cooler as if he had invented it and showed Nelson the bowl with the single spigot where the travelers brushed their teeth. They went through several cars and came to the diner.

This was the most elegant car in the train. It was painted a rich egg-yellow and had a wine-colored carpet on the floor. There were wide windows over the tables and great spaces of the rolling view were caught in miniature in the sides of the coffee pots and in the glasses. Three very black Negroes in white suits and aprons were running up and down the aisle, swinging trays and bowing and bending over the travelers eating breakfast. One of them
240   rushed up to Mr. Head and Nelson and said, holding up two fingers, "Space for two!" but Mr. Head replied in a loud voice, "We eaten before we left!"

The waiter wore large brown spectacles that increased the size of his eye whites. "Stan' aside then please," he said with an airy wave of the arm as if he were brushing aside flies.

Neither Nelson nor Mr. Head moved a fraction of an inch. "Look," Mr. Head said.

The near corner of the diner, containing two tables, was set off from the rest by a saffron-colored curtain. One table was set but empty but at the other, facing them, his back to the drape, sat the tremendous Negro. He was
250   speaking in a soft voice to the two women while he buttered a muffin. He had a heavy sad face and his neck bulged over his white collar on either side. "They rope them off," Mr. Head explained. Then he said, "Let's go see the kitchen," and they walked the length of the diner but the black waiter was coming fast behind them.

"Passengers are not allowed in the kitchen!" he said in a haughty voice. "Passengers are NOT allowed in the kitchen!"

Mr. Head stopped where he was and turned. "And there's good reason for that," he shouted into the Negro's chest, "because the cockroaches would run the passengers out!"

260   All the travelers laughed and Mr. Head and Nelson walked out, grinning. Mr. Head was known at home for his quick wit and Nelson felt a sudden keen pride in him. He realized the old man would be his only support in the

strange place they were approaching. He would be entirely alone in the world if he were ever lost from his grandfather. A terrible excitement shook him and he wanted to take hold of Mr. Head's coat and hold on like a child.

As they went back to their seats they could see through the passing windows that the countryside was becoming speckled with small houses and shacks and that a highway ran alongside the train. Cars sped by on it, very small and fast. Nelson felt that there was less breath in the air than there had been thirty minutes ago. The man across the aisle had left and there was no   270
one near for Mr. Head to hold a conversation with so he looked out the window, through his own reflection, and read aloud the names of the buildings they were passing. "The Dixie Chemical Corp!" he announced. "Southern Maid Flour! Dixie Doors! Southern Belle Cotton Products! Patty's Peanut Butter! Southern Mammy Cane Syrup!"

"Hush up!" Nelson hissed.

All over the car people were beginning to get up and take their luggage off the overhead racks. Women were putting on their coats and hats. The conductor stuck his head in the car and snarled, "Firstopppppmry," and Nelson lunged out of his sitting position, trembling. Mr. Head pushed him   280
down by the shoulder.

"Keep your seat," he said in dignified tones. "The first stop is on the edge of town. The second stop is at the main railroad station." He had come by this knowledge on his first trip when he had got off at the first stop and had had to pay a man fifteen cents to take him into the heart of town. Nelson sat back down, very pale. For the first time in his life, he understood that his grandfather was indispensable to him.

The train stopped and let off a few passengers and glided on as if it had never ceased moving. Outside, behind rows of brown rickety houses, a line of blue buildings stood up, and beyond them a pale rose-gray sky faded away   290
to nothing. The train moved into the railroad yard. Looking down, Nelson saw lines and lines of silver tracks multiplying and criss-crossing. Then before he could start counting them, the face in the window started out at him, gray but distinct, and he looked the other way. The train was in the station. Both he and Mr. Head jumped up and ran to the door. Neither noticed that they had left the paper sack with the lunch in it on the seat.

They walked stiffly through the small station and came out of a heavy door into the squall of traffic. Crowds were hurrying to work. Nelson didn't know where to look. Mr. Head leaned against the side of the building and glared in front of him.   300

Finally Nelson said, "Well, how do you see what all it is to see?"

Mr. Head didn't answer. Then as if the sight of people passing had given him the clue, he said, "You walk," and started off down the street. Nelson followed, steadying his hat. So many sights and sounds were flooding in on him that for the first block he hardly knew what he was seeing. At the second corner, Mr. Head turned and looked behind him at the station they had left, a putty-colored terminal with a concrete dome on top. He thought that if he

Same experience for Mr. Head?

could keep the dome always in sight, he would be able to get back in the afternoon to catch the train again.

310 As they walked along, Nelson began to distinguish details and take note of the store windows, jammed with every kind of equipment—hardware, drygoods, chicken feed, liquor. They passed one that Mr. Head called his particular attention to where you walked in and sat on a chair with your feet upon two rests and let a Negro polish your shoes. They walked slowly and stopped and stood at the entrances so he could see what went on in each place but they did not go into any of them. Mr. Head was <u>determined not to go into any city store because on his first trip here, he had got lost in a large one and had found his way out only after many people had insulted him.</u>

They came in the middle of the next block to a store that had a weighing
320 machine in front of it and they both in turn stepped up on it and put in a penny and received a ticket. Mr. Head's ticket said, "You weigh 120 pounds. You are upright and brave and all your friends admire you." He put the ticket in his pocket, surprised that the machine should have got <u>his character correct but his weight wrong, for he had weighed on a grain scale not long before and knew he weighed 110.</u> Nelson's ticket said, "You weigh 98 pounds. You have a great destiny ahead of you but beware of dark women." Nelson did not know any women and he weighed only 68 pounds but Mr. Head pointed out that the machine had probably printed the number upside down, meaning the 9 for a 6.

330 They walked on and at the end of five blocks the dome of the terminal sank out of sight and Mr. Head turned to the left. Nelson could have stood in front of every store window for an hour if there had not been another more interesting one next to it. Suddenly he said, "I was born here!" Mr. Head turned and looked at him with horror. There was a sweaty brightness about his face. "<u>This is where I come from!</u>" he said.

Mr. Head was appalled. He saw the moment had come for drastic action. "Lemme show you one thing you ain't seen yet," he said and took him to the corner where there was a sewer entrance. "Squat down," he said, "and stick you head in there," and he held the back of the boy's coat while he got down
340 and put his head in the sewer. He drew it back quickly, hearing a gurgling in the depths under the sidewalk. Then Mr. Head explained the sewer system, how the entire city was underlined with it, how it contained all the drainage and was full of rats and how a man could slide into it and be sucked along down endless pitchblack tunnels. At any minute any man in the city might be sucked into the sewer and never heard from again. He described it so well that Nelson was for some seconds shaken. He connected the sewer passages with the entrance to hell and understood for the first time how the world was <u>put together in its lower parts</u>. He drew away from the curb.

Then he said, "Yes, but you can stay away from the holes," and his face
350 took on that stubborn look that was so exasperating to his grandfather. "<u>This is where I come from!</u>" he said.

[margin handwritten note:] The grain scale is shorting people? The scales—did they print tickets at weighing or ahead?

[margin handwritten note:] "This is where I come from!"

Mr. Head was dismayed but he only muttered, "You'll get your fill," and
they walked on. At the end of two more blocks he turned to the left, feeling
that he was circling the dome; and he was correct for in a half-hour they
passed in front of the railroad station again. At first Nelson did not notice
that he was seeing the same stores twice but when they passed the one where
you put your feet on the rests while the Negro polished your shoes, he perceived that they were walking in a circle.

"We done been here!" he shouted. "I don't believe you know where
you're at!"

"The direction just slipped my mind for a minute," Mr. Head said and
they turned down a different street. He still did not intend to let the dome
get too far away and after two blocks in their new direction, he turned to the
left. This street contained two- and three-story wooden dwellings. Anyone
passing on the sidewalk could see into the rooms and Mr. Head, glancing
through one window, saw a woman lying on an iron bed, looking out, with
a sheet pulled over her. Her knowing expression shook him. A fierce-looking
boy on a bicycle came driving down out of nowhere and he had to jump to
the side to keep from being hit. "It's nothing to them if they knock you
down," he said. "You better keep closer to me."

They walked on for some time on streets like this before he remembered
to turn again. The houses they were passing now were all unpainted and the
wood in them looked rotten; the street between was narrower. Nelson saw a
colored man. Then another. Then another. "Niggers live in these houses," he
observed.

"Well come on and we'll go somewheres else," Mr. Head said. "We didn't
come to look at niggers," and they turned down another street but they
continued to see Negroes everywhere. Nelson's skin began to prickle and
they stepped along at a faster pace in order to leave the neighborhood as soon
as possible. There were colored men in their undershirts standing in the doors
and colored women rocking on the sagging porches. Colored children played
in the gutters and stopped what they were doing to look at them. Before long
they began to pass rows of stores with colored customers in them but they
didn't pause at the entrances of these. Black eyes in black faces were watching
them from every direction. "Yes," Mr. Head said, "this is where you were
born—right here with all these niggers."

Nelson scowled. "I think you done got us lost," he said.

Mr. Head swung around sharply and looked for the dome. It was nowhere
in sight. "I ain't got us lost either," he said. "You're just tired of walking."

"I ain't tired, I'm hungry," Nelson said. "Give me a biscuit."

They discovered then that they had lost the lunch.

"You were the one holding the sack," Nelson said. "I would have kepa-
holt of it."

"If you want to direct this trip, I'll go on by myself and leave you right
here," Mr. Head said and was pleased to see the boy turn white. However, he

360

370

380

390

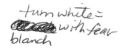

realized they were lost and drifting farther every minute from the station. He
was hungry himself and beginning to be thirsty and since they had been in
the colored neighborhood, they had both begun to sweat. Nelson had on his
shoes and he was unaccustomed to them. The concrete sidewalks were very
400   hard. They both wanted to find a place to sit down but this was impossible
and they kept on walking, the boy muttering under his breath, "First you lost
the sack and then you lost the way," and Mr. Head growling from time to
time, "Anybody wants to be from this nigger heaven can be from it!"

By now the sun was well forward in the sky. The odor of dinners cooking
drifted out to them. The Negroes were all at their doors to see them pass.
"Whyn't you ast one of these niggers the way?" Nelson said. "You got us lost."

"This is where you were born," Mr. Head said. "You can ast one yourself
if you want to."

Nelson was afraid of the colored men and he didn't want to be laughed at
410   by the colored children. Up ahead he saw a large colored woman leaning in
a doorway that opened onto the sidewalk. Her hair stood straight out from
her head for about four inches all around and she was resting on bare brown
feet that turned pink at the sides. She had on a pink dress that showed her
exact shape. As they came abreast of her, she lazily lifted one hand to her head
and her fingers disappeared into her hair.

Nelson stopped. He felt his breath drawn up by the woman's dark eyes.
"How do you get back to town?" he said in a voice that did not sound like
his own.

After a minute she said, "You in town now," in a rich low tone that made
420   Nelson feel as if a cool spray had been turned on him.

"How do you get back to the train?" he said in the same reed-like voice.

"You can catch you a car," she said.

He understood she was making fun of him but he was too paralyzed even
to scowl. He stood drinking in every detail of her. His eyes traveled up from
her great knees to her forehead and then made a triangular path from the glis-
tening sweat on her neck down and across her tremendous bosom and over
her bare arm back to where her fingers lay hidden in her hair. He suddenly
wanted her to reach down and pick him up and draw him against her and
then he wanted to feel her breath on his face. He wanted to look down and
430   down into her eyes while she held him tighter and tighter. He had never had
such a feeling before. He felt as if he were reeling down through a pitchblack
tunnel.

"You can go a block down yonder and catch you a car take you to the railroad station, Sugarpie," she said.

Nelson would have collapsed at her feet if Mr. Head had not pulled him
roughly away. "You act like you don't have any sense!" the old man growled.

They hurried down the street and Nelson did not look back at the
woman. He pushed his hat sharply forward over his face which was already
burning with shame. The sneering ghost he had seen in the train window and
440   all the foreboding feelings he had on the way returned to him and he remem-

bered that his ticket from the scale had said to beware of dark women and that his grandfather's had said he was upright and brave. He took hold of the old man's hand, a sign of dependence that he seldom showed.

They headed down the street toward the car tracks where a long yellow rattling trolley was coming. Mr. Head had never boarded a streetcar and he let that one pass. Nelson was silent. From time to time his mouth trembled slightly but his grandfather, occupied with his own problems, paid him no attention. They stood on the corner and neither looked at the Negroes who were passing, going about their business just as if they had been white, except that most of them stopped and eyed Mr. Head and Nelson. It occurred to   450
Mr. Head that since the streetcar ran on tracks, they could simply follow the tracks. He gave Nelson a slight push and explained that they would follow the tracks on into the railroad station, walking, and they set off.

Presently to their great relief they began to see white people again and Nelson sat down on the sidewalk against the wall of a building. "I got to rest myself some," he said. "You lost the sack and the direction. You can just wait on me to rest myself."

"There's the tracks in front of us," Mr. Head said. "All we got to do is keep them in sight and you could have remembered the sack as good as me. This is where you were born. This is your old home town. This is your sec-   460
ond trip. You ought to know how to do," and he squatted down and continued in this vein but the boy, easing his burning feet out of his shoes, did not answer.

"And standing there grinning like a chim-pan-zee while a nigger woman gives you direction. Great Gawd!" Mr. Head said.

"I never said I was nothing but born here," the boy said in a shaky voice. "I never said I would or wouldn't like it. I never said I wanted to come. I only said I was born here and I never had nothing to do with that. I want to go home. I never wanted to come in the first place. It was all your big idea. How you know you ain't following the tracks in the wrong direction?"   470

This last had occurred to Mr. Head too. "All these people are white," he said.

"We ain't passed here before," Nelson said. This was a neighborhood of brick buildings that might have been lived in or might not. A few empty automobiles were parked along the curb and there was an occasional passerby. The heat of the pavement came up through Nelson's thin suit. His eyelids began to droop, and after a few minutes his head tilted forward. His shoulders twitched once or twice and then he fell over on his side and lay sprawled in an exhausted fit of sleep.

Mr. Head watched him silently. He was very tired himself but they could   480
not both sleep at the same time and he could not have slept anyway because he did not know where he was. In a few minutes Nelson would wake up, refreshed by his sleep and very cocky, and would begin complaining that he had lost the sack and the way. You'd have a mighty sorry time if I wasn't here, Mr. Head thought; and then another idea occurred to him. He looked at the

sprawled figure for several minutes; presently he stood up. He justified what he was going to do on the grounds that it is sometimes necessary to teach a child a lesson he won't forget, particularly when the child is always reasserting his position with some new impudence. He walked without a sound to

490 the corner about twenty feet away and sat down on a covered garbage can in the alley where he could look out and watch Nelson wake up alone.

The boy was dozing fitfully, half conscious of vague noises and black forms moving up from some dark part of him into the light. His face worked in his sleep and he had pulled his knees up under his chin. The sun shed a dull dry light on the narrow street; everything looked like exactly what it was. After a while Mr. Head, hunched like an old monkey on the garbage can lid, decided that if Nelson didn't wake up soon, he would make a loud noise by bamming his foot against the can. He looked at his watch and discovered that it was two o'clock. Their train left at six and the possibility of missing it was

500 too awful for him to think of. He kicked his foot backwards on the can and a hollow boom reverberated in the alley.

Nelson shot up onto his feet with a shout. He looked where his grandfather should have been and stared. He seemed to whirl several times and then, picking up his feet and throwing his head back, he dashed down the street like a wild maddened pony. Mr. Head jumped off the can and galloped after but the child was almost out of sight. He saw a streak of gray disappearing diagonally a block ahead. He ran as fast as he could, looking both ways down every intersection, but without sight of him again. Then as he passed the third intersection, completely winded, he saw about half a block down the

510 street a scene that stopped him altogether. He crouched behind a trash box to watch and get his bearings.

Nelson was sitting with both legs spread out and by his side lay an elderly woman, screaming. Groceries were scattered about the sidewalk. A crowd of women had already gathered to see justice done and Mr. Head distinctly heard the old woman on the pavement shout, "You've broken my ankle and your daddy'll pay for it! Every nickel! Police! Police!" Several of the women were plucking at Nelson's shoulder but the boy seemed too dazed to get up.

Something forced Mr. Head from behind the trash box and forward, but

520 only at a creeping pace. He had never in his life been accosted by a policeman. The women were milling around Nelson as if they might suddenly all dive on him at once and tear him to pieces, and the old woman continued to scream that her ankle was broken and to call for an officer. Mr. Head came on so slowly that he could have been taking a backward step after each forward one, but when he was about ten feet away, Nelson saw him and sprang. The child caught him around the hips and clung panting against him.

The women all turned on Mr. Head. The injured one sat up and shouted, "You sir! You'll pay every penny of my doctor's bill that your boy has caused. He's a juve-nile deliquent! Where is an officer? Somebody take this man's

530 name and address!"

Mr. Head was trying to detach Nelson's fingers from the flesh in the back of his legs. The old man's head had lowered itself into his collar like a turtle's; his eyes were glazed with fear and caution.

"Your boy has broken my ankle!" the old woman shouted. "Police!"

Mr. Head sensed the approach of the policeman from behind. He stared straight ahead at the women who were massed in their fury like a solid wall to block his escape, "This is not my boy," he said. "I never seen him before."

But it wasn't

He felt Nelson's fingers fall out of his flesh.

The women dropped back, staring at him with horror, as if they were so repulsed by a man who would deny his own image and likeness that they could not bear to lay hands on him. Mr. Head walked on, through a space they silently cleared, and left Nelson behind. Ahead of him he saw nothing but a hollow tunnel that had once been the street.   540

The boy remained standing where he was, his neck craned forward and his hands hanging by his sides. His hat was jammed on his head so that there were no longer any creases in it. The injured woman got up and shook her fist at him and the others gave him pitying looks, but he didn't notice any of them. There was no policeman in sight.

In a minute he began to move mechanically, making no effort to catch up with his grandfather but merely following at about twenty paces. They   550 walked on for five blocks in this way. Mr. Head's shoulders were sagging and his neck hung forward at such an angle that it was not visible from behind. He was afraid to turn his head. Finally he cut a short hopeful glance over his shoulder. Twenty feet behind him, he saw two small eyes piercing into his back like pitchfork prongs.

The boy was not of a forgiving nature but this was the first time he had ever had anything to forgive. Mr. Head had never disgraced himself before. After two more blocks, he turned and called over his shoulder in a high desperately gay voice, "Let's us go get us a Co' Cola somewheres!"

Nelson, with a dignity he had never shown before, turned and stood with   560 his back to his grandfather.

Mr. Head began to feel the depth of his denial. His face as they walked on became all hollows and bare ridges. He saw nothing they were passing but he perceived that they had lost the car tracks. There was no dome to be seen anywhere and the afternoon was advancing. He knew that if dark overtook them in the city, they would be beaten and robbed. The speed of God's justice was only what he expected for himself, but he could not stand to think that his sins would be visited upon Nelson and that even now, he was leading the boy to his doom.

robbed of what?

They continued to walk on block after block through an endless section   570 of small brick houses until Mr. Head almost fell over a water spigot sticking up about six inches off the edge of a grass plot. He had not had a drink of water since early morning but he felt he did not deserve it now. Then he thought that Nelson would be thirsty and they would both drink and be brought together. He squatted down and put his mouth to the nozzle and turned a cold stream of water into his throat. Then he called out in the high desperate voice, "Come on and getcher some water!"

This time the child stared through him for nearly sixty seconds. Mr. Head got up and walked on as if he had drunk poison. Nelson, though he had not 580 had water since some he had drunk out of a paper cup on the train, passed by the spigot, disdaining to drink where his grandfather had. When Mr. Head realized this, he lost all hope. His face in the waning afternoon light looked ravaged and abandoned. He could feel the boy's steady hate, traveling at an even pace behind him and he knew that (if by some miracle they escaped being murdered in the city) it would continue just that way for the rest of his life. He knew that now he was wandering into a black strange place where nothing was like it had ever been before, a long old age without respect and an end that would be welcome because it would be the end.

As for Nelson, his mind had frozen around his grandfather's treachery as 590 if he were trying to preserve it intact to present at the final judgment. He walked without looking to one side or the other, but every now and then his mouth would twitch and this was when he felt, from some remote place inside himself, a black mysterious form reach up as if it would melt his frozen vision in one hot grasp.

The sun dropped down behind a row of houses and hardly noticing, they passed into an elegant suburban section where mansions were set back from the road by lawns with birdbaths on them. Here everything was entirely deserted. For blocks they didn't pass even a dog. The big white houses were like partially submerged icebergs in the distance. There were no sidewalks, 600 only drives, and these wound around and around in endless ridiculous circles. Nelson made no move to come nearer to Mr. Head. The old man felt that if he saw a sewer entrance he would drop down into it and let himself be carried away; and he could imagine the boy standing by, watching with only a slight interest, while he disappeared.

A loud bark jarred him to attention and he looked up to see a fat man approaching with two bulldogs. He waved both arms like someone shipwrecked on a desert island. "I'm lost!" he called. "I'm lost and can't find my way and me and this boy have got to catch this train and I can't find the station. Oh Gawd I'm lost! Oh hep me Gawd I'm lost!"

610 The man, who was bald-headed and had on golf knickers, asked him what train he was trying to catch and Mr. Head began to get out his tickets, trembling so violently he could hardly hold them. Nelson had come up to within fifteen feet and stood watching.

"Well," the fat man said, giving him back the tickets, "you won't have time to get back to town to make this but you can catch it at the suburb stop. That's three blocks from here," and he began explaining how to get there.

Mr. Head stared as if he were slowly returning from the dead and when the man had finished and gone off with the dogs jumping at his heels, he turned to Nelson and said breathlessly, "We're going to get home!"

[handwritten margin note: "Negro/Colored" faucets, aversion/revulsion/moral impulse]

The child was standing about ten feet away, his face bloodless under the   620
gray hat. His eyes were triumphantly cold. There was no light in them, no
feeling, no interest. He was merely there, a small figure, waiting. Home was
nothing to him.

Mr. Head turned slowly. He felt he knew now what time would be like
without seasons and what heat would be like without light and what man
would be like without salvation. He didn't care if he never made the train and
if it had not been for what suddenly caught his attention, like a cry out of
the gathering dusk, he might have forgotten there was a station to go to.

He had not walked five hundred yards down the road when he saw,
within reach of him, the plaster figure of a Negro sitting bent over on a low   630
yellow brick fence that curved around a wide lawn. The Negro was about
Nelson's size and he was pitched forward at an unsteady angle because the
putty that held him to the wall had cracked. One of his eyes was entirely
white and he held a piece of brown watermelon.

Mr. Head stood looking at him silently until Nelson stopped at a little
distance. Then as the two of them stood there, Mr. Head breathed, "An artificial nigger!"

It was not possible to tell if the artificial Negro were meant to be young
or old; he looked too miserable to be either. He was meant to look happy
because his mouth was stretched up at the corners but the chipped eye and   640
the angle he was cocked at gave him a wild look of misery instead.

"An artificial nigger!" Nelson repeated in Mr. Head's exact tone.

The two of them stood there with their necks forward at almost the same
angle and their shoulders curved in almost exactly the same way and their
hands trembling identically in their pockets. Mr. Head looked like an ancient
child and Nelson like a miniature old man. They stood gazing at the artificial Negro as if they were faced with some great mystery, some monument to
another's victory that brought them together in their common defeat. They
could both feel it dissolving their differences like an action of mercy.
Mr. Head had never known before what mercy felt like because he had been   650
too good to deserve any, but he felt he knew now. He looked at Nelson and
understood that he must say something to the child to show that he was still
wise and in the look the boy returned he saw a hungry need for that assurance. Nelson's eyes seemed to implore him to explain once and for all the
mystery of existence.

Mr. Head opened his lips to make a lofty statement and heard himself say,
"They ain't got enough real ones here. They got to have an artificial one."

After a second, the boy nodded with a strange shivering about his mouth,
and said, "Let's go home before we get ourselves lost again."

Their train glided into the suburb stop just as they reached the station   660
and they boarded it together, and ten minutes before it was due to arrive at
the junction, they went to the door and stood ready to jump off if it did not
stop; but it did, just as the moon, restored to its full splendor, sprang from a

cloud and flooded the clearing with light. As they stepped off, the sage grass was shivering gently in shades of silver and the clinkers under their feet glittered with a fresh black light. The treetops, fencing the junction like the protecting walls of a garden, were darker than the sky which was hung with gigantic white clouds illuminated like lanterns.

670   Mr. Head stood very still and felt the action of mercy touch him again but this time he knew that there were no words in the world that could name it. He understood that it grew out of agony, which is not denied to any man and which is given in strange ways to children. He understood it was all a man could carry into death to give his Maker and he suddenly burned with shame that he had so little of it to take with him. He stood appalled, judging himself with the thoroughness of God, while the action of mercy covered his pride like a flame and consumed it. He had never thought himself a great sinner before but he saw now that his true depravity had been hidden from him lest it cause him despair. He realized that he was forgiven for sins from the beginning of time, when he had conceived in his own heart the sin of

680   Adam, until the present, when he had denied poor Nelson. He saw that no sin was too monstrous for him to claim as his own, and since God loved in proportion as He forgave, he felt ready at that instant to enter Paradise.

Nelson, composing his expression under the shadow of his hat brim, watched him with a mixture of fatigue and suspicion, but as the train glided past them and disappeared like a frightened serpent into the woods, even his face lightened and he muttered, "I'm glad I've went once, but I'll never go back again!"

How do you know the family's economic situation?

What's the worst thing you've ever done to somebody &
how did it resolve in your feelings?

What is "mercy"?

Is this a story of redemption?

The ties of tribe that seemed so strong
could be severed by fear. Then the ties
were reknit in the face of another ⟶ of moral annihilation
other — the jeopardy they were in left   loneliness
them seeking one another's company on   lostress
whatever terms were most familiar.   separation

Better read the Scripture passages first for context.

THE MORAL INSTINCT
Steven Pinker

Steven Pinker is the Johnstone Family Professor of Psychology at Harvard University and the author of "The Language Instinct" and "The Stuff of Thought: Language as a Window Into Human Nature."

Which of the following people would you say is the most admirable: 1
Mother Teresa, Bill Gates or Norman Borlaug? And which do you
think is the least admirable? For most people, it's an easy question. Mother
Teresa, famous for ministering to the poor in Calcutta, has been beatified by
the Vatican, awarded the Nobel Peace Prize and ranked in an American poll
as the most admired person of the 20th century. Bill Gates, infamous for giving us the Microsoft dancing paper clip and the blue screen of death, has
been decapitated in effigy in "I Hate Gates" Web sites and hit with a pie in
the face. As for Norman Borlaug . . . who the heck is Norman Borlaug?

Yet a deeper look might lead you to rethink your answers. Borlaug, father   10
of the "Green Revolution" that used agricultural science to reduce world
hunger, has been credited with saving a billion lives, more than anyone else
in history. Gates, in deciding what to do with his fortune, crunched the numbers and determined that he could alleviate the most misery by fighting
everyday scourges in the developing world like malaria, diarrhea and para-
sites. Mother Teresa, for her part, extolled the virtue of suffering and ran her
well-financed missions accordingly: their sick patrons were offered plenty of
prayer but harsh conditions, few analgesics and dangerously primitive medical care.

It's not hard to see why the moral reputations of this trio should be so out   20
of line with the good they have done. Mother Teresa was the very embodi-
ment of saintliness: white-clad, sad-eyed, ascetic and often photographed with
the wretched of the earth. Gates is a nerd's nerd and the world's richest man,
as likely to enter heaven as the proverbial camel squeezing through the nee-
dle's eye. And Borlaug, now 93, is an agronomist who has spent his life in labs
and nonprofits, seldom walking onto the media stage, and hence into our consciousness, at all.

Obit?

I doubt these examples will persuade anyone to favor Bill Gates over
Mother Teresa for sainthood. But they show that our heads can be turned by
an aura of sanctity, distracting us from a more objective reckoning of the   30
actions that make people suffer or flourish. It seems we may all be vulnerable to moral illusions the ethical equivalent of the bending lines that trick the
eye on cereal boxes and in psychology textbooks. Illusions are a favorite tool

of perception scientists for exposing the workings of the five senses, and of philosophers for shaking people out of the naive belief that our minds give us a transparent window onto the world (since if our eyes can be fooled by an illusion, why should we trust them at other times?). Today, a new field is using illusions to unmask a sixth sense, the moral sense. Moral intuitions are being drawn out of people in the lab, on Web sites and in brain scanners, and
40 are being explained with tools from game theory, neuroscience and evolutionary biology.

"Two things fill the mind with ever new and increasing admiration and awe, the oftener and more steadily we reflect on them," wrote Immanuel Kant, "the starry heavens above and the moral law within." These days, the moral law within is being viewed with increasing awe, if not always admiration. The human moral sense turns out to be an organ of considerable complexity, with quirks that reflect its evolutionary history and its neurobiological foundations.

These quirks are bound to have implications for the human predicament.
50 Morality is not just any old topic in psychology but close to our conception of the meaning of life. Moral goodness is what gives each of us the sense that we are worthy human beings. We seek it in our friends and mates, nurture it in our children, advance it in our politics and justify it with our religions. A disrespect for morality is blamed for everyday sins and history's worst atrocities. To carry this weight, the concept of morality would have to be bigger than any of us and outside all of us.

So dissecting moral intuitions is no small matter. If morality is a mere trick of the brain, some may fear, our very grounds for being moral could be eroded. Yet as we shall see, the science of the moral sense can instead be seen
60 as a way to strengthen those grounds, by clarifying what morality is and how it should steer our actions.

THE MORALIZATION SWITCH

The starting point for appreciating that there is a distinctive part of our psychology for morality is seeing how moral judgments differ from other kinds of opinions we have on how people ought to behave. Moralization is a psychological state that can be turned on and off like a switch, and when it is on, a distinctive mind-set commandeers our thinking. This is the mind-set that makes us deem actions immoral ("killing is wrong"), rather than merely disagreeable ("I hate brussels sprouts"), unfashionable ("bell-bottoms are out") or imprudent ("don't scratch mosquito bites").
70 The first hallmark of moralization is that the rules it invokes are felt to be universal. Prohibitions of rape and murder, for example, are felt not to be matters of local custom but to be universally and objectively warranted. One can easily say, "I don't like brussels sprouts, but I don't care if you eat them," but no one would say, "I don't like killing, but I don't care if you murder someone."

The other hallmark is that people feel that those who commit immoral acts <u>deserve to be punished</u>. Not only is it allowable to inflict pain on a person who has broken a moral rule; it is <u>wrong not to</u>, to "let them get away with it." People are thus untroubled in inviting divine retribution or the power of the state to harm other people they deem immoral. Bertrand Russell wrote, "The infliction of cruelty with a good conscience is a delight to moralists—that is why they invented hell."

②Deserving of punishment

80

We all know what it feels like when the moralization switch flips inside us—the righteous glow, the burning dudgeon, the drive to recruit others to the cause. The psychologist Paul Rozin has studied the toggle switch by comparing two kinds of people who engage in the same behavior but with different switch settings. Health vegetarians avoid meat for practical reasons, like lowering cholesterol and avoiding toxins. Moral vegetarians avoid meat for ethical reasons: to avoid complicity in the suffering of animals. By investigating their feelings about meat-eating, Rozin showed that the moral motive sets off a cascade of opinions. Moral vegetarians are more likely to treat meat as a contaminant—they refuse, for example, to eat a bowl of soup into which a drop of beef broth has fallen. They are more likely to think that other people ought to be vegetarians, and are more likely to imbue their dietary habits with other virtues, like believing that meat avoidance makes people less aggressive and bestial.

90

Much of our recent social history, <u>including the culture wars between liberals and conservatives, consists of the moralization or amoralization of particular kinds of behavior</u>. Even when people agree that an outcome is desirable, they may disagree on whether it should be treated as a matter of preference and prudence or as a matter of sin and virtue. Rozin notes, for example, that <u>smoking has lately been moralized</u>. Until recently, it was understood that some people didn't enjoy smoking or avoided it because it was hazardous to their health. But with the discovery of the harmful effects of secondhand smoke, smoking is now treated as immoral. Smokers are ostracized; images of people smoking are censored; and entities touched by smoke are felt to be contaminated (so hotels have not only nonsmoking rooms but nonsmoking floors). The desire for retribution has been visited on tobacco companies, who have been slapped with staggering "punitive damages."

100

At the same time, many <u>behaviors have been amoralized</u>, switched from moral failings to lifestyle choices. They include divorce, illegitimacy, being a working mother, marijuana use and homosexuality. Many afflictions have been reassigned from payback for bad choices to unlucky misfortunes. There used to be people called "bums" and "tramps"; today they are "homeless." Drug addiction is a "disease"; syphilis was rebranded from the price of wanton behavior to a "sexually transmitted disease" and more recently a "sexually transmitted infection."

110

This wave of amoralization has led the cultural right to lament that morality itself is under assault, as we see in the group that anointed itself the Moral Majority. In fact there seems to be a Law of Conservation of Moralization, so

120

that as old behaviors are taken out of the moralized column, new ones are added to it. Dozens of things that past generations treated as practical matters are now ethical battlegrounds, including disposable diapers, I.Q. tests, poultry farms, Barbie dolls and research on breast cancer. Food alone has become a minefield, with critics sermonizing about the size of sodas, the chemistry of fat, the freedom of chickens, the price of coffee beans, the species of fish and now the distance the food has traveled from farm to plate.

130   Many of these moralizations, like the assault on smoking, may be understood as practical tactics to reduce some recently identified harm. But whether an activity flips our mental switches to the "moral" setting isn't just a matter of how much harm it does. We don't show contempt to the man who fails to change the batteries in his smoke alarms or takes his family on a driving vacation, both of which multiply the risk they will die in an accident. Driving a gas-guzzling Hummer is reprehensible, but driving a gas-guzzling old Volvo is not; eating a Big Mac is unconscionable, but not imported cheese or creme brulee. The reason for these double standards is obvious: people tend to align their moralization with their own lifestyles.

REASONING AND RATIONALIZING

[handwritten margin note: moral judgments flawed — process of making them — flawed as well]

It's not just the content of our moral judgments that is often questionable, but the way we arrive at them. We like to think that when we have a conviction,
140   tion, there are good reasons that drove us to adopt it. That is why an older approach to moral psychology, led by Jean Piaget and Lawrence Kohlberg, tried to document the lines of reasoning that guided people to moral conclusions. But consider these situations, originally devised by the psychologist Jonathan Haidt:

Julie is traveling in France on summer vacation from college with her brother Mark. One night they decide that it would be interesting and fun if they tried making love. Julie was already taking birth-control pills, but Mark uses a condom, too, just to be safe. They both enjoy the sex but decide not to do it again. They keep the night as a special secret, which makes them feel
150   closer to each other. What do you think about that—was it O.K. for them to make love?

A woman is cleaning out her closet and she finds her old American flag. She doesn't want the flag anymore, so she cuts it up into pieces and uses the rags to clean her bathroom.

A family's dog is killed by a car in front of their house. They heard that dog meat was delicious, so they cut up the dog's body and cook it and eat it for dinner.

Most people immediately declare that these acts are wrong and then grope to justify why they are wrong. It's not so easy. In the case of Julie and
160   Mark, people raise the possibility of children with birth defects, but they are reminded that the couple were diligent about contraception. They suggest that the siblings will be emotionally hurt, but the story makes it clear that

they weren't. They submit that the act would offend the community, but then recall that it was kept a secret. Eventually many people admit, "I don't know, I can't explain it, I just know it's wrong." People don't generally engage in moral reasoning, Haidt argues, but moral rationalization: they begin with the conclusion, coughed up by an unconscious emotion, and then work backward to a plausible justification.

The gap between people's convictions and their justifications is also on display in the favorite new sandbox for moral psychologists, a thought experiment devised by the philosophers Philippa Foot and Judith Jarvis Thomson called the Trolley Problem. On your morning walk, you see a trolley car hurtling down the track, the conductor slumped over the controls. In the path of the trolley are five men working on the track, oblivious to the danger. You are standing at a fork in the track and can pull a lever that will divert the trolley onto a spur, saving the five men. Unfortunately, the trolley would then run over a single worker who is laboring on the spur. Is it permissible to throw the switch, killing one man to save five? Almost everyone says "yes."

Consider now a different scene. You are on a bridge overlooking the tracks and have spotted the runaway trolley bearing down on the five workers. Now the only way to stop the trolley is to throw a heavy object in its path. And the only heavy object within reach is a fat man standing next to you. Should you throw the man off the bridge? Both dilemmas present you with the option of sacrificing one life to save five, and so, by the utilitarian standard of what would result in the greatest good for the greatest number, the two dilemmas are morally equivalent. But most people don't see it that way: though they would pull the switch in the first dilemma, they would not heave the fat man in the second. When pressed for a reason, they can't come up with anything coherent, though moral philosophers haven't had an easy time coming up with a relevant difference, either.

When psychologists say "most people" they usually mean "most of the two dozen sophomores who filled out a questionnaire for beer money." But in this case it means most of the 200,000 people from a hundred countries who shared their intuitions on a Web-based experiment conducted by the psychologists Fiery Cushman and Liane Young and the biologist Marc Hauser. A difference between the acceptability of switch-pulling and man-heaving, and an inability to justify the choice, was found in respondents from Europe, Asia and North and South America; among men and women, blacks and whites, teenagers and octogenarians, Hindus, Muslims, Buddhists, Christians, Jews and atheists; people with elementary-school educations and people with Ph.D.'s.

Joshua Greene, a philosopher and cognitive neuroscientist, suggests that evolution equipped people with a revulsion to manhandling an innocent person. This instinct, he suggests, tends to overwhelm any utilitarian calculus that would tote up the lives saved and lost. The impulse against roughing up a fellow human would explain other examples in which people abjure killing one to save many, like euthanizing a hospital patient to harvest his organs and save five dying patients in need of transplants, or throwing someone out of a crowded lifeboat to keep it afloat.

210   By itself this would be no more than a plausible story, but Greene teamed up with the cognitive neuroscientist Jonathan Cohen and several Princeton colleagues to peer into people's brains using functional M.R.I. They sought to find signs of a conflict between brain areas associated with emotion (the ones that recoil from harming someone) and areas dedicated to rational analysis (the ones that calculate lives lost and saved).

MRI study

When people pondered the dilemmas that required killing someone with their bare hands, several networks in their brains lighted up. One, which included the medial (inward-facing) parts of the frontal lobes, has been impli-
220   cated in emotions about other people. A second, the dorsolateral (upper and outer-facing) surface of the frontal lobes, has been implicated in ongoing mental computation (including nonmoral reasoning, like deciding whether to get somewhere by plane or train). And a third region, the anterior cingulate cortex (an evolutionarily ancient strip lying at the base of the inner surface of each cerebral hemisphere), registers a conflict between an urge coming from one part of the brain and an advisory coming from another.

But when the people were pondering a hands-off dilemma, like switching the trolley onto the spur with the single worker, the brain reacted differently: only the area involved in rational calculation stood out. Other studies have shown that neurological patients who have blunted emotions because of
230   damage to the frontal lobes become utilitarians: they think it makes perfect sense to throw the fat man off the bridge. Together, the findings corroborate Greene's theory that our nonutilitarian intuitions come from the victory of an emotional impulse over a cost-benefit analysis.

utilitarianism as a disease process!

A UNIVERSAL MORALITY?

The findings of trolleyology—complex, instinctive and worldwide moral intuitions—led Hauser and John Mikhail (a legal scholar) to revive an analogy from the philosopher John Rawls between the moral sense and language. According to Noam Chomsky, we are born with a "universal grammar" that forces us to analyze speech in terms of its grammatical structure, with no conscious awareness of the rules in play. By analogy, we are born with a univer-
240   sal moral grammar that forces us to analyze human action in terms of its moral structure, with just as little awareness.

The idea that the moral sense is an innate part of human nature is not farfetched. A list of human universals collected by the anthropologist Donald E. Brown includes many moral concepts and emotions, including a distinction between right and wrong; empathy; fairness; admiration of generosity; rights and obligations; proscription of murder, rape and other forms of violence; redress of wrongs; sanctions for wrongs against the community; shame; and taboos.

Get Donald Brown's whole list

The stirrings of morality emerge early in childhood. Toddlers spontaneously offer toys and help to others and try to comfort people they see in distress. And according to the psychologists Elliot Turiel and Judith Smetana,
preschoolers have an inkling of the difference between societal conventions
and moral principles. Four-year-olds say that it is not O.K. to wear pajamas
to school (a convention) and also not O.K. to hit a little girl for no reason (a
moral principle). But when asked whether these actions would be O.K. if the
teacher allowed them, most of the children said that wearing pajamas would
now be fine but that hitting a little girl would still not be.

Though no one has identified genes for morality, there is circumstantial
evidence they exist. The character traits called "conscientiousness" and
"agreeableness" are far more correlated in identical twins separated at birth
(who share their genes but not their environment) than in adoptive siblings
raised together (who share their environment but not their genes). People
given diagnoses of "antisocial personality disorder" or "psychopathy" show
signs of morality blindness from the time they are children. They bully
younger children, torture animals, habitually lie and seem incapable of empathy or remorse, often despite normal family backgrounds. Some of these children grow up into the monsters who bilk elderly people out of their savings,
rape a succession of women or shoot convenience-store clerks lying on the
floor during a robbery.

Though psychopathy probably comes from a genetic predisposition, a
milder version can be caused by damage to frontal regions of the brain
(including the areas that inhibit intact people from throwing the hypothetical fat man off the bridge). The neuroscientists Hanna and Antonio Dama-
sio and their colleagues found that some children who sustain severe injuries
to their frontal lobes can grow up into callous and irresponsible adults,
despite normal intelligence. They lie, steal, ignore punishment, endanger
their own children and can't think through even the simplest moral dilemmas, like what two people should do if they disagreed on which TV channel
to watch or whether a man ought to steal a drug to save his dying wife.

The moral sense, then, may be rooted in the design of the normal human
brain. Yet for all the awe that may fill our minds when we reflect on an innate
moral law within, the idea is at best incomplete. Consider this moral
dilemma: A runaway trolley is about to kill a schoolteacher. You can divert
the trolley onto a sidetrack, but the trolley would trip a switch sending a signal to a class of 6-year-olds, giving them permission to name a teddy bear
Muhammad. Is it permissible to pull the lever?

This is no joke. Last month a British woman teaching in a private school
in Sudan allowed her class to name a teddy bear after the most popular boy
in the class, who bore the name of the founder of Islam. She was jailed for
blasphemy and threatened with a public flogging, while a mob outside the
prison demanded her death. To the protesters, the woman's life clearly had
less value than maximizing the dignity of their religion, and their judgment

on whether it is right to divert the hypothetical trolley would have differed from ours. Whatever grammar guides people's moral judgments can't be all that universal. Anyone who stayed awake through Anthropology 101 can offer many other examples.

Of course, languages vary, too. In Chomsky's theory, languages conform to an abstract blueprint, like having phrases built out of verbs and objects, while the details vary, like whether the verb or the object comes first. <u>Could</u>
300   <u>we be wired with an abstract spec sheet that embraces all the strange ideas</u> <u>that people in different cultures moralize?</u>

THE VARIETIES OF MORAL EXPERIENCE

When anthropologists like Richard Shweder and Alan Fiske survey moral concerns across the globe, they find that a few themes keep popping up from amid the diversity. People everywhere, at least in some circumstances and with certain other folks in mind, think it's bad to harm others and good to help them. They have a sense of fairness: that one should reciprocate favors, reward benefactors and punish cheaters. They value loyalty to a group, sharing and solidarity among its members and conformity to its norms. They believe that it is right to defer to legitimate authorities and to respect people with high sta-
310   tus. And they exalt purity, cleanliness and sanctity while loathing defilement, contamination and carnality.

The exact number of themes depends on whether you're a lumper or a splitter, but Haidt counts five—<u>harm</u>, <u>fairness</u>, <u>community</u> (or group loyalty), <u>authority</u> and <u>purity</u>—and suggests that they are the primary colors of our moral sense. Not only do they keep reappearing in cross-cultural surveys, but each one tugs on the moral intuitions of people in our own culture. Haidt asks us to consider how much money someone would have to pay us to do hypothetical acts like the following:

Stick a pin into your palm.
320   Stick a pin into the palm of a child you don't know. (Harm.)
Accept a wide-screen TV from a friend who received it at no charge
    because of a computer error.
Accept a wide-screen TV from a friend who received it from a thief who
    had stolen it from a wealthy family. (Fairness.)
Say something bad about your nation (which you don't believe) on a
    talk-radio show in your nation.
Say something bad about your nation (which you don't believe) on a
    talk-radio show in a foreign nation. (Community.)
Slap a friend in the face, with his permission, as part of a comedy skit.
330   Slap your minister in the face, with his permission, as part of a comedy
    skit. (Authority.)
Attend a performance-art piece in which the actors act like idiots for
    30 minutes, including flubbing simple problems and falling down
    on stage.

Attend a performance-art piece in which the actors act like animals for
30 minutes, including crawling around naked and urinating on stage.
(Purity.)

In each pair, the second action feels far more repugnant. Most of the moral
illusions we have visited come from an unwarranted intrusion of one of the
moral spheres into our judgments. A violation of community led people to   340
frown on using an old flag to clean a bathroom. Violations of purity repelled
the people who judged the morality of consensual incest and prevented the
moral vegetarians and nonsmokers from tolerating the slightest trace of a vile
contaminant. At the other end of the scale, displays of extreme purity lead
people to venerate religious leaders who dress in white and affect an aura of
chastity and asceticism.

THE GENEALOGY OF MORALS

The five spheres are good candidates for a periodic table of the moral sense
not only because they are ubiquitous but also because they appear to have
deep evolutionary roots. The impulse to avoid harm, which gives trolley pon-
derers the willies when they consider throwing a man off a bridge, can also   350
be found in rhesus monkey, who go hungry rather than pull a chain that
delivers food to them and a shock to another monkey. Respect for authority
is clearly related to the pecking orders of dominance and appeasement that
are widespread in the animal kingdom. The purity-defilement contrast taps
the emotion of disgust that is triggered by potential disease vectors like bodily effluvia, decaying flesh and unconventional forms of meat, and by risky
sexual practices like incest.

The other two moralized spheres match up with the classic examples of
how altruism can evolve that were worked out by sociobiologists in the 1960s
and 1970s and made famous by Richard Dawkins in his book *The Selfish Gene*.   360
Fairness is very close to what scientists call reciprocal altruism, where a willingness to be nice to others can evolve as long as the favor helps the recipient
more than it costs the giver and the recipient returns the favor when fortunes
reverse. The analysis makes it sound as if reciprocal altruism comes out of a
robotlike calculation, but in fact Robert Trivers, the biologist who devised the
theory, argued that it is implemented in the brain as a suite of moral emotions.
Sympathy prompts a person to offer the first favor, particularly to someone in
need for whom it would go the furthest. Anger protects a person against
cheaters who accept a favor without reciprocating, by impelling him to punish
the ingrate or sever the relationship. Gratitude impels a beneficiary to reward   370
those who helped him in the past. Guilt prompts a cheater in danger of being
found out to repair the relationship by redressing the misdeed and advertising
that he will behave better in the future (consistent with Mencken's definition
of conscience as "the inner voice which warns us that someone might be looking"). Many experiments on who helps whom, who likes whom, who punishes
whom and who feels guilty about what have confirmed these predictions.

[handwritten margin notes: Community (4) evolutionarily!]

380   Community, the very different emotion that prompts people to share and sacrifice without an expectation of payback, may be rooted in nepotistic altruism, the empathy and solidarity we feel toward our relatives (and which evolved because any gene that pushed an organism to aid a relative would have helped copies of itself sitting inside that relative). In humans, of course, communal feelings can be lavished on nonrelatives as well. Sometimes it pays people (in an evolutionary sense) to love their companions because their interests are yoked, like spouses with common children, in-laws with common relatives, friends with common tastes or allies with common enemies. And sometimes it doesn't pay them at all, but their kinship-detectors have been tricked into treating their groupmates as if they were relatives by tactics like kinship metaphors (blood brothers, fraternities, the fatherland), origin myths, communal meals and other bonding rituals.

[handwritten margin note: church nation music]

JUGGLING THE SPHERES

390   All this brings us to a theory of how the moral sense can be universal and variable at the same time. The five moral spheres are universal, a legacy of evolution. But how they are ranked in importance, and which is brought in to moralize which area of social life—sex, government, commerce, religion, diet and so on—depends on the culture. Many of the flabbergasting practices in faraway places become more intelligible when you recognize that the same moralizing impulse that Western elites channel toward violations of harm and fairness (our moral obsessions) is channeled elsewhere to violations in the other spheres. Think of the Japanese fear of nonconformity (community), the holy ablutions and dietary restrictions of Hindus and Orthodox

400   Jews (purity), the outrage at insulting the Prophet among Muslims (authority). In the West, we believe that in business and government, fairness should trump community and try to root out nepotism and cronyism. In other parts of the world this is incomprehensible—what heartless creep would favor a perfect stranger over his own brother?

The ranking and placement of moral spheres also divides the cultures of liberals and conservatives in the United States. Many bones of contention, like homosexuality, atheism and one-parent families from the right, or racial imbalances, sweatshops and executive pay from the left, reflect different weightings of the spheres. In a large Web survey, Haidt found that liberals

410   put a lopsided moral weight on harm and fairness while playing down group loyalty, authority and purity. Conservatives instead place a moderately high weight on all five. It's not surprising that each side thinks it is driven by lofty ethical values and that the other side is base and unprincipled.

[handwritten margin note: liberals conservatives]

Reassigning an activity to a different sphere, or taking it out of the moral spheres altogether, isn't easy. People think that a behavior belongs in its sphere as a matter of sacred necessity and that the very act of questioning an assignment is a moral outrage. The psychologist Philip Tetlock has shown

[handwritten margin note: asking if it should be thus causes moral outrage]

[handwritten margin note: 5]

that the mentality of taboo—a conviction that some thoughts are sinful to think—is not just a superstition of Polynesians but a mind-set that can easily be triggered in college-educated Americans. Just ask them to think about applying the sphere of reciprocity to relationships customarily governed by community or authority. When Tetlock asked subjects for their opinions on whether adoption agencies should place children with the couples willing to pay the most, whether people should have the right to sell their organs and whether they should be able to buy their way out of jury duty, the subjects not only disagreed but felt personally insulted and were outraged that anyone would raise the question.

The institutions of modernity often question and experiment with the way activities are assigned to moral spheres. Market economies tend to put everything up for sale. Science amoralizes the world by seeking to understand phenomena rather than pass judgment on them. Secular philosophy is in the business of scrutinizing all beliefs, including those entrenched by authority and tradition. It's not surprising that these institutions are often seen to be morally corrosive.

IS NOTHING SACRED?

And "morally corrosive" is exactly the term that some critics would apply to the new science of the moral sense. The attempt to dissect our moral intuitions can look like an attempt to debunk them. Evolutionary psychologists seem to want to unmask our noblest motives as ultimately self-interested—to show that our love for children, compassion for the unfortunate and sense of justice are just tactics in a Darwinian struggle to perpetuate our genes. The explanation of how different cultures appeal to different spheres could lead to a spineless relativism, in which we would never have grounds to criticize the practice of another culture, no matter how barbaric, because "we have our kind of morality and they have theirs." And the whole enterprise seems to be dragging us to an amoral nihilism, in which morality itself would be demoted from a transcendent principle to a figment of our neural circuitry.

In reality, none of these fears are warranted, and it's important to see why not. The first misunderstanding involves the logic of evolutionary explanations. Evolutionary biologists sometimes anthropomorphize DNA for the same reason that science teachers find it useful to have their students imagine the world from the viewpoint of a molecule or a beam of light. One shortcut to understanding the theory of selection without working through the math is to imagine that the genes are little agents that try to make copies of themselves.

Unfortunately, the meme of the selfish gene escaped from popular biology books and mutated into the idea that organisms (including people) are ruthlessly self-serving. And this doesn't follow. Genes are not a reservoir of our dark unconscious wishes. "Selfish" genes are perfectly compatible with

[handwritten margin notes: relativism gone amuck; why does it seem to demean morality to think it's hardwired or flexible?; "meme" do students know this word?]

460 selfless organisms, because a gene's metaphorical goal of selfishly replicating itself can be implemented by wiring up the brain of the organism to do unselfish things, like being nice to relatives or doing good deeds for needy strangers. When a mother stays up all night comforting a sick child, the genes that endowed her with that tenderness were "selfish" in a metaphorical sense, but by no stretch of the imagination is she being selfish.

Nor does reciprocal altruism—the evolutionary rationale behind fairness—imply that people do good deeds in the cynical expectation of repayment down the line. We all know of unrequited good deeds, like tipping a waitress in a city you will never visit again and falling on a grenade to save platoonmates. These bursts of goodness are not as anomalous to a biologist as they might appear.

470 In his classic 1971 article, Trivers, the biologist, showed how natural selection could push in the direction of true selflessness. The emergence of tit-for-tat reciprocity, which lets organisms trade favors without being cheated, is just a first step. A favor-giver not only has to avoid blatant cheaters (those who would accept a favor but not return it) but also prefer generous reciprocators (those who return the biggest favor they can afford) over stingy ones (those who return the smallest favor they can get away with). Since it's good to be chosen as a recipient of favors, a competition arises to be the most generous partner around. More accurately, a competition arises to appear to be the most generous partner around, since the favor-giver can't lit-480 erally read minds or see into the future. A reputation for fairness and generosity becomes an asset.

Now this just sets up a competition for potential beneficiaries to inflate their reputations without making the sacrifices to back them up. But it also pressures the favor-giver to develop ever-more-sensitive radar to distinguish the genuinely generous partners from the hypocrites. This arms race will eventually reach a logical conclusion. The most effective way to seem generous and fair, under harsh scrutiny, is to be generous and fair. In the long run, then, reputation can be secured only by commitment. At least some agents evolve to be genuinely high-minded and self-sacrificing—they are 490 moral not because of what it brings them but because that's the kind of people they are.

Of course, a theory that predicted that everyone always sacrificed themselves for another's good would be as preposterous as a theory that predicted that no one ever did. Alongside the niches for saints there are niches for more grudging reciprocators, who attract fewer and poorer partners but don't make the sacrifices necessary for a sterling reputation. And both may coexist with outright cheaters, who exploit the unwary in one-shot encounters. An ecosystem of niches, each with a distinct strategy, can evolve when the payoff of each strategy depends on how many players are playing the other strategies. 500 The human social environment does have its share of generous, grudging and crooked characters, and the genetic variation in personality seems to bear the fingerprints of this evolutionary process.

IS MORALITY A FIGMENT?

So a biological understanding of the moral sense does not entail that people are calculating maximizers of their genes or self-interest. But where does it leave the concept of morality itself?

Here is the worry. The scientific outlook has taught us that some parts of our subjective experience are products of our biological makeup and have no objective counterpart in the world. The qualitative difference between red and green, the tastiness of fruit and foulness of carrion, the scariness of heights and prettiness of flowers are design features of our common nervous system, and if our species had evolved in a different ecosystem or if we were missing a few genes, our reactions could go the other way. Now, if the distinction between right and wrong is also a product of brain wiring, why should we believe it is any more real than the distinction between red and green? And if it is just a collective hallucination, how could we argue that evils like genocide and slavery are wrong for everyone, rather than just distasteful to us?

Putting God in charge of morality is one way to solve the problem, of course, but Plato made short work of it 2,400 years ago. Does God have a good reason for designating certain acts as moral and others as immoral? If not—if his dictates are divine whims—why should we take them seriously? Suppose that God commanded us to torture a child. Would that make it all right, or would some other standard give us reasons to resist? And if, on the other hand, God was forced by moral reasons to issue some dictates and not others—if a command to torture a child was never an option—then why not appeal to those reasons directly?

This throws us back to wondering where those reasons could come from, if they are more than just figments of our brains. They certainly aren't in the physical world like wavelength or mass. The only other option is that moral truths exist in some abstract Platonic realm, there for us to discover, perhaps in the same way that mathematical truths (according to most mathematicians) are there for us to discover. On this analogy, we are born with a rudimentary concept of number, but as soon as we build on it with formal mathematical reasoning, the nature of mathematical reality forces us to discover some truths and not others. (No one who understands the concept of two, the concept of four and the concept of addition can come to any conclusion but that 2 + 2 = 4.) Perhaps we are born with a rudimentary moral sense, and as soon as we build on it with moral reasoning, the nature of moral reality forces us to some conclusions but not others.

Moral realism, as this idea is called, is too rich for many philosophers' blood. Yet a diluted version of the idea—if not a list of cosmically inscribed Thou-Shalts, then at least a few If-Thens—is not crazy. Two features of reality point any rational, self-preserving social agent in a moral direction. And they could provide a benchmark for determining when the judgments of our moral sense are aligned with morality itself.

510

520

530

540

[margin handwritten notes:] would we posit similar ethical/moral norms would evolve in a community in other worlds? A truly universal morality that would be recognizable? Has a science fiction person ever written a piece describing a different set of outcomes that yet were consistent?

[margin handwritten note:] Moral realism

One is the prevalence of nonzero-sum games. In many arenas of life, two parties are objectively better off if they both act in a nonselfish way than if each of them acts selfishly. You and I are both better off if we share our surpluses, rescue each other's children in danger and refrain from shooting at each other, compared with hoarding our surpluses while they rot, letting the other's child drown while we file our nails or feuding like the Hatfields and McCoys. Granted, I might be a bit better off if I acted selfishly at your expense and you played the sucker, but the same is true for you with me, so if each of us tried for these advantages, we'd both end up worse off. Any neutral observer, and you and I if we could talk it over rationally, would have to conclude that the state we should aim for is the one in which we both are unselfish. These spreadsheet projections are not quirks of brain wiring, nor are they dictated by a supernatural power; they are in the nature of things.

[margin note: The "things" in this sentence are part of creation.]

The other external support for morality is a feature of rationality itself: that it cannot depend on the egocentric vantage point of the reasoner. If I appeal to you to do anything that affects me—to get off my foot, or tell me the time or not run me over with your car—then I can't do it in a way that privileges my interests over yours (say, retaining my right to run you over with my car) if I want you to take me seriously. Unless I am Galactic Overlord, I have to state my case in a way that would force me to treat you in kind. I can't act as if my interests are special just because I'm me and you're not, any more than I can persuade you that the spot I am standing on is a special place in the universe just because I happen to be standing on it.

[margin note: 5]

Not coincidentally, the core of this idea—the interchangeability of perspectives—keeps reappearing in history's best-thought-through moral philosophies, including the Golden Rule (itself discovered many times); Spinoza's Viewpoint of Eternity; the Social Contract of Hobbes, Rousseau and Locke; Kant's Categorical Imperative; and Rawls's Veil of Ignorance. It also underlies Peter Singer's theory of the Expanding Circle—the optimistic proposal that our moral sense, though shaped by evolution to overvalue self, kin and clan, can propel us on a path of moral progress, as our reasoning forces us to generalize it to larger and larger circles of sentient beings.

DOING BETTER BY KNOWING OURSELVES

Morality, then, is still something larger than our inherited moral sense, and the new science of the moral sense does not make moral reasoning and conviction obsolete. At the same time, its implications for our moral universe are profound.

[margin note: morality larger than just inherited moral sense, but does have implications →]

At the very least, the science tells us that even when our adversaries' agenda is most baffling, they may not be amoral psychopaths but in the throes of a moral mind-set that appears to them to be every bit as mandatory and universal as ours does to us. Of course, some adversaries really are psychopaths, and others are so poisoned by a punitive moralization that they are beyond the pale of reason. (The actor Will Smith had many historians on his side when he recently speculated to the press that Hitler thought he was acting morally.) But in any conflict in which a meeting of the minds is not completely hopeless, a recognition that the other guy is acting from moral rather than venal reasons can be a first patch of common ground. One side can acknowledge the other's concern for community or stability or fairness or dignity, even while arguing that some other value should trump it in that instance. With affirmative action, for example, the opponents can be seen as arguing from a sense of fairness, not racism, and the defenders can be seen as acting from a concern with community, not bureaucratic power. Liberals can ratify conservatives' concern with families while noting that gay marriage is perfectly consistent with that concern.

The science of the moral sense also alerts us to ways in which our psychological makeup can get in the way of our arriving at the most defensible moral conclusions. The moral sense, we are learning, is as vulnerable to illusions as the other senses. It is apt to confuse morality per se with purity, status and conformity. It tends to reframe practical problems as moral crusades and thus see their solution in punitive aggression. It imposes taboos that make certain ideas indiscussible. And it has the nasty habit of always putting the self on the side of the angels.

Though wise people have long reflected on how we can be blinded by our own sanctimony, our public discourse still fails to discount it appropriately. In the worst cases, the thoughtlessness of our brute intuitions can be celebrated as a virtue. In his influential essay "The Wisdom of Repugnance," Leon Kass, former chair of the President's Council on Bioethics, argued that we should disregard reason when it comes to cloning and other biomedical technologies and go with our gut: "We are repelled by the prospect of cloning human beings . . . because we intuit and feel, immediately and without argument, the violation of things that we rightfully hold dear. . . . In this age in which everything is held to be permissible so long as it is freely done . . . repugnance may be the only voice left that speaks up to defend the central core of our humanity. Shallow are the souls that have forgotten how to shudder."

There are, of course, good reasons to regulate human cloning, but the shudder test is not one of them. People have shuddered at all kinds of morally irrelevant violations of purity in their culture: touching an untouchable, drinking from the same water fountain as a Negro, allowing Jewish blood to mix with Aryan blood, tolerating sodomy between consenting men. And if our ancestors' repugnance had carried the day, we never would have had autopsies, vaccinations, blood transfusions, artificial insemination, organ transplants and in vitro fertilization, all of which were denounced as immoral when they were new.

There are many other issues for which we are too quick to hit the moralization button and look for villains rather than bug fixes. What should we do when a hospital patient is killed by a nurse who administers the wrong drug in a patient's intravenous line? Should we make it easier to sue the hospital for damages? Or should we redesign the IV fittings so that it's physically impossible to connect the wrong bottle to the line?

And nowhere is moralization more of a hazard than in our greatest global challenge. The threat of human-induced climate change has become the occasion for a moralistic revival meeting. In many discussions, the cause of climate change is overindulgence (too many S.U.V.'s) and defilement (sullying the atmosphere), and the solution is temperance (conservation) and expiation (buying carbon offset coupons). Yet the experts agree that these numbers don't add up: even if every last American became conscientious about his or her carbon emissions, the effects on climate change would be trifling, if for no other reason than that two billion Indians and Chinese are unlikely to copy our born-again abstemiousness. Though voluntary conservation may be one wedge in an effective carbon-reduction pie, the other wedges will have to be morally boring, like a carbon tax and new energy technologies, or even taboo, like nuclear power and deliberate manipulation of the ocean and atmosphere. Our habit of moralizing problems, merging them with intuitions of purity and contamination, and resting content when we feel the right feelings, can get in the way of doing the right thing.

Far from debunking morality, then, the science of the moral sense can advance it, by allowing us to see through the illusions that evolution and culture have saddled us with and to focus on goals we can share and defend. As Anton Chekhov wrote, "Man will become better when you show him what he is like."

Plato, "Selections from The Republic" in The ITHC,

5th ed.

SELECTIONS FROM *THE REPUBLIC*
Plato

BOOK II

JUSTICE WRIT LARGE IN THE STATE (367E–369B)

Socrates: The inquiry we are undertaking is not trivial, but requires sharp   1
sight, as it appears to me. So since we are not clever, I said, I think we should
make this sort of inquiry as though we were not very sharp-sighted and someone ordered us to read small letters at a distance. If one next realized that the
same letters exist elsewhere, larger and on a larger surface, it would appear to
be a stroke of luck, I think, to be able to read those first and in this way examine the smaller, to see if they happen to be the same.

Of course, said Adeimantus. But what do you see of this sort in the
inquiry about justice, Socrates?

I will tell you, I said. Justice, we say, belongs to one man, but surely also   10
to a whole city?

Of course, he replied.

Now, a city is greater than one man?

Yes, he said.

Perhaps then justice would be larger and easier to understand in what is
greater. If you will, then, let us first seek to discover what it is in cities; afterward, we will thus also examine it in the individual, looking for the likeness
of the greater in the character of the less.

Why, I think that is an excellent suggestion, he said.

Then if we should watch a city come to be in discourse, I replied, we   20
would also see the justice and the injustice of it come to be?

Perhaps, he replied.

So if that happened, there is hope that what we seek would be easier
to see?

Yes, much easier.

Do you think we should try to go through with it? For I suspect it is no
small task. Think about it.

I have Adeimantus replied. Please continue.

THE GUARDIANS' NATIVE DISPOSITION (374E–376E)

Then in as much as the work of the Guardians is of greatest importance, I
replied, it would by so much require utmost leisure from other activities, and   30
again, the greatest amount of art and training.

Yes, I think so, he replied.

Does it also require a nature suited to the occupation itself?

Of course.

Reprinted from *The Republic* (2006), by permission of Yale University Press.

So it would be our task, it seems, to pick out, if we can, which and what sorts of nature are suitable for guardianship of a city.

Indeed.

Really then, I replied, we have perhaps taken on ourselves no mean task. Nevertheless, it is not to be shirked, so far as ability permits.

40   No, he said.

Do you suppose then, I replied, in respect to guardianship, that there is any difference in nature between a well-bred young pup and a well-born young lad?

How do you mean?

For example, each of the two must be sharp of perception and quick in pursuit of what he perceives, and strong too, if he must subdue what he has caught.

Why, they require all this, he said.

Yes, and courage too, if they are to fight well.

50   Of course.

Will a horse or dog or any other animal be courageous if it is not spirited? Or have you not realized how irresistible and invincible spirit is? Its presence makes every soul fearless and indomitable in everything.

Yes.

It is clear then what bodily characteristics the Guardian must have.

Yes.

And further, those of his soul—at least that it be spirited.

That too.

Then if their natures are of this sort, Glaucon, I replied, how will they not
60   be savage with one another and the other citizens?

Really, it is not easy to see, he replied.

Nevertheless, they must be hard on their enemies but gentle with their friends. Otherwise, they will not need to wait around for others to destroy them; they will be beforehand in doing it themselves.

True, he said.

What shall we do, then? I replied. Where shall we find a character at once gentle and high spirited? For gentle nature is surely opposite to spirited.

It appears so.

A nature deprived of either would never become a good guardian. Yet
70   they seem incompatible, and thus then it follows that a good guardian is impossible.

Very likely, he said.

I was at a loss, and reflected on what had gone before. We are rightly perplexed, my friend, I said, for we have departed from the image we set before ourselves.

How do you mean?

We did not realize that there are, after all, natures which have these opposites, of a sort we did not consider.

Where?

One might see it even in other animals, but especially in the animal we 80
compared to the guardian. For you surely know that it is the natural character of well-bred dogs to be as gentle as possible to those they know and are
accustomed to, but the opposite to those they do not know.

Yes, certainly.

So it is possible, I replied, and the sort of guardian we are seeking is not
contrary to nature.

It seems not.

Now, in addition to being spirited, do you think our future guardian will
in nature still further need to be a philosopher?

How so? he said. I don't understand. 90

You see it even in dogs, I replied. Indeed, it is worth admiring in the
beast.

What's that?

The dog is roused to anger at seeing someone he does not know, without
ever having suffered any evil; but he welcomes someone he knows even if he
has never experienced anything good at the other's hands. Have you never yet
wondered at that?

I had not paid much attention to it before this, he said. But clearly, they
do act that way.

But surely this shows a fine trait of his nature, and that it is truly 100
philosophical.

How so?

Because, I replied, he distinguishes a friendly from an unfriendly face on
no other basis than having learned to know the one but not the other. And
yet, if he can distinguish what is his own and what is alien on the basis of
knowledge and ignorance, how would he not be a lover of learning?

He must be, he replied.

Again, I said, love of learning and love of wisdom are the same?

Yes, he said.

Then we may confidently assume also in man, that if he is to be gentle 110
toward his own and those he knows, he must by nature be a philosopher and
lover of learning?

Let's assume it, he said.

Then anyone who is to be a good and noble Guardian of our city will be
a lover of wisdom, and spirited and quick and strong in nature.

Most assuredly, he said.

So that is their natural disposition. But how will they be raised and educated? Is it helpful to examine the question relative to discerning the object
of our whole inquiry: how justice and injustice come to be present in a city?
We must not curtail argument, nor yet draw it out at length. 120

And Glaucon's brother said, I certainly think this inquiry is helpful in
respect to that.

Then we surely must not give it up, dear Adeimantus, I replied, even if it happens to be rather lengthy.

No.

Come then. As though telling a story at our leisure, we will educate these men in discourse.

Why, so we must.

BOOK V

PHILOSOPHERS AND LOVERS OF SIGHTS AND SOUNDS: THE THEORY OF FORMS (475D–476B)

And Glaucon said, Then many strange folk will be philosophers. For all
130   lovers of sights and spectacles, it seems to me, are like this, because they delight in learning. And lovers of sounds are among the strangest to rank as philosophers, because they will not willingly engage in arguments and such pursuits as that, but run around to Dionysiac festivals as though they had rented out their ears to every chorus, omitting no performance either in city or country village. Shall we then say that all these are philosophers too? And others who learn other things of this same sort, or practice the minor arts?

No, I said, but they are like philosophers.

Who do you say are the genuine philosophers? he said.

Those who love the sight and spectacle of truth, I replied.
140   No doubt, he said. But what do you mean?

It's not easily explained to another, I replied, but I think you will agree with me in this.

What?

Since beautiful is opposite to ugly, they are two.

Of course.

Then since two, each is also one?

Yes.

And the same account for just and unjust, good and evil, and all the forms: each in itself is one, but by communion with actions and bodies and
150   each other, they make their appearance everywhere, and each appears many.

You are right, he said.

In this way, then, I replied, I distinguish separately on one side those whom you just now described as lovers of sights and spectacles and lovers of arts and practical men, and separately again on the other side those with whom the argument is concerned, and whom one alone would rightly call philosophers or lovers of wisdom.

How do you mean? he said.

Lovers of sights and sounds, I replied, surely delight in beautiful tones and colors and figures and all that is fashioned from such things, but their
160   understanding is incapable of seeing and delighting in the nature of the beautiful itself.

Yes, that is certainly so, he said.

KNOWLEDGE AND OPINION (476D–477B)

Then we would rightly say that the understanding of the one is knowledge, since he knows, but that of the other is opinion, since he judges by appearances.

Of course.

What if this person whom we say judges by appearances but does not know became angry at us, and contended that we do not speak truly? Can we soothe and gently persuade him, while disguising the fact that he is unsound?

We must at least try, he said.

Come then, consider what we will say to him. Or would you have us   170
inquire of him in this way, suggesting that if he knows something no one begrudges him; on the contrary, we would be delighted to see that he knows something. But he must please tell us this: does someone who knows, know something or nothing? You answer me in his behalf.

I will answer that he knows something, he said.

Something that is, or is not?

Something that is. For how could something be known if it is not?

Then we are sufficiently assured, from whatever point of view we may examine it, that the perfectly real is perfectly knowable, but what in no way is, is in every way utterly unknowable?   180

Yes.

Very well. But if there is something such that it both exists and does not exist, would it not lie intermediate between what purely is, and again, what in no way is?

Yes.

Then since knowledge is directed to what is, but ignorance of necessity to what is not, something intermediate between knowledge and ignorance must also be sought, if there happens to be such a thing, directed to this intermediate.

Of course.   190

Now, we say that opinion or judgment of appearances is something?

Certainly.

Is it a power other than knowledge, or the same?

Other.

So judgment of appearances is ordered to one object, knowledge to another, each according to its own respective power.

That is so.

BOOK VI

PHILOSOPHERS AND GUARDIANS (484A–487A)

Then following out a somewhat lengthy way, Glaucon, I replied, those who are philosophers and those who are not have, with some difficulty, revealed who they each are.   200

Perhaps the way could not easily have been shortened, he said.

It appears not, I said. At any rate, I think it might have been still better revealed if this were the only thing we had to talk about, and so many other things did not also require explanation in order to discern how a just life differs from an unjust life.

What is next, then? he said.

Then next consider whether people who are to be such as we described necessarily have this additional element in their nature:

What?

210   Lack of falseness and refusal willingly to accept falsehood in any way, but to hate it and desire the truth.

Likely enough, he said.

Not only likely, my friend, but there is every necessity that someone in love by nature delights in everything akin and closely related to what he loves.

Right, he said.

Now, would you find anything more closely related to wisdom than truth?

No, he replied.

Then is it possible for the same nature to love wisdom and love falsehood?

Surely not.

220   So the real lover of learning must, from childhood up, strive as much as possible after all truth.

Certainly.

Why, Momus himself could not find fault with it, he said.

But when such people are perfected by education and age, I replied, you would turn the city over only to them?

ADEIMANTUS OBJECTS:
PEOPLE THINK PHILOSOPHERS USELESS (487B–E)

And Adeimantus said, No one can gainsay you in this, Socrates. Still, when you talk this way, your hearers are often affected somewhat like this: they believe that through inexperience in question and answer, they are little by little led astray by the argument at every question, and when the little mis-
230   takes are collected at the end, they turn out to be a big slip and opposite to what was said at first. Just as less skillful players at backgammon are finally shut out by clever ones and can't make a move, so also they themselves are finally shut out in this other kind of game where the counters are not pebbles but words, and don't have a thing to say.

Well, but do you think it just to speak of what one does not know as if he thought he knew? I replied.

Certainly not as if he thought he knew, he said, but nevertheless as one who is willing to say what he thinks, given that he thinks it.

Are you not aware, I said, that all opinions without knowledge are
240   flawed? The best of them are blind. Or do you think those who judge something truly without thought differ at all from blind men traveling the right road?

No, he said.

Would you then contemplate flawed things, halt and blind, when it is possible to hear bright and beautiful things from others?

THE SUN AND THE IDEA OF THE GOOD (506D–509C)

How do you mean? he said. Please explain further.

You know that eyes, I replied, when one no longer turns them toward those things whose colors are overspread by the light of day, but by moonlight or starlight, become dull and appear nearly blind, as if pure vision were not present.

Indeed, he said.

Yes, but I suppose when the Sun illuminates their object, they see clearly, and vision proves to be present in these same eyes.

Of course.

So also then conceive what belongs to the soul: when it is fixed upon what truth and reality illuminate, it conceives and knows it, and proves to possess thought. But when it is fixed upon what is mixed with darkness, upon what comes to be and passes away, it judges and becomes dull and changes opinions back and forth, and seems not to possess thought.

Yes.

BOOK VII

THE CAVE (514A–517A)

Next then, I said, concerning education and the lack of it, compare our own nature to a situation like this: Picture people as dwelling in a cavernous underground chamber, with an entrance opening upward to the light, and a long passageway running down the whole length of the cave. They have been there since childhood, legs and necks fettered so they cannot move: they see only what is in front of them, unable to turn their heads because of the bonds. But light reaches them from a fire burning some distance behind and above them. Between the fire and the prisoners, picture a track a bit higher up, and a little wall built along it like the screens in front of the performers at puppet shows, above which they show the puppets.

I see it, he said.

See also then people carrying all sorts of artificial objects alongside this little wall, statues of men and other animals, made of wood and stone and all sorts of things. Some of the carriers are talking, it is likely, others silent.

A strange image, he said, and strange prisoners.

Like ourselves, I replied. For first, do you think such prisoners see anything of themselves or one another except the shadows cast by the fire on the wall of the cave in front of them?

250

260

270

280

Why, how could they, he said, if they had been compelled to hold their heads motionless throughout life?

What about the objects being carried along. Isn't it the same?

Of course.

Then if they were able to converse with one another, don't you think they would acknowledge as things which are, the things that they saw?

Necessarily.

What if the prison also had an echo from the wall opposite. Whenever some one of those passing gave utterance, do you think they would believe anything except the passing shadow spoke?

Emphatically not, he said.

Such prisoners, then, I replied, would not acknowledge as true anything except shadows of artificial objects.

Quite necessarily, he said.

Consider then, I replied, what release and healing from the bonds of unwisdom would consist in, if it by nature occurred to them in this way: whenever one of them was released, and suddenly compelled to stand upright and turn his head and walk and look upward to the light, he would feel pain in doing all this, and because his eyes were dazzled, he would be unable to discern those things yonder whose shadows he had seen before. What do you suppose he would say, if someone told him that what he had seen before was foolishness, but that now, being somewhat nearer to what is and turned toward more real objects, he would see more correctly? Especially if, after being shown each of the things which are passing, he was compelled by questioning to answer what it is? Don't you suppose he would be perplexed and at a loss, and believe the things he saw before more true than those pointed out to him now?

Yes, he said.

Then suppose he were also compelled to look toward the light itself. It would hurt his eyes, and he would turn away in order to escape to the things he was able to see, and acknowledge them as really more clear than what was being shown him.

That's so, he said.

But if someone forcibly dragged him from there up the rugged steep ascent, I replied, and did not let go until he had hauled him into the light of the sun, wouldn't he suffer and be distressed as he was dragged along? And when he came to the light, his eyes would be so filled with its brightness that he would be unable to see even one among the things now claimed to be true?

No, he said, at least not immediately.

Then I suppose he would have to become accustomed to it, if he is going to see the things above. It would be easiest first to look at shadows, next, at images in water of men and other things, and afterward at the things themselves; after this, it would be easier to contemplate things in the heaven and the heaven itself by night, and gaze at the light of the stars and the moon, than at the sun and its light by day.

Of course.

Finally then, I suppose, the sun. Not appearances of it in water or in alien seats: he would be able to look at it alone by itself in its own place, and contemplate it as it is.

Necessarily, he said.

After this, he would at that point infer of it that it is this which produces 330 the seasons and the years and governs everything in the visible place, and is in some manner cause of all the things they used to see.

It is clear, he said, that he would arrive next at this conclusion along with that.

Suppose he were to recall his first dwelling place, and the wisdom there, and his fellow prisoners then. Wouldn't he think himself happy in the change, and pity them?

Indeed.

Suppose they had honors and prizes for those who most acutely discern and best remember the shadows that pass—which of them usually comes 340 before, and after, and at the same time—and from this was then best able to guess what was coming next. Do you think he would want what they have, and envy them their honors and positions of power? Or would he feel, as Homer has it, that he would much prefer to be the slave of a landless man and suffer anything at all, rather than believe those things and live that life?

Yes, he said, I think he would suffer anything rather than accept that life.

Consider this too, I replied. If such a man went down again and sat upon the same seat, would not his eyes be filled with darkness, coming suddenly from the sun?

Yes, indeed, he said.　　350

Suppose then he had to compete again in judging those shadows with people who had always been prisoners, while his vision was dim, before his eyes settled down—and it would take some little time to get used to the darkness. Wouldn't he be laughed at? Wouldn't it be said of him that he had journeyed upward only to return with his eyes ruined, that it wasn't worth it even to try to go up? And if they were able somehow to lay hands on the man trying to release them and lead them up, and kill him, they would kill him.

Certainly, he said.

THE CAVE APPLIED TO THE SUN AND THE LINE (517A–518B)

This image, my dear Glaucon, I replied, must be applied as a whole to what was said before, likening the seat which appears through sight to the prison 360 dwelling, and the light of the fire in it to the power of the sun. If you assume that the ascent upward and the vision of things above is the upward journey of the soul to the intelligible place, you will not mistake my surmise, since you desire to hear it. God alone knows whether it happens to be true, but these appearances appear thus to me. In the intelligible place, the Idea of the

Good is seen finally and with difficulty, but once seen, it must be inferred that it is the cause of all things right and beautiful. In the visible place it gives birth to Light and to the Sun, the Lord of Light; in the intelligible place it is itself Lord, and provides intelligence and truth. It must also be inferred that
370   whoever intends to act wisely in public or private must see it.

So far as I am able, he said, I concur.

Come then, I replied, and concur also in this: do not be surprised that those who arrive here refuse to take part in the affairs of men; rather, their souls ever press on to spend their time above. For it is surely likely to be so, if the foregoing image once again applies.

Yes, he said.

Then do you think it at all surprising, I replied, if someone who has come from contemplation of divine things to the evils of human life is awkward, and appears quite ridiculous when, with vision still dim and before becom-
380   ing sufficiently accustomed to the present darkness, he is compelled, in law courts or elsewhere, to contend about the shadows of what is just, or about images of the things of which they are shadows, and to dispute about how they are understood by those who have never seen justice itself?

It would not at all be surprising, he said.

But a reasonable man might remember, I replied, that eyes become disturbed in two ways and for two reasons: by shifting from light to darkness, and from darkness to light. He would acknowledge that this same thing also happens with soul, and whenever he saw it disturbed and unable to see something, he would not thoughtlessly laugh, but inquire whether it had been
390   blinded by unaccustomed darkness after coming from a brighter life, or whether in passing from greater ignorance to a brighter life it had been dazzled by yet more light; and thus he would count one soul happy in its experience and its life, but pity the other, and if he wished to laugh at it, his laughter would be less ridiculous than laughter at a soul come down from the light above.

A very fair statement, he said.

EDUCATION AND VIRTUE (518B–519D)

If this is true, I said, we must acknowledge that education is not what it is said to be by some, who profess to be able to put knowledge into a soul where it is not present, as though putting sight into blind eyes.
400   They do claim that, he said.

The present account signifies, I replied, that this power is present in the soul of each person, along with the instrument by which each person understands. It is as if an eye could not turn from darkness to what is bright except in company with the whole body. Just so, this instrument must be converted from what becomes by turning in company with the whole soul until it has become capable of being lifted up to contemplate what is, and the brightest of what is. But this, we say, is the Good. Not so?

Yes.

Then there would be an art whose object is to effect this very thing, this conversion, I replied, to turn the soul around in the easiest and most effec-   410
tive way. Not to put sight into it, for we may suppose it already has it, but to contrive that it not be turned to look in the wrong direction, but where it should.

It seems so, he said.

The other virtues commonly said to belong to the soul are not far removed from things of the body—for they are afterward produced by habits and practices where they were not really present before—but the virtue of intelligence assuredly happens to be something more divine, it seems: it never loses its power, but becomes useful and beneficial or useless and harmful because of the way it is turned. Or have you never noticed, among those said   420
to be bad but wise, how shrewd is the vision of their petty souls and how keenly it sees the things toward which it is turned? There's nothing the matter with their vision, but it is compelled to the service of evil, so that the more keenly it sees, the more evils it works.

Of course, he replied.

And yet, I replied, if such a nature were pruned from childhood up—cleared, as it were, of those leaden weights, akin to becoming, which are attached to it by gluttony and greedy pleasures of that kind and bend the vision of the soul downward—if, freed from these, it were turned round at last to things which are true, then this same thing belonging to these same   430
people would see things yonder most keenly, even as the objects toward which it is now turned.

Yes, likely enough, he said.

But isn't it also likely, I replied, and even necessary from what has been said, that a city cannot ever sufficiently be governed by those who are uneducated and without experience of truth, nor again by those allowed to pass their whole time in education? Not the one, because they have no single target in life at which to aim in every action, public and private; not the other, because they'll be unwilling to act, believing they've been transported to the Isles of the Blessed while still alive.   440

True, he said.

Then it is our own task as founders, I replied, to compel the best natures to attain to the knowledge which we formerly described as most important: to see the Good and rise upward in that ascent. And when they have ascended and sufficiently seen, not to allow to them what is now allowed.

What is that?

To abide there, I replied, and refuse to go back down again among the prisoners and share their labors and honors, whether of lesser or more serious worth.

HOW GUARDIANS ARE LED UPWARD TO THE LIGHT (521C–522D)

450

Would you then have us at this point consider how such people as this will come to be present and how to lead them upward to the light, as some are said to have ascended from the Underworld to the gods?

How could I not wish it? he said.

This then, it seems, is no mere flip of an oystershell, but a conversion of soul from a day which is like night to genuine day, an ascent to what is real which we say is true philosophy.

Of course.

Then we must examine which studies have this power?

Certainly.

DIALECTIC (531C–535A)

460

Well, Glaucon, I said, is this at last the very law which dialectic fulfills, the song which it performs? Being intelligible, the power of vision, which we said undertakes to look at the animals by themselves, and at the stars by themselves and finally at the Sun itself, would imitate it. So also, when one undertakes by dialectical conversation, without any of the senses, to begin to make his way through reason to what each thing is by itself, and does not give over until he grasps by thought itself what the Good is by itself, he reaches the end of the intelligible, even as, before, the power of vision reached the end of the visible.

Certainly, he said.

Well then, don't you call this journey dialectic?

470

Of course.

Yes, I replied. It is release from bondage and conversion from shadows to images and the light, and ascent out of the cave into the sunlight—and there, even still, inability to look at animals and plants and the light of the sun, but only at divine appearances in water and shadows of things which are, though not shadows of images cast by that different sort of light which is itself a shadow compared to the Sun. This whole business of the arts we have described has this power to lead what is noblest in soul upward to the vision of what is best among things which are, even as before what was clearest in body led upward to the vision of what is brightest in the bodily and visible place.

480

I accept this, he said. And yet, I think it is very hard to accept, though in another way hard to reject.

At any rate, I replied, no one will dispute us and claim that any other method of inquiry undertakes to grasp in every case what each thing by itself is. On the contrary: the other arts are all directed either to the beliefs and desires of men, or to generation and combination, or to the service of things which grow and are put together. And we see that the remaining arts—geometry and the studies which follow on it, which we said grasp something of what is—merely dream about reality. They cannot see with waking vision so long as they make use of hypotheses and leave them undisturbed, unable to render an account of them. For with a starting point which one does not know, and a conclusion and intermediate premises woven together from what one does not know—by what device can this sort of agreement and implication ever become knowledge?

490

None, he replied.

Dialectic, I rejoined, is the only method of inquiry which proceeds in this way: it does away with hypotheses and proceeds to the starting point and the first principle itself in order to make its results secure. Finding that the eye of the soul is really sunk in a slough of barbarous mud, dialectic gently draws and leads it upward, using as assistants and helpers the arts we have described—which we often through force of habit call branches of knowl-edge, though they need another name, in that they are more clear than opin-ion but more obscure than knowledge. In what went before we marked this off as understanding; but when an inquiry of such great magnitude lies before us, the dispute, I think, is not about a name.

500

Of course not, he said.

Then as before, I replied, it suffices to call the first portion knowledge, the second understanding, the third belief, and the fourth imagination. The latter two together are opinion, the former two, thought. And opinion is concerned with becoming, thought with being. And being is to becoming as thought is to opinion, and thought is to opinion as knowledge is to belief, and understanding to imagination. But let us dismiss the proportionality of that to which they are directed, Glaucon, and the twofold division of each of the two, opinable and intelligible, so that we do not get involved in discus-sions many times as long as those we've had.

510

Why, I agree with you about the others, he said, in so far as I am able to follow.

And do you also call a dialectician one who accepts a reasoned account of the nature and reality of each thing? Will you deny that insofar as one can-not render a reasoned account to himself and to another, he in that degree cannot be said to have intelligence about it?

520

How could I deny it, he replied?

Then so in like manner about the Good. Whoever cannot distinguish the Idea of the Good by reason and set it apart from all other things, and, as though in battle, fight his way through all refutations in his eagerness to argue not according to opinion but according to reality, and proceed in all this without tripping up in argument—you will claim that someone like that knows neither the Good itself nor any other good. Rather, if in some way he grasps a deficient image of it, he does so by opinion, not knowledge, and sleeps and dreams away his present life. Before ever he awakens here, he will go to the place of the dead and fall asleep completely.

530

Yes, he replied. I shall emphatically assert all of this.

Moreover, these children of yours whom you are raising and educating in discourse—if ever you should raise them in fact, you would not, I think, allow them to be rulers in the city and to control matters of utmost importance, while being, as it were, irrational quantities?

Of course not, he said.

Then you will provide by law that they should instead receive this education, from which they will be able to ask and answer questions with utmost knowledge?

540   I will so provide, he said, in company with you.

Do you think then, I said, that dialectic is set like a copingstone over the subjects of study, and that no other study higher than it would rightly be put above it, but at this point the subjects of study have an end?

Yes, he said.

ARTS OF THE CONTACT ZONE
Mary Louise Pratt

CONTACT AND COMMUNITY

The idea of the contact zone is intended in part to contrast with ideas of community that underlie much of the thinking about language, communication, and culture that gets done in the academy. A couple of years ago, thinking about the linguistic theories I knew, I tried to make sense of a utopian quality that often seemed to characterize social analyses of language by the academy. Languages were seen as living in "speech communities,"[1] and these tended to be theorized as discrete, self-defined, coherent entities, held together by a homogeneous competence or grammar shared identically and equally among all the members. This abstract idea of the speech community seemed to reflect, among other things, the utopian way modern nations conceive of themselves as what Benedict Anderson calls "imagined communities." In a book of that title, Anderson observes that with the possible exception of what he calls "primordial villages," human communities exist as *imagined* entities in which people "will never know most of their fellow-members, meet them or even hear of them, yet in the mind of each lives the image of their communion." "Communities are distinguished," he goes on to say, "not by their falsity/genuineness, but by *the style in which they are imagined*" (15; emphasis mine). Anderson proposes three features that characterize the style in which the modern nation is imagined. First, it is imagined as *limited*, by "finite, if elastic, boundaries"; second, it is imagined as *sovereign*; and, third, it is imagined as *fraternal*, "a deep, horizontal comradeship" for which millions of people are prepared "not so much to kill as willingly to die" (15). As the image suggests, the nation-community is embodied metonymically in the finite, sovereign, fraternal figure of the citizen-soldier.

Anderson argues that European bourgeoisies were distinguished by their ability to "achieve solidarity on an essentially imagined basis" (74) on a scale far greater than that of elites of other times and places. Writing and literacy play a central role in this argument. Anderson maintains, as have others, that the main instrument that made bourgeois nation-building projects possible was print capitalism. The commercial circulation of books in the various European vernaculars, he argues, was what first created the invisible networks that would eventually constitute the literate elites and those they ruled as nations. (Estimates are that 180 million books were put into circulation in Europe between the years 1500 and 1600 alone.)

Now obviously this style of imagining of modern nations, as Anderson describes it, is strongly utopian, embodying values like equality, fraternity, liberty, which the societies often profess but systematically fail to realize. The prototype of the modern nation as imagined community was, it seemed to

Reprinted from *Profession 91* (1991), Modern Language Association of America.

me, mirrored in ways people thought about language and the speech community. Many commentators have pointed out how modern views of language
as code and competence assume a unified and homogeneous social world in
which language exists as a shared patrimony—as a device, precisely, for imagining community. An image of a universally shared literacy is also part of the
picture. The prototypical manifestation of language is generally taken to be
the speech of individual adult native speakers face-to-face (as in Saussure's
famous diagram) in monolingual, even monodialectal situations—in short,
the most homogeneous case linguistically and socially. The same goes for written communication. Now one could certainly imagine a theory that assumed
different things—that argued, for instance, that the most revealing speech situation for understanding language was one involving a gathering of people
each of whom spoke two languages and understood a third and held only
one language in common with any of the others. It depends on what workings of language you want to see or want to see first, on what you choose to
define as normative.

In keeping with autonomous, fraternal models of community, analyses of
language use commonly assume that principles of cooperation and shared
understanding are normally in effect. Descriptions of interactions between
people in conversation, classrooms, medical and bureaucratic settings, readily take it for granted that the situation is governed by a single set of rules or
norms shared by all participants. The analysis focuses then on how those rules
produce or fail to produce an orderly, coherent exchange. Models involving
games and moves are often used to describe interactions. Despite whatever
conflicts or systematic social differences might be in play, it is assumed that
all participants are engaged in the same game and that the game is the same
for all players. Often it is. But of course it often is not, as, for example, when
speakers are from different classes or cultures, or one party is exercising authority and another is submitting to it or questioning it. Last year one of my
children moved to a new elementary school that had more open classrooms
and more flexible curricula than the conventional school he started out in. A
few days into the term, we asked him what it was like at the new school.
"Well," he said, "they're a lot nicer, and they have a lot less rules. But know
why they're nicer?" "Why?" I asked. "So you'll obey all the rules they don't
have," he replied. This is a very coherent analysis with considerable elegance
and explanatory power, but probably not the one his teacher would have given.

When linguistic (or literate) interaction is described in terms of orderli-
ness, games, moves, or scripts, usually only legitimate moves are actually named
as part of the system, where legitimacy is defined from the point of view of
the party in authority—regardless of what other parties might see themselves
as doing. Teacher-pupil language, for example, tends to be described almost
entirely from the point of view of the teacher and teaching, not from the point
of view of pupils and pupiling (the word doesn't even exist, though the thing
certainly does). If a classroom is analyzed as a social world unified and homog-
enized with respect to the teacher, whatever students do other than what the

teacher specifies is invisible or anomalous to the analysis. This can be true in practice as well. On several occasions my fourth grader, the one busy obeying all the rules they didn't have, was given writing assignments that took the form of answering a series of questions to build up a paragraph. These questions often asked him to identify with the interests of those in power over him—parents, teachers, doctors, public authorities. He invariably sought ways to resist or subvert these assignments. One assignment, for instance, called for imagining "a helpful invention." The students were asked to write single-sentence responses to the following questions:

What kind of invention would help you?
How would it help you?
Why would you need it?
What would it look like?
Would other people be able to use it also?
What would be an invention to help your teacher?
What would be an invention to help your parents?

Manuel's reply read as follows:

A grate adventchin

Some inventchins are GRATE!!!!!!!!!!! My inventchin would be a shot that would put every thing you learn at school in your brain. It would help me by letting me graduate right now!! I would need it because it would let me play with my friends, go on vacachin and, do fun a lot more. It would look like a regular shot. Ather peaple would use to. This inventchin would help my teacher parents get away from a lot of work. I think a shot like this would be GRATE!

Despite the spelling, the assignment received the usual star to indicate the task had been fulfilled in an acceptable way. No recognition was available, however, of the humor, the attempt to be critical or contestatory, to parody the structures of authority. On that score, Manuel's luck was only slightly better than Guaman Poma's. What is the place of unsolicited oppositional discourse, parody, resistance, critique in the imagined classroom community? Are teachers supposed to feel that their teaching has been most successful when they have eliminated such things and unified the social world, probably in their own image? Who wins when we do that? Who loses?

Such questions may be hypothetical, because in the United States in the 1990s, many teachers find themselves less and less able to do that even if they want to. The composition of the national collectivity is changing and so are the styles, as Anderson put it, in which it is being imagined. In the 1980s in many nation-states, imagined national syntheses that had retained hegemonic force began to dissolve. Internal social groups with histories and lifeways different from the official ones began insisting on those histories and

model of education - Mills

Poma—indigenous Peruvian disillusioned w/ Spanish treatment of Andeans. Wrote illustrated book Nueva Coronica y Buen Gobierno (1615) sent to King Philip III of Spain No evidence of response.

lifeways *as part of their citizenship, as the very mode of their membership in the national collectivity*. In their dialogues with dominant institutions, many groups began asserting a rhetoric of belonging that made demands beyond those of representation and basic rights granted from above. In universities we started to hear, "I don't just want you to let me be here, I want to belong here; this institution should belong to me as much as it does to anyone else." Institutions have responded with, among other things, rhetorics of diversity and multiculturalism whose import at this moment is up for grabs across the ideological spectrum.

These shifts are being lived out by everyone working in education today, and everyone is challenged by them in one way or another. Those of us committed to educational democracy are particularly challenged as that notion finds itself besieged on the public agenda. Many of those who govern us display, openly, their interest in a quiescent, ignorant, manipulable electorate. Even as an ideal, the concept of an enlightened citizenry seems to have disappeared from the national imagination. A couple of years ago the university where I work went through an intense and wrenching debate over a narrowly defined Western-culture requirement that had been instituted there in 1980. It kept boiling down to a debate over the ideas of national patrimony, cultural citizenship, and imagined community. In the end, the requirement was transformed into a much more broadly defined course called Cultures, Ideas, Values.[2] In the context of the change, a new course was designed that centered on the Americas and the multiple cultural histories (including European ones) that have intersected here. As you can imagine, the course attracted a very diverse student body. The classroom functioned not like a homogeneous community or a horizontal alliance but like a contact zone. Every single text we read stood in specific historical relationships to the students in the class, but the range and variety of historical relationships in play were enormous. Everybody had a stake in nearly everything we read, but the range and kind of stakes varied widely.

It was the most exciting teaching we had ever done, and also the hardest. We were struck, for example, at how anomalous the formal lecture became in a contact zone (who can forget Atahuallpa throwing down the Bible because it would not speak to him?). The lecturer's traditional (imagined) task—unifying the world in the class's eyes by means of a monologue that rings equally coherent, revealing, and true for all, forging an ad hoc community, homogeneous with respect to one's own words—this task became not only impossible but anomalous and unimaginable. Instead, one had to work in the knowledge that whatever one said was going to be systematically received in radically heterogeneous ways that we were neither able nor entitled to prescribe.

The very nature of the course put ideas and identities on the line. All the students in the class had the experience, for example, of hearing their culture discussed and objectified in ways that horrified them; all the students saw their roots traced back to legacies of both glory and shame; all the students experienced face-to-face the ignorance and incomprehension, and occasionally the hostility, of others. In the absence of community values and the hope of synthesis, it was easy to forget the positives; the fact, for instance, that kinds of marginalization once taken for granted were gone. Virtually every student was having the experience of seeing the world described with him or her in it. Along with rage, incomprehension, and pain, there were exhilarating moments of wonder and revelation, mutual understanding, and new wisdom—the joys of the contact zone. The sufferings and revelations were, at different moments to be sure, experienced by every student. No one was excluded, and no one was safe.

The fact that no one was safe made all of us involved in the course appreciate the importance of what we came to call "safe houses." We used the term to refer to social and intellectual spaces where groups can constitute themselves as horizontal, homogeneous, sovereign communities with high degrees of trust, shared understandings, temporary protection from legacies of oppression. This is why, as we realized, multicultural curricula should not seek to replace ethnic or women's studies, for example. Where there are legacies of subordination, groups need places for healing and mutual recognition, safe houses in which to construct shared understandings, knowledges, claims on the world that they can then bring into the contact zone.

Meanwhile, our job in the Americas course remains to figure out how to make that crossroads the best site for learning that it can be. We are looking for the pedagogical arts of the contact zone. These will include, we are sure, exercises in storytelling and in identifying with the ideas, interests, histories, and attitudes of others; experiments in transculturation and collaborative work and in the arts of critique, parody, and comparison (including unseemly comparisons between elite and vernacular cultural forms); the redemption of the oral; ways for people to engage with suppressed aspects of history (including their own histories), ways to move *into and out of* rhetorics of authenticity; ground rules for communication across lines of difference and hierarchy that go beyond politeness but maintain mutual respect; a systematic approach to the all-important concept of *cultural mediation*. These arts were in play in every room at the extraordinary Pittsburgh conference on literacy. I learned a lot about them there, and I am thankful.

NOTES

1. The discussion of community here is summarized from my essay "Linguistic Utopias."
2. For information about this program and the contents of courses taught in it, write Program in Cultures, Ideas, Values (CIV), Stanford Univ., Stanford, CA 94305.

Language essay

THINKING ABOUT SOCIAL CHANGE IN AMERICA
Robert D. Putnam

What happened next to civic and social life in American communities is the subject of this book. In recent years social scientists have framed concerns about the changing character of American society in terms of the concept of "social capital." By analogy with notions of physical capital and human capital—tools and training that enhance individual productivity—the core idea of social capital theory is that social networks have value. Just as a screwdriver (physical capital) or a college education (human capital) can increase productivity (both individual and collective), so too social contacts affect the productivity of individuals and groups.

Whereas physical capital refers to physical objects and human capital refers to properties of individuals, social capital refers to connections among individuals—social networks and the norms of reciprocity and trustworthiness that arise from them. In that sense social capital is closely related to what some have called "civic virtue." The difference is that "social capital" calls attention to the fact that civic virtue is most powerful when embedded in a dense network of reciprocal social relations. A society of many virtuous but isolated individuals is not necessarily rich in social capital.

The term *social capital* itself turns out to have been independently invented at least six times over the twentieth century, each time to call attention to the ways in which our lives are made more productive by social ties. The first known use of the concept was not by some cloistered theoretician, but by a practical reformer of the Progressive Era—L. J. Hanifan, state supervisor of rural schools in West Virginia. Writing in 1916 to urge the importance of community involvement for successful schools, Hanifan invoked the idea of "social capital" to explain why. For Hanifan, social capital referred to

> those tangible substances [that] count for most in the daily lives of people: namely good will, fellowship, sympathy, and social intercourse among the individuals and families who make up a social unit. . . . The individual is helpless socially, if left to himself. . . . If he comes into contact with his neighbor, and they with other neighbors, there will be an accumulation of social capital, which may immediately satisfy his social needs and which may bear a social potentiality sufficient to the substantial improvement of living conditions in the whole community. The community as a whole will benefit by the cooperation of all its parts, while the individual will find in his associations the advantages of the help, the sympathy, and the fellowship of his neighbors.[1]

Reprinted from *Bowling Alone: The Collapse and Revival of American Community* (2000), by permission of Simon & Schuster, Inc.

225

example of history of an idea and the way individuals contribute to knowledge

Hanifan's account of social capital anticipated virtually all the crucial elements in later interpretations, but his conceptual invention apparently attracted no notice from other social commentators and disappeared without a trace. But like sunken treasure recurrently revealed by shifting sands and tides, the same idea was independently rediscovered in the 1950s by Canadian sociologists to characterize the club memberships of arriviste suburbanites, in the 1960s by urbanist Jane Jacobs to laud neighborliness in the modern metropolis, in the 1970s by economist Glenn Loury to analyze the social legacy of slavery, and in the 1980s by French social theorist Pierre Bourdieu and by German economist Ekkehart Schlicht to underline the social and economic resources embodied in social networks. Sociologist James S. Coleman put the term firmly and finally on the intellectual agenda in the late 1980s, using it (as Hanifan had originally done) to highlight the social context of education.[2]

As this array of independent coinages indicates, social capital has both an individual and a collective aspect—a private face and a public face. First, individuals form connections that benefit our own interests. One pervasive strategem of ambitious job seekers is "networking," for most of us get our jobs because of whom we know, not what we know—that is, our social capital, not our human capital. Economic sociologist Ronald Burt has shown that executives with bounteous Rolodex files enjoy faster career advancement. Nor is the private return to social capital limited to economic rewards. As Claude S. Fischer, a sociologist of friendship, has noted, "Social networks are important in all our lives, often for finding jobs, more often for finding a helping hand, companionship, or a shoulder to cry on.[3]

If individual clout and companionship were all there were to social capital, we'd expect foresighted, self-interested individuals to invest the right amount of time and energy in creating or acquiring it. However, social capital also can have "externalities" that affect the wider community, so that not all the costs and benefits of social connections accrue to the person making the contact.[4] As we shall see later in this book, a well-connected individual in a poorly connected society is not as productive as a well-connected individual in a well-connected society. And even a poorly connected individual may derive some of the spillover benefits from living in a well-connected community. If the crime rate in my neighborhood is lowered by neighbors keeping an eye on one another's homes, I benefit even if I personally spend most of my time on the road and never even nod to another resident on the street.

explain externalities

Social capital can thus be simultaneously a "private good" and a "public good." Some of the benefit from an investment in social capital goes to bystanders, while some of the benefit redounds to the immediate interest of the person making the investment. For example, service clubs, like Rotary or Lions, mobilize local energies to raise scholarships or fight disease at the same time that they provide members with friendships and business connections that pay off personally.

Students should be able to speak to this connection in their own lives

Social connections are also important for the rules of conduct that they sustain. Networks involve (almost by definition) mutual obligations; they are not interesting as mere "contacts." Networks of community engagement foster sturdy norms of reciprocity: I'll do this for you now, in the expectation that you (or perhaps someone else) will return the favor. "Social capital is akin to what Tom Wolfe called 'the favor bank' in his novel *The Bonfire of the Vanities*," notes economist Robert Frank.[5] It was, however, neither a novelist nor an economist, but Yogi Berra who offered the most succinct definition of reciprocity: "If you don't go to somebody's funeral, they won't come to yours."

Sometimes, as in these cases, reciprocity is *specific:* I'll do this for you if you do that for me. Even more valuable, however, is a norm of *generalized* reciprocity: I'll do this for you without expecting anything specific back from you, in the confident expectation that someone else will do something for me down the road. The Golden Rule is one formulation of generalized reciprocity. Equally instructive is the T-shirt slogan used by the Gold Beach, Oregon, Volunteer Fire Department to publicize their annual fund-raising effort: "Come to our breakfast, we'll come to your fire." "We act on a norm of specific reciprocity," the firefighters seem to be saying, but onlookers smile because they recognize the underlying norm of generalized reciprocity—the firefighters will come even if *you* don't. When Blanche DuBois depended on the kindness of strangers, she too was relying on generalized reciprocity.

A society characterized by generalized reciprocity is more efficient than a distrustful society, for the same reason that money is more efficient than barter. If we don't have to balance every exchange instantly, we can get a lot more accomplished. Trustworthiness lubricates social life. Frequent interaction among a diverse set of people tends to produce a norm of generalized reciprocity. Civic engagement and social capital entail mutual obligation and responsibility for action. As L. J. Hanifan and his successors recognized, social networks and norms of reciprocity can facilitate cooperation for mutual benefit. When economic and political dealing is embedded in dense networks of social interaction, incentives for opportunism and malfeasance are reduced. This is why the diamond trade, with its extreme possibilities for fraud, is concentrated within close-knit ethnic enclaves. Dense social ties facilitate gossip and other valuable ways of cultivating reputation—an essential foundation for trust in a complex society.

Physical capital is not a single "thing," and different forms of physical capital are not interchangeable. An eggbeater and an aircraft carrier both appear as physical capital in our national accounts, but the eggbeater is not much use for national defense, and the carrier would not be much help with your morning omelet. Similarly, social capital—that is, social networks and the associated norms of reciprocity—comes in many different shapes and sizes with many different uses. Your extended family represents a form of social capital, as do your Sunday school class, the regulars who play poker on your commuter train, your college roommates, the civic organizations to which you belong, the Internet chat group in which you participate, and the network of professional acquaintances recorded in your address book.

Sometimes "social capital," like its conceptual cousin "community," sounds warm and cuddly. Urban sociologist Xavier de Souza Briggs, however, properly warns us to beware of a treacly sweet, "kumbaya" interpretation of social capital.[6] Networks and the associated norms of reciprocity are generally good for those inside the network, but the external effects of social capital are by no means always positive. It was social capital, for example, that enabled Timothy McVeigh to bomb the Alfred P. Murrah Federal Building in Oklahoma City. McVeigh's network of friends, bound together by a norm of reciprocity, enabled him to do what he could not have done alone. Similarly, urban gangs, NIMBY ("not in my backyard") movements, and power elites often exploit social capital to achieve ends that are antisocial from a wider perspective. Indeed, it is rhetorically useful for such groups to obscure the difference between the pro-social and antisocial consequences of community organizations. When Floridians objected to plans by the Ku Klux Klan to "adopt a highway," Jeff Coleman, grand wizard of the Royal Knights of the KKK, protested, "Really, we're just like the Lions or the Elks. We want to be involved in the community."[7]

Social capital, in short, can be directed toward malevolent, antisocial purposes, just like any other form of capital.[8] (McVeigh also relied on physical capital, like the explosive-laden truck, and human capital, like bomb-making expertise, to achieve his purposes.) Therefore it is important to ask how the positive consequences of social capital—mutual support, cooperation, trust, institutional effectiveness—can be maximized and the negative manifestations—sectarianism, ethnocentrism, corruption—minimized. Toward this end, scholars have begun to distinguish many different forms of social capital.

Some forms involve repeated, intensive, multistranded networks—like a group of steelworkers who meet for drinks every Friday after work and see each other at mass on Sunday—and some are episodic, single stranded, and anonymous, like the faintly familiar face you see several times a month in the supermarket checkout line. Some types of social capital, like a Parent-Teacher Association, are formally organized, with incorporation papers, regular meetings, a written constitution, and connection to a national federation, whereas others, like a pickup basketball game, are more informal. Some forms of social capital, like a volunteer ambulance squad, have explicit public-regarding purposes; some, like a bridge club, exist for the private enjoyment of the members; and some, like the Rotary club mentioned earlier, serve both public and private ends.

Of all the dimensions along which forms of social capital vary, perhaps the most important is the distinction between *bridging* (or inclusive) and *bonding* (or exclusive).[9] Some forms of social capital are, by choice or necessity, inward looking and tend to reinforce exclusive identities and homogeneous groups. Examples of bonding social capital include ethnic fraternal organizations, church-based women's reading groups, and fashionable country clubs. Other networks are outward looking and encompass people across diverse social cleavages. Examples of bridging social capital include the civil rights movement, many youth service groups, and ecumenical religious organizations.

Bonding social capital is good for undergirding specific reciprocity and mobilizing solidarity. Dense networks in ethnic enclaves, for example, provide crucial social and psychological support for less fortunate members of the community, while furnishing start-up financing, markets, and reliable labor for local entrepreneurs. Bridging networks, by contrast, are better for linkage to external assets and for information diffusion. Economic sociologist Mark Granovetter has pointed out that when seeking jobs—or political allies—the "weak" ties that link me to distant acquaintances who move in different circles from mine are actually more valuable than the "strong" ties that link me to relatives and intimate friends whose sociological niche is very like my own. Bonding social capital is, as Xavier de Souza Briggs puts it, good for "getting by," but bridging social capital is crucial for "getting ahead."[10]

Moreover, bridging social capital can generate broader identities and reciprocity, whereas bonding social capital bolsters our narrower selves. In 1829 at the founding of a community lyceum in the bustling whaling port of New Bedford, Massachusetts, Thomas Greene eloquently expressed this crucial insight:

> We come from all the divisions, ranks and classes of society . . . to teach and to be taught in our turn. While we mingle together in these pursuits, we shall learn to know each other more intimately; we shall remove many of the prejudices which ignorance or partial acquaintance with each other had fostered. . . . In the parties and sects into which we are divided, we sometimes learn to love our brother at the expense of him whom we do not in so many respects regard as a brother. . . . We may return to our homes and firesides [from the lyceum] with kindlier feelings toward one another, because we have learned to know one another better.[11]

Bonding social capital constitutes a kind of sociological superglue, whereas bridging social capital provides a sociological WD-40. Bonding social capital, by creating strong in-group loyalty, may also create strong out-group antagonism; as Thomas Greene and his neighbors in New Bedford knew, and for that reason we might expect negative external effects to be more common with this form of social capital. Nevertheless, under many circumstances both bridging and bonding social capital can have powerfully positive social effects.

Many groups simultaneously bond along some social dimensions and bridge across others. The black church, for example, brings together people of the same race and religion across class lines. The Knights of Columbus was created to bridge cleavages among different ethnic communities while bonding along religious and gender lines. Internet chat groups may bridge across

Think of an example of bridging + bonding social capital in your own life

geography, gender, age, and religion, while being tightly homogeneous in education and ideology. In short, bonding and bridging are not "either-or" categories into which social networks can be neatly divided, but "more or less" dimensions along which we can compare different forms of social capital.

It would obviously be valuable to have distinct measures of the evolution of these various forms of social capital over time. However, like researchers on global warming, we must make do with the imperfect evidence that we can find, not merely lament its deficiencies. Exhaustive descriptions of social networks in America—even at a single point in time—do not exist. I have found no reliable, comprehensive, nationwide measures of social capital that neatly distinguish "bridgingness" and "bondingness." In our empirical account of recent social trends in this book, therefore, this distinction will be less prominent than I would prefer. On the other hand, we must keep this conceptual differentiation at the back of our minds as we proceed, recognizing that bridging and bonding social capital are not interchangeable.

"Social Capital" is to some extent merely new language for a very old debate in American intellectual circles. Community has warred incessantly with individualism for preeminence in our political hagiology. Liberation from ossified community bonds is a recurrent and honored theme in our culture, from the Pilgrims' storied escape from religious convention in the seventeenth century to the lyric nineteenth-century paeans to individualism by Emerson ("Self-Reliance"), Thoreau ("Civil Disobedience"), and Whitman ("Song of Myself") to Sherwood Anderson's twentieth-century celebration of the struggle against conformism by ordinary citizens in *Winesburg, Ohio* to the latest Clint Eastwood film. Even Alexis de Tocqueville, patron saint of American communitarians, acknowledged the uniquely democratic claim of individualism, "a calm and considered feeling which disposes each citizen to isolate himself from the mass of his fellows and withdraw into the circle of family and friends; with this little society formed to his taste, he gladly leaves the greater society to look after itself."[12]

Our national myths often exaggerate the role of individual heroes and understate the importance of collective effort. Historian David Hackett Fischer's gripping account of opening night in the American Revolution, for example, reminds us that Paul Revere's alarm was successful only because of networks of civic engagement in the Middlesex villages. Towns without well-organized local militia, no matter how patriotic their inhabitants, were AWOL from Lexington and Concord.[13] Nevertheless, the myth of rugged individualism continues to strike a powerful inner chord in the American psyche.

Debates about the waxing and waning of "community" have been endemic for at least two centuries. "Declensionist narrative"—postmodernist jargon for tales of decline and fall—have a long pedigree in our letters. We seem perennially tempted to contrast our tawdry todays with past golden ages. We apparently share this nostalgic predilection with the rest of humanity. As sociologist Barry Wellman observes,

It is likely that pundits have worried about the impact of social change on communities ever since human beings ventured beyond their caves. . . . In the [past] two centuries many leading social commentators have been gainfully employed suggesting various ways in which large-scale social changes associated with the Industrial Revolution may have affected the structure and operation of communities. . . . This ambivalence about the consequences of large-scale changes continued well into the twentieth century. Analysts have kept asking if things have, in fact, fallen apart.[14]

At the conclusion of the twentieth century, ordinary Americans shared this sense of civic malaise. We were reasonably content about our economic prospects, hardly a surprise after an expansion of unprecedented length, but we were not equally convinced that we were on the right track morally or culturally. Of baby boomers interviewed in 1987, 53 percent thought their parents' generation was better in terms of "being a concerned citizen, involved in helping others in the community," as compared with only 21 percent who thought their own generation was better. Fully 77 percent said the nation was worse off because of "less involvement in community activities." In 1992 three-quarters of the U.S. workforce said that "the breakdown of community" and "selfishness" were "serious" or "extremely serious" problems in America. In 1996 only 8 percent of all Americans said that "the honesty and integrity of the average American" were improving, as compared with 50 percent of us who thought we were becoming less trustworthy. Those of us who said that people had become less civil over the preceding ten years outnumbered those who thought people had become more civil, 80 percent to 12 percent. In several surveys in 1999 two-thirds of Americans said that America's civic life had weakened in recent years, that social and moral values were higher when they were growing up, and that our society was focused more on the individual than the community. More than 80 percent said there should be more emphasis on community, even if that put more demands on individuals.[15] Americans' concern about weakening community bonds may be misplaced or exaggerated, but a decent respect for the opinion of our fellow citizens suggests that we should explore the issue more thoroughly.

It is emphatically not my view that community bonds in America have weakened steadily throughout our history—or even throughout the last hundred years. On the contrary, American history carefully examined is a story of ups and downs in civic engagement, *not just downs*—a story of collapse *and* of renewal. As I have already hinted in the opening pages of this book, within living memory the bonds of community in America were becoming stronger, not weaker, and as I shall argue in the concluding pages, it is within our power to reverse the decline of the last several decades.

Nevertheless, my argument is, at least in appearance, in the declensionist tradition, so it is important to avoid simple nostalgia. Precisely because the theme of this book might lend itself to gauzy self-deception, our methods must be transparent. Is life in communities as we enter the twenty-first century really so different after all from the reality of American communities in the 1950s and 1960s? One way of curbing nostalgia is to count things. Are club meetings really less crowded today than yesterday, or does it just seem so? Do we really know our neighbors less well than our parents did, or is our childhood recollection of neighborhood barbecues suffused with a golden glow of wishful reminiscence? Are friendly poker games less common now, or is it merely that we ourselves have outgrown poker? League bowling may be passé, but how about softball and soccer? Are strangers less trustworthy now? Are boomers and X'ers really less engaged in community life? After all, it was the preceding generation that was once scorned as "silent." Perhaps the younger generation today is no less engaged than their predecessors, but engaged in new ways. In the chapters that follow we explore these questions with the best available evidence.

The challenge of studying the evolving social climate is analogous in some respects to the challenge facing meteorologists who measure global warming: We know what kind of evidence we would ideally want from the past, but time's arrow means that we can't go back to conduct those well-designed studies. Thus if we are to explore how our society is like or unlike our parents', we must make imperfect inferences from all the evidence that we can find.

The most powerful strategy for paleometeorologists seeking to assess global climate change is to triangulate among diverse sources of evidence. If pollen counts in polar ice, and the width of southwestern tree rings, and temperature records of the British Admiralty all point in a similar direction, the inference of global warming is stronger than if the cord of evidence has only a single strand. For much the same reason, prudent journalists follow a "two source" rule: Never report anything unless at least two independent sources confirm it.

In this book I follow that same maxim. Nearly every major generalization here rests on more than one body of independent evidence, and where I have discovered divergent results from credible sources, I note that disparity as well. I have a case to make, but like any officer of the court, I have a professional obligation to present all relevant evidence I have found, exculpatory as well as incriminating. To avoid cluttering the text with masses of redundant evidence, I have typically put confirmatory evidence from multiple studies in the notes, so skeptical "show me" readers should examine those notes as well as the text.[16]

I have sought as diverse a range of evidence as possible on continuities and change in American social life. If the transformation that I discern is as broad and deep as I believe it to be, it ought to show up in many different places, so I have cast a broad net. Of course, social change, like climatic change, is inevitably uneven. Life is not lived in a single dimension. We should not expect to find everything changing in the same direction and at the same speed, but those very anomalies may contain important clues to what is happening.

American society, like the continent on which we live, is massive and *polymorphous*, and our civic engagement historically has come in many sizes and shapes. A few of us still share plowing chores with neighbors, while many more pitch in to wire classrooms to the Internet. Some of us run for Congress, and others join self-help groups. Some of us hang out at the local bar association and others at the local bar. Some of us attend mass once a day, while others struggle to remember to send holiday greetings once a year. The forms of our social capital—the ways in which we connect with friends and neighbors and strangers—are varied.

So our review of trends in social capital and civic engagement ranges widely across various sectors of this complex society. In the chapters that follow we begin by charting Americans' participation in the most public forum—politics and public affairs. We next turn to the institutions of our communities—clubs and community associations, religious bodies, and work-related organizations, such as unions and professional societies. Then we explore the almost infinite variety of informal ties that link Americans— card parties and bowling leagues, bar cliques and ball games, picnics and parties. Next we examine the changing patterns of trust and altruism in America—philanthropy, volunteering, honesty, reciprocity. Finally we turn to three apparent counterexamples to the decline of connectedness—small groups, social movements, and the Internet.

In each domain we shall encounter currents and crosscurrents and eddies, but in each we shall also discover common, powerful tidal movements that have swept across American society in the twentieth century. The dominant theme is simple: For the first two-thirds of the twentieth century a powerful tide bore Americans into ever deeper engagement in the life of their communities, but a few decades ago—silently, without warning—that tide reversed and we were overtaken by a treacherous rip current. Without at first noticing, we have been pulled apart from one another and from our communities over the last third of the century.

350

Polymorphous

360

370

ENDNOTES

1. Lyda Judson Hanifan, "The Rural School Community Center," *Annals of the American Academy of Political and Social Science* 67 (1916): 130–138, quotation at 130. Ever the practical reformer, Hanifan was self-conscious about using the term *capital* to encourage hard-nosed businessmen and economists to recognize the productive importance of social assets. Having introduced the idea of social capital, he observes, "That there is a great lack of such social capital in some rural districts need not be retold in this chapter. The important question at this time is: How can these conditions be improved? The story which follows is an account of the way a West Virginia rural community in a single year actually developed social capital and then used this capital in the improvement of its recreational, intellectual, moral, and economic conditions." His essay,

which included a list of practical exercises for community-based activists, was originally prepared in 1913 for West Virginia schoolteachers as "a handbook for community meetings at rural schoolhouses," and it was subsequently incorporated in L. J. Hanifan, *The Community Center* (Boston: Silver, Burdett, 1920). I am grateful to Brad Clarke for first spotting this usage of the term *social capital.*

2. John R. Seeley, Alexander R. Sim, and Elizabeth W. Loosley, *Crestwood Heights: A Study of the Culture of Suburban Life* (New York: Basic Books, 1956); Jane Jacobs, *The Death and Life of Great American Cities* (New York: Random House, 1961); Glenn Loury, "A Dynamic Theory of Racial Income Differences; in *Women, Minorities, and Employment Discrimination,* ed. P. A. Wallace and A. LeMund (Lexington, Mass.: Lexington Books, 1977), 153–188; Pierre Bourdieu, "Forms of Capital," in *Handbook of Theory and Research for the Sociology of Education,* ed. John G. Richardson (New York: Greenwood Press, 1983), 241–258; Ekkehart Schlicht, "Cognitive Dissonance in Economics," in *Normengeleitetes Verhalten in den Sozialwissenschaften* (Berlin: Duncker and Humblot, 1984), 61–81; James S. Coleman, "Social Capital in the Creation of Human Capital," *American Journal of Sociology* 94 (1988): S95–SI20; and James S. Coleman, *Foundations of Social Theory* (Cambridge, Mass.: Harvard University Press, 1990). See also George C. Homans, *Social Behavior: Its Elementary Forms* (New York: Harcourt, Brace & World, 1961), 378–98. Except for a brief acknowledgment by Coleman of Loury's work, I can find no evidence that any of these theorists were aware of any of the preceding usages. For a comprehensive overview of the conceptual history of "social capital," see Michael Woolcock, "Social Capital and Economic Development: Toward a Theoretical Synthesis and Policy Framework," *Theory and Society* 27 (1998): 151–208.

3. Ronald S. Burt, *Structural Holes: The Social Structure of Competition* (Cambridge, Mass.: Harvard University Press, 1992); Ronald S. Burt, "The Contingent Value of Social Capital," *Administrative Science Quarterly* 42 (1997): 339–365; and Ronald S. Burt, "The Gender of Social Capital," *Rationality & Society* 10 (1998): 5–46; Claude S. Fischer, "Network Analysis and Urban Studies," in *Networks and Places: Social Relations in the Urban Setting,* ed. Claude S. Fischer (New York: Free Press, 1977), 19; James D. Montgomery, "Social Networks and Labor-Market Outcomes: Toward an Economic Analysis," *American Economic Review* 81 (1991): 1408–1418, esp. table 1.

4. In earlier work I emphasized this public dimension of social capital almost to the exclusion of the private returns to social capital. See Robert D. Putnam, "The Prosperous Community: Social Capital and Public Affairs," *The American Prospect* 13 (1993): 35–42, on which the present text draws. For a literature review that highlights the private returns almost to the exclusion of the collective dimension, see

Alejandro Portes, "Social Capital: Its Origins and Applications in Modern Sociology," *Annual Review of Sociology* 22 (1998): 1–24.

5. Robert Frank in private conversation.

6. Xavier de Souza Briggs, "Social Capital and the Cities: Advice to Change Agents," *National Civic Review* 86 (summer 1997): 111–117.

7. *U.S. News & World Report* (August 4, 1997): 18. Fareed Zakaria, "Bigger Than the Family, Smaller Than the State," *New York Times Book Review,* August 13, 1995: 1, pointed out that McVeigh and his co-conspirators spent evenings together in a bowling alley and concluded that "we would all have been better off if Mr. McVeigh had gone bowling alone." Sometimes, as in certain cults or clans, even the *internal* effects of social capital can be negative, but these are less common than negative *external* effects.

8. In *Making Democracy Work: Civic Traditions in Modern Italy* (Princeton, N.J.: Princeton University Press, 1993), I ignored the possibility that social capital might have antisocial effects, but I recognized this possibility explicitly in "The Prosperous Community," published that same year.

9. So far as I can tell, credit for coining these labels belongs to Ross Gittell and Avis Vidal, *Community Organizing Building Social Capital as a Development Strategy* (Thousand Oaks, Calif.: Sage, 1998), 8.

10. Mark S. Granovetter, "The Strength of Weak Ties," *American Journal of Sociology* 78 (1973): 1360–1380; Xavier de Souza Briggs, "Doing Democracy Up Close: Culture, Power, and Communication in Community Building," *Journal of Planning Education and Research* 18 (1998): 1–13.

11. As quoted in Richard D. Brown, "The Emergence of Voluntary Associations in Massachusetts," *Journal of Voluntary Action Research* 2 (April 1973): 64–73, at 69. See also Ashutosh Varshney, *Ethnic Conflict and Civic Life: Hindus and Muslims in India* (New Haven, Conn.: Yale University Press, 2000).

12. Alexis de Tocqueville, *Democracy in America,* ed. J. P. Mayer, trans. George Lawrence (Garden City, N.Y.: Doubleday, 1969), 506. See also Wilson Carey McWilliams, *The Idea of Fraternity in America,* (Berkeley: University of California Press, 1973), and Thomas Bender, *Community and Social Change in America* (Baltimore, Md.: Johns Hopkins University Press, 1978).

13. David Hackett Fischer, *Paul Revere's Ride* (New York: Oxford University Press, 1994).

14. Barry Wellman, "The Community Question Re-Evaluated," in *Power, Community, and the City,* Michael Peter Smith, ed. (New Brunswick, N.J.: Transaction 1988), 81–107, quotation at 82–83. Pamela Paxton, "Is Social Capital Declining in the United States? A Multiple Indicator Assessment," *American Journal of Sociology* 105 (1999): 88–127.

15. *The Public Perspective* 8 (December/January 1997): 64; Robert Wuthnow, "Changing Character of Social Capital in the United States," in *The Dynamics of Social Capital in Comparative Perspective*, Robert D. Putnam, ed. (2000, forthcoming); *The Public Perspective* 10 (April/May 1999): 15; *Wall Street Journal*, June 24, 1999, A12; Mark J. Penn, "The Community Consensus," *Blueprint: Ideas for a New Century* (spring 1999). Respondents with no opinion are excluded.

16. For example, figures 31–33 present data from six independent sources on trends in philanthropy, but I have also discovered four additional sources that confirm the basic pattern, and those sources are mentioned briefly in the notes. For additional discussion of methodology, see the appendixes.

Reading this right before 9/11 makes me conscious that there can be trends and also fulcrum points in community. What would it have been like if Bush had said – 'become more a part of your neighbors' lives' as a post 9/11 effort?

THE SOCIAL CONTRACT
Jean-Jacques Rousseau

Translated by George Douglas and Howard Cole

BOOK I

1. Subject of the First Book

Man is born free; and everywhere he is in chains. One thinks himself the 1
master of others, and still remains a greater slave than they. How did this
change come about? I do not know. What can make it legitimate? That question I think I can answer.

If I took into account only force, and the effects derived from it, I should
say: "As long as a people is compelled to obey, and obeys, it does well; as soon
as it can shake off the yoke, and shakes it off, it does still better; for, regain-
ing its liberty by the same right as took it away, either it is justified in resum-
ing it, or there was no justification for those who took it away." But the social
order is a sacred right which is the basis of all other rights. Nevertheless, this 10
right does not come from nature, and must therefore be founded on conventions. Before coming to that, I have to prove what I have just asserted.

2. The First Societies

The most ancient of all societies, and the only one that is natural, is the family: and even so the children remain attached to the father only so long as they
need him for their preservation. As soon as this need ceases, the natural bond
is dissolved. The children, released from the obedience they owed to the father,
and the father, released from the care he owed his children, return equally to
independence. If they remain united, they continue so no longer naturally, but
voluntarily; and the family itself is then maintained only by convention.

This common liberty results from the nature of man. His first law is to 20
provide for his own preservation, his first cares are those which he owes to
himself; and, as soon as he reaches years of discretion, he is the sole judge of
the proper means of preserving himself, and consequently becomes his own
master.

The family then may be called the first model of political societies: the
ruler corresponds to the father, and the people to the children; and all, being
born free and equal, alienate their liberty only for their own advantage. The
whole difference is that, in the family, the love of the father for his children
repays him for the care he takes of them, while, in the State, the pleasure of
commanding takes the place of the love which the chief cannot have for the 30
peoples under him.

Reprinted from *The Social Contract* (2010).

Grotius denies that all human power is established in favour of the governed, and quotes slavery as an example. His usual method of reasoning is constantly to establish right by fact. It would be possible to employ a more logical method, but none could be more favourable to tyrants.

It is then, according to Grotius, doubtful whether the human race belongs to a hundred men, or that hundred men to the human race: and, throughout his book, he seems to incline to the former alternative, which is also the view of Hobbes. On this showing, the human species is divided into so many herds of cattle, each with its ruler, who keeps guard over them for the purpose of devouring them.

As a shepherd is of a nature superior to that of his flock, the shepherds of men, i.e., their rulers, are of a nature superior to that of the peoples under them. Thus, Philo tells us, the Emperor Caligula reasoned, concluding equally well either that kings were gods, or that men were beasts.

The reasoning of Caligula agrees with that of Hobbes and Grotius. Aristotle, before any of them, had said that men are by no means equal naturally, but that some are born for slavery, and others for dominion.

Aristotle was right; but he took the effect for the cause. Nothing can be more certain than that every man born in slavery is born for slavery. Slaves lose everything in their chains, even the desire of escaping from them: they love their servitude, as the comrades of Ulysses loved their brutish condition. If then there are slaves by nature, it is because there have been slaves against nature. Force made the first slaves, and their cowardice perpetuated the condition.

I have said nothing of King Adam, or Emperor Noah, father of the three great monarchs who shared out the universe, like the children of Saturn, whom some scholars have recognised in them. I trust to getting due thanks for my moderation; for, being a direct descendant of one of these princes, perhaps of the eldest branch, how do I know that a verification of titles might not leave me the legitimate king of the human race? In any case, there can be no doubt that Adam was sovereign of the world, as Robinson Crusoe was of his island, as long as he was its only inhabitant; and this empire had the advantage that the monarch, safe on his throne, had no rebellions, wars, or conspiracies to fear.

3. The Right of the Strongest

The strongest is never strong enough to be always the master, unless he transforms strength into right, and obedience into duty. Hence the right of the strongest, which, though to all seeming meant ironically, is really laid down as a fundamental principle. But are we never to have an explanation of this phrase? Force is a physical power, and I fail to see what moral effect it can have. To yield to force is an act of necessity, not of will—at the most, an act of prudence. In what sense can it be a duty?

Suppose for a moment that this so-called "right" exists. I maintain that the sole result is a mass of inexplicable nonsense. For, if force creates right, the effect changes with the cause: every force that is greater than the first succeeds to its right. As soon as it is possible to disobey with impunity, disobedience is legitimate; and, the strongest being always in the right, the only thing that matters is to act so as to become the strongest. But what kind of right is that which perishes when force fails? If we must obey perforce, there is no need to obey because we ought; and if we are not forced to obey, we are under no obligation to do so. Clearly, the word "right" adds nothing to force: in this connection, it means absolutely nothing.

Obey the powers that be. If this means yield to force, it is a good precept, but superfluous: I can answer for its never being violated. All power comes from God, I admit; but so does all sickness: does that mean that we are forbidden to call in the doctor? A brigand surprises me at the edge of a wood: must I not merely surrender my purse on compulsion; but, even if I could withhold it, am I in conscience bound to give it up? For certainly the pistol he holds is also a power.

Let us then admit that force does not create right, and that we are obliged to obey only legitimate powers. In that case, my original question recurs.

4. Slavery

Since no man has a natural authority over his fellow, and force creates no right, we must conclude that conventions form the basis of all legitimate authority among men.

If an individual, says Grotius, can alienate his liberty and make himself the slave of a master, why could not a whole people do the same and make itself subject to a king? There are in this passage plenty of ambiguous words which would need explaining; but let us confine ourselves to the word *alienate*. To alienate is to give or to sell. Now, a man who becomes the slave of another does not give himself; he sells himself, at the least for his subsistence: but for what does a people sell itself? A king is so far from furnishing his subjects with their subsistence that he gets his own only from them; and, according to Rabelais, kings do not live on nothing. Do subjects then give their persons on condition that the king takes their goods also? I fail to see what they have left to preserve.

It will be said that the despot assures his subjects civil tranquillity. Granted; but what do they gain, if the wars his ambition brings down upon them, his insatiable avidity, and the vexatious conduct of his ministers press harder on them than their own dissensions would have done? What do they gain, if the very tranquillity they enjoy is one of their miseries? Tranquillity is found also in dungeons; but is that enough to make them desirable places to live in? The Greeks imprisoned in the cave of the Cyclops lived there very tranquilly, while they were awaiting their turn to be devoured.

To say that a man gives himself gratuitously, is to say what is absurd and inconceivable; such an act is null and illegitimate, from the mere fact that he who does it is out of his mind. To say the same of a whole people is to suppose a people of madmen; and madness creates no right.

Even if each man could alienate himself, he could not alienate his children: they are born men and free; their liberty belongs to them, and no one but they has the right to dispose of it. Before they come to years of discretion, the father can, in their name, lay down conditions for their preservation and well-being, but he cannot give them irrevocably and without conditions: such a gift is contrary to the ends of nature, and exceeds the rights of paternity. It would therefore be necessary, in order to legitimise an arbitrary government, that in every generation the people should be in a position to accept or reject it; but, were this so, the government would be no longer arbitrary.

To renounce liberty is to renounce being a man, to surrender the rights of humanity and even its duties. For him who renounces everything no indemnity is possible. Such a renunciation is incompatible with man's nature; to remove all liberty from his will is to remove all morality from his acts. Finally, it is an empty and contradictory convention that sets up, on the one side, absolute authority, and, on the other, unlimited obedience. Is it not clear that we can be under no obligation to a person from whom we have the right to exact everything? Does not this condition alone, in the absence of equivalence or exchange, in itself involve the nullity of the act? For what right can my slave have against me, when all that he has belongs to me, and, his right being mine, this right of mine against myself is a phrase devoid of meaning?

So, from whatever aspect we regard the question, the right of slavery is null and void, not only as being illegitimate, but also because it is absurd and meaningless. The words *slave* and *right* contradict each other, and are mutually exclusive. It will always be equally foolish for a man to say to a man or to a people: "I make with you a convention wholly at your expense and wholly to my advantage; I shall keep it as long as I like, and you will keep it as long as I like."

5. That We Must Always Go Back to a First Convention

Even if I granted all that I have been refuting, the friends of despotism would be no better off. There will always be a great difference between subduing a multitude and ruling a society. Even if scattered individuals were successively enslaved by one man, however numerous they might be, I still see no more than a master and his slaves, and certainly not a people and its ruler; I see what may be termed an aggregation, but not an association; there is as yet neither public good nor body politic. The man in question, even if he has enslaved half the world, is still only an individual; his interest, apart from that of others, is still a purely private interest. If this same man comes to die, his

[margin note: Even if one could sell oneself, not one's children]

[margin note: We call that democracy]

[margin line numbers: 120, 130, 140, 150]

empire, after him, remains scattered and without unity, as an oak falls and dissolves into a heap of ashes when the fire has consumed it.

A people, says Grotius, can give itself to a king. Then, according to Grotius, a people is a people before it gives itself. The gift is itself a civil act, and implies public deliberation. It would be better, before examining the act by which a people gives itself to a king, to examine that by which it has become a people; for this act, being necessarily prior to the other, is the true foundation of society.

Indeed, if there were no prior convention, where, unless the election were unanimous, would be the obligation on the minority to submit to the choice of the majority? How have a hundred men who wish for a master the right to vote on behalf of ten who do not? The law of majority voting is itself something established by convention, and presupposes unanimity, on one occasion at least.

6. The Social Compact

I suppose men to have reached the point at which the obstacles in the way of their preservation in the state of nature show their power of resistance to be greater than the resources at the disposal of each individual for his maintenance in that state. That primitive condition can then subsist no longer; and the human race would perish unless it changed its manner of existence.

But, as men cannot engender new forces, but only unite and direct existing ones, they have no other means of preserving themselves than the formation, by aggregation, of a sum of forces great enough to overcome the resistance. These they have to bring into play by means of a single motive power, and cause to act in concert.

This sum of forces can arise only where several persons come together: but, as the force and liberty of each man are the chief instruments of his self-preservation, how can he pledge them without harming his own interests, and neglecting the care he owes to himself? This difficulty, in its bearing on my present subject, may be stated in the following terms:

> "*The problem is to find a form of association which will defend and protect with the whole common force the person and goods of each associate, and in which each, while uniting himself with all, may still obey himself alone, and remain as free as before.*" This is the fundamental problem of which the *Social Contract* provides the solution.

The clauses of this contract are so determined by the nature of the act that the slightest modification would make them vain and ineffective; so that, although they have perhaps never been formally set forth, they are everywhere the same and everywhere tacitly admitted and recognised, until, on the violation of the social compact, each regains his original rights and resumes his natural liberty, while losing the conventional liberty in favour of which he renounced it.

These clauses, properly understood, may be reduced to one—the total alienation of each associate, together with all his rights, to the whole community; for, in the first place, as each gives himself absolutely, the conditions are the same for all; and, this being so, no one has any interest in making them burdensome to others.

Moreover, the alienation being without reserve, the union is as perfect as it can be, and no associate has anything more to demand: for, if the individuals retained certain rights, as there would be no common superior to decide between them and the public, each, being on one point his own judge, would ask to be so on all; the state of nature would thus continue, and the association would necessarily become inoperative or tyrannical.

Finally, each man, in giving himself to all, gives himself to nobody; and as there is no associate over whom he does not acquire the same right as he yields others over himself, he gains an equivalent for everything he loses, and an increase of force for the preservation of what he has.

If then we discard from the social compact what is not of its essence, we shall find that it reduces itself to the following terms:

> *"Each of us puts his person and all his power in common under the supreme direction of the general will, and, in our corporate capacity, we receive each member as an indivisible part of the whole."*

At once, in place of the individual personality of each contracting party, this act of association creates a moral and collective body, composed of as many members as the assembly contains votes, and receiving from this act its unity, its common identity, its life and its will. This public person, so formed by the union of all other persons formerly took the name of *city,* and now takes that of *Republic* or *body politic;* it is called by its members *State* when passive, *Sovereign* when active, and *Power* when compared with others like itself. Those who are associated in it take collectively the name of *people,* and severally are called *citizens,* as sharing in the sovereign power, and *subjects,* as being under the laws of the State. But these terms are often confused and taken one for another: it is enough to know how to distinguish them when they are being used with precision.

7. The Sovereign

This formula shows us that the act of association comprises a mutual undertaking between the public and the individuals, and that each individual, in making a contract, as we may say, with himself, is bound in a double capacity; as a member of the Sovereign he is bound to the individuals, and as a member of the State to the Sovereign. But the maxim of civil right, that no one is bound by undertakings made to himself, does not apply in this case;

for there is a great difference between incurring an obligation to yourself and incurring one to a whole of which you form a part.

Attention must further be called to the fact that public deliberation, while competent to bind all the subjects to the Sovereign, because of the two different capacities in which each of them may be regarded, cannot, for the opposite reason, bind the Sovereign to itself; and that it is consequently against the nature of the body politic for the Sovereign to impose on itself a law which it cannot infringe. Being able to regard itself in only one capacity, it is in the position of an individual who makes a contract with himself; and this makes it clear that there neither is nor can be any kind of fundamental law binding on the body of the people—not even the social contract itself. This does not mean that the body politic cannot enter into undertakings with others, provided the contract is not infringed by them; for in relation to what is external to it, it becomes a simple being, an individual.

But the body politic or the Sovereign, drawing its being wholly from the sanctity of the contract, can never bind itself, even to an outsider, to do anything derogatory to the original act, for instance, to alienate any part of itself, or to submit to another Sovereign. Violation of the act by which it exists would be self-annihilation; and that which is itself nothing can create nothing.

As soon as this multitude is so united in one body, it is impossible to offend against one of the members without attacking the body, and still more to offend against the body without the members resenting it. Duty and interest therefore equally oblige the two contracting parties to give each other help; and the same men should seek to combine, in their double capacity, all the advantages dependent upon that capacity.

Again, the Sovereign, being formed wholly of the individuals who compose it, neither has nor can have any interest contrary to theirs; and consequently the sovereign power need give no guarantee to its subjects, because it is impossible for the body to wish to hurt all its members. We shall also see later on that it cannot hurt any in particular. The Sovereign, merely by virtue of what it is, is always what it should be.

This, however, is not the case with the relation of the subjects to the Sovereign, which, despite the common interest, would have no security that they would fulfil their undertakings, unless it found means to assure itself of their fidelity.

In fact, each individual, as a man, may have a particular will contrary or dissimilar to the general will which he has as a citizen. His particular interest may speak to him quite differently from the common interest: his absolute and naturally independent existence may make him look upon what he owes to the common cause as a gratuitous contribution, the loss of which will do less harm to others than the payment of it is burdensome to himself; and, regarding the moral person which constitutes the State as a *persona ficta*, because not a man, he may wish to enjoy the rights of citizenship without being ready to fulfil the duties of a subject. The continuance of such an injustice could not but prove the undoing of the body politic.

[margin note: so it goes without saying you will participate]

280   In order then that the social compact may not be an empty formula, it tacitly includes the undertaking, which alone can give force to the rest, that whoever refuses to obey the general will shall be compelled to do so by the whole body. This means nothing less than that he will be forced to be free; for this is the condition which, by giving each citizen to his country, secures him against all personal dependence. In this lies the key to the working of the political machine; this alone legitimises civil undertakings, which, without it, would be absurd, tyrannical, and liable to the most frightful abuses.

8. The Civil State

[margin note: movement from state of nature to civilized society]

The passage from the state of nature to the civil state produces a very remarkable change in man, by substituting justice for instinct in his conduct, and giving his actions the morality they had formerly lacked. Then only, when the
290   voice of duty takes the place of physical impulses and right of appetite, does man, who so far had considered only himself, find that he is forced to act on different principles, and to consult his reason before listening to his inclinations. Although, in this state, he deprives himself of some advantages which he got from nature, he gains in return others so great, his faculties are so stimulated and developed, his ideas so extended, his feelings so ennobled, and his whole soul so uplifted, that, did not the abuses of this new condition often degrade him below that which he left, he would be bound to bless continually the happy moment which took him from it for ever, and, instead of a stupid and unimaginative animal, made him an intelligent being and a man.

[margin note: abuses are what make people reluctant to thank God for the social contract]

300   Let us draw up the whole account in terms easily commensurable. What man loses by the social contract is his natural liberty and an unlimited right to everything he tries to get and succeeds in getting; what he gains is civil liberty and the proprietorship of all he possesses. If we are to avoid mistake in weighing one against the other, we must clearly distinguish natural liberty, which is bounded only by the strength of the individual, from civil liberty, which is limited by the general will; and possession, which is merely the effect of force or the right of the first occupier, from property, which can be founded only on a positive title.

[margin note: basis of property ownership]

We might, over and above all this, add, to what man acquires in the civil
310   state, moral liberty, which alone makes him truly master of himself; for the mere impulse of appetite is slavery, while obedience to a law which we prescribe to ourselves is liberty. But I have already said too much on this head, and the philosophical meaning of the word liberty does not now concern us.

[margin note: moral liberty also]

9. Real Property

Each member of the community gives himself to it, at the moment of its foundation, just as he is, with all the resources at his command, including the goods he possesses. This act does not make possession, in changing hands, change its nature, and become property in the hands of the Sovereign; but, as the forces of the city are incomparably greater than those of an individual, public possession is also, in fact, stronger and more irrevocable, without being any more legitimate, at any rate from the point of view of foreigners. For the State, in relation to its members, is master of all their goods by the social contract, which, within the State, is the basis of all rights; but, in relation to other powers, it is so only by the right of the first occupier, which it holds from its members.

The right of the first occupier, though more real than the right of the strongest, becomes a real right only when the right of property has already been established. Every man has naturally a right to everything he needs; but the positive act which makes him proprietor of one thing excludes him from everything else. Having his share, he ought to keep to it, and can have no further right against the community. This is why the right of the first occupier, which in the state of nature is so weak, claims the respect of every man in civil society. In this right we are respecting not so much what belongs to another as what does not belong to ourselves.

The peculiar fact about this alienation is that, in taking over the goods of individuals, the community, so far from despoiling them, only assures them legitimate possession, and changes usurpation into a true right and enjoyment into proprietorship. Thus the possessors, being regarded as depositaries of the public good, and having their rights respected by all the members of the State and maintained against foreign aggression by all its forces, have, by a cession which benefits both the public and still more themselves, acquired, so to speak, all that they gave up. This paradox may easily be explained by the distinction between the rights which the Sovereign and the proprietor have over the same estate, as we shall see later on.

It may also happen that men begin to unite one with another before they possess anything, and that, subsequently occupying a tract of country which is enough for all, they enjoy it in common, or share it out among themselves, either equally or according to a scale fixed by the Sovereign. However the acquisition be made, the right which each individual has to his own estate is always subordinate to the right which the community has over all: without this, there would be neither stability in the social tie, nor real force in the exercise of Sovereignty.

I shall end this chapter and this book by remarking on a fact on which the whole social system should rest: i.e., that, instead of destroying natural inequality, the fundamental compact substitutes, for such physical inequality as nature may have set up between men, an equality that is moral and legitimate, and that men, who may be unequal in strength or intelligence, become every one equal by convention and legal right.

BOOK II

1. That Sovereignty Is Inalienable

The first and most important deduction from the principles we have so far laid down is that the general will alone can direct the State according to the object for which it was instituted, i.e., the common good: for if the clashing of particular interests made the establishment of societies necessary, the agreement of these very interests made it possible. The common element in these different interests is what forms the social tie; and, were there no point of agreement between them all, no society could exist. It is solely on the basis of this common interest that every society should be governed.

3. Whether the General Will Is Fallible

It follows from what has gone before that the general will is always right and tends to the public advantage; but it does not follow that the deliberations of the people are always equally correct. Our will is always for our own good, but we do not always see what that is; the people is never corrupted, but it is often deceived, and on such occasions only does it seem to will what is bad.

There is often a great deal of difference between the will of all and the general will; the latter considers only the common interest, while the former takes private interest into account, and is no more than a sum of particular wills: but take away from these same wills the pluses and minuses that cancel one another, and the general will remains as the sum of the differences.

If, when the people, being furnished with adequate information, held its deliberations, the citizens had no communication one with another, the grand total of the small differences would always give the general will, and the decision would always be good. But when factions arise, and partial associations are formed at the expense of the great association, the will of each of these associations becomes general in relation to its members, while it remains particular in relation to the State: it may then be said that there are no longer as many votes as there are men, but only as many as there are associations. The differences become less numerous and give a less general result. Lastly, when one of these associations is so great as to prevail over all the rest, the result is no longer a sum of small differences, but a single difference; in this case there is no longer a general will, and the opinion which prevails is purely particular.

It is therefore essential, if the general will is to be able to express itself, that there should be no partial society within the State, and that each citizen should think only his own thoughts: which was indeed the sublime and unique system established by the great Lycurgus. But if there are partial societies, it is best to have as many as possible and to prevent them from being unequal, as was done by Solon, Numa and Servius. These precautions are the only ones that can guarantee that the general will shall be always enlightened, and that the people shall in no way deceive itself.

4. The Limits of the Sovereign Power

If the State is a moral person whose life is in the union of its members, and if the most important of its cares is the care for its own preservation, it must have a universal and compelling force, in order to move and dispose each part as may be most advantageous to the whole. As nature gives each man absolute power over all his members, the social compact gives the body politic absolute power over all its members also; and it is this power which, under the direction of the general will, bears, as I have said, the name of Sovereignty.

But, besides the public person, we have to consider the private persons composing it, whose life and liberty are naturally independent of it. We are bound then to distinguish clearly between the respective rights of the citizens and the Sovereign, and between the duties the former have to fulfil as subjects, and the natural rights they should enjoy as men.

Each man alienates, I admit, by the social compact, only such part of his powers, goods and liberty as it is important for the community to control; but it must also be granted that the Sovereign is sole judge of what is important.

Every service a citizen can render the State he ought to render as soon as the Sovereign demands it; but the Sovereign, for its part, cannot impose upon its subjects any fetters that are useless to the community, nor can it even wish to do so; for no more by the law of reason than by the law of nature can anything occur without a cause.

The undertakings which bind us to the social body are obligatory only because they are mutual; and their nature is such that in fulfilling them we cannot work for others without working for ourselves. Why is it that the general will is always in the right, and that all continually will the happiness of each one, unless it is because there is not a man who does not think of "each" as meaning him, and consider himself in voting for all? This proves that equality of rights and the idea of justice which such equality creates originate in the preference each man gives to himself, and accordingly in the very nature of man. It proves that the general will, to be really such, must be general in its object as well as its essence; that it must both come from all and apply to all; and that it loses its natural rectitude when it is directed to some particular and determinate object, because in such a case we are judging of something foreign to us, and have no true principle of equity to guide us.

Indeed, as soon as a question of particular fact or right arises on a point not previously regulated by a general convention, the matter becomes contentious. It is a case in which the individuals concerned are one party, and the public the other, but in which I can see neither the law that ought to be followed nor the judge who ought to give the decision. In such a case, it would be absurd to propose to refer the question to an express decision of the general will, which can be only the conclusion reached by one of the parties and in consequence will be, for the other party, merely an external and particular will, inclined on this occasion to injustice and subject to error. Thus, just as a particular will cannot stand for the general will, the general will, in turn, changes its nature, when its object is particular, and, as general, cannot pronounce on a man or a fact. When, for instance, the people of Athens nominated or displaced its rulers, decreed honours to one, and imposed penalties

[margin notes:]
400 Social compact gives total power over members

But "we are bound" to distinguish rights of Sov + citizen

410 Indiv only gives what society has need of. but Sov determines what that is.

420

430

440

The 3 branches of our gov't spring from different aspects of functional need + the impartiality of the judiciary from this principle

on another, and, by a multitude of particular decrees, exercised all the functions of government indiscriminately, it had in such cases no longer a general will in the strict sense; it was acting no longer as Sovereign, but as magistrate. This will seem contrary to current views; but I must be given time to expound my own.

450   It should be seen from the foregoing that what makes the will general is less the number of voters than the common interest uniting them; for, under this system, each necessarily submits to the conditions he imposes on others: and this admirable agreement between interest and justice gives to the common deliberations an equitable character which at once vanishes when any particular question is discussed, in the absence of a common interest to unite and identify the ruling of the judge with that of the party.

From whatever side we approach our principle, we reach the same conclusion, that the social compact sets up among the citizens an equality of such a kind, that they all bind themselves to observe the same conditions and

460   should therefore all enjoy the same rights. Thus, from the very nature of the compact, every act of Sovereignty, i.e., every authentic act of the general will, binds or favours all the citizens equally; so that the Sovereign recognises only the body of the nation, and draws no distinctions between those of whom it is made up. What, then, strictly speaking, is an act of Sovereignty? It is not a convention between a superior and an inferior, but a convention between the body and each of its members. It is legitimate, because based on the social contract, and equitable, because common to all; useful, because it can have no other object than the general good, and stable, because guaranteed by the public force and the supreme power. So long as the subjects have to submit

470   only to conventions of this sort, they obey no-one but their own will; and to ask how far the respective rights of the Sovereign and the citizens extend, is to ask up to what point the latter can enter into undertakings with themselves, each with all, and all with each.

We can see from this that the sovereign power, absolute, sacred and inviolable as it is, does not and cannot exceed the limits of general conventions, and that every man may dispose at will of such goods and liberty as these conventions leave him; so that the Sovereign never has a right to lay more charges on one subject than on another, because, in that case, the question becomes particular, and ceases to be within its competency.

480   When these distinctions have once been admitted, it is seen to be so untrue that there is, in the social contract, any real renunciation on the part of the individuals, that the position in which they find themselves as a result of the contract is really preferable to that in which they were before. Instead of a renunciation, they have made an advantageous exchange: instead of an uncertain and precarious way of living they have got one that is better and more secure; instead of natural independence they have got liberty, instead of the power to harm others security for themselves, and instead of their strength, which others might overcome, a right which social union makes invincible. Their very life, which they have devoted to the State, is by

it constantly protected; and when they risk it in the State's defence, what 490
more are they doing than giving back what they have received from it? What
are they doing that they would not do more often and with greater danger in
the state of nature, in which they would inevitably have to fight battles at the
peril of their lives in defence of that which is the means of their preservation?
All have indeed to fight when their country needs them; but then no one has
ever to fight for himself. Do we not gain something by running, on behalf of
what gives us our security, only some of the risks we should have to run for
ourselves, as soon as we lost it?

5. The Right of Life and Death

The question is often asked how individuals, having no right to dispose of
their own lives, can transfer to the Sovereign a right which they do not pos- 500
sess. The difficulty of answering this question seems to me to lie in its being
wrongly stated. Every man has a right to risk his own life in order to preserve it. Has it ever been said that a man who throws himself out of the window to escape from a fire is guilty of suicide? Has such a crime ever been
laid to the charge of him who perishes in a storm because, when he went on
board, he knew of the danger?

The social treaty has for its end the preservation of the contracting parties.
He who wills the end wills the means also, and the means must involve some
risks, and even some losses. He who wishes to preserve his life at others' expense
should also, when it is necessary, be ready to give it up for their sake. Further- 510
more, the citizen is no longer the judge of the dangers to which the law desires
him to expose himself; and when the prince says to him: "It is expedient for the
State that you should die," he ought to die, because it is only on that condition
that he has been living in security up to the present, and because his life is no
longer a mere bounty of nature, but a gift made conditionally by the State.

The Sovereign can ask for one's life back.

6. Law

By the social compact we have given the body politic existence and life; we
have now by legislation to give it movement and will. For the original act by
which the body is formed and united still in no respect determines what it
ought to do for its preservation.

What is well and in conformity with order is so by the nature of things and 520
independently of human conventions. All justice comes from God, who is its
sole source; but if we knew how to receive so high an inspiration, we should
need neither government nor laws. Doubtless, there is a universal justice ema-
nating from reason alone; but this justice, to be admitted among us, must be
mutual. Humanly speaking, in default of natural sanctions, the laws of justice
are ineffective among men: they merely make for the good of the wicked and
the undoing of the just, when the just man observes them towards everybody
and nobody observes them towards him. Conventions and laws are therefore

If no punishments, good guys are fools.

530 needed to join rights to duties and refer justice to its object. In the state of
nature, where everything is common, I owe nothing to him whom I have promised nothing; I recognise as belonging to others only what is of no use to me. In
the state of society all rights are fixed by law, and the case becomes different.

But what, after all, is a law? As long as we remain satisfied with attaching
purely metaphysical ideas to the word, we shall go on arguing without arriving at an understanding; and when we have defined a law of nature, we shall
be no nearer the definition of a law of the State.

"law" of nature not the same as state "law"

I have already said that there can be no general will directed to a particular object. Such an object must be either within or outside the State. If outside, a will which is alien to it cannot be, in relation to it, general; if within,
540 it is part of the State, and in that case there arises a relation between whole
and part which makes them two separate beings, of which the part is one,
and the whole minus the part the other. But the whole minus a part cannot
be the whole; and while this relation persists, there can be no whole, but only
two unequal parts; and it follows that the will of one is no longer in any
respect general in relation to the other.

But when the whole people decrees for the whole people, it is considering only itself; and if a relation is then formed, it is between two aspects of
the entire object, without there being any division of the whole. In that case
the matter about which the decree is made is, like the decreeing will, general.
550 This act is what I call a law.

When I say that the object of laws is always general, I mean that law considers subjects *en masse* and, actions in the abstract, and never a particular
person or action. Thus the law may indeed decree that there shall be privileges, but cannot confer them on anybody by name. It may set up several
classes of citizens, and even lay down the qualifications for membership of
these classes, but it cannot nominate such and such persons as belonging to
them; it may establish a monarchical government and hereditary succession,
but it cannot choose a king, or nominate a royal family. In a word, no function which has a particular object belongs to the legislative power.

560 On this view, we at once see that it can no longer be asked whose business it is to make laws, since they are acts of the general will; nor whether the
prince is above the law, since he is a member of the State; nor whether the
law can be unjust, since no one is unjust to himself; nor how we can be both
free and subject to the laws, since they are but registers of our wills.

Changing the questions

Laws are, properly speaking, only the conditions of civil association.
The people, being subject to the laws, ought to be their author: the conditions of the society ought to be regulated solely by those who come
together to form it. But how are they to regulate them? Is it to be by common agreement, by a sudden inspiration? Has the body politic an organ
570 to declare its will? Who can give it the foresight to formulate and
announce its acts in advance? Or how is it to announce them in the hour
of need? How can a blind multitude, which often does not know what it
wills, because it rarely knows what is good for it, carry out for itself so

great and difficult an enterprise as a system of legislation? Of itself the people wills always the good, but of itself it by no means always sees it. The general will is always in the right, but the judgment which guides it is not always enlightened. It must be got to see objects as they are, and sometimes as they ought to appear to it; it must be shown the good road it is in search of, secured from the seductive influences of individual wills, taught to see times and spaces as a series, and made to weigh the attrac- 580 tions of present and sensible advantages against the danger of distant and hidden evils. The individuals see the good they reject; the public wills the good it does not see. All stand equally in need of guidance. The former must be compelled to bring their wills into conformity with their reason; the latter must be taught to know what it wills. If that is done, public enlightenment leads to the union of understanding and will in the social body: the parts are made to work exactly together, and the whole is raised to its highest power. This makes a legislator necessary.

BOOK III

4. Democracy

He who makes the law knows better than anyone else how it should be exe- cuted and interpreted. It seems then impossible to have a better constitution 590 than that in which the executive and legislative powers are united; but this very fact renders the government in certain respects inadequate, because things which should be distinguished are confounded, and the prince and the Sovereign, being the same person, form, so to speak, no more than a gov- ernment without government.

It is not good for him who makes the laws to execute them, or for the body of the people to turn its attention away from a general standpoint and devote it to particular objects. Nothing is more dangerous than the influence of private interests in public affairs, and the abuse of the laws by the govern- ment is a less evil than the corruption of the legislator, which is the inevitable 600 sequel to a particular standpoint. In such a case, the State being altered in substance, all reformation becomes impossible, a people that would never misuse governmental powers would never misuse independence; a people that would always govern well would not need to be governed.

If we take the term in the strict sense, there never has been a real democ- racy, and there never will be. It is against the natural order for the many to govern and the few to be governed. It is unimaginable that the people should remain continually assembled to devote their time to public affairs, and it is clear that they cannot set up commissions for that purpose without the form of administration being changed. 610

In fact, I can confidently lay down as a principle that, when the functions of government are shared by several tribunals, the less numerous sooner or later acquire the greatest authority, if only because they are in a position to expedite affairs, and power thus naturally comes into their hands.

[margin note: Checks & balances]

[margin note: danger of indiv interests in public affairs]

[margin note: Rejects pure democracy

"I prefer liberty with danger to peace with slavery."]

It may be added that there is no government so subject to civil wars and intestine agitations as democratic or popular government, because there is none which has so strong and continual a tendency to change to another form, or which demands more vigilance and courage for its maintenance as it is. Under such a constitution above all, the citizen should arm himself with strength and constancy, and say, every day of his life, what a virtuous Count Palatine said in the Diet of Poland: *Malo periculosam libertatem quam quietum servitium.*

Were there a people of gods, their government would be democratic. So perfect a government is not for men.

11. The Death of the Body Politic

Such is the natural and inevitable tendency of the best constituted governments. If Sparta and Rome perished, what State can hope to endure for ever? If we would set up a long-lived form of government, let us not even dream of making it eternal. If we are to succeed, we must not attempt the impossible, or flatter ourselves that we are endowing the work of man with a stability of which human conditions do not permit.

The body politic, as well as the human body, begins to die as soon as it is born, and carries in itself the causes of its destruction. But both may have a constitution that is more or less robust and suited to preserve them a longer or a shorter time. The constitution of man is the work of nature; that of the State the work of art. It is not in men's power to prolong their own lives; but it is for them to prolong as much as possible the life of the State, by giving it the best possible constitution. The best constituted State will have an end; but it will end later than any other, unless some unforeseen accident brings about its untimely destruction.

[margin note: legislature = heart executive = brain]

The life-principle of the body politic lies in the sovereign authority. The legislative power is the heart of the State; the executive power is its brain, which causes the movement of all the parts. The brain may become paralysed and the individual still live. A man may remain an imbecile and live; but as soon as the heart ceases to perform its functions, the animal is dead.

The State subsists by means not of the laws, but of the legislative power. Yesterday's law is not binding to-day; but silence is taken for tacit consent, and the Sovereign is held to confirm incessantly the laws it does not abrogate as it might. All that it has once declared itself to will it wills always, unless it revokes its declaration.

Why then is so much respect paid to old laws? For this very reason. We must believe that nothing but the excellence of old acts of will can have preserved them so long: if the Sovereign had not recognised them as throughout salutary, it would have revoked them a thousand times. This is why, so far from growing weak, the laws continually gain new strength in any well constituted State; the precedent of antiquity makes them daily more venerable: while wherever the laws grow weak as they become old, this proves that there is no longer a legislative power, and that the State is dead.

[margin note: Old laws: tested by time become more + more compelling

unless they don't]

15. Deputies or Representatives

As soon as public service ceases to be the chief business of the citizens, and they would rather serve with their money than with their persons, the State is not far from its fall. When it is necessary to march out to war, they pay troops and stay at home: when it is necessary to meet in council, they name deputies and stay at home. By reason of idleness and money, they end by having soldiers to enslave their country and representatives to sell it.

660

It is through the hustle of commerce and the arts, through the greedy self-interest of profit, and through softness and love of amenities that personal services are replaced by money payments. Men surrender a part of their profits in order to have time to increase them at leisure. Make gifts of money, and you will not be long without chains. The word *finance* is a slavish word, unknown in the city-state. In a country that is truly free, the citizens do everything with their own arms and nothing by means of money; so far from paying to be exempted from their duties, they would even pay for the privilege of fulfilling them themselves. I am far from taking the common view: I hold enforced labour to be less opposed to liberty than taxes.

670

what would it look like if we required churches etc. to provide the services?

wow

The better the constitution of a State is, the more do public affairs encroach on private in the minds of the citizens. Private affairs are even of much less importance, because the aggregate of the common happiness furnishes a greater proportion of that of each individual, so that there is less for him to seek in particular cares. In a well-ordered city every man flies to the assemblies: under a bad government no one cares to stir a step to get to them, because no one is interested in what happens there, because it is foreseen that the general will will not prevail, and lastly because domestic cares are all-absorbing. Good laws lead to the making of better ones; bad ones bring about worse. As soon as any man says of the affairs of the State *What does it matter to me?* the State may be given up for lost.

680

But what if all seems well—won't outrage what gets people involved?

16. That the Institution of Government Is Not a Contract

The legislative power once well established, the next thing is to establish similarly the executive power; for this latter, which operates only by particular acts, not being of the essence of the former, is naturally separate from it. Were it possible for the Sovereign, as such, to possess the executive power, right and fact would be so confounded that no one could tell what was law and what was not; and the body politic, thus disfigured, would soon fall a prey to the violence it was instituted to prevent.

690

As the citizens, by the social contract, are all equal, all can prescribe what all should do, but no one has a right to demand that another shall do what he does not do himself. It is strictly this right, which is indispensable for giving the body politic life and movement, that the Sovereign, in instituting the government, confers upon the prince.

It has been held that this act of establishment was a contract between the people and the rulers it sets over itself,—a contract in which conditions were laid down between the two parties binding the one to command and the other to obey. It will be admitted, I am sure, that this is an odd kind of contract to enter into. But let us see if this view can be upheld.

First, the supreme authority can no more be modified than it can be alienated; to limit it is to destroy it. It is absurd and contradictory for the Sovereign to set a superior over itself; to bind itself to obey a master would be to return to absolute liberty.

Moreover, it is clear that this contract between the people and such and such persons would be a particular act; and from this it follows that it can be neither a law nor an act of Sovereignty, and that consequently it would be illegitimate.

It is plain too that the contracting parties in relation to each other would be under the law of nature alone and wholly without guarantees of their mutual undertakings, a position wholly at variance with the civil state. He who has force at his command being always in a position to control execution, it would come to the same thing if the name "contract" were given to the act of one man who said to another: "I give you all my goods, on condition that you give me back as much of them as you please."

There is only one contract in the State, and that is the act of association, which in itself excludes the existence of a second. It is impossible to conceive of any public contract that would not be a violation of the first.

BOOK IV

1. That the General Will Is Indestructible

As long as several men in assembly regard themselves as a single body, they have only a single will which is concerned with their common preservation and general well-being. In this case, all the springs of the State are vigorous and simple and its rules clear and luminous; there are no embroilments or conflicts of interests; the common good is everywhere clearly apparent, and only good sense is needed to perceive it.

But when the social bond begins to be relaxed and the State to grow weak, when particular interests begin to make themselves felt and the smaller societies to exercise an influence over the larger, the common interest changes and finds opponents: opinion is no longer unanimous; the general will ceases to be the will of all; contradictory views and debates arise; and the best advice is not taken without question.

Finally, when the State, on the eve of ruin, maintains only a vain, illusory and formal existence, when in every heart the social bond is broken, and the meanest interest brazenly lays hold of the sacred name of "public good," the general will becomes mute: all men, guided by secret motives, no more give their views as citizens than if the State had never been; and iniquitous decrees directed solely to private interest get passed under the name of laws.

Does it follow from this that the general will is exterminated or corrupted? Not at all: it is always constant, unalterable and pure; but it is sub-

The relationship of people with prince ≠ contract

ordinated to other wills which encroach upon its sphere. Each man, in
detaching his interest from the common interest, sees clearly that he cannot   740
entirely separate them; but his share in the public mishaps seems to him negligible beside the exclusive good he aims at making his own. Apart from this
particular good, he wills the general good in his own interest, as strongly as
anyone else. Even in selling his vote for money, he does not extinguish in
himself the general will, but only eludes it. The fault he commits is that of
changing the state of the question, and answering something different from
what he is asked. Instead of saying, by his vote, "It is to the advantage of the
State," he says, "It is of advantage to this or that man or party that this or
that view should prevail." Thus the law of public order in assemblies is not
so much to maintain in them the general will as to secure that the question   750
be always put to it, and the answer always given by it.

I could here set down many reflections on the simple right of voting in
every act of Sovereignty—a right which no one can take from the citizens—
and also on the right of stating views, making proposals, dividing and discussing, which the government is always most careful to leave solely to its
members, but this important subject would need a treatise to itself, and it is
impossible to say everything in a single work.

2. Voting

There is but one law which, from its nature, needs unanimous consent.
This is the social compact; for civil association is the most voluntary of all
acts. Every man being born free and his own master, no one, under any pre-   760
text whatsoever, can make any man subject without his consent. To decide
that the son of a slave is born a slave is to decide that he is not born a man.

If then there are opponents when the social compact is made, their opposition does not invalidate the contract, but merely prevents them from being
included in it. They are foreigners among citizens. When the State is instituted, residence constitutes consent; to dwell within its territory is to submit
to the Sovereign.

Apart from this primitive contract, the vote of the majority always binds
all the rest. This follows from the contract itself. But it is asked how a man
can be both free and forced to conform to wills that are not his own. How   770
are the opponents at once free and subject to laws they have not agreed to?

I retort that the question is wrongly put. The citizen gives his consent to
all the laws, including those which are passed in spite of his opposition, and
even those which punish him when he dares to break any of them. The constant will of all the members of the State is the general will; by virtue of it
they are citizens and free. When in the popular assembly a law is proposed,
what the people is asked is not exactly whether it approves or rejects the proposal, but whether it is in conformity with the general will, which is their
will. Each man, in giving his vote, states his opinion on that point; and the
general will is found by counting votes. When therefore the opinion that is   780

contrary to my own prevails, this proves neither more nor less than that I was mistaken, and that what I thought to be the general will was not so. If my particular opinion had carried the day I should have achieved the opposite of what was my will; and it is in that case that I should not have been free.

This presupposes, indeed, that all the qualities of the general will still reside in the majority: when they cease to do so, whatever side a man may take, liberty is no longer possible.

BLACK? WHITE? ASIAN? MORE YOUNG AMERICANS CHOOSE ALL OF THE ABOVE
Susan Saulny

COLLEGE PARK, Md.—In another time or place, the game of "What Are You?" that was played one night last fall at the University of Maryland might have been mean, or menacing: Laura Wood's peers were picking apart her every feature in an effort to guess her race.

"How many mixtures do you have?" one young man asked above the chatter of about 50 students. With her tan skin and curly brown hair, Ms. Wood's ancestry could have spanned the globe.

"I'm mixed with two things," she said politely.

"Are you mulatto?" asked Paul Skym, another student, using a word once tinged with shame that is enjoying a comeback in some young circles. When Ms. Wood confirmed that she is indeed black and white, Mr. Skym, who is Asian and white, boasted, "Now that's what I'm talking about!" in affirmation of their mutual mixed lineage.

Then the group of friends—formally, the Multiracial and Biracial Student Association—erupted into laughter and cheers, a routine show of their mixed-race pride.

The crop of students moving through college right now includes the largest group of mixed-race people ever to come of age in the United States, and they are only the vanguard: the country is in the midst of a demographic shift driven by immigration and intermarriage.

One in seven new marriages is between spouses of different races or ethnicities, according to data from 2008 and 2009 that was analyzed by the Pew Research Center. Multiracial and multiethnic Americans (usually grouped together as "mixed race") are one of the country's fastest-growing demographic groups. And experts expect the racial results of the 2010 census, which will start to be released next month, to show the trend continuing or accelerating.

Many young adults of mixed backgrounds are rejecting the color lines that have defined Americans for generations in favor of a much more fluid sense of identity. Ask Michelle López-Mullins, a 20-year-old junior and the president of the Multiracial and Biracial Student Association, how she marks her race on forms like the census, and she says, "It depends on the day, and it depends on the options."

They are also using the strength in their growing numbers to affirm roots that were once portrayed as tragic or pitiable.

"I think it's really important to acknowledge who you are and everything that makes you that," said Ms. Wood, the 19-year-old vice president of the group. "If someone tries to call me black I say, 'yes—and white.' People have the right not to acknowledge everything, but don't do it because society tells you that you can't."

No one knows quite how the growth of the multiracial population will change the country. Optimists say the blending of the races is a step toward

Reprinted from *The New York Times*, 2011, by permission of PARS International Corporation.

transcending race, to a place where America is free of bigotry, prejudice and programs like affirmative action.

Pessimists say that a more powerful multiracial movement will lead to more stratification and come at the expense of the number and influence of other minority groups, particularly African-Americans.

And some sociologists say that grouping all multiracial people together glosses over differences in circumstances between someone who is, say, black and Latino, and someone who is Asian and white. (Among interracial cou-

50   ples, white-Asian pairings tend to be better educated and have higher incomes, according to Reynolds Farley, a professor emeritus at the University of Michigan.)

Along those lines, it is telling that the rates of intermarriage are lowest between blacks and whites, indicative of the enduring economic and social distance between them.

Prof. Rainier Spencer, director of the Afro-American Studies Program at the University of Nevada, Las Vegas, and the author of "Reproducing Race: The Paradox of Generation Mix," says he believes that there is too much "emotional investment" in the notion of multiracialism as a panacea for the nation's

60   age-old divisions. "The mixed-race identity is not a transcendence of race, it's a new tribe," he said. "A new Balkanization of race."

But for many of the University of Maryland students, that is not the point. They are asserting their freedom to identify as they choose.

"All society is trying to tear you apart and make you pick a side," Ms. Wood said. "I want us to have a say."

THE WAY WE WERE

Americans mostly think of themselves in singular racial terms. Witness President Obama's answer to the race question on the 2010 census: Although his mother was white and his father was black, Mr. Obama checked only one box, black, even though he could have checked both races.

70   Some proportion of the country's population has been mixed-race since the first white settlers had children with Native Americans. What has changed is how mixed-race Americans are defined and counted.

Long ago, the nation saw itself in more hues than black and white: the 1890 census included categories for racial mixtures such as quadroon (one-fourth black) and octoroon (one-eighth black). With the exception of one survey from 1850 to 1920, the census included a mulatto category, which was for people who had any perceptible trace of African blood.

But by the 1930 census, terms for mixed-race people had all disappeared, replaced by the so-called one-drop rule, an antebellum convention that held

80   that anyone with a trace of African ancestry was only black. (Similarly, people who were "white and Indian" were generally to be counted as Indian.)

It was the census enumerator who decided.

By the 1970s, Americans were expected to designate themselves as members of one officially recognized racial group: black, white, American Indian, Japanese, Chinese, Filipino, Hawaiian, Korean or "other," an option used frequently by people of Hispanic origin. (The census recognizes Hispanic as an ethnicity, not a race.)

what is the difference between race and ethnicity?

Starting with the 2000 census, Americans were allowed to mark one or more races.

The multiracial option came after years of complaints and lobbying, mostly   90 by the white mothers of biracial children who objected to their children being allowed to check only one race. In 2000, seven million people—about 2.4 percent of the population—reported being more than one race.

According to estimates from the Census Bureau, the mixed-race population has grown by roughly 35 percent since 2000.

And many researchers think the census and other surveys undercount the mixed population.

The 2010 mixed-race statistics will be released, state by state, over the first half of the year.

Research

"There could be some big surprises," said Jeffrey S. Passel, a senior demog-   100 rapher at the Pew Hispanic Center, meaning that the number of mixed-race Americans could be high. "There's not only less stigma to being in these groups, there's even positive cachet."

MOVING FORWARD

The faces of mixed-race America are not just on college campuses. They are in politics, business and sports. And the ethnically ambiguous are especially ubiquitous in movies, television shows and advertising. There are news, social networking and dating Web sites focusing on the mixed-race audience, and even consumer products like shampoo. There are mixed-race film festivals and conferences. And student groups like the one at Maryland, offering peer support and activism, are more common.   110

Such a club would not have existed a generation ago—when the question at the center of the "What Are You?" game would have been a provocation rather than an icebreaker.

"It's kind of a taking-back in a way, taking the reins," Ms. López-Mullins said. "We don't always have to let it get us down," she added, referring to the question multiracial people have heard for generations.

"The No. 1 reason why we exist is to give people who feel like they don't want to choose a side, that don't want to label themselves based on other people's interpretations of who they are, to give them a place, that safe space," she said. Ms. López-Mullins is Chinese and Peruvian on one side, and white   120 and American Indian on the other.

That safe space did not exist amid the neo-Classical style buildings of the campus when Warren Kelley enrolled in 1974. Though his mother is Japanese and his father is African-American, he had basically one choice when it came to his racial identity. "I was black and proud to be black," Dr. Kelley said. "There was no notion that I might be multiracial. Or that the public discourse on college campuses recognized the multiracial community."

Almost 40 years later, Dr. Kelley is the assistant vice president for student affairs at the university and faculty adviser to the multiracial club, and he is
130   often in awe of the change on this campus.

When the multiracial group was founded in 2002, Dr. Kelley said, "There was an instant audience."

They did not just want to hold parties. The group sponsored an annual weeklong program of discussions intended to raise awareness of multiracial identities—called Mixed Madness—and conceived a new class on the experience of mixed-race Asian-Americans that was made part of the curriculum last year.

"Even if someone had formed a mixed-race group in the '70s, would I have joined?" Dr. Kelley said. "I don't know. My multiracial identity wasn't promi-
140   nent at the time. I don't think I even conceptualized the idea."

By the 2000 census, Dr. Kelley's notion of his racial identity had evolved to include his mother's Asian heritage; he modified his race officially on the form. After a lifetime of checking black, he checked Asian and black.

(Dr. Kelley's mother was born in Kyoto. She met her future husband, a black soldier from Alabama, while he was serving in the Pacific during World War II.)

Checking both races was not an easy choice, Dr. Kelley said, "as a black man, with all that means in terms of pride in that heritage as well as reasons to give back and be part of progress forward."
150   "As I moved into adulthood and got a professional job, I started to respect my parents more and see the amount of my mom's culture that's reflected in me," he said. "Society itself also moved."

FINDING CAMARADERIE

In fall 2009, a question tugged at Sabrina Garcia, then a freshman at Maryland, a public university with 26,500 undergraduates: "Where will I fit in?" recalled Ms. Garcia, who is Palestinian and Salvadoran.

"I considered the Latina student union, but I'm only half," she said. "I didn't want to feel like I was hiding any part of me. I went to an M.B.S.A. meeting and it was really great. I really feel like part of a group that understands."

The group holds weekly meetings, in addition to hosting movie nights,
160   dinners, parties and, occasionally, posts broadcasts on YouTube.

Not all of its 100 or so members consider themselves mixed race, and the club welcomes everyone.

At a meeting in the fall, David Banda, who is Hispanic, and Julicia Coleman, who is black, came just to unwind among supportive listeners. They discussed the frustrations of being an interracial couple, even today, especially back in their hometown, Upper Marlboro, Md.

"When we go back home, let's say for a weekend or to the mall, they see us walking and I get this look, you know, sort of giving me the idea: 'Why are you with her? You're not black, so she should be with a black person.' Or comments," Mr. Banda, 20, said at a meeting of the group. "Even some of my friends tell me, 'Why don't you date a Hispanic girl?'"

Mr. Banda and Ms. Coleman are thinking about having children someday. "One of the main reasons I joined is to see the struggles mixed people go through," he said, "so we can be prepared when that time comes."

And despite the growth of the mixed-race population, there are struggles.

Ian Winchester, a junior who is part Ghanaian, part Scottish-Norwegian, said he felt lucky and torn being biracial. His Scottish grandfather was keen on dressing him in kilts as a boy. The other side of the family would put him in a dashiki. "I do feel empowered being biracial," he said. "The ability to question your identity—identity in general—is really a gift."

But, he continued, "I don't even like to identify myself as a race anymore. My family has been pulling me in two directions about what I am. I just want to be a person."

Similarly, Ms. López-Mullins sees herself largely in nonracial terms.

"I hadn't even learned the word 'Hispanic' until I came home from school one day and asked my dad what I should refer to him as, to express what I am," she said. "Growing up with my parents, I never thought we were different from any other family."

But it was not long before Ms. López-Mullins came to detest what was the most common question put to her in grade school, even from friends. "What are you?" they asked, and "Where are you from?" They were fascinated by her father, a Latino with Asian roots, and her mother with the long blond hair, who was mostly European in ancestry, although mixed with some Cherokee and Shawnee.

"I was always having to explain where my parents are from because just saying 'I'm from Takoma Park, Maryland,' was not enough," she said. "Saying 'I'm an American' wasn't enough."

"Now when people ask what I am, I say, 'How much time do you have?'" she said. "Race will not automatically tell you my story."

What box does she check on forms like the census? "Hispanic, white, Asian American, Native American," she said. "I'm pretty much checking everything."

At one meeting of the Multiracial and Biracial Student Association, Ms. Wood shared a story about surprises and coming to terms with them. "Until I was 8 years old, I thought I was white," she told the group. "My mother and aunt sat me down and said the guy I'd been calling Dad was not my father. I started crying. And she said, 'Your real father is black.'"

Ms. Wood's mother, Catherine Bandele, who is white, and her biological father split up before she was born. Facing economic troubles and resistance

from her family about raising a mixed-race child, Ms. Bandele gave her daugh-
210   ter up for adoption to a couple who had requested a biracial baby. But after
two weeks, she changed her mind. "I had to fight to get her back, but I got
her," Ms. Bandele said. "And we're so proud of Laura."

Eventually Ms. Wood's closest relatives softened, embracing her.

But more distant relatives never came around. "They can't see past the
color of my skin and accept me even though I share DNA with them," she
said. "It hurts a lot because I don't even know my father's side of the family."

Ms. Wood has searched the Internet for her father, to no avail.

"Being in M.B.S.A., it really helps with that," she said. "Finding a group
of people who can accept you for who you are and being able to accept your-
220   self, to just be able to look in the mirror and say, 'I'm O.K. just the way I
am!'—honestly, I feel that it's a blessing."

"It took a long time," she said.

Now Ms. Wood is one of the group's foremost advocates.

Over dinner with Ms. López-Mullins one night, she wondered: "What if
Obama had checked white? There would have been an uproar because he's
the first 'black president,' even though he's mixed. I would like to have a
conversation with him about why he did that."

Absent that opportunity, Ms. Wood took her concerns about what
Mr. Obama checked to a meeting of the campus chapter of the N.A.A.C.P.
230   last year. Vicky Key, a past president of the Multiracial and Biracial Student
Association, who is Greek and black, joined her. The question for discussion
was whether Mr. Obama is the first black president or the first multiracial
president.

Ms. Key, a senior, remembered someone answering the question without
much discussion: "One-drop rule, he's black."

"But we were like, 'Wait!'" she said. "That's offensive to us. We sat there
and tried to advocate, but they said, 'No, he's black and that's it.' Then someone said, 'Stop taking away our black president.' I didn't understand where
they were coming from, and they didn't understand me."

240   Whether Mr. Obama is considered black or multiracial, there is a wider
debate among mixed-race people about what the long-term goals of their advocacy should be, both on campus and off.

"I don't want a color-blind society at all," Ms. Wood said. "I just want
both my races to be acknowledged."

Ms. López-Mullins countered, "I want mine not to matter."

Is Obama the first black president?

YouTube videos mentioned p. 262

THE DEVELOPMENT OF WHITE IDENTITY
"I'M NOT ETHNIC, I'M JUST NORMAL"
Beverly Daniel Tatum

I often begin the classes and workshops I lead by asking participants to   1
reflect on their own social class and ethnic background in small discussion
groups. The first question I pose is one that most people of color answer
without hesitation: "What is your class and ethnic background?" White participants, however, often pause before responding. On one such occasion a
young White woman quickly described herself as middle-class but seemed
stumped as to how to describe herself ethnically. Finally, she said, "I'm just
normal!" What did she mean? She explained that she did not identify with
any particular ethnic heritage, and that she was a lot like the other people
who lived in her very homogeneous White middle-class community. But her   10
choice of words was telling. If she is just normal, are those who are different
from her "just abnormal"?

Like many White people, this young woman had never really considered her own racial and ethnic group membership. For her, Whiteness was
simply the unexamined norm. Because they represent the societal norm,
Whites can easily reach adulthood without thinking much about their
racial group. For example, one White teacher who was taking a professional
development course on racism with me wrote in one of her papers: "I am
thirty-five years old and I never really started thinking about race too much
until now, and that makes me feel uncomfortable. . . . I just think for some   20
reason I didn't know. No one taught us." There is a lot of silence about race
in White communities, and as a consequence Whites tend to think of racial
identity as something that other people have, not something that is salient
for them. But when, for whatever reason, the silence is broken, a process of
racial identity development for Whites begins to unfold.

Counseling psychologist Janet Helms has described this process of development for Whites in her book *Black and White Racial Identity Development:
Theory, Research, and Practice.* She assumes, as do I, that in a race-conscious
society, racial group membership has psychological implications. The messages we receive about assumed superiority or inferiority shape our percep-   30
tions of reality and influence our interactions with others. While the task for
people of color is to resist negative societal messages and develop an empowered sense of self in the face of a racist society, Helms says the task for Whites
is to develop a positive White identity based in reality, not on assumed superiority. In order to do that each person must become aware of his or her
Whiteness, accept it as personally and socially significant, and learn to feel

Reprinted from *Why Are All the Black Kids Sitting Together in the Cafeteria?: A Psychologist
Explains the Development of Racial Identity* (1997), by permission of Perseus Books Group.

good about it, not in the sense of a Klan member's "White pride," but in the context of a commitment to a just society.

It comes as a surprise to some White people to think about their race in this way. "Of course White people feel good about being White," they say. But that is not my experience with my students or with the people who come to my workshops. Most of the White people I talk to either have not thought about their race and so don't feel anything, or have thought about it and felt guilt and shame. These feelings of guilt and shame are part of the hidden costs of racism.

How can White people achieve a healthy sense of White identity? Helms's model is instructive. For Whites, there are two major developmental tasks in this process, the abandonment of individual racism and the recognition of and opposition to institutional and cultural racism. These tasks occur over six stages: *contact, disintegration, reintegration, pseudo-independent, immersion/emersion,* and *autonomy.*

developmental stages

ABANDONING RACISM

At the contact stage, the first step in the process, Whites pay little attention to the significance of their racial identity. As exemplified by the "I'm just normal" comment, individuals at this point of development rarely describe themselves as White. If they have lived, worked, or gone to school in predominantly White settings, they may simply think of themselves as being part of the racial norm and take this for granted without conscious consideration of their White privilege, the systematically conferred advantages they receive simply because they are White.

While they have been breathing the "smog" and have internalized many of the prevailing societal stereotypes of people of color, they typically are unaware of this socialization process. They often perceive themselves as color-blind, completely free of prejudice, unaware of their own assumptions about other racial groups. In addition, they usually think of racism as the prejudiced behaviors of individuals rather than as an institutionalized system of advantage benefiting Whites in subtle as well as blatant ways. Peggy McIntosh speaks for many Whites at the contact level when she writes, "I was taught to recognize racism only in individual acts of meanness by members of my group, never in invisible systems conferring unsought racial dominance on my group from birth."

While some Whites may grow up in families where they are encouraged to embrace the ideology of White superiority (children of Klan members, for example), for many Whites this early stage of racial identity development represents the passive absorption of subtly communicated messages. Robert Carter, another racial identity researcher, illustrates this point when he quotes a forty-four-year-old White male who grew up in upstate New York, where he had limited direct contact with Blacks.

There was no one to compare ourselves to. As you would drive through other neighborhoods, I think there was a clear message of difference or even superiority. The neighborhoods were poorer, and it was probably subtle, I don't remember my parents being bigoted, although by today's standards they clearly were. I think there was probably a message of superiority. The underlying messages were subtle. No one ever came out and said, White people are this and Black people are like this. I think the underlying message is that White people are generally good and they're like us, us and them.

These messages may go unchallenged and unexamined for a long time. However, the next level, disintegration, is marked by a growing awareness of racism and White privilege as a result of personal encounters in which the social significance of race is made visible. For some White people, disintegration occurs when they develop a close friendship or a romantic relationship with a person of color. The White person then sees firsthand how racism can operate. For example, one female college student described her experiences shopping with a Puerto Rican roommate. She couldn't help noticing how her Latina friend was followed around in stores and was asked for more identification than Whites when writing checks. She also saw how her friend's Black boyfriend was frequently asked to show his college ID when he visited their residence hall, while young White men came and went without being questioned. For other White people, disintegration may result from seeing racist incidents such as the police beating of Rodney King or participating in an "unlearning racism" workshop. Certainly being in a classroom where the social consequences of racial group membership are explicitly discussed as part of the course content is likely to trigger the process.

Once the silence is broken, the cycle of racism becomes increasingly visible. For example, in my class I show a very powerful video, *Ethnic Notions,* on the dehumanizing images of African Americans in the popular culture from before the Civil War through the twentieth century. The video links the nineteenth-century caricatures of Black physical features, commonly published racial epithets, and the early cinematic portrayals of stupid but happy "darkies," menacing Black "savages," and heavyset, caretaking "mammies," to their updated forms in today's media. After seeing this film, students can't help but notice the pervasiveness of racial stereotyping on television each night. The same programs they used to find entertaining now offend them. They start to notice the racism in the everyday language of family and friends. For example, one White student reported that when she asked her roommate to get her a glass of water, the White roommate jokingly replied, "Do I look Black to you?" Although I had never heard of this expression, it was very familiar to the student. Yet, before then, she had never recognized the association of Blackness with servitude, and the assumed superiority of Whiteness being conveyed in the remark.

This new awareness is characterized by <u>discomfort</u>. The uncomfortable emotions of guilt, shame, and anger are often related to a new awareness of one's personal prejudices or the prejudices within one's family. The following excerpts from the journals of two White students illustrate this point:

> Today was the first class on racism. . . . Before today I didn't think I was exposed to any form of racism. Well, except for my father. He is about as prejudiced as they come.
>
>   It really bothers me that stereotypes exist because it is from them that I originally became uninformed. My grandmother makes all kinds of decisions based on stereotypes—who to hire, who to help out. When I was growing up, the only Black people that I knew were adults [household help], but I admired them just as much as any other adult. When I expressed these feelings to my parents, I was always told that the Black people that I knew were the exceptions and that the rest of the race were different. I, too, was taught to be afraid.

Others' parents were silent on the subject of racism, simply accepting the status quo.

Those whose parents were actively antiracist may feel less guilt, but often still feel unprepared for addressing racism outside the family, a point highlighted by the comments of this young woman:

> Talking with other class members, I realized how exceptional my parents were. Not only were they not overtly racist but they also tried to keep society's subtle racism from reaching me. Basically I grew up believing that racism was no longer an issue and all people should be treated as equals. Unfortunately, my parents were not being very realistic as society's racism did begin to reach me. They did not teach me how to support and defend their views once I was interacting in a society without them as a buffer.

<u>At the disintegration stage, White individuals begin to see how much their lives and the lives of people of color have been affected by racism in our society.</u> The societal inequities they now notice directly contradict the idea of an American meritocracy, a concept that has typically been an integral part of their belief system. The cognitive dissonance that results is part of the discomfort which is experienced at this point in the process of development. Responses to this discomfort may include denying the validity of the information that is being presented, or psychologically or physically withdrawing from it. The logic is, "If I don't read about racism, talk about racism, watch those documentaries or special news programs, or spend time with those people of color, I won't have to feel uncomfortable." (In the case of my students, this is usually not an option. By the time they have to deal with these emotional responses, it is too late to drop the course.)

meritocracy

If the individual remains engaged, he or she can turn the discomfort into action. Once they have an awareness of the cycle of racism, many people are angered by it and want to interrupt it. Often action comes in the form of educating others—pointing out the stereotypes as they watch television, interrupting the racial jokes, writing letters to the editor, sharing articles with friends and family. Like new converts, people experiencing disintegration can be quite zealous in their efforts. A White woman in her forties who participated in an antiracist professional development course for educators described herself at this stage:

> What it was like for me when I was taking the course [one year ago] and just afterwards, hell, because this dissonance stuff doesn't feel all that great. And trying to put it in a perspective and figure out what to do with it is very hard. . . . I was on the band wagon so I'm not going to be quiet about it. So there was dissonance everywhere. Personally, I remember going home for Thanksgiving, the first Thanksgiving [while taking the course], back to our families . . . and turning to my brother-in-law and saying, "I really don't want you to say that in front of me— I don't want to hear that joke—I am not interested." . . . At every turn it seemed like there, I was *responsible* for saying something. . . . My husband, who I think is a very good, a very liberal person, but who really hasn't been through [this], saying, "You know I think you're taking yourself too seriously here and where is your sense of humor? You have lost your sense of humor." And my saying, "It isn't funny; you don't understand, it just isn't funny to me." Not that he would ever tell a racial joke, but there were these things that would come up and he would just sort of look back and say, "I don't understand where you're coming from now." So there was a lot of dissonance. . . . I don't think anybody was too comfortable with me for a while.

My college students have similar experiences with family members and friends. Though they want to step off the cycle of racism, the message from the surrounding White community seems to be, "Get back on!" A very poignant example of this was shared with me by a young White man from a very privileged background. He wrote:

> I realized that it was possible to simply go through life totally oblivious to the entire situation or, even if one realizes it, one can totally repress it. It is easy to fade into the woodwork, run with the rest of society, and never have to deal with these problems. So many people I know from home are like this. They have simply accepted what society has taught them with little, if any, question. My father is a prime example of this. . . . It has caused much friction in our relationship, and he often tells me as a father he has failed in raising me correctly. Most of my high school friends will never deal with these issues and

propagate them on to their own children. It's easy to see how the cycle
continues. I don't think I could ever justify within myself simply turning my back on the problem. I finally realized that my position in all
of these dominant groups gives me power to make change occur. . . .
It is an unfortunate result often though that I feel alienated from
friends and family. It's often played off as a mere stage that I'm going
210   through. I obviously can't tell if it's merely a stage, but I know that
they say this to take the attention off of the truth of what I'm saying.
By belittling me, they take the power out of my argument. It's very
depressing that being compassionate and considerate are seen as only
phases that people go through. I don't want it to be a phase for me,
but as obvious as this may sound, I look at my environment and often
wonder how it will not be.

The social pressure from friends and acquaintances to collude, to not
notice racism, can be quite powerful.
But it is very difficult to stop noticing something once it has been pointed
220   out. The conflict between noticing and not noticing generates internal tension, and there is a great desire to relieve it. Relief often comes through what
Helms calls reintegration. At this stage, the previous feelings of guilt or denial
may be transformed into fear and anger directed toward people of color. The
logic is, "If there is a problem with racism, then you people of color must
have done something to cause it. And if you would just change your behavior, the problem would go away." The elegance of this argument is that it
relieves the White person of all responsibility for social change.
I am sometimes asked if it is absolutely necessary to go through this
phase. Must one blame the victim? Although it is not inevitable, most White
230   people who speak up against racism will attest to the temptation they sometimes feel to slip back into collusion and silence. Because the pressure to
ignore racism and to accept the socially sanctioned stereotypes is so strong,
and the system of advantage so seductive, many White people get stuck in
reintegration thinking. The psychological tension experienced at this stage is
clearly expressed by Connie, a White woman of Italian ancestry who took my
course on the psychology of racism. After reading about the stages of White
identity development, she wrote:

There was a time when I never considered myself a color. I never
described myself as a "White, Italian female" until I got to college and
240   noticed that people of color always described themselves by their
color/race. While taking this class, I have begun to understand that
being White makes a difference. I never thought about it before, but
there are many privileges to being White. In my personal life, I cannot say that I have ever felt that I have had the advantage over a Black
person, but I am aware that my race has the advantage.

I am feeling really guilty lately about that. I find myself thinking: "I didn't mean to be White, I really didn't mean it." I am starting to feel angry toward my race for ever using this advantage toward personal gains. But at the same time I resent the minority groups. I mean, it's not my fault that society has deemed us "superior." I don't feel any better than a Black person. But it really doesn't matter because I am a member of the dominant race. . . . I can't help it . . . and I sometimes get angry and feel like I'm being attacked.

I guess my anger toward a minority group would enter me into the next stage of Reintegration where I am once again starting to blame the victim. This is all very trying for me and it has been on my mind a lot. I really would like to be able to reach the last stage . . . where I can accept being White without hostility and anger. That is really hard to do.

"BUT I'M AN INDIVIDUAL!"

Another source of the discomfort and anger that Whites often experience in this phase stems from the frustration of being seen as a group member, rather than as an individual. People of color learn early in life that they are seen by others as members of a group. For Whites, thinking of oneself only as an individual is a legacy of White privilege. As McIntosh writes, "I can swear, or dress in second hand clothes, or not answer letters, without having people attribute these choices to the bad morals, the poverty, or the illiteracy of my race. . . . I can do well in a challenging situation without being called a credit to my race. . . . I am never asked to speak for all the people of my racial group." In short, she and other Whites are perceived as individuals most of the time.

The view of oneself as an individual is very compatible with the dominant ideology of rugged individualism and the American myth of meritocracy. Understanding racism as a system of advantage that structurally benefits Whites and disadvantages people of color on the basis of group membership threatens not only beliefs about society but also beliefs about one's own life accomplishments. For example, organizational consultant Nancie Zane writes that senior White male managers "were clearly invested in the notion that their hard work, ingenuity and skills had won them their senior-level positions." As others talked about the systemic racist and sexist barriers to their own achievement, "white men heard it as a condemnation that they somehow didn't 'deserve' their position." If viewing oneself as a group member threatens one's self-definition, making the paradigm shift from individual to group member will be painful.

In the case of White men, both maleness and Whiteness are normative, so acknowledging group status may be particularly difficult. Those White women who have explored their subordinate gender identity have made at least some

250

260

270

280

movement away from the notion of a strictly individual self-definition and may find it easier to grasp the significance of their racial group membership. However, as McIntosh and others have pointed out, understanding one form of oppression does not guarantee recognition of another.

Those Whites who are highly identified with a particular subordinate identity may also struggle with claiming Whiteness as a meaningful group category because they feel far from the White male norm. For example, Jewish people of European ancestry sometimes do not think of themselves as White because for them the term means White Christian. Also, in Nazi Germany, Jews were defined as a distinct, non-Aryan racial group. In the context of an anti-Jewish culture, the salient identity may be the targeted Jewish identity. However, in terms of U.S. racial ideology, Jews of European ancestry are also the beneficiaries of White racial privilege. My White Jewish students often struggle with the tension between being targeted and receiving privilege. In this case, as in others, the reality of multiple identities complicates the process of coming to terms with one particular dimension of identity. For example, one student wrote:

> I am constantly afraid that people will see my assertion of my Jewish identity as a denial of whiteness, as a way of escaping the acknowledgment of white privilege. I feel I am both part of and not part of whiteness. I am struggling to be more aware of my white privilege . . . but I will not do so at the cost of having my Jewishness erased.

Similarly, White lesbians sometimes find it hard to claim privileged status as Whites when they are so targeted by homophobia and heterosexism, often at the hands of other Whites.

These complexities notwithstanding, when White men and women begin to understand that they are viewed as members of a dominant racial group not only by other Whites but also by people of color, they are sometimes troubled, even angered, to learn that simply because of their group status they are viewed with suspicion by many people of color. "I'm an individual, view me as an individual!" For example, in a racially mixed group of educators participating in an antiracist professional development course, a Black man commented about using his "radar" to determine if the group would be a safe place for him. Many of the White people in the room, who believed that their very presence in the course was proof of their trustworthiness, were upset by the comment, initially unprepared to acknowledge the invisible legacy of racism that accompanied any and every interaction they had with people of color. The White people in the course found some comfort in reading Lois Stalvey's memoir, *The Education of a WASP,* in which she described her own responses to the ways Black people tested her trustworthiness. She writes,

I could never resent the tests as some white people have told me they do. . . . But to me, the longest tests have always indicated the deepest hurts. We whites would have to be naive to expect that hundreds of years of humiliation can be forgotten the moment we wish it to be. At times, the most poignant part of the test is that black people have enough trust left to give it. Testing implies we might pass the test. It is safer and easier for a black person to turn his back on us. If he does not gamble on our sincerity, he cannot be hurt if we prove false. Testing shows an optimism I doubt I could duplicate if I were black.

Sometimes poorly organized antiracism workshops or other educational experiences can create a scenario that places participants at risk for getting stuck in their anger. Effective consciousness-raising about racism must also point the way toward constructive action. When people don't have the tools for moving forward, they tend to return to what is familiar, often becoming more vigorous in their defense of the racial status quo than they were initially.

As we have seen, many White people experience themselves as powerless, even in the face of privilege. But the fact is that we all have a sphere of influence, some domain in which we exercise some level of power and control. The task for each of us, White and of color, is to identify what our own sphere of influence is (however large or small) and to consider how it might be used to interrupt the cycle of racism.

DEFINING A POSITIVE WHITE IDENTITY

As a White person's understanding of the complexity of institutional racism in our society deepens, the less likely he or she is to resort to explanations that blame the victim. Instead, deepening awareness usually leads to a commitment to unlearn one's racism, and marks the emergence of the pseudo-independent stage.

Sometimes epitomized by the "guilty White liberal" persona, the pseudo-independent individual has an intellectual understanding of racism as a system of advantage, but doesn't quite know what to do about it. Self-conscious and guilty about one's own Whiteness, the individual often desires to escape it by associating with people of color. Ruth Frankenberg, author of *White Women, Race Matters: The Social Construction of Whiteness,* describes the confusing emotions of this process in an autobiographical essay. "I viewed my racial privilege as total. I remember months when I was terrified to speak in gatherings that were primarily of color, since I feared that anything I did say would be marked by my whiteness, my racial privilege (which in my mind meant the same)." When her friends of color were making casual conversation—chatting about their mothers, for example—she would worry that anything she might say about her own mother would somehow reveal her race privilege, and by the time she had sorted it out mentally, the topic of conversation would have changed. She writes, "In that silence, I tried to 'pass' (as what? as racially unmarked? as exceptional? as the one white girl who could 'hang'?)."

370   Similarly, a student of mine writes:

> One of the major and probably most difficult steps in identity development is obtaining or finding the consciousness of what it means to be White. I definitely remember many a time that I wished I was not White, ashamed of what I and others have done to the other racial groups in the world. . . . I wanted to pretend I was Black, live with them, celebrate their culture, and deny my Whiteness completely. Basically, I wanted to escape the responsibility that came with identifying myself as "White."

How successful these efforts to escape Whiteness via people of color will
380   be depends in part on the racial identity development of the people of color involved. Remember the Black students at the cafeteria table? If they are in the encounter or immersion/emersion stages, they are not likely to be interested in cultivating White friendships. If a White person reaches out to a Black person and is rebuffed, it may cause the White person to retreat into "blame the victim" thinking. However, even if these efforts to build interracial relationships are successful, the White individual must eventually confront the reality of his or her own Whiteness.

We all must be able to embrace who we are in terms of our racial and cultural heritage, not in terms of assumed superiority or inferiority, but as an
390   integral part of our daily experience in which we can take pride. But, as we see in these examples, for many White people who at this stage have come to understand the everyday reality of racism, Whiteness is still experienced as a source of shame rather than as a source of pride.

Recognizing the need to find a more positive self-definition is a hallmark of the next phase of White racial identity development, the immersion/ emersion stage. Bob, a White male student in my racism class, clearly articulated this need.

> I'm finding that this idea of White identity is more important than I thought. Yet White identity seems very hard to pin hole. I seem to
400   have an idea and feel myself understanding what I need to do and why and then something presents itself that throws me into mass confusion. I feel that I need some resources that will help me through the process of finding White identity.

The resource Bob needs most at this point are not people of color, but other Whites who are further along in the process and can help show him the way.

It is at just this point that White individuals intensify their efforts to see their Whiteness in a positive light. Just as Cross describes the period of Black redefinition as a time for Black people to seek new ways of thinking about Blackness, ways that take them beyond the role of victim, White people must seek new ways of thinking about Whiteness, ways that take them beyond the role of victimizer. 410

THE SEARCH FOR WHITE ALLIES
AND THE RESTORATION OF HOPE

In fact, another role does exist. There is a history of White protest against racism, a history of Whites who have resisted the role of oppressor and who have been allies to people of color. Unfortunately these Whites are often invisible to us. While the names of active racists are easily recalled—past and present Klan leaders and Southern segregationists, for example—the names of White allies are often unknown. I have had the experience of addressing roomfuls of classroom teachers who have been unable to name even one White person who has worked against racism without some prompting from me. If they can't do it, it is likely that their students can't either. 420

Those who have studied or lived through the Civil Rights era (many of my students have not) may know the names of Viola Liuzzo, James Reeb, or Michael Schwerner, White civil rights workers who were killed for their antiracist efforts. But most people don't want to be martyrs. There is a need to know about White allies who spoke up, who worked for social change, who resisted racism and lived to tell about it. How did these White allies break free from the confines of the racist socialization they surely experienced to claim this identity for themselves? These are the voices that many White people at this stage in the process are hungry to hear.

Biographies of or autobiographies by White individuals who have been engaged in antiracist activities can be very helpful. For example, there is *A Season of Justice,* the autobiography of Morris Dees, the executive director of the Southern Poverty Law Center and a vigorous anti-Klan litigator. There is *Outside the Magic Circle,* the oral history of Virginia Foster Durr, a Southern belle turned civil rights activist. And there is *The Education of a WASP,* the story of Lois Stalvey, a mother struggling to create a nonracist environment for her children. Such books can be an antidote to the feelings of isolation and loneliness that White people often feel at this point. There is comfort in knowing that others have traveled this terrain. 430

One of the consequences of racism in our society is that those who oppose racism are often marginalized, and as a result, their stories are not readily accessed. Yet having access to these stories makes a difference to those Whites who are looking for ways to be agents of change. White people who are doing this work need to make their stories known to serve as guides for others. 440

In my class I try to address the lack of knowledge of White role models by providing concrete examples of such people. In addition to assigning reading material, my strategy has been to invite a local White antiracist activist, Andrea Ayvazian, to my class to speak about her own personal journey

450 toward an awareness of racism and her development as a White ally. Students typically ask questions that reflect their fears about social isolation at this phase of development. "Did you lose friends when you started to speak up?" "My boyfriend makes a lot of racist comments. What can I do?" "What do you say to your father at Thanksgiving when he tells those jokes?" These are not just the questions of late adolescents. The mature White teachers I work with ask the same things.

My White students, who often comment about how depressing it is to study racism, typically say that the opportunity to talk with this ally gave them renewed hope. Through her example, they see that the role of the ally is not to help victims of racism, but to speak up against systems of oppres-
460 sion and to challenge other Whites to do the same. One point that Andrea emphasizes in her speaking and writing is the idea that "allies need allies," others who will support their efforts to swim against the tide of cultural and institutional racism. This point was especially helpful for one young woman who had been struggling with feelings of isolation. She wrote:

> About being an ally, a positive role model: . . . it enhanced my positive feelings about the difference each individual (me!) can make. I don't need to feel helpless when there is so much I can do. I still can see how easily things can back-up and start getting depressing, but I can also see how it is possible to keep going strong and powerful. One of the most
> 470 important points she made was the necessity of a support group/ system; people to remind me of what I have done, why I should keep going, of why I'm making a difference, why I shouldn't feel helpless. I think our class started to help me with those issues, as soon as I started to let it, and now I've found similar supports in friends and family. They're out there, it's just finding and establishing them—it really is a necessity. Without support, it would be too easy to give up, burn-out, become helpless again. In any endeavor support is important, but when the forces against you are so prevalent and deep-rooted as racism is in this society, it is the only way to keep moving forward.

480 Participation in White consciousness-raising groups organized specifically for the purpose of examining one's own racism are another way to "keep moving forward." At Mount Holyoke College such a group, White Women Against Racism, was formed following the 1992 acquittal of the Los Angeles police officers involved in the beating of Rodney King. There are similar groups with different names operating formally and informally in local communities around the country. Support groups of this nature help to combat the social isolation that antiracist Whites often experience, and provide places to forge new identities.

I am sometimes asked why such groups need to be made up of Whites
490 only. To many Whites it seems inconceivable that there would be any value in participating in all-White discussions of racism. While of course there is

value in cross-racial dialogue, all-White support groups serve a unique function. Particularly when Whites are trying to work through their feelings of guilt and shame, separate groups give White people the "space to speak with honesty and candor rarely possible in racially-mixed groups." Even when Whites feel comfortable sharing these feelings with people of color, frankly, people of color don't necessarily want to hear about it. The following comment, written by a Black woman in my class, illustrates this dilemma:

> Many times in class I feel uncomfortable when White students use the term Black because even if they aren't aware of it they say it with all or at least a lot of the negative connotations they've been taught goes along with Black. Sometimes it just causes a stinging feeling inside of me. Sometimes I get real tired of hearing White people talk about the conditions of Black people. I think it's an important thing for them to talk about, but still I don't always like being around when they do it. I also get tired of hearing them talk about how hard it is for them, though I understand it, and most times I am very willing to listen and be open, but sometimes I can't. Right now I can't.

[margin note: 500]
[margin note: Tired of it]

Though a White person may need to describe the racist things a parent or spouse has said or done, to tell the story to a person of color may reopen that person's wounds. Listening to those stories and problem-solving about them is a job that White people can do for each other.

[margin note: 510]
[margin note: Re injury]

It is at this stage of redefining Whiteness, immersion/emersion, that the feelings of guilt and shame start to fade. Reflecting on her own White identity development, sociologist Becky Thompson chronicles this process:

> [I understood] that I didn't have to recreate the wheel in my own life. I began to actively seek writing by white women who have historically stood up against racism—Elly Bulkin, Lillian Smith, Sara Evans, Angelina Grimke, Ruth Frankenberg, Helen Joseph, Melanie Kaye/ Kantrowitz, Tillie Olsen, Minnie Bruce Pratt, Ruth Seid, Mab Segrest, and others.

[margin note: 520]

She also realized that she needed antiracist White people in her daily life with whom she could share stories and whom she could trust to give her honest feedback. Her experience in a White antiracism group helped her to stop feeling bad because she was White. She writes, "I started seeing ways to channel my energies without trying to leave a piece of my identity behind."

The last stage, autonomy, represents the culmination of the White racial developmental process. At this point, a person incorporates the newly defined view of Whiteness as part of a personal identity. The positive feelings associated with this redefinition energize the person's efforts to confront racism and oppression in daily life. Clayton Alderfer, a White man with many years of personal and professional experience, describes the thinking that characterizes

[margin note: 530]

this stage. "We have a more complete awareness of ourselves and of others to the degree that we neither negate the uniqueness of each person, regardless of that person's group memberships nor deny the ever-present effects of group memberships for each individual."

While autonomy might be described as racial self-actualization, racial identity development never really ends. The person at this level is continually open to new information and new ways of thinking about racial and cultural variables. Helms describes each of the six stages as representing patterns of thinking that predominate at particular points of development. But even when active antiracist thinking predominates, there may still be particular situations that trigger old modes of responding. Whites, like people of color, continue to be works in progress.

A major benefit of this racial identity development process is increased effectiveness in multiracial settings. The White person who has worked through his or her own racial identity process has a deep understanding of racism and an appreciation and respect for the identity struggles of people of color. When we see strong, mutually respectful relationships between people of color and Whites, we are usually looking at the tangible results of both people's identity processes. If we want to promote positive cross-group relations, we need to help young White people engage in the kind of dialogue that precipitates this kind of identity development just as we need to help youth of color achieve an empowered sense of racial and ethnic identity.

Though the process of examining their racial identity can be uncomfortable and even frightening for Whites, those who persist in the struggle are rewarded with an increasingly multiracial and multicultural existence. In our still quite segregated society, this "borderland" is unfamiliar to many Whites and may be hard to envision. Becky Thompson has experienced it, and she writes: "We need to talk about what living in this borderland feels like, how we get there, what sustains us, and how we benefit from it. For me, this place of existence is tremendously exciting, invigorating, and life-affirming." Though it can also be "complicated and lonely," it is also liberating, opening doors to new communities, creating possibilities for more authentic connections with people of color, and in the process, strengthening the coalitions necessary for genuine social change.

Stages   Janet Helms   A Race Is a Nice Thing to Have

1) Contact
2) Disintegration
3) Reintegration
4) Pseudo-Independence
5) Immersion/Emersion
6) Autonomy

                              John + Jony Hoffman
        Whites   P of Color
    Conformity   Conformity
    Acceptance
                              Dissonance
                              Immersion

    Resistance
    Retreat
                              Emersion
                              Internalization

    Emergence
    Integrative Awareness   Integrative Awareness

THE UNITED STATES CONSTITUTION

PREAMBLE

We the People of the United States, in Order to form a more perfect   1
Union, establish Justice, insure domestic Tranquility, provide for the
common defense, promote the general Welfare, and secure the Blessings of
Liberty to ourselves and our Posterity, do ordain and establish this Constitution for the United States of America.

ARTICLE I.

Section 8.*

Clause 1: The Congress shall have Power To lay and collect Taxes, Duties,
  Imposts and Excises, to pay the Debts and provide for the common
  Defense and general Welfare of the United States; but all Duties,
  Imposts and Excises shall be uniform throughout the United States;

Clause 2: To borrow Money on the credit of the United States;   10

Clause 3: To regulate Commerce with foreign Nations, and among the
  several States, and with the Indian Tribes;

Clause 4: To establish an uniform Rule of Naturalization, and uniform
  Laws on the subject of Bankruptcies throughout the United States;

Clause 5: To coin Money, regulate the Value thereof, and of foreign
  Coin, and fix the Standard of Weights and Measures;

Clause 6: To provide for the Punishment of counterfeiting the Securities
  and current Coin of the United States;

Clause 7: To establish Post Offices and post Roads;

Clause 8: To promote the Progress of Science and useful Arts, by secur-   20
  ing for limited Times to Authors and Inventors the exclusive Right to
  their respective Writings and Discoveries;

Clause 9: To constitute Tribunals inferior to the supreme Court;

Clause 10: To define and punish Piracies and Felonies committed on
  the high Seas, and offenses against the Law of Nations;

Clause 11: To declare War, grant Letters of Marque and Reprisal, and
  make Rules concerning Captures on Land and Water;

Clause 12: To raise and support Armies, but no Appropriation of
  Money to that Use shall be for a longer Term than two Years;

Clause 13: To provide and maintain a Navy;   30

Clause 14: To make Rules for the Government and Regulation of the
  land and naval Forces;

Clause 15: To provide for calling forth the Militia to execute the Laws
  of the Union, suppress Insurrections and repel Invasions;

What was the Law of Nations then?

→ hardly saw us as a world power, then

What kind of insurrection did they imagine?

---

*We begin our nation's founding legal contract with its citizens by focusing on Section 8. Sec-
tion 8 details the responsibilities and powers of the Government. Readers can then move
directly to the "Bill of Rights"—the Amendments which grant the governed ("We, the People")
inalienable rights and certain freedoms from government power.

Clause 16: To provide for organizing, arming, and disciplining, the Militia, and for governing such Part of them as may be employed in the Service of the United States, reserving to the States respectively, the Appointment of the Officers, and the Authority of training the Militia according to the discipline prescribed by Congress;

40   Clause 17: To exercise exclusive Legislation in all Cases whatsoever, over such District (not exceeding ten Miles square) as may, by Cession of particular States, and the Acceptance of Congress, become the Seat of the Government of the United States, and to exercise like Authority over all Places purchased by the Consent of the Legislature of the State in which the Same shall be, for the Erection of Forts, Magazines, Arsenals, dock-Yards, and other needful Buildings;—And

Clause 18: To make all Laws which shall be necessary and proper for carrying into Execution the foregoing Powers, and all other Powers vested by this Constitution in the Government of the United States,

50   or in any Department or Officer thereof.

AMENDMENTS TO THE CONSTITUTION OF THE UNITED STATES

Amendment I (1791)

Congress shall make no law respecting an establishment of religion, or prohibiting the free exercise thereof; or abridging the freedom of speech, or of the press; or the right of the people peaceably to assemble, and to petition the government for a redress of grievances.

Amendment II (1791)

A well regulated militia, being necessary to the security of a free state, the right of the people to keep and bear arms, shall not be infringed.

Amendment III (1791)

No soldier shall, in time of peace be quartered in any house, without the consent of the owner, nor in time of war, but in a manner to be prescribed by law.

Amendment IV (1791)

The right of the people to be secure in their persons, houses, papers, and

60   effects, against unreasonable searches and seizures, shall not be violated, and no warrants shall issue, but upon probable cause, supported by oath or affirmation, and particularly describing the place to be searched, and the persons or things to be seized.

Amendment V (1791)

No person shall be held to answer for a capital, or otherwise infamous crime, unless on a presentment or indictment of a grand jury, except in cases arising in the land or naval forces, or in the militia, when in actual service in time of war or public danger; nor shall any person be subject for the same offense to

be twice put in jeopardy of life or limb; nor shall be compelled in any criminal case to be a witness against himself, nor be deprived of life, liberty, or property, without due process of law; nor shall private property be taken for   70
public use, without just compensation.

Amendment VI (1791)

In all criminal prosecutions, the accused shall enjoy the right to a speedy and public trial, by an impartial jury of the state and district wherein the crime shall have been committed, which district shall have been previously ascertained by law, and to be informed of the nature and cause of the accusation; to be confronted with the witnesses against him; to have compulsory process for obtaining witnesses in his favor, and to have the assistance of counsel for his defense.

Amendment VII (1791)

In suits at common law, where the value in controversy shall exceed twenty dollars, the right of trial by jury shall be preserved, and no fact tried by a jury,   80
shall be otherwise reexamined in any court of the United States, than according to the rules of the common law.

Amendment VIII (1791)

Excessive bail shall not be required, nor excessive fines imposed, nor cruel and unusual punishments inflicted.

Amendment IX (1791)

The enumeration in the Constitution, of certain rights, shall not be constructed to deny or disparage others retained by the people.

Amendment X (1791)

The powers not delegated to the United States by the Constitution, nor prohibited by it to the states, are reserved to the states respectively, or to the people.

Amendment XI (1798)

The judicial power of the United States shall not be construed to extend to   90
any suit in law or equity, commenced or prosecuted against one of the United States by citizens of another state, or by citizens or subjects of any foreign state.

Amendment XIII (1865)

Section 1.

Neither slavery nor involuntary servitude, except as a punishment for crime whereof the party shall have been duly convicted, shall exist within the United States, or any place subject to their jurisdiction.

Section 2.

Congress shall have power to enforce this article by appropriate legislation.

Amendment XIV (1868)

Section 1.

All persons born or naturalized in the United States, and subject to the jurisdiction thereof, are citizens of the United States and of the state wherein they reside. No state shall make or enforce any law which shall abridge the privileges or immunities of citizens of the United States; nor shall any state deprive any person of life, liberty, or property, without due process of law; nor deny to any person within its jurisdiction the equal protection of the laws.

Section 2.

Representatives shall be apportioned among the several states according to their respective numbers, counting the whole number of persons in each state, excluding Indians not taxed. But when the right to vote at any election for the choice of electors for President and Vice President of the United States, Representatives in Congress, the executive and judicial officers of a state, or the members of the legislature thereof, is denied to any of the male inhabitants of such state, being twenty-one years of age, and citizens of the United States, or in any way abridged, except for participation in rebellion, or other crime, the basis of representation therein shall be reduced in the proportion which the number of such male citizens shall bear to the whole number of male citizens twenty-one years of age in such state.

Section 3.

No person shall be a Senator or Representative in Congress, or elector of President and Vice President, or hold any office, civil or military, under the United States, or under any state, who, having previously taken an oath, as a member of Congress, or as an officer of the United States, or as a member of any state legislature, or as an executive or judicial officer of any state, to support the Constitution of the United States, shall have engaged in insurrection or rebellion against the same, or given aid or comfort to the enemies thereof. But Congress may by a vote of two-thirds of each House, remove such disability.

Section 4.

The validity of the public debt of the United States, authorized by law, including debts incurred for payment of pensions and bounties for services in suppressing insurrection or rebellion, shall not be questioned. But neither the United States nor any state shall assume or pay any debt or obligation incurred in aid of insurrection or rebellion against the United States, or any claim for the loss or emancipation of any slave; but all such debts, obligations and claims shall be held illegal and void.

Section 5.

The Congress shall have power to enforce, by appropriate legislation, the   130
provisions of this article.

Amendment XV (1870)
Section 1.

The right of citizens of the United States to vote shall not be denied or abridged by the United States or by any state on account of race, color, or previous condition of servitude.

Section 2.

The Congress shall have power to enforce this article by appropriate legislation.

Amendment XVI (1913)

The Congress shall have power to lay and collect taxes on incomes, from whatever source derived, without apportionment among the several states, and without regard to any census of enumeration.   _?_

Amendment XVII (1913)

The Senate of the United States shall be composed of two Senators from each state, elected by the people therefore, for six years; and each Senator shall   140
have one vote. The electors in each state shall have the qualifications requisite for electors of the most numerous branch of the state legislatures.

different rules for voting eligibility by state + House!

When vacancies happen in the representation of any state in the Senate, the executive authority of such state shall issue writs of election to fill such vacancies: Provided, that the legislature of any state may empower the executive thereof to make temporary appointments until the people fill the vacancies by election as the legislature may direct.

This amendment shall not be so construed as to affect the election or term of any Senator chosen before it becomes valid as part of the Constitution.

Amendment XVIII (1919)

Section 1.

150   After one year from the ratification of this article the manufacture, sale, or transportation of intoxicating liquors within, the importation thereof into, or the exportation thereof from the United States and all territory subject to the jurisdiction thereof for beverage purposes is hereby prohibited.

Section 2.

The Congress and the several states shall have concurrent power to enforce this article by appropriate legislation.

Section 3.

This article shall be inoperative unless it shall have been ratified as an amendment to the Constitution by the legislatures of the several states, as provided in the Constitution, within seven years from the date of the submission hereof to the states by the Congress.

Amendment XIX (1920)

160   The right of citizens of the United States to vote shall not be denied or abridged by the United States or by any state on account of sex.

Congress shall have power to enforce this article by appropriate legislation.

Amendment XXI (1933)

Section 1.

The eighteenth article of amendment to the Constitution of the United States is hereby repealed.

Section 2.

The transportation or importation into any state, territory, or possession of the United States for delivery or use therein of intoxicating liquors, in violation of the laws thereof, is hereby prohibited.

Amendment XXII (1951)

Section 1.

No person shall be elected to the office of the President more than twice, and no person who has held the office of President, or acted as President, for

170   more than two years of a term to which some other person was elected Pres-

ident shall be elected to the office of the President more than once. But this article shall not apply to any person holding the office of President when this article was proposed by the Congress, and shall not prevent any person who may be holding the office of President, or acting as President, during the term within which this article becomes operative from holding the office of President or acting as President during the remainder of such term.

Section 2.

This article shall be inoperative unless it shall have been ratified as an amendment to the Constitution by the legislatures of three-fourths of the several states within seven years from the date of its submission to the states by the Congress.   180

Amendment XXIV (1964)

Section 1.

The right of citizens of the United States to vote in any primary or other election for President or Vice President, for electors for President or Vice President, or for Senator or Representative in Congress, shall not be denied or abridged by the United States or any state by reason of failure to pay any poll tax or other tax.

Section 2.

The Congress shall have power to enforce this article by appropriate legislation.

Amendment XXVI (1971)

Section 1.

The right of citizens of the United States, who are 18 years of age or older, to vote, shall not be denied or abridged by the United States or any state on account of age.

Section 2.

The Congress shall have the power to enforce this article by appropriate   190
legislation.

SELECTIONS FROM *SONG OF MYSELF*
Walt Whitman

1

I CELEBRATE myself, and sing myself,
And what I assume you shall assume,
For every atom belonging to me as good belongs to you.

I loafe and invite my soul,
I lean and loafe at my ease observing a spear of summer grass.

My tongue, every atom of my blood, form'd from this soil, this air,
Born here of parents born here from parents the same, and their parents
    the same,
I, now thirty-seven years old in perfect health begin,   10
Hoping to cease not till death. . . .

2

. . . . Have you reckon'd a thousand acres much? have you reckon'd the
    earth much?
Have you practis'd so long to learn to read?
Have you felt so proud to get at the meaning of poems?

Stop this day and night with me and you shall possess the origin of all
    poems,
You shall possess the good of the earth and sun, (there are millions of suns
    left,)   20
You shall no longer take things at second or third hand, nor look through
    the eyes of the dead, nor feed on the spectres in books,
You shall not look through my eyes either, nor take things from me,
You shall listen to all sides and filter them from your self.

3

I have heard what the talkers were talking, the talk of the beginning and
    the end,
But I do not talk of the beginning or the end.

There was never any more inception than there is now,
Nor any more youth or age than there is now,   30
And will never be any more perfection than there is now,
Nor any more heaven or hell than there is now.
Urge and urge and urge,
Always the procreant urge of the world.

Out of the dimness opposite equals advance, always substance and increase, always sex,
Always a knit of identity, always distinction, always a breed of life.
To elaborate is no avail, learn'd and unlearn'd feel that it is so. . . .

4

40 Trippers and askers surround me,
People I meet, the effect upon me of my early life or the ward and city I
    live in, or the nation,
The latest dates, discoveries, inventions, societies, authors old and new,
My dinner, dress, associates, looks, compliments, dues,
The real or fancied indifference of some man or woman I love,
The sickness of one of my folks or of myself, or ill-doing or loss or lack of
    money, or depressions or exaltations,
Battles, the horrors of fratricidal war, the fever of doubtful news, the fitful
    events;
50 These come to me days and nights and go from me again,
But they are not the Me myself.

Apart from the pulling and hauling stands what I am,
Stands amused, complacent, compassionating, idle, unitary,
Looks down, is erect, or bends an arm on an impalpable certain rest,
Looking with side-curved head curious what will come next,
Both in and out of the game and watching and wondering at it.

Backward I see in my own days where I sweated through fog with linguists
    and contenders,
I have no mockings or arguments, I witness and wait.

60 15
. . . . The city sleeps and the country sleeps,
The living sleep for their time, the dead sleep for their time,
The old husband sleeps by his wife and the young husband sleeps by his wife;
And these tend inward to me, and I tend outward to them,
And such as it is to be of these more or less I am,
And of these one and all I weave the song of myself.

16
I am of old and young, of the foolish as much as the wise,
Regardless of others, ever regardful of others,
70 Maternal as well as paternal, a child as well as a man,
Stuff'd with the stuff that is coarse and stuff'd with the stuff that is fine,
One of the Nation of many nations, the smallest the same and the largest
    the same. . . .

. . . A learner with the simplest, a teacher of the thoughtfullest,
A novice beginning yet experient of myriads of seasons,
Of every hue and caste am I, of every rank and religion,
A farmer, mechanic, artist, gentleman, sailor, quaker,
Prisoner, fancy-man, rowdy, lawyer, physician, priest.

I resist any thing better than my own diversity,
Breathe the air but leave plenty after me,   80
And am not stuck up, and am in my place. . . .
The bright suns I see and the dark suns I cannot see are in their place,
The palpable is in its place and the impalpable is in its place.

17
These are really the thoughts of all men in all ages and lands, they are not
    original with me,
If they are not yours as much as mine they are nothing, or next to
    nothing,
If they are not the riddle and the untying of the riddle they are nothing,
If they are not just as close as they are distant they are nothing.   90

This is the grass that grows wherever the land is and the water is,
This the common air that bathes the globe.

20
Who goes there? . . . What am I? What are you?

All I mark as my own you shall offset it with your own,
Else it·were time lost listening to me. . . .

In all people I see myself, none more and not one a barley-corn less,
And the good or bad I say of myself I say of them.

I know I am solid and sound,
To me the converging objects of the universe perpetually flow,   100
All are written to me, and I must get what the writing means. . . .

I exist as I am, that is enough,
If no other in the world be aware I sit content,
And if each and all be aware I sit content.

One world is aware and by far the largest to me, and that is myself,
And whether I come to my own to-day or in ten thousand or ten million
    years,
I can cheerfully take it now, or with equal cheerfulness I can wait. . . .

21

110   I am the poet of the Body and I am the poet of the Soul,
The pleasures of heaven are with me and the pains of hell are with me,
The first I graft and increase upon myself, the latter I translate into new
   tongue.

I am the poet of the woman the same as the man,
And I say it is as great to be a woman as to be a man,
And I say there is nothing greater than the mother of men. . . .

24

Walt Whitman, a kosmos, of Manhattan the son,
Turbulent, fleshy, sensual, eating, drinking and breeding,
120   No sentimentalist, no stander above men and women or apart from
   them,
No more modest than immodest.

Unscrew the locks from the doors!
Unscrew the doors themselves from their jambs!

Whoever degrades another degrades me,
And whatever is done or said returns at last to me.

Through me the afflatus surging and surging, through me the current and
   index.

I speak the pass-word primeval, I give the sign of democracy,
130   By God! I will accept nothing which all cannot have their counterpart of
   on the same terms.

Through me many long dumb voices,
Voices of the interminable generations of prisoners and slaves,
Voices of the diseas'd and despairing and of thieves and dwarfs,
Voices of cycles of preparation and accretion,
And of the threads that connect the stars, and of wombs and of the father-
   stuff,

And of the rights of them the others are down upon,
Of the deform'd, trivial, flat, foolish, despised,
140   Fog in the air, beetles rolling balls of dung.

Through me forbidden voices,
Voices of sexes and lusts, voices veil'd and I remove the veil,
Voices indecent by me clarified and transfigur'd.

I do not press my fingers across my mouth,
I keep as delicate around the bowels as around the head and heart,
Copulation is no more rank to me than death is.

I believe in the flesh and the appetites,
Seeing, hearing, feeling, are miracles, and each part and tag of me is a
    miracle.

Divine am I inside and out, and I make holy whatever I touch or am   150
    touch'd from,
The scent of these arm-pits aroma finer than prayer,
This head more than churches, bibles, and all the creeds.

If I worship one thing more than another it shall be the spread of my own
    body, or any part of it,
Translucent mould of me it shall be you!
Shaded ledges and rests it shall be you!
Firm masculine colter it shall be you!
Whatever goes to the tilth of me it shall be you!
You my rich blood! your milky stream pale strippings of my life!   160
Breast that presses against other breasts it shall be you!
My brain it shall be your occult convolutions!
Root of wash'd sweet-flag! timorous pond-snipe! nest of guarded duplicate
    eggs! it shall be you!
Mix'd tussled hay of head, beard, brawn, it shall be you!
Trickling sap of maple, fibre of manly wheat, it shall be you!
Sun so generous it shall be you!
Vapors lighting and shading my face it shall be you!
You sweaty brooks and dews it shall be you!
Winds whose soft-tickling genitals rub against me it shall be you!   170
Broad muscular fields, branches of live oak, loving lounger in my winding
    paths, it shall be you!
Hands I have taken, face I have kiss'd, mortal I have ever touch'd, it shall
    be you.

I dote on myself, there is that lot of me and all so luscious,
Each moment and whatever happens thrills me with joy,
I cannot tell how my ankles bend, nor whence the cause of my faintest wish,
Nor the cause of the friendship I emit, nor the cause of the friendship I
    take again. . . .

26   180
Now I will do nothing but listen,
To accrue what I hear into this song, to let sounds contribute toward it.

I hear bravuras of birds, bustle of growing wheat, gossip of flames, clack of
    sticks cooking my meals,
I hear the sound I love, the sound of the human voice,
I hear all sounds running together, combined, fused or following,
Sounds of the city and sounds out of the city, sounds of the day and night,
Talkative young ones to those that like them, the loud laugh of work-
    people at their meals,
190   The angry base of disjointed friendship, the faint tones of the sick,
The judge with hands tight to the desk, his pallid lips pronouncing a
    death-sentence. . . .

27

To be in any form, what is that?
(Round and round we go, all of us, and ever come back thither,)
If nothing lay more develop'd the quahaug in its callous shell were enough.

Mine is no callous shell,
I have instant conductors all over me whether I pass or stop,
They seize every object and lead it harmlessly through me.

200   I merely stir, press, feel with my fingers, and am happy,
To touch my person to some one else's is about as much as I can stand.

42

A call in the midst of the crowd,
My own voice, orotund sweeping and final. . . .

orotund:
marked by
fullness, strength
+ clarity of sound

. . . This is the city and I am one of the citizens,
Whatever interests the rest interests me, politics, wars, markets, newspapers,
    schools,
The mayor and councils, banks, tariffs, steamships, factories, stocks, stores,
    real estate and personal estate.
210   The little plentiful manikins skipping around in collars and tail'd coats
I am aware who they are, (they are positively not worms or fleas,)
I acknowledge the duplicates of myself, the weakest and shallowest is death-
    less with me,
What I do and say the same waits for them,
Every thought that flounders in me the same flounders in them.

I know perfectly well my own egotism,
Know my omnivorous lines and must not write any less,
And would fetch you whoever you are flush with myself.

Not words of routine this song of mine,
220   But abruptly to question, to leap beyond yet nearer bring;

This printed and bound book—but the printer and the printing-office boy?
The well-taken photographs—but your wife or friend close and solid in
    your arms?

. . . The sky up there—yet here or next door, or across the way?
The saints and sages in history—but you yourself?
Sermons, creeds, theology—but the fathomless human brain,
And what is reason? and what is love? and what is life?

44
It is time to explain myself—let us stand up.

What is known I strip away,   230
I launch all men and women forward with me into the Unknown.

The clock indicates the moment—but what does eternity indicate?

We have thus far exhausted trillions of winters and summers,
There are trillions ahead, and trillions ahead of them.

Births have brought us richness and variety,
And other births will bring us richness and variety.

I do not call one greater and one smaller,
That which fills its period and place is equal to any.

Were mankind murderous or jealous upon you, my brother, my sister?
I am sorry for you, they are not murderous or jealous upon me,   240
All has been gentle with me, I keep no account with lamentation,
(What have I to do with lamentation?)
I am an acme of things accomplish'd, and I an encloser of things to be.

My feet strike an apex of the apices of the stairs,
On every step bunches of ages, and larger bunches between the steps,
All below duly travel'd, and still I mount and mount.

apices – plural of apex

Rise after rise bow the phantoms behind me,
Afar down I see the huge first Nothing, I know I was even there,
I waited unseen and always, and slept through the lethargic mist,
And took my time, and took no hurt from the fetid carbon.   250

Long I was hugg'd close—long and long.

Immense have been the preparations for me,
Faithful and friendly the arms that have help'd me.

Cycles ferried my cradle, rowing and rowing like cheerful boatmen,
For room to me stars kept aside in their own rings,
They sent influences to look after what was to hold me.

Before I was born out of my mother generations guided me,
My embryo has never been torpid, nothing could overlay it.

For it the nebula cohered to an orb,
260   The long slow strata piled to rest it on,
Vast vegetables gave it sustenance,
Monstrous sauroids transported it in their mouths and deposited it with
     care.

Sauropod-dinosaur

All forces have been steadily employ'd to complete and delight me,
Now on this spot I stand with my robust soul.

48

I have said that the soul is not more than the body,
And I have said that the body is not more than the soul,
And nothing, not God, is greater to one than one's self is,
270   And whoever walks a furlong without sympathy walks to his own funeral
     drest in his shroud,
And I or you pocketless of a dime may purchase the pick of the earth,
And to glance with an eye or show a bean in its pod confounds the learn-
     ing of all times,
And there is no trade or employment but the young man following it may
     become a hero,
And there is no object so soft but it makes a hub for the wheel'd universe,
And I say to any man or woman, Let your soul stand cool and composed
     before a million universes.

280   And I say to mankind, Be not curious about God,
For I who am curious about each am not curious about God,
(No array of terms can say how much I am at peace about God and about
     death.)

I hear and behold God in every object, yet understand God not in the
     least,
Nor do I understand who there can be more wonderful than myself.

Why should I wish to see God better than this day?
I see something of God each hour of the twenty-four, and each moment then,
In the faces of men and women I see God, and in my own face in the glass,
290   I find letters from God dropt in the street, and every one is sign'd by God's
     name,

And I leave them where they are, for I know that wheresoe'er I go,
Others will punctually come for ever and ever.

49
And as to you Death, and you bitter hug of mortality, it is idle to try to
    alarm me.

To his work without flinching the accoucheur comes,
I see the elder-hand pressing receiving supporting,
I recline by the sills of the exquisite flexible doors,
And mark the outlet, and mark the relief and escape.

Accoucheur - one that assists at a birth

300

And as to you Corpse I think you are good manure, but that does not
    offend me,
I smell the white roses sweet-scented and growing,
I reach to the leafy lips, I reach to the polish'd breasts of melons.

And as to you Life I reckon you are the leavings of many deaths,
(No doubt I have died myself ten thousand times before.)

I hear you whispering there O stars of heaven,
O suns—O grass of graves—O perpetual transfers and promotions,
If you do not say any thing how can I say any thing?

Of the turbid pool that lies in the autumn forest,
Of the moon that descends the steeps of the soughing twilight,
Toss, sparkles of day and dusk—toss on the black stems that decay in the
    muck,
Toss to the moaning gibberish of the dry limbs.

310

Turbid. obscured, muddy, thick/opaque

Sough to make a moaning or sighing sound

I ascend from the moon, I ascend from the night,
I perceive that the ghastly glimmer is noonday sunbeams reflected,
And debouch to the steady and central from the offspring great or small.

Debouch to cause to emerge, discharge, to march out into open ground

50
There is that in me—I do not know what it is—but I know it is in me.

320

Wrench'd and sweaty—calm and cool then my body becomes,
I sleep—I sleep long.

I do not know it—it is without name—it is a word unsaid,
It is not in any dictionary, utterance, symbol.

Something it swings on more than the earth I swing on,
To it the creation is the friend whose embracing awakes me.

Perhaps I might tell more. Outlines! I plead for my brothers and sisters.

Do you see O my brothers and sisters?
It is not chaos or death—it is form, union, plan—it is eternal life—it is
    Happiness.

330   51
. . . Do I contradict myself?
Very well then I contradict myself,
(I am large, I contain multitudes.)

I concentrate toward them that are nigh, I wait on the door-slab.

Who has done his day's work? Who will soonest be through with his
    supper?
Who wishes to walk with me?

Will you speak before I am gone? Will you prove already too late?

  52
340 The spotted hawk swoops by and accuses me, he complains of my gab and
    my loitering.

I too am not a bit tamed, I too am untranslatable,
I sound my barbaric yawp over the roofs of the world.

The last scud of day holds back for me,
It flings my likeness after the rest and true as any on the shadow'd wilds,
It coaxes me to the vapor and the dusk. . . .

I bequeath myself to the dirt to grow from the grass I love,
If you want me again look for me under your boot-soles.

You will hardly know who I am or what I mean,
350 But I shall be good health to you nevertheless,
And filter and fibre your blood.

Failing to fetch me at first keep encouraged,
Missing me one place search another,
I stop somewhere waiting for you.

Grass — interconnected web
prairie grasses wild varieties
grew together + root systems
intertwined

also growing out of the graves

NPR Discussion of <u>L of Grass</u>

A SITUATIONIST PERSPECTIVE
ON THE PSYCHOLOGY OF EVIL
UNDERSTANDING HOW GOOD PEOPLE
ARE TRANSFORMED INTO PERPETRATORS
Philip G. Zimbardo

I endorse the application of a situationist perspective to the ways in which the antisocial behavior of individuals and the violence sanctioned by nations can be best understood, treated, and prevented. This view, which has both influenced and been informed by a body of social-psychological research and theory, contrasts with the traditional perspective that explains evil behavior in dispositional terms: Internal determinants of antisocial behavior locate evil within individual predispositions—genetic "bad seeds," personality traits, psychopathological risk factors, and other organismic variables. The situationist approach is to the dispositional as public health models of disease are to medical models. Following basic principles of Lewinian theory, the situationist perspective propels external determinants of behavior to the foreground, well beyond the status as merely extenuating background circumstances. Unique to this situationist approach is the use of experimental laboratory and field research to demonstrate vital phenomena, that other approaches only analyze verbally or rely on archival or correlational data for answers. The basic paradigm presented in this chapter illustrates the relative ease with which ordinary, "good" men and women can be induced into behaving in "evil" ways by turning on or off one or another social situational variable.

I begin the chapter with a series of "oldies but goodies"—my laboratory and field studies on deindividuation, aggression, vandalism, and the Stanford prison experiment, along with a process analysis of Milgram's obedience studies, and Bandura's analysis of "moral disengagement." My analysis is extended to the evil of inaction by considering bystander failures of helping those in distress. This body of research demonstrates the underrecognized power of social situations to alter the mental representations and behavior of individuals, groups, and nations. Finally, I explore extreme instances of "evil" behavior for their dispositional or situational foundations: torturers, death-squad violence workers, and terrorist suicide bombers.

Evil can be defined as intentionally behaving, or causing others to act, in ways that demean, dehumanize, harm, destroy, or kill innocent people. This behaviorally focused definition makes the individual or group responsible for purposeful, motivated actions that have a range of negative consequences for other people. The definition excludes accidental or unintended harmful outcomes, as well as the broader, generic forms of institutional evil, such as poverty, prejudice, or destruction of the environment by agents of corporate

Reprinted from *The Social Psychology of Good and Evil: Understanding Our Capacity for Kindness and Cruelty*, edited by Arthur G. Miller (2005), by permission of Guilford Publications, Inc.

greed. However, it does include corporate forms of wrongdoing, such as the marketing and selling of products with known disease-causing, death-dealing properties (e.g., cigarette manufacturers or other substance/drug dealers). The definition also extends beyond the proximal agent of aggression, as stud-
40　ied in research on interpersonal violence, to encompass those in distal positions of authority whose orders or plans are carried out by functionaries. Such agents include military commanders and national leaders, such as Hitler, Stalin, Mao, Pol Pot, Idi Amin, and others whom history has identified as tyrants for their complicity in the deaths of untold millions of innocent people.

History will also have to decide on the evil status of President George W. Bush's role in declaring a pre-emptive, aggressive war against Iraq in March 2003, with dubious justification, that resulted in widespread death, injury, destruction, and enduring chaos. We might also consider a simpler definition
50　of evil, proposed by my colleague, Irving Sarnoff: "Evil is knowing better but doing worse."

We live in a world cloaked in the evils of civil and international wars, of terrorism (home-grown and exported), homicides, rapes, domestic and child abuse, and countless other forms of devastation. The same human mind that creates the most beautiful works of art and extraordinary marvels of technology is equally responsible for the perversion of its own perfection. This most dynamic organ in the universe has served as a seemingly endless source of ever viler torture chambers and instruments of horror in earlier centuries, the "bestial machinery" unleashed on Chinese citizens by Japanese soldiers in
60　their rape of Nanking (see Chang, 1997), and the recent demonstration of "creative evil" in the destruction of the World Trade Center by "weaponizing" commercial airlines. We continue to ask, *why*? Why and how is it possible for such deeds to continue to occur? How can the unimaginable become so readily imagined? These are the same questions that have been asked by generations before ours.

I wish I had answers to these profound questions about human existence and human nature. Here I can offer modest versions of possible answers. My concern centers around how good, ordinary people can be recruited, induced, seduced into behaving in ways that could be classified as evil. In
70　contrast to the traditional approach of trying to identify "evil people" to account for the evil in our midst, I focus on trying to outline some of the central conditions that are involved in the transformation of good people into perpetrators of evil.

LOCATING EVIL WITHIN PARTICULAR PEOPLE: THE RUSH TO THE DISPOSITIONAL

"Who is responsible for evil in the world, given that there is an all-powerful, omniscient God who is also all-Good?" That conundrum began the intellectual scaffolding of the Inquisition in the 16th and 17th centuries in Europe.

As revealed in *Malleus Maleficarum*, the handbook of the German Inquisitors from the Roman Catholic Church, the inquiry concluded that "the Devil" was the source of all evil. However, these theologians argued the Devil works his evil through intermediaries, lesser demons, and, of course, human witches. So the hunt for evil focused on those marginalized people who looked or acted differently from ordinary people, who might qualify, under rigorous examination of conscience and torture, as "witches," and then put them to death. The victims were mostly women who could be readily exploited without sources of defense, especially when they had resources that could be confiscated. An analysis of this legacy of institutionalized violence against women is detailed by historian Anne Barstow (1994) in *Witchcraze*. Paradoxically, this early effort of the Inquisition to understand the origins of evil and develop interventions to cope with it instead fomented new forms of evil that fulfill all facets of my definition. The phenomenon of the Inquisition exemplifies the notion of simplifying the complex problem of widespread evil by identifying *individuals* who might be the guilty parties and then making them "pay" for their evil deeds.

Most traditional psychiatry as well as psychodynamic theory also locate the source of individual violence and antisocial behavior within the psyches of disturbed people, often tracing it back to early roots in unresolved infantile conflicts. Like genetic views of pathology, such psychological approaches seek to link behaviors society judges as pathological to pathological origins—be they defective genes, "bad seeds," or premorbid personality structures. However, this view overlooks the fact that the same violent outcomes can be generated by very different types of people, all of whom give no hint of evil impulses. My colleagues and I (Lee, Zimbardo, & Berthoff, 1977) interviewed and tested 19 inmates in California prisons who had all recently been convicted of homicide. Ten of these killers had a long history of violence, showed lack of impulse control (on the Minnesota Multiphasic Personality Inventory), were decidedly masculine in sexual identity, and generally extraverted. The other murderers were totally different. They had never committed any criminal offense prior to the homicide—their murders were totally unexpected, given their mild manner and gentle disposition. Their problem was an *excessive* impulse control that inhibited their expression of any feelings. Their sexual identity was feminine or androgynous, and the majority were shy. These "shy sudden murderers" killed just as violently as did the habitual criminals, and their victims died just as surely, but it would have been impossible to predict this outcome from any prior knowledge of their personalities, which were so different from the more obvious habitual criminals.

The concept of an authoritarian personality syndrome was developed by a team of psychologists (Adorno, Frenkel-Brunswick, Levinson, & Sanford, 1950) after World War II who were trying to make sense of the Holocaust and the broad appeal of fascism and Hitler. Their dispositional bias led them to focus on identifying a set of personality factors that might underlie the fascist mentality. However, they over-looked the host of processes operating at political, economic, societal, and historical levels, all of which influenced and directed so many millions of individuals into a constrained behavioral channel of hating Jews and other minority groups, while endorsing and even applauding the views and policies of their dictator.

This tendency to explain observed behavior by reference to internal dispositional factors while ignoring or minimizing the impact of situational variables has been termed the fundamental attribution error (FAE) by my colleague Lee Ross (1977). We are all subject to this dual bias of overutilizing dispositional

130 analyses and underutilizing situational explanations when faced with ambiguous causal scenarios we want to understand. We succumb to this effect because our educational institutions, social and professional training programs, and societal agencies are all geared toward a focus on individual, dispositional orientations. Dispositional analyses are a central operating feature of cultures that are based on individualistic rather than collectivist values (see Triandis, 1994). Thus, it is individuals who are lauded with praise and fame and wealth for achievement and are honored for their uniqueness, but it is also individuals who are blamed for the ills of society. Our legal, medical, educational, and religious systems all are founded on principles of individualism.

140 Dispositional analyses of antisocial, or non-normative, behaviors typically include strategies for behavior modification, whereby deviant individuals learn to conform better to social norms, or facilities for excluding them from society via imprisonment, exile, or execution. Locating evil within selected individuals or groups carries with it the "social virtue" of taking society "off the hook" as blameworthy; societal structures and political decision making are exonerated from bearing any burden of the more fundamental circumstances that create racism, sexism, elitism, poverty, and marginal existence for some citizens. Furthermore, this dispositional orientation to understanding evil implies a simplistic, binary world of good people, like us, and bad peo-

150 ple, like them. That clear-cut dichotomy is divided by a manufactured line that separates good and evil. We then take comfort in the illusion that such a line constrains crossovers in either direction. We could never imagine being like *them*, of doing their unthinkable dirty deeds, and do not admit them into our company because they are so essentially different as to be unchangeable. This extreme position also means we forfeit the motivation to understand how they came to engage in what we view as evil behavior. I find it helpful to remind myself of the geopolitical analysis of the Russian novelist Alexander Solzhenitsyn, a victim of persecution by the Soviet KGB, that the line between good and evil lies in the center of every human heart.

THE TRANSFORMATION OF GOOD PEOPLE INTO AGENTS OF DESTRUCTION

160 My bias is admittedly more toward situational analyses of behavior and comes from my training as an experimental social psychologist as well as from having grown up in poverty, in a New York City ghetto of the South Bronx. I

believe that dispositional orientations are more likely to correlate with afflu-ence: The rich want to take full credit for their success, whereas the situa-tionists hail more from the lower classes who want to explain the obvious dys-functional lifestyles of those around them in terms of external circumstances rather than internal failures. I am primarily concerned with understanding the psychological and social dynamics involved when an ordinary, "good" per-son begins to act in antisocial ways and, in the extreme, behaves destructively toward the property or person of others. I saw, firsthand, my childhood   170 friends go through such transformations, and I wondered how and why they changed so drastically and whether I could also change like that (e.g., they were bullied, failed in school, parents fought all the time, nothing to look forward to). I was similarly fascinated with the tale of the behavioral trans-formation of Robert Louis Stevenson's good Dr. Jekyll into the murderous Mr. Hyde. What was in his chemical formula that could have such an imme-diate and profound impact? Even as a child, I wondered if there were other ways to induce such changes, since my friends did not have access to his elixir of evil before they did such bad things to other people. I would later discover that social psychology had recipes for such transformations.   180

Our mission is to understand better how virtually anyone could be recruited to engage in evil deeds that deprive other human beings of their dignity, humanity, and life. The dispositional analysis has the comforting side effect of enabling those who have not yet done wrong to righteously assert, "Not *me*, I am different from those kinds of people who did that evil deed!" By positing a "me-us-them" distinction, we live with the illusion of moral superiority firmly entrenched in the pluralistic ignorance that comes from not recognizing the set of situational and structural circumstances that empowered others—like ourselves—to engage in deeds that they too once thought were alien to their nature. We take false pride in believing that "I am   190 not that kind of person."

I argue that the human mind is so marvelous that it can adapt to virtu-ally any known environmental circumstance in order to survive, to create, and to destroy, as necessary. We are not born with tendencies toward good or evil but with mental templates to do *either*. What I mean is that we have the potential to be better or worse than anyone who has existed in the past, to be more creative and more destructive, to make the world a better place or a worse place than before. It is only through the recognition that no one of us is an island, that we all share the human condition, that humility takes prece-dence over unfounded pride in acknowledging our vulnerability to situa-   200 tional forces. If we want to develop mechanisms for combating such malev-olent transformations, then it seems essential to learn to appreciate the extent to which ordinary people can be seduced or initiated into the performance of evil deeds. We need to focus on discovering the mechanisms among the causal factors that influence so many to do so much bad, to commit so much evil throughout the globe. (See also the breadth of ideas presented by Baumeister, 1997; Darley, 1992; Staub, 1989; Waller, 2002.)

THE MILGRAM OBEDIENCE EXPERIMENTS

The most obvious power of the experimental demonstration by Stanley Milgram (1974) of blind obedience to authority lies in the unexpectedly high rates of such compliance, with the majority—two-thirds—of the subjects "going all the way" in shocking a victim with apparently lethal consequences. His finding was indeed shocking to most of those who read about it or saw his movie version of the study, because it revealed that a variety of ordinary American citizens could so readily be led to engage in "electrocuting a nice stranger." But the more significant importance of his research comes from what he did after that initial classic study with Yale College undergraduates. Milgram conducted 18 experimental variations on more than a *thousand* subjects from a variety of backgrounds, ages, both genders, and all educational levels. In each of these studies he varied one social-psychological variable and observed its impact on the extent of obedience to the unjust authority's pressure to continue to shock the "learner-victim." He was able to demonstrate that compliance rates of those who delivered the maximum 450 volts to the hapless victim could soar to 90% or could be reduced to less than 10% by introducing a single variable into the compliance recipe.

Milgram found that obedience was maximized when subjects first observed peers behaving obediently; it was dramatically reduced when peers rebelled or when the victim acted like a masochist asking to be shocked. What is especially interesting to me about this last result are the data Milgram provides on the predictions of his outcome by 40 psychiatrists who were given the basic description of the classic experiment. Their average estimate of the percentage of U.S. citizens who would give the full 450 volts was fewer than 1%. Only sadists would engage in such sadistic behavior, they believed. In a sense, this is the comparison level for appreciating the enormity of Milgram's finding. These experts on human behavior were *totally* wrong because they ignored the situational determinants of behavior in the procedural description of the experiment and overrelied on the dispositional perspective that comes from their professional training. Their error is a classic instance of the FAE at work. In fact, in this research, the average person does *not* behave like a sadist when an apparently masochistic victim encourages him or her to do so.

Milgram's intention was to provide a paradigm in which it was possible to quantify "evil" by the number of buttons a subject pushed on a shock generator, which allegedly delivered shocks to a mild-mannered confederate, playing the role of the pupil or learner, while the subject enacted the teacher role. Some of the procedures in this research paradigm that seduced many ordinary citizens to engage in evil offer parallels to compliance strategies used by "influence professionals" in real-world settings, such as salespeople, cult recruiters, and our national leaders (see Cialdini, 2001).

TEN INGREDIENTS IN THE SITUATIONIST'S RECIPE FOR BEHAVIORAL TRANSFORMATIONS

Among the influence principles in Milgram's paradigm for getting ordinary people to do things they originally believed they would not do are the following: 250

1. Presenting an acceptable justification, or rationale, for engaging in the undesirable action, such as wanting to help people improve their memory by judicious use of punishment strategies. In experiments this justification is known as the "cover story" because it is intended to cover up the procedures that follow, which might not make sense on their own. The real-world equivalent of the cover story is an ideology, such as "national security," that often provides the nice big lie for instituting a host of bad, illegal, and immoral policies.

2. Arranging some form of contractual obligation, verbal or written, to   260
enact the behavior.

3. Giving participants meaningful roles to play (e.g., teacher, student) that carry with them previously learned positive values and response scripts.

4. Presenting basic rules to be followed, which seem to make sense prior to their actual use, but then can be arbitrarily used to justify mindless compliance. "Failure to respond must be treated as an error" was a Milgram rule for shock omissions as well as for false commissions. But then what happens when the learner complains of a heart condition, wants to quit, then screams, followed by a thud and silence? The   270
learner's apparent inability to respond to the teacher's testing due to death or unconsciousness must be continually challenged by further shocks, since omission equals commission. The proceedings do not make sense at all: How could the teacher be helping to improve the memory of a learner who is incapacitated or dead? All too many participants stopped engaging in such basic, obvious critical thinking endeavors as their confusion and stress mounted.

5. Altering the semantics of the act and action: from hurting victims to helping learners by punishing them.

6. Creating opportunities for diffusion of responsibility for negative   280
outcomes; others will be responsible, or it will not be evident that the actor will be held liable.

7. Starting the path toward the ultimate evil act with a small, insignificant first step (only 15 volts).

8. Increasing each level of aggression in gradual steps that do not seem like noticeable differences (only 30 volts).

9. Gradually changing the nature of the influence authority from "just" to "unjust," from reasonable and rational to unreasonable and irrational.

290   10. Making the "exit costs" high and the process of exiting difficult by not permitting usual forms of verbal dissent to qualify as behavioral disobedience.

Such procedures are utilized across varied influence situations, in which those in authority want others to do their bidding but know that few would engage in the "end game" final solution without first being properly prepared psychologically to do the "unthinkable." I would encourage readers to engage in the thought exercise of applying these compliance principles to the tactics used by the Bush administration to cajole Americans into endorsing the preemptive invasion of Iraq (discussed further later in the chapter).

LORD OF THE FLIES AND THE PSYCHOLOGY OF DEINDIVIDUATION

300   William Golding's (1954) Noble prize-winning novel of the transformation of good British choir boys into murderous beasts centers on the point of change in mental state and behavior that follows a change in physical appearance. Painting themselves, changing their outward appearance, made it possible for some of Golding's characters to disinhibit previously restrained impulses to kill a pig for food. Once that alien deed of killing another creature was accomplished, they could then continue on to kill, with pleasure, both animals and people alike. Was Golding describing a psychologically valid principle in his use of external appearance as catalyst to dramatic changes in internal and behavioral processes? That is the question I answered

310   with a set of experiments and field studies on the psychology of deindividuation (Zimbardo, 1970).

The basic procedure involved having young women deliver a series of painful electric shocks to each of two other young women whom they could see and hear in a one-way mirror before them. Half were randomly assigned to a condition of anonymity, or deindividuation, half to one of uniqueness, or individuation. The appearance of the four college student subjects in each deindividuation group was concealed, and they were given identifying numbers in place of their names. The comparison individuation subjects in the four-woman groups were called by their names and

320   made to feel unique. They were asked to make the same responses of shocking each of two female "victims"—all with a suitable cover story, the big lie that they never questioned.

The results were clear: Women in the deindividuation condition delivered twice as much shock to both victims as did the women in the individuated comparison condition. Moreover, the deindividuated subjects shocked both victims, the one previously rated as pleasant and the other as unpleasant, more over the course of the 20 trials, whereas the individuated subjects shocked the pleasant woman less over time than they did the unpleasant one. One important conclusion flows from this research and its various replica-

tions and extensions, some using military personnel: Anything that makes   330
a person feel anonymous, as if no one knows who he or she is, creates the
potential for that person to act in evil ways—if the situation gives permission
for violence.

HALLOWEEN DISGUISES AND AGGRESSION IN CHILDREN

Outside the laboratory, *masks* may be used to create the anonymity needed
to disinhibit typically restrained behavior. For example, people mask themselves at Carnival rituals in many Catholic countries. Children in the United
States don masks and costumes for Mardi Gras and Halloween parties.
Bringing the laboratory to the party, so to speak, Fraser (1974) arranged for
elementary school children to go to a special, experimental Halloween party
given by their teacher. There were many games to play and for each game   340
won, tokens were earned that could be exchanged for gifts at the end of the
party. Half the games were nonaggressive in nature, and half were matched
in content but involved aggression: Physical confrontations between two
children were necessary to reach the goal and win the contest. The experimental design was a within-subject (A-B-A) format: in the first phase the
games were played without costumes; then the costumes arrived and were
worn as the games continued; finally, the costumes were removed and the
games went on for the third phase (each phase lasted about an hour). The
data are striking testimony to the power of anonymity. Aggression increased
significantly as soon as the costumes were worn, more than doubling from   350
the initial base level average. When the costumes were removed, aggression
dropped back well below the initial base rate. Equally interesting was the second result: that aggression had negative instrumental consequences on winning tokens—that is, it costs money to be aggressive—but that cost did not
matter when the children were anonymous in their costumes. The least number of tokens won occurred during the costumed anonymity phase, when
aggression was highest.

CULTURAL WISDOM OF CHANGING WARRIORS' APPEARANCES

Let us leave the laboratory and the fun and games of children's parties to enter
the real world, where these issues of anonymity and violence may take on life-
and-death significance. Some societies go to war without having the young   360
male warriors change their appearance, whereas others always include ritual
transformations of appearance by painting or masking the warriors (as in *Lord
of the Flies*). Does that change in external appearance make a difference in how
warring enemies are treated? After reading my Nebraska Symposium chapter,
Harvard anthropologist John Watson (1973) posed a research question, then
went to the human area files to find the answer, then published the data:
(1) the societies that did or did not change appearance of warriors prior to
going to war; and (2) the extent to which they killed, tortured, or mutilated

their victims. The results are striking confirmation of the prediction that
370   anonymity promotes destructive behavior, when permission is also given to
behave in aggressive ways that are ordinarily prohibited. Of the 23 societies for
which these two data sets were present, the majority (12 of 15, 80%) of societies in which warriors changed their appearance were those noted as most
destructive, whereas only one of the eight societies in which the warriors did
not change appearance before going to battle was noted as destructive. Cultural wisdom dictates that when old men want usually peaceful young men to
harm and kill other young men like themselves in a war, it is easier to do so if
they first change their appearance by putting on uniforms or masks or painting their faces. With that anonymity in place, out goes their usual internal
380   focus of compassion and concern for others.

THE THEORETICAL MODEL OF DEINDIVIDUATION AND BANDURA'S MODEL OF MORAL DISENGAGEMENT

The psychological mechanisms involved in getting good people to do evil are
embodied in two theoretical models, the first elaborated by me (Zimbardo,
1970) and modified by input from subsequent variants on my deindividuation conceptions, notably by Diener (1980). The second is Bandura's model
of moral disengagement (1998, 2003), which specifies the conditions under
which anyone can be led to act immorally, even those who usually ascribe to
high levels of morality.

Bandura's model outlines how it is possible to morally disengage from
destructive conduct by using a set of cognitive mechanisms that alter (1) one's
390   perception of the reprehensible conduct (e.g., by engaging in moral justifications, making palliative comparisons, using euphemistic labeling for one's
conduct); (2) one's sense of the detrimental effects of that conduct (e.g., by
minimizing, ignoring, or misconstruing the consequences); (3) one's sense of
responsibility for the link between reprehensible conduct and the detrimental
effects (e.g., by displacing or diffusing responsibility); and (4) one's view of the
victim (e.g., by dehumanizing him or her, attributing the blame for the outcome to the victim).

Dehumanization in Action: "Animals" by Any Other Name Are College Students

A remarkable experiment by Bandura, Underwood, and Fromson (1975)
reveals how easy it is to induce intelligent college students to accept a dehu-
400   manizing label of other people and then to act aggressively based on that
stereotyped term. Four participants were led to believe they were overhearing
the research assistant tell the experimenter that the students from another
college were present to start the study in which they were to deliver electric
shocks of varying intensity to the participants (according to the dictates of a
reasonable cover story). In one of the three randomly assigned conditions,

the subjects overheard the assistant say to the experimenter that the other students seemed "nice"; in a second condition, they heard the other students described as "animals"; in the third group, the assistant did not label the students in the alleged other group.

The dependent variable of shock intensity clearly reflected this situational manipulation. The subjects gave the highest levels of shock to those labeled in the dehumanizing way as "animals," and their shock level increased linearly over the 10 trials. Those labeled "nice" were given the least shock, whereas the unlabelled group fell in the middle of these two extremes. Thus, a single word—*animals*—was sufficient to incite intelligent college students to treat those so labeled as if they deserved to be harmed. On the plus side, the labeling effect resulted in others being treated with greater respect if someone in authority labeled them positively. The graphed data is also of interest: On the first trial there is no difference across the three experimental treatments in the level of shock administered, but with each successive opportunity, the shock levels diverge. Those shocking the so-called "animals" shock them more and more over time, a result comparable to the escalating shock level of the deindividuated female students in my earlier study. That rise in aggressive responding over time, with practice, or with experience belies a self-reinforcing effect of aggressive or violent responding: It is experienced as increasingly pleasurable.

What my model adds to the mix of what is needed to get good people to engage in evil deeds is a focus on the role of cognitive controls that usually guide behavior in socially desirable and personally acceptable ways. The shift from good to evil behavior can be accomplished by knocking out these control processes, blocking them, minimizing them, or reorienting them. Doing so suspends conscience, self-awareness, sense of personal responsibility, obligation, commitment, liability, morality, and analyses in terms of costs-benefits of given actions. The two general strategies for accomplishing this objective are (1) reducing cues of social accountability of the actor (i.e., "No one knows who I am, nor cares to know"), and (2) reducing concerns for self-evaluation by the actor. The first eliminates concerns for social evaluation and social approval by conveying a sense of anonymity to the actor and diffusing personal responsibility across others in the situation. The second strategy stops self-monitoring and consistency monitoring by relying on tactics that alter states of consciousness (e.g., via drugs, arousing strong emotions or hyperintense actions, creating a highly focused present-time orientation wherein there is no concern for past or future), and by projecting responsibility outside the self and onto others.

My research and that of other social psychologists (see Prentice-Dunn & Rogers, 1983) on deindividuation differs from the paradigm in Milgram's studies in that there is no authority figure present, urging the subject to obey. Rather, the situation is created in such a way that subjects act in accordance to paths made available to them, without thinking through the meaning or consequences of those actions. Their actions are not cognitively guided, as they are typically, but directed by the actions of others in proximity to them or by their strongly aroused emotional states and situationally available cues, such as the presence of weapons.

Environmental Anonymity Breeds Vandalism

It is possible for certain environments to convey a sense of anonymity on those who live in, or pass through, their midst. The people living in such environments do not have a sense of community. Vandalism and graffiti may be interpreted as an individual's attempt for public notoriety in a society that deindividuates him or her.

I conducted a simple field study to demonstrate the ecological differences between places ruled by anonymity versus those conveying a sense of community. I abandoned used but good-condition cars in the Bronx, New York City, and in Palo Alto, California, one block away from New York University and Stanford University, respectively. License plates were removed and hoods raised slightly to serve as ethological "releaser cues" for the potential vandals' attack behavior. It worked swiftly in the Bronx, as we watched and filmed from a vantage point across the street. Within 10 minutes of officially beginning this study, the first vandals surfaced. This parade of vandals continued for 2 days, by which time there was nothing of value left to strip; then they simply began destroying the remains. In 48 hours we recorded 23 separate "destructive contacts" by individuals or groups, who either took something from the abandoned vehicle or did something to wreck it. Curiously, only one of these episodes involved adolescents; the rest of the vandals were adults, many well dressed and many driving cars, so that they might qualify as, at least, lower middle class. Anonymity can make brazen vandals of us all. But what about the fate of the abandoned car in Palo Alto? Our time-lapse film revealed that no one vandalized any part of the car over a 5-day period. When we removed the car, three local residents called the police to say that an abandoned car was being stolen (the local police had been notified of our field study). That is one definition of "community," where people care about what happens on their turf, even to the person or property of strangers, with the reciprocal assumption that they would also care about them.

I now feel that any environmental or societal conditions that contribute to making some members of society feel that they are anonymous—that no one knows or cares who they are, that no one recognizes their individuality and thus their humanity—makes them potential assassins and vandals, a danger to my person and my property—and yours (Zimbardo, 1976).

THE FACES OF THE "ENEMY": PROPAGANDA IMAGES CONDITION US TO KILL ABSTRACTIONS

We need to add a few more operational principles to our arsenal of variables that trigger the commission of evil acts by men and women who are ordinarily good people. We can learn about some of these principles by considering

how nations prepare their young men (admittedly, women are now members   490
of the armed forces in many countries, but it is primarily the men who are sent
into combat zones) to engage in deadly wars, and how they prepare citizens to
support the risks of going to war, especially a war of aggression. This difficult
transformation is accomplished by a special form of cognitive conditioning.
Images of "The Enemy" are created by national propaganda to prepare the
minds of soldiers and citizens alike to hate those who fit the new category of
"your enemy." This mental conditioning is a soldier's most potent weapon, for
without it, he could probably never fire his weapon to kill another young man
in the cross-hairs of his gun sight. A fascinating account of how this "hostile
imagination" is created in the minds of soldiers and their families is presented   500
in *Faces of the Enemy* by Sam Keen (1986; see also his companion video).
Archetypal images of the enemy are created by propaganda fashioned by the
governments of most nations against those judged to be the dangerous
"them"—the outsiders who are also "our" enemies. These visual images create
a consensual societal paranoia that is focused on the enemy who would do
harm to the women, children, homes, and god of the soldier's nation, way of
life, and so forth. Keen's analysis of this propaganda on a worldwide scale
reveals that there are a select number of attributes utilized by "homo hostilis"
to invent an evil enemy in the minds of good members of righteous tribes.
The enemy is aggressive, faceless, a rapist, godless, barbarian, greedy, criminal,   510
a torturer, harbinger of death, a dehumanized animal, or just an abstraction.
Finally, there is the enemy as worthy, heroic opponent to be crushed in mortal combat—as in the video game of the same name.

Ordinary Men Murder Ordinary Men, Women, and Children: Jewish Enemies

One of the clearest illustrations of my fundamental theme of how ordinary
people can be transformed into engaging in evil deeds that are alien to their
past history and to their moral development comes from the analysis of British
historian Christopher Browning. In *Ordinary Men: Reserve Police Battalion 101
and the Final Solution in Poland* (1992) he recounts that in March 1942 about
80% of all victims of the Holocaust were still alive, but a mere 11 months later
about 80% were dead. In this short period of time, the *Endlösung* (Hitler's   520
"Final Solution") was galvanized by means of an intense wave of mass mobile
murder squads in Poland. This genocide required mobilization of a large-scale
killing machine at the same time as able-bodied soldiers were needed on the
Russian front. Since most Polish Jews lived in small towns and not the large
cities, the question that Browning raised about the German High Command
was "where had they found the manpower during this pivotal year of the war
for such an astounding logistical achievement in mass murder?" (p. xvi).

His answer came from archives of Nazi war crimes, in the form of the
activities of Reserve Battalion 101, a unit of about 500 men from Hamburg,
Germany. They were elderly family men, too old to be drafted into the army,   530
from working-class and lower middle-class backgrounds, with no military or
police experience, just raw recruits sent to Poland without warning of, or any

training in, their secret mission: the total extermination of all Jews living in the remote villages of Poland. In just 4 months they had shot to death at point blank range at least 38,000 Jews and had deported another 45,000 to the concentration camp at Treblinka. Initially, their commander told them that this was a difficult mission which must be obeyed by the battalion, but any individual could refuse to execute these men, women, and children. Records indicate that at first about half the men refused, letting the others 540 commit the mass murder. But over time, social modeling processes took their toll, as did any guilt-induced persuasion by buddies who did the killing, until by the end, up to 90% of the men in Battalion 101 had participated in the shootings, even proudly taking photographs of their up-close and personal slaughter of Jews.

Browning makes clear that there was no special selection of these men, only that they were as "ordinary" as could be imagined—until they were put into a situation in which they had "official" permission, even encouragement, to act sadistically and brutishly against those arbitrarily labeled, as "the enemy."

550 Let us go from the abstract to the personal for a moment: Imagine you witnessed your own father shooting to death a helpless mother and her infant child, and then imagine his answer to your question, "Why did you do it, Daddy?"

The War on Iraq: A Spurious Creation of Evil Terrorists and Infusion of National Fears

Fast forward to our time, our nation, our citizenry, and the fears of terrorism instilled by the destruction of the World Trade Center towers since that unforgettable day of September 11, 2001. The initial press and official reaction was to label the perpetrators of this horrific deed as "hijackers," "murderers," "criminals." Soon the label changed to "terrorists" and their deeds described as "evil." *Evil* became the coin of the realm, used repeatedly by the 560 media as fed by the administration, and with an ever-widening net of inclusiveness. Osama bin Laden, the mastermind of 9/11, was the first culprit designated as evil. But when he proved elusive, escaping from the war zone in Afghanistan, it became necessary for the administration's war on terrorism campaign to put a new face and a new place on terrorism. Of course, terrorism works its generation of fear and anxiety by its very facelessness and nonlocal ubiquity. Several countries were labeled by our president as the "axis of evil," with the leader of one of those countries, Iraq, designated as so evil that he, Saddam Hussein, had to be removed from power by all means necessary.

570 A propaganda campaign was created to justify a preemptive war against Saddam Hussein's regime by identifying the clear and imminent threat to the national security of the United States posed by the alleged weapons of mass destruction (WMD) this evil leader had at his disposal. Then a link was erected between him and the terrorist networks to whom, allegedly, he would sell or gift these WMD. Over time, many Americans began to believe the

falsehoods that Saddam Hussein was involved in the 9/11 terrorist attacks, was in complicity with Osama bin Laden, and had ready and operational an arsenal of deadly weapons that threatened U.S. security and well-being. Magazine images, newspaper accounts, and vivid TV stories contributed to the "evilization" of Saddam Hussein over the course of a year.

The vulnerability to terrorism that Americans continued to experience on deep, personal levels—in part, sustained and magnified by the administration's issuance of repeated (false) alarms of imminent terrorist attacks on the homeland—was relieved by the action of officially going to war. The public and Congress strongly supported a symmetrical war of "shock and awe"—to rid Iraq of the feared WMD and destroy Hussein's evil menace. Thus, for the first time in its history, the United States endorsed what the majority believed to be a justified aggressive war that has already cost billions of dollars, untold thousands of deaths (soldiers *and* civilians), totally destroyed a nation, weakened the United Nations, and will enmesh the United States in a prolonged, Vietnam-like, "no exit" scenario for years to come.

When no WMD were uncovered, despite the alleged best intelligence reports and aerial photos of them presented by the Secretary of State to the United Nations, collective cognitive dissonance reduction seeped in to maintain the belief that it was still a "necessary" and "good" war against evil (Festinger, 1957). After many months of an all-out, desperately intense search of every part of Iraq, American troops and intelligence forces have not unearthed a single WMD! So the original reason for going to war is being played down and is being replaced by the mantra that Iraq is the new front in our worldwide fight against terrorism, thus it is good we are in control of the destiny of Iraq. But who cares what the truth really is regarding the deceptive reasons for going to war, if the United States is now safer and the president is a commander-in-chief of decisive action—as his image crafters have carefully depicted him in the media. This national mind control experiment deserves careful documenting by unbiased social historians for the current and future generations to appreciate the power of images, words, and framing that can lead a democratic nation to support *and even relish* the unthinkable evil of an aggressive war.

The Socialization of Evil: How the "Nazi Hate Primers" Prepared and Conditioned the Minds of German Youth to Hate Jews

The second broad class of operational principles by which otherwise good people can be recruited into evil is through education/socialization processes that are sanctioned by the government in power, enacted within school programs, and supported by parents and teachers. A prime example is the way in which German children in the 1930s and 1940s were systematically indoctrinated to hate Jews, to view them as the all-purpose enemy of the new (post–World War I) German nation. Space limitations do not allow full documentation of this process, but I touch on several examples of one way in which governments are responsible for sanctioning evil.

In Germany, as the Nazi party rose to power in 1933, no target of Nazification took higher priority than the reeducation of Germany's youth. Hitler wrote: "I will have no intellectual training. Knowledge is ruin to my young men. A violently active, dominating, brutal youth—that is what I am after" (*The New Order*, 1989, pp. 101–102). To teach the youth about geography and race, special primers were created and ordered to be read starting in the first grade of elementary school (see *The New Order*, 1989). These "hate primers" were brightly colored comic books that contrasted the beautiful blond Aryans with the despicably ugly caricatured Jew. They sold in the hundreds of thousands. One was titled *Trust No Fox in the Green Meadows and No Jew on His Oath*. What is most insidious about this kind of hate conditioning is that the misinformation was presented as facts to be learned and tested upon, or from which to practice penmanship. In the copy of the *Trust No Fox* text that I reviewed, a series of cartoons illustrates all the ways in which Jews supposedly deceive Aryans, get rich and fat from dominating them, and are lascivious, mean, and without compassion for the plight of the poor and the elderly Aryans.

The final scenarios depict the retribution of Aryan children when they expel Jewish teachers and children from their school, so that "proper discipline and order" could then be taught. Initially, Jews were prohibited from community areas, like public parks, then expelled altogether from Germany. The sign in the cartoon reads, ominously, "One-way street." Indeed, it was a unidirectional street that led eventually to the death camps and crematoria that were the centerpiece of Hitler's Final Solution: the genocide of the Jews. Thus, this institutionalized evil was spread pervasively and insidiously through a perverted educational system that turned away from the types of critical thinking exercises that open students' minds to new ideas and toward thinking uncritically and close-mindedly about those targeted as the enemy of the people. By controlling education and the propaganda media, any national leader could produce the fantastic scenarios depicted in George Orwell's (1981) frightening novel *1984*.

The institutionalized evil that Orwell vividly portrays in his fictional account of state dominance over individuals goes beyond the novelist's imagination when its prophetic vision is carried into operational validity by powerful cult leaders or by agencies and departments within the current national administration of the United States. Previously I have outlined the direct parallels between the mind control strategies and tactics Orwell attributes to "The Party" and those that Reverend Jim Jones used in dominating the members of his religious/political cult, Peoples Temple (Zimbardo, 2003a). Jones orchestrated the suicide/murders of more than 900 U.S. citizens in the jungles of Guyana 25 years ago, perhaps as the grand finale of his experiment in institutionalized mind control. I learned from former members of this group that not only did Jones read *1984*, he talked about it often and even had a song commissioned by the church's singer, entitled "1984 Is Coming," that everyone had to sing at some services. I will leave it to the reader to explore the similarities between the mind control practices in *1984* and those being practiced on U.S. citizens in the past few years (see Zimbardo, 2003b).

THE STANFORD PRISON EXPERIMENT: A CRUCIBLE OF HUMAN NATURE WHERE GOOD BOYS ENCOUNTERED AN EVIL PLACE

Framing the issues we have been considering as, in essence, who wins when good boys are put in an evil place casts it as a neo-Greek tragedy scenario, wherein "the situation" stands in for the externally imposed forces of "the gods and destiny." As such, we can anticipate an outcome unfavorable to humanity. In more mundane psychological terms, this research on the Stanford prison experiment synthesized many of the processes and variables outlined earlier: those of place and person anonymity that contribute to the deindividuation of the people involved, the dehumanization of victims, giving some actors (guards) permission to control others (prisoners), and placing it all within a unique setting (the prison) that most societies throughout the world acknowledge provides some form of institutionally approved sanctions for evil through the extreme differentials in control and power fostered in prison environments.

In 1971, I designed a dramatic experiment that would extend over a 2-week period to provide our research participants with sufficient time for them to become fully engaged in their experimentally assigned roles of either guards or prisoners. Having participants live in a simulated prison setting day and night, if prisoners, or work there for long 8-hour shifts, if guards, would also allow sufficient time for situational norms to develop and patterns of social interaction to emerge, change, and crystallize. The second feature of this study was to ensure that all research participants would be as normal as possible initially, healthy both physically and mentally, and without any history of involvement in drugs or crime or violence. This baseline was essential to establish if we were to untangle the situational versus dispositional knot: What the situation elicited from this collection of similar, interchangeable young men versus what was emitted by the research participants based on the unique dispositions they brought into the experiment. The third feature of the study was the novelty of the prisoner and guard roles: Participants had no prior training in how to play the randomly assigned roles. Each subject's prior societal learning of the meaning of prisons and the behavioral scripts associated with the oppositional roles of prisoner and guard was the sole source of guidance. The fourth feature was to create an experimental setting that came as close to a *functional simulation* of the psychology of imprisonment as possible. The details of how we went about creating a mindset comparable to that of real prisoners and guards are given in several of the articles I wrote about the study (see Zimbardo, 1975; Zimbardo, Haney, Banks, & Jaffe, 1973).

Central to this mind set were the oppositional issues of power and powerlessness, dominance and submission, freedom and servitude, control and rebellion, identity and anonymity, coercive rules and restrictive roles. In general, these social-psychological constructs were operationalized by putting all subjects in appropriate uniforms, using assorted props (e.g., handcuffs, police clubs, whistles, signs on doors and halls), replacing corridor hall doors with prison bars to create prison cells, using windowless and clock-less cells that afforded no clues as to time of day, applying institutional rules that removed/ substituted individual names with numbers (prisoners) or titles for staff (Mr. Correctional Officer, Warden, Superintendent), and that gave guards control power over prisoners.

710   Subjects were recruited from among nearly 100 men between the ages of 18 and 30 who answered our advertisements in the local city newspaper. They were given a background evaluation that consisted of a battery of five psychological tests, personal history, and in-depth interviews. The 24 who were evaluated as most normal and healthiest in every respect were randomly assigned, half to the role of prisoner and half to that of guard. The student-prisoners underwent a realistic surprise arrest by officers from the Palo Alto Police Department, who cooperated with our plan. The arresting officer proceeded with a formal arrest, taking the "felons" to the police station for booking, after which each prisoner was brought to our prison in the reconstructed
720   basement of our psychology department.

The prisoner's uniform was a smock/dress with a prison ID number. The guards wore military-style uniforms and silver-reflecting sunglasses to enhance anonymity. At any one time there were nine prisoners on "the yard," three to a cell, and three guards working 8-hour shifts. Data were collected via systematic video recordings, secret audio recordings of conversations of prisoners in their cells, interviews and tests at various times during the study, postexperiment reports, and direct, concealed observations.

For a detailed chronology and fuller account of the behavioral reactions that followed, readers are referred to the above references, to Zimbardo,
730   Maslach, and Haney (1999), and to our new website: *www.prisonexp.org*. For current purposes, let me simply summarize that the negative situational forces overwhelmed the positive dispositional tendencies. The Evil Situation triumphed over the Good People. Our projected 2-week experiment had to be terminated after only 6 days because of the pathology we were witnessing. Pacifistic young men were behaving sadistically in their role as guards, inflicting humiliation and pain and suffering on other young men who had the inferior status of prisoner. Some "guards" even reported enjoying doing so. Many of the intelligent, healthy college students who were occupying the role of prisoner showed signs of "emotional breakdown" (i.e., stress disorders)
740   so extreme that five of them had to be removed from the experiment within that first week. The prisoners who adapted better to the situation were those who mindlessly followed orders and who allowed the guards to dehumanize and degrade them ever more with each passing day and night. The only personality variable that had any significant predictive value was that of *F*-scale authoritarianism: The higher the score, the more days the prisoner survived in this totally authoritarian environment.

I terminated the experiment not only because of the escalating level of violence and degradation by the guards against the prisoners that was apparent when viewing the videotapes of their interactions, but also because I was
750   made aware of the transformation that I was undergoing personally (see the

analysis by Christina Maslach of how she intervened to help bring light to that dark place and end the study; in Zimbardo et al., 1999). I had become a Prison Superintendent in addition to my role as Principal Investigator. I began to talk, walk, and act like a rigid institutional authority figure more concerned about the security of "my prison" than the needs of the young men entrusted to my care as a psychological researcher. In a sense, I consider the extent to which I was transformed to be the most profound measure of the power of this situation. We held extended debriefing sessions of guards and prisoners at the end of the study and conducted periodic checkups over many years. Fortunately, there were no lasting negative consequences of this pow-   760
erful experience.

Before moving on, I would like to share parts of a letter sent to me recently (e-mail communication, October 18, 2002) by a young psychology student, recently discharged from military service. It outlines some of the direct parallels between the aversive aspects of our simulated prison many years ago and current despicable practices still taking place in some military boot-camp training. It also points up the positive effects that research and education can have:

> I am a 19-year-old student of psychology [who watched] the slide show of your prison experiment. Not too far into it, I was almost in   770
> tears. . . . I joined the United States Marine Corps, pursuing a child-hood dream. To make a long story short, I had become the victim of repeated illegal physical and mental abuse. An investigation showed I suffered more than 40 unprovoked beatings. Eventually, as much as I fought it, I became suicidal, thus received a discharge from boot camp. . . .
>
> The point I am trying to make is that the manner in which your guards carried about their duties and the way that military drill instructors do is unbelievable. I was amazed at all the parallels of your guards and one particular D. I. who comes to mind. I was treated   780
> much the same way, and even worse, in some cases.
>
> One incident that stands out was the time, in an effort to break platoon solidarity, I was forced to sit in the middle of my squad bay (living quarters) and shout to the other recruits "If you guys would have moved faster, we wouldn't be doing this for hours," referencing every single recruit who was holding over his head a very heavy foot locker. The event was very similar to the prisoners saying #819 was a bad prisoner. After my incident, and after I was home safe some months later, all I could think about was how much I wanted to go   790
> back to show the other recruits that as much as the D. I.s told the pla-toon that I was a bad recruit, I wasn't.
>
> Other behaviors come to mind, like the push-ups we did for punish-ment, the shaved heads, not having any identity other than being addressed as, and referring to other people as, "Recruit So-and-So"—

which replicates your study. The point of it all is that even though your experiment was conducted 31 years ago, my reading the study has helped me gain an understanding I was previously unable to gain before, even after therapy and counseling. What you have demonstrated really gave me insight into something I've been dealing with for almost a year now. 800 Although, it is certainly not an excuse for their behavior, I now can understand the rationale behind the D. I.'s actions as far as being sadistic and power hungry.

THE FAILURE OF THE SOCIAL EXPERIMENT OF THE U.S. CORRECTIONAL SYSTEM

As much joy that such personal reactions bring to someone whose vision has always been for psychological research to make a difference in people's lives, I have been saddened by the lack of impact the Stanford prison experiment has had on the correctional system in the United States. When Craig Haney and I recently did a retrospective analysis of our study, with contrasting views of U.S. and California correctional policies over the past 30 years, our conclusions were disheartening (Haney & Zimbardo, 1998). Prisons continue to 810 be failed social experiments that rely on a dispositional model of punishment and isolation of offenders. Gone is any sense of the modifiable situational determinants of crime or of basic rehabilitation practices that might reduce persistently high rates of recidivism. The United States is now the prison center of the universe, with more than 2 million citizens incarcerated, *greater than any other nation*, and growing. Our analysis revealed that prison conditions had significantly worsened in the decades since our study, as a consequence of the politicization of prisons, with politicians, prosecutors, DAs, and other officials taking a hard line on crime as a means of currying favor of an electorate made fearful of crime by media exaggerations. Misguided 820 policies about sentencing for crack cocaine use and sale and the "Three Strikes" rulings have put a disproportionately large number of African American and Hispanic men behind bars for long sentences. There are now more African American men wasting away in the nation's prison system than fulfilling their potentials in our higher educational system.

THE EVIL OF INACTION

Our usual take on evil focuses on violent, destructive actions, but *non*action can also become a form of evil, when assistance, dissent, and disobedience are needed. Social psychologists heeded the alarm when the infamous Kitty Genovese case made national headlines. As she was being stalked, stabbed, and eventually murdered, 39 people in a housing complex heard her screams and 830 did nothing to help. It seemed obvious that this was a prime example of the callousness of New Yorkers, as many media accounts reported. A counter to this dispositional analysis came in the form of a series of classic studies by

Latané and Darley (1970) on bystander intervention. One key finding was that people are less likely to help when they are in a group, when they perceive that others are available who could help, than when those people are alone. The presence of others diffuses the sense of personal responsibility of any individual.

A powerful demonstration of the failure to help strangers in distress was staged by Darley and Batson (1973). Imagine you are a theology student on your way to deliver the sermon of the Good Samaritan in order to have it videotaped for a psychology study on effective communication. Further imagine that as you are heading from the psychology department to the video taping center, you pass a stranger huddled up in an alley in dire distress. Are there any conditions that you could conceive that would not make you stop to be that Good Samaritan? What about "time press"? Would it make a difference to you if you were late for your date to give that sermon? I bet you would like to believe it would not make a difference, that you would stop and help no matter what the circumstances. Right? Remember, you are a theology student, thinking about helping a stranger in distress, which is amply rewarded in the Biblical tale.

The researchers randomly assigned students of the Princeton Theological Seminary to three conditions that varied in how much time they thought they had between receiving their assignment from the researchers and getting to the communication department to tape their Good Samaritan speeches. The conclusion: Do not be a victim in distress when people are late and in a hurry, because 90% of them are likely to pass you by, giving you no help at all! The more time the seminarians believed they had, the more likely they were to stop and help. So the situational variable of *time press* accounted for the major variance in extending or withholding help, without any need to resort to dispositional explanations about theology students being callous or cynical or indifferent, as Kitty Genovese's nonhelpers were assumed to be—another instance of the FAE, one that needs to be reversed.

THE WORST OF THE APPLES IN THE EVIL BARREL: TORTURERS AND EXECUTIONERS?

There is little debate but that the systematic torture by men and women of their fellow men and women represents one of the darkest sides of human nature. Surely, my colleagues and I reasoned, here was a place where dispositional evil would be manifest among torturers who did their dirty deeds daily, for years, in Brazil as policemen sanctioned by the government to extract confessions through torturing so-called enemies of the state. We began by focusing solely on the torturers, trying to understand both their psyches and the ways they were shaped by their circumstances, but we had to expand our analytical net to capture their comrades-in-arms who chose, or were assigned to, another branch of violence work—death-squad executioners. They shared a "common enemy": men, women, and children who, though citizens of

840

850

860

870

their state, even neighbors, were declared by "the authorities" to be threats to the country's national security. Some had to be eliminated efficiently, whereas those who might hold secret information had to be made to yield it up and confess to their treason.

In carrying out this mission, these torturers could rely, in part, on the "creative evil" embodied in the torture devices and techniques that had been refined over centuries since the Inquisition by officials of The Church and, later, of the National State. But our current-day torturers added a measure of improvisation to accommodate the particular resistances and resiliencies of the enemy standing before them, claiming innocence, refusing to acknowledge their culpability, or not succumbing to intimidation. It took time and emerging insights into exploitable human weaknesses for these torturers to become adept at their craft, in contrast to the task of the death-squad executioners, who, wearing hoods for anonymity and sporting good guns and group support, could dispatch their duty to country swiftly and impersonally. For the torturer, it could never be "just business." Torture always involves a personal relationship, essential for understanding what kind of torture to employ, what intensity of torture to use on this person at this time: wrong kind or too little, no confession; too much, and the victim dies before confessing. In either case, the torturer fails to deliver the goods. Learning to select the right kind and degree of torture that yields up the desired information makes rewards abound and praise flow from the superiors.

What kind of men could do such deeds? Did they need to rely on sadistic impulses and a history of sociopathic life experiences to rip and tear flesh of fellow beings day in and day out for years on end? Were these violence workers a breed apart from the rest of humanity—bad seeds, bad tree trunks, bad flowers? Or, is it conceivable that they were programmed to carry out their deplorable deeds by means of some identifiable and replicable training processes? Could a set of external conditions—that is, situational variables—that contributed to the making of these torturers and killers be identified? If their evil deeds were not traceable to inner defects but attributable to outer forces acting upon them—the political, economic, social, historical, and experiential components of their police training—then we might be able to generalize, across cultures and settings, those principles responsible for this remarkable transformation. Martha Huggins, Mika Haritos-Fatouros, and I interviewed several dozen of these violence workers in depth and recently published a summary of our methods and findings (Huggins, Haritos-Fatouros, & Zimbardo, 2002). Mika had done a similar, earlier study of torturers trained by the Greek military junta, and our results were largely congruent with hers (Haritos-Fatouros, 2003).

We learned that sadists are *selected out* of the training process by trainers because they are not controllable, get off on the pleasure of inflicting pain, and thus do not sustain the focus on the goal of confession extraction. From all the evidence we could muster, these violence workers were not unusual or deviant in any way prior to practicing this new role, nor were there any per-

sisting deviant tendencies or pathologies among any of them in the years following their work as torturers and executioners. Their transformation was 920
entirely understandable as a consequence of (1) the training they were given
to play this new role, (2) group camaraderie, (3) acceptance of the national
security ideology, and (4) the belief in socialist-communists as enemies of
their state. They were also influenced by being made to feel special—above
and better than peers in public service—by the secrecy of their duties and by
the constant pressure to produce desired results regardless of fatigue or personal problems. We report many detailed case studies that document the
ordinariness of these men engaged in the most heinous of deeds, sanctioned
by their government at that time in history, but reproducible at this time in
any nation whose obsession with national security and fears of terrorism per-   930
mit suspension of basic individual freedoms.

SUICIDE BOMBERS: SENSELESS FANATICS OR MARTYRS FOR A CAUSE?

Not surprisingly, what holds true for the Brazilian violence workers is comparable to the nature of the transformation of young Palestinians from students to suicide bombers killing Israelis. Recent media accounts converge on
the findings from more systematic analyses of the process of becoming a suicidal killer (see Atran, 2003; Bennet, 2003; Hoffman, 2003; Merari, 1990,
2002; Myer, 2003). There have been more than 95 suicide bombings by
Palestinians against Israelis since September, 2000. Originally, and most frequently, the bombers were young men, but recently a half dozen women have
joined the ranks of suicidal bombers. What has been declared as senseless,   940
mindless murder by those attacked and by outside observers is anything but
to those intimately involved. It was mistakenly believed that it was poor, desperate, socially isolated, illiterate young people with no career and no future
who adopted this fatalistic role. That stereotype has been shattered by the
actual portraits of these young men and women, many of whom were students with hopes for a better future, intelligent and attractive youth, connected with their family and community.

Ariel Merari, an Israeli psychologist who has studied this phenomenon for
many years, outlines the common steps on the path to these explosive deaths.
Senior members of an extremist group first identify particular young people   950
who appear to have an intense patriotic fervor, based on their declarations at
public rallies against Israel or their support of some Islamic cause or Palestinian action. These individuals are invited to discuss how serious they are in
their love of their country and their hatred of Israel. They are then asked to
commit to being trained in how to put their hatred into action. Those who
make the commitment are put into a small group of three to five similar youth
who are at varying stages of "progress" toward becoming agents of death. They
learn the tricks of the trade from elders: bomb making, disguise, selecting and
timing targets. Then they publicize their private commitment by making a

960 videotape on which they declare themselves to be "living martyrs" for Islam and for the love of Allah. In one hand they hold the Koran, a rifle in the other, their head-band declaring their new status. This video binds them to the final deed, since it is sent home to the family of the recruit before they execute the final plan. The recruits also realize that not only will they earn a place beside Allah, but their relatives will also be entitled to a high place in heaven because of their martyrdom. A sizable financial incentive is bestowed on their family as a gift for their sacrifice.

Their photo is emblazoned on posters that will be put on walls everywhere in the community the moment they succeed in their mission. They 970 will be immortalized as inspirational models. To stifle concerns about the pain from wounds inflicted by exploding nails and other bomb parts, they are told that before the first drop of their blood touches the ground, they will already be seated at the side of Allah, feeling no pain, only pleasure. An ultimate incentive for the young males is the promise of heavenly bliss with scores of virgins in the next life. They become heroes and heroines, modeling self-sacrifice to the next cadre of young suicide bombers.

We can see that this program utilizes a variety of social-psychological and motivational principles in turning collective hatred and general frenzy into a dedicated, seriously calculated program of indoctrination and training for 980 individuals to become youthful "living martyrs." It is neither mindless nor senseless, only a very different mind set and with different sensibilities than we have been used to witnessing among young adults in our country. A recent television program on female suicide bombers went so far as to describe them in terms more akin to the girl next door than to alien fanatics. Indeed, that very normalcy is what is so frightening about the emergence of this new social phenomena—that so many intelligent young people could be persuaded to envision and welcome their lives ending in a suicidal explosive blast.

To counteract the powerful tactics of these recruiting agents requires the provision of meaningful, life-affirming alternatives to this next generation. It 990 requires new national leadership that is willing and able to explore every negotiating strategy that could lead to peace instead of death. It requires these young people across national boundaries to openly share their values, their education, and their resources and to explore their commonalities, not highlight their differences. The suicide, the murder, of any young person is a gash in the fabric of the human connection that we elders from every nation must unite to prevent. To encourage the sacrifice of youth for the sake of advancing ideologies of the old might be considered a form of evil from a more cosmic perspective that transcends local politics and expedient strategies.

CONCLUSIONS

It is a truism in psychology that personality and situations interact to gener-
1000 ate behavior, as do cultural and societal influences. However, I have tried to show in my research over the past 30 years that situations exert more power

over human actions than has been generally acknowledged by most psychologists or recognized by the general public. Along with a hardy band of experimental social psychologists, I have conducted research demonstrations designed, in part, to provide a corrective balance to the pervasive fundamental attribution error. Nevertheless, the traditional dispositional perspective continues to dominate Anglo-American psychology fueled by reliance on the individualist orientation central in our institutions of medicine, education, psychiatry, law, and religion. Acknowledging the power of situational forces does not excuse the behaviors evoked in response to their operation. Rather, 1010 it provides a knowledge base that shifts attention away from simplistic "blaming the victim" mentality and ineffective individualistic treatments designed to change the evil doer, toward more profound attempts to discover causal networks that should be modified. Sensitivity to situational determinants of behavior also affords "risk alerts" that allow us to avoid or modify prospective situations of vulnerability.

Please consider this Zimbardo homily that captures the essence of the difference between dispositional and situational orientations: "While a few bad apples might spoil the barrel (filled with good fruit/people), a barrel filled with vinegar will *always* transform sweet cucumbers into sour pickles—regardless 1020 of the best intentions, resilience, and genetic nature of those cucumbers." So, does it make more sense to spend our resources on attempts to identify, isolate, and destroy the few bad apples or to learn how vinegar works so that we can teach cucumbers how to avoid undesirable vinegar barrels?

My situational sermon has several related dimensions. First, we should be aware that a range of apparently simple situational factors can impact our behavior more compellingly than we would expect or predict. The research outlined here, along with that of my colleagues presented in this volume, points to the influential force of numerous variables: role playing, rules, presence of others, emergent group norms, group identity, uniforms, anonymity, 1030 social modeling, authority presence, symbols of power, time pressures, semantic framing, stereotypical images and labels, among others.

Second, the situationist approach redefines heroism. When the majority of ordinary people can be overcome by such pressures toward compliance and conformity, the minority who resist should be considered *heroic*. Acknowledging the special nature of this resistance means that we should learn from their example by studying how they have been able to rise above such compelling pressures. That suggestion is coupled with another that encourages the development of an essential but ignored domain of psychology—heroes and heroism. 1040

Third, the situationist approach should, in my view, encourage us all to share a profound sense of personal humility when trying to understand those "unthinkable," "unimaginable," "senseless" acts of evil. Instead of immediately embracing the high moral ground that distances us good folks from those bad ones and gives short shrift to analyses of causal factors in the situations that form the context of the evil acts, the situational approach gives all others the benefit of "attributional charity." This means that any deed, for good or evil, that any human being has ever performed or committed, you and I could also perform or commit—given the same situational forces. If so, it becomes imperative to constrain our immediate moral outrage that seeks vengeance against wrongdoers and turn our efforts toward uncovering the causal factors that could have led them in that aberrant direction.

Do students believe this?

The obvious current instantiation of these principles is the rush to characterize terrorists and suicide bombers as "evil" people, instead of working to understand the nature of the psychological, social, economic, and political conditions that have fostered such generalized hatred of an enemy nation, including our own, that young people are willing to sacrifice their lives and murder other human beings. The "war on terrorism" can never be won solely by the current administration's plans to find and destroy terrorists—since any individual, anywhere, at any time, can become an active terrorist. It is only by understanding the *situational determinants of terrorism* that programs can be developed to win the hearts and minds of potential terrorists away from destruction and toward creation—not a simple task, but an essential one that requires implementation of social-psychological perspectives and methods in a comprehensive, long-term plan of attitude, value, and behavior change.

REFERENCES

Adorno, T. W., Frenkel-Brunswick, E., Levenson, D. J., & Sanford, R. N. (1950). *The authoritarian personality*. New York: Harper & Row.

Atran, S. (2003, May 5), Who wants to be a martyr? *The New York Times*, p. A23.

Bandura, A. (1998). Mechanisms of moral disengagement. In W. Reich (Ed.), *Origins of terrorism: Psychologies, ideologies, theologies, states of mind* (pp. 161–191). New York: Cambridge University Press.

Bandura, A. (2003). The role of selective moral disengagement in terrorism and counterterrorism. In F. M. Mogahaddam & A. J. Marsella (Eds.), *Understanding terrorism* (pp. 121–150). Washington, DC: American Psychological Association.

Bandura, A., Underwood, B., & Fromson, M. E. (1975). Disinhibition of aggression through diffusion of responsibility and dehumanization of victims. *Journal of Personality and Social Psychology, 9*, 253–269.

Barstow, A. L. (1994). *Witchcraze: A new history of the European witch hunts*. New York: HarperCollins.

Baumeister, R. F. (1997). *Evil: Inside human cruelty and violence*. New York: Freeman.

Bennett, J. (2003, May 30). A scholar of English who clung to the veil. *The New York Times*, pp. A1, A14.

Browning, C. R. (1992). *Ordinary men: Reserve police battalion 101 and the final solution in Poland*. New York: HarperPerennial.

Chang, I. (1997). *The rape of Nanking: The forgotten holocaust of World War II*. New York: Basic Books.

Cialdini, R. B. (2001). *Influence: Science and practice* (4th ed.). Boston: Allyn & Bacon.

Dailey, J. M. (1992). Social organization for the production of evil. *Psychological Inquiry 3*, 199–218.

Darley, J. M., & Batson, D. (1973). From Jerusalem to Jericho: A study of situational and dispositional variables in helping behavior. *Journal of Personality and Social Psychology, 27*, 100–108.

Diener, E. (1980). Deindividuation: The absence of self-awareness and self-regulation in group members. In P. B. Paulus (Ed.), *The psychology of group influence* (pp. 209–243). Hillsdale, NJ: Erlbaum.

Festinger, L. (1957). *A theory of cognitive dissonance*. Palo Alto, CA: Stanford University Press.

Fraser, S. C. (1974). *Deindividuation: Effects of anonymity on aggression in children*. Unpublished manuscript, University of Southern California, Los Angeles.

Golding, W. (1954). *Lord of the flies*. New York: Capricorn Books.

Haney, C., & Zimbardo, P. G. (1998). The past and future of U.S. prison policy: Twenty-five years after the Stanford Prison Experiment. *American Psychologist, 53*, 709–727.

Haritos-Fatouros, M. (2002). *The psychological origins of institutionalized torture*. London: Routledge.

Hoffman, B. (2003, June). The logic of suicide terrorism. *The Atlantic Monthly*, 40–47.

Huggins, M., Haritos-Fatouros, M., & Zimbardo, P. G. (2002). *Violence workers: Police torturers and murderers reconstruct Brazilian atrocities*. Berkeley: University of California Press.

Keen, S. (1986). *Faces of the enemy: Reflections of the hostile imagination*. New York: HarperCollins.

Kramer, H., & Sprenger, J. (1971). *The malleus maleficarum*. New York: Dover. (Original work published 1486)

Latané, B., & Darley, J. M. (1970). *The unresponsive bystander: Why doesn't he help?* New York: Appleton-Century-Crofts.

Lee, M., Zimbardo, P. G., & Berthof, M. (1977). Shy murderers. *Psychology Today, 11*, 69–70, 76, 148.

Merari, A. (1990). The readiness to kill and die: Suicidal terrorism in the Middle East. In W. Reich (Ed.), *Origins of terrorism: Psychologies, theologies, states of mind* (pp. 192–200). New York: Cambridge University Press.

Merari, A. (2002, October). *Suicide terrorism*. Paper presented at the First Conference of the National Center for Disaster Psychology and Terrorism, Palo Alto, CA.

Milgram, S. (1974). *Obedience to authority*. New York: Harper & Row.

Myer, G. (2003, May 30). A young man radicalized by his months in jail. *The New York Times*, pp. A1, A14.

The new order (The Third Reich). (1989). Alexandria, VA: Time Life Books.

Orwell, G. (1981). *1984*. New York: Signet.

Prentice-Dunn, S., & Rogers, R. W. (1983). Deindividuation and aggression. In R. G. Geen & E. I. Donnerstein (Eds.), *Aggression: Theoretical and empirical reviews—issues in research* (Vol. 2, pp. 155–171). New York: Academic Press.

Ross, L. (1977). The intuitive psychologist and his shortcomings. In L. Berkowitz (Ed.), *Advances in experimental social psychology* (Vol. 10, pp. 173–220). New York: Academic Press.

Staub, E. (1989). *The roots of evil: The origins of genocide and other group violence*. New York: Cambridge University Press.

Waller, J. (2002). *Becoming evil: How ordinary people commit genocide and mass killing*. New York: Oxford University Press.

Watson, R. I., Jr. (1973). Investigation into deindividuation using a cross-cultural survey technique. *Journal of Personality and Social Psychology, 25*, 342–345.

Zimbardo, P. G. (1970). The human choice: Individuation, reason, and order versus deindividuation, impulse, and chaos. In W. J. Arnold & D. Levine (Eds.), *1969 Nebraska Symposium on Motivation* (pp. 237–307). Lincoln: University of Nebraska Press.

Zimbardo, P. G. (1975). On transforming experimental research into advocacy for social change. In M. Deutsch & H. Hornstein (Eds.), *Applying social psychology: implications for research, practice, and training* (pp. 33–66). Hillsdale, NJ: Erlbaum.

Zimbardo, P. G. (1976). Making sense of senseless vandalism. In E. P. Hollander & R. G. Hunt (Eds.), *Current perspectives in social psychology* (4th ed., pp. 129–134). Oxford, UK: Oxford University Press.

Zimbardo, P. G. (2003a). Mind control in Orwell's *1984*: Fictional concepts become operational realities in Jim Jones' jungle experiment. In M. Nussbaum, J. Goldsmith, & A. Gleason (Eds.), *1984: Orwell and our future*. Princeton: Princeton University Press.

Zimbardo, P. G. (2003b). Phantom menace: Is Washington terrorizing us more than Al Qaeda? *Psychology Today, 36*, pp. 34–36.

Zimbardo, P. G., Haney, C., Banks, C., & Jaffe, D. (1973, April 8). The mind is a formidable jailer: A Pirandellian prison. *The New York Times Magazine*, pp. 38 ff.

Zimbardo, P. G., Maslach, C., & Haney, C. (1999). Reflections on the Stanford Prison Experiment: Genesis, transformation, consequences. In T. Blass (Ed.), *Obedience to authority: Current perspectives on the Milgram Paradigm* (pp. 193–237). Mahwah, NJ: Erlbaum.